China

WORLD BIBLIOGRAPHICAL SERIES

General Editors:
Robert L. Collison (Editor-in-chief)
Sheila R. Herstein
Louis J. Reith
Hans H. Wellisch

VOLUMES IN THE SERIES

1 *Yugoslavia*, John J. Horton
2 *Lebanon*, Shereen Khairallah
3 *Lesotho*, Shelagh M. Willet and David Ambrose
4 *Rhodesia/Zimbabwe*, Oliver B. Pollack and Karen Pollack
5 *Saudi Arabia*, Frank A. Clements
6 *USSR*, Anthony Thompson
7 *South Africa*, Reuben Musiker
8 *Malawi*, Robert B. Boeder
9 *Guatemala*, Woodman B. Franklin
11 *Uganda*, Robert L. Collison
12 *Malaysia*, Lim Huck Tee and Wong Sook Jean
13 *France*, Frances Chambers
14 *Panama*, Eleanor DeSelms Langstaff
15 *Hungary*, Thomas Kabdebo
16 *USA*, Sheila R. Herstein and Naomi Robbins
17 *Greece*, Richard Clogg and Mary Jo Clogg
18 *New Zealand*, R. F. Grover
19 *Algeria*, Richard I. Lawless
21 *Belize*, Ralph Lee Woodward, Jr.
23 *Luxembourg*, Carlo Hury and Jul Christophory
24 *Swaziland*, Balam Nyeko
25 *Kenya*, Robert L. Collison
26 *India*, Brijen Gupta and Datta Kharbas
27 *Turkey*, Meral Güçlü
28 *Cyprus*, P. M. Kitromilides and M. L. Evriviades
29 *Oman*, Frank A. Clements
30 *Italy*, Emiliana P. Noether
31 *Finland*, J. E. O. Screen
32 *Poland*, Richard C. Lewanski
33 *Tunisia*, Allan M. Findlay, Anne M. Findlay and Richard I. Lawless
34 *Scotland*, Eric G. Grant
35 *China*, Peter Cheng
36 *Qatar*, P. T. H. Unwin
37 *Iceland*, John J. Horton
38 *Nepal*, Dina Nath Wadhwa
39 *Haiti*, Frances Chambers
40 *Sudan*, M. W. Daly
41 *Vatican City State*, Michael J. Walsh
42 *Iraq*, Abdul Jabbar Abdulrahman
43 *United Arab Emirates*, Frank A. Clements
44 *Nicaragua*, Ralph Lee Woodward, Jr.

VOLUME 35

China

Peter Cheng
Compiler

CLIO PRESS
OXFORD, ENGLAND · SANTA BARBARA, CALIFORNIA

British Library Cataloguing in Publication Data
Cheng, Peter
China. — (World bibliographical series; 35)
1. China — Bibliography
I. Title II. Series
016.951   Z3101

ISBN 0-903450-81-X

Clio Press Ltd.,
55 St. Thomas' Street,
Oxford OX1 1JG, England.
Providing the services of the European
Bibliographical Centre and the American
Bibliographical Center

American Bibliographical Center-Clio Press,
Riviera Campus, 2040 Alameda Padre Serra,
Santa Barbara, Ca. 93103, U.S.A.

Designed by Bernard Crossland
Computer typeset by Peter Peregrinus Ltd.
Printed in Great Britain
by the Camelot Press, Southampton

THE WORLD BIBLIOGRAPHICAL SERIES

This series will eventually cover every country in the world, each in a separate volume comprising annotated entries on works dealing with its history, geography, economy and politics; and with its people, their culture, customs, religion and social organization. Attention will also be paid to current living conditions – housing, education, newspapers, clothing, etc. – that are all too often ignored in standard bibliographies; and to those particular aspects relevant to individual countries. Each volume seeks to achieve, by use of careful selectivity and critical assessment of the literature, an expression of the country and an appreciation of its nature and national aspirations, to guide the reader towards an understanding of its importance. The keynote of the series is to provide, in a uniform format, an interpretation of each country that will express its culture, its place in the world, and the qualities and background that make it unique.

SERIES EDITORS

Robert L. Collison (Editor-in-chief) is Professor Emeritus, Library and Information Studies, University of California, Los Angeles, and is currently the President of the Society of Indexers. Following the war, he served as Reference Librarian for the City of Westminster and later became Librarian to the BBC. During his fifty years as a professional librarian in England and the USA, he has written more than twenty works on bibliography, librarianship, indexing and related subjects.

Sheila R. Herstein is Reference Librarian and Library Instruction Coordinator at the City College of the City University of New York. She has extensive bibliographic experience and recently described her innovations in the field of bibliographic instruction in 'Team teaching and bibliographic instruction', *The Bookmark*, Autumn 1979. In addition, Doctor Herstein co-authored a basic annotated bibliography in history for Funk & Wagnalls *New encyclopedia*, and for several years reviewed books for *Library Journal*.

Louis J. Reith is librarian with the Franciscan Institute, St. Bonaventure University, New York. He received his PhD from Stanford University, California, and later studied at Eberhard-Karls-Universität, Tübingen. In addition to his activities as a librarian, Dr. Reith is a specialist on 16th century German history and the Reformation and has published many articles and papers in both German and English. He was also editor of the *American Society for Reformation Research Newsletter*.

Hans H. Wellisch is Associate Professor at the College of Library and Information Services, University of Maryland, and a member of the American Society of Indexers and the International Federation for Documentation. He is the author of numerous articles and several books on indexing and abstracting, and has most recently published *Indexing and abstracting: an international bibliography*. He also contributes frequently to *Journal of the American Society for Information Science, Library Quarterly*, and *The Indexer*.

Contents

INTRODUCTION xi

THE COUNTRY AND ITS PEOPLE 1

GEOGRAPHY 11
    General 11   Maps and atlases 14

TOURISM AND TRAVELLERS' ACCOUNTS 16
    General 16   Guidebooks 26

FLORA AND FAUNA 28

PREHISTORY AND ARCHAEOLOGY 30

HISTORY 35
    Pre-20th century 35   Post 1949 62
    1900-1949 49

BIOGRAPHICAL WORKS 70
    Mao Zedong 70   Who's Who 86
    Others 78

RELIGION AND PHILOSOPHY 89
    Religion 89   Philosophy 95

SOCIETY AND SOCIAL STRUCTURE 103
    General 103   Women's status 111
    Family 109

POPULATION 114

OVERSEAS CHINESE 117

EDUCATION 123

Contents

MEDICINE AND HEALTH 130

LAW 135

POLITICS AND GOVERNMENT 139
    History 139   Political philosophy 160
    Contemporary 144

FOREIGN RELATIONS 164
    History 164   Contemporary 170

ECONOMY 195

FINANCE AND BANKING 208

TRADE 211

INDUSTRY 216

AGRICULTURE AND RURAL DEVELOPMENT 220

LABOUR AND EMPLOYMENT 227

SCIENCE AND TECHNOLOGY 230

LANGUAGE 236
    Beginners' textbooks 236   English-Chinese dictionaries 242
    Intermediate textbooks 238   Chinese-Chinese dictionaries 243
    Chinese-English   Linguistic studies 243
      dictionaries 240

LITERATURE 246
    Texts 246   Fiction 261
    Lu Xun 254   Non-fiction 271
    Poetry 256

THE ARTS 277
    History 277   Music and dance 287
    Painting and calligraphy 279 Theatre and film 288
    Pottery, sculpture and   Cooking 290
      crafts 284

SPORT AND RECREATION 293

LIBRARIES, MUSEUMS AND ARCHIVES 295

Contents

MASS MEDIA 299

PERIODICALS AND NEWSPAPERS 301
    Periodicals 301   Newspapers 306

BIBLIOGRAPHIES AND DIRECTORIES 307

INDEX OF AUTHORS, TITLES AND SUBJECTS 319

MAP OF CHINA 391

Introduction

Purpose of this Bibliography
The goal is to present a selection of over 1,450 works in English which will provide basic information on China, including its culture, its place in the world and the qualities which make it unique. Like the other volumes in the *World Bibliographical Series*, this book is designed for 'an audience ranging from the informed general reader to the scholar who wishes to obtain background information in a field other than his own'. It is hoped that this volume will meet the needs of new students of China and those anticipating a long stay in China or requiring a greater acquaintance with it as a result of business or professional contacts. It should also be useful to librarians seeking to enlarge or improve their Chinese collections.

The People's Republic of China: Past, Present and Future
China has an area of 3.7 million square miles, slightly more than the 3.6 million square miles of the United States (including Alaska and Hawaii). Although the country extends through slightly more than 35° of latitude, nearly all of its densely populated agricultural lands and significant industrial areas are situated between 46°N and 23°N, comparable to the latitudes of Montreal and Havana, respectively. Beijing is 1° further north than Washington, DC; Najing and Savannah and Muken and Boston are latitudinally comparable. Nearly all of South China, however, representing about 20% of the total area of the country, lies south of the latitude of the continental United States (with the exception of the Florida peninsula).

Nearly one-fourth of the world's population lives in China. The official 1982 Chinese census showed a population of 1,008,175,288. Population density varies strikingly within the country, with the greatest contrast being between the eastern half of China and the lands of the West and the North-west. The high mountains, plateaux and arid basins of the Xizang Highlands and Xixiang-Mongolian Region comprise

Introduction

slightly more than 50% of the area of China, but this vast territory contains only about 5% of the total population. In the eastern half of China, which contains almost all of the agricultural land, population densities generally range upward from 130 persons per square mile. Major areas in which the population density is in excess of 520 persons per square mile include the North China Plain, the middle and lower Yangzi Valley and the Sichuan Basin. Smaller and discontinuous high-density areas occur along the South-eastern coast, in river valleys and basins in the hilly interior of South China, in the Wei and Fen River valleys of North China, and in parts of the Manchurian Plain. Exceptionally high population densities − for example, more than 1,500 persons per square mile − occur in the lower Yangzi Valley and the western Sichuan Basin. Most of the extremely high-density areas are coterminous with the level-to-rolling alluvial plains on which intensive agriculture is centred. A major exception is the moderately hilly Sichuan Basin; it contains little level land, but many man-made terraces, which combined with a long growing season, have permitted a very high rural population density.

Agriculture in China accounts for almost 50% of the national income, employs about 80% of the labour force and provides a major proportion of China's exports. The size of the yearly harvest vitally affects consumption, industrial production, capital investment, revenue, foreign and retail trade and other economic variables. Thus, China's need to increase agricultural productivity, and the continuing debate over policies to achieve this end, provide the leadership with its most serious and persistent economic problem. Most plans for significant increases in agricultural output are geared towards improving yields through expansion of irrigation and multiple cropping, application of chemical fertilizers and the use of improved varieties of seed, better land management and coordination of land and water conservancy programmes. Wheat, barley, corn, kaoliang, millet and other cereals, peas and soy beans are produced in the North; rice, sugar and indigo in the South. Rice is the staple food of the Chinese. Fruit is grown in abundance. Fibre crops are important and include abutilon, hemp, jute, ramie and flax. Cotton is produced mostly in the Yangzi and Yellow River valleys. Tea is cultivated principally in the West and South.

China's energy resources vary, but they are sufficient to support a major industrialization programme. Coal reserves and hydroelectric potential are very large, comparing favourably with those in the United States and the USSR. The supply of petroleum is much more limited, but it is adequate for the relatively modest present requirements of China. The distribution of coal and hydroelectric resources is complementary; North and North-east China are major coal producers, with

Introduction

large coal reserves and relatively limited water power resources; in contrast, South China and areas in the South-west apparently lack large coal reserves but possess immense hydroelectric resources. Many of the best potential hydroelectric sites are located in Yunnan, western Sichuan, and eastern Xizang — in sparsely populated areas, distant from urban and industrial centres. Most of China's electric power facilities are concentrated in three areas — in the industrialized North-east in the vicinity of Anshan and Fushun, in the North around Beijing, and in the East in the Shanghai-Nanjing region.

China is relatively well endowed with most minerals and metals and is a significant world producer of several mineral products. Antimony and tungsten reserves are believed to be the largest in the world, and the supply of aluminous ores, lead, magnetics, manganese, molybdenum, mercury, tin, and a number of lesser minerals and metals is also very great. Major mineral deposits occur in the South-eastern part of Liaoning province and Southern China from eastern Guizhou to north-east Guangdong. Important mining areas are also located in northern Hebei, along the middle and lower Yangzi valley, in central Hunan, and in southern Yunnan. Scattered and often sizeable mineral deposits are located elsewhere, particularly in the western provinces, where they are, for the most part, still untapped.

Industry in China has expanded impressively from the small base inherited by the present government three decades ago. Nevertheless, Chinese industry remains relatively undeveloped in relation to the country's natural resources, huge population and the ambitions of its leadership. Factories and mines are still concentrated in the eastern third of the country, and they probably produce only about 20% of the gross national product.

North-east China, which is comprised of most of former Manchuria, continues to rank as China's largest industrial concentration and the foremost centre of heavy industry. The region is the largest producer of electric power, iron and steel, gold, natural and synthetic petroleum, timber, paper, trucks and a variety of machinery and equipment. Although heavy industry continues to be concentrated in the southern part of the region (Mukden, Anshan, Fushun and Dairen), perhaps one-fifth of the projects that were completed with Soviet aid are located to the North in Kirin and Heilongjiang.

East China, though smallest in area, has nearly one-third of China's population, a factor that helps explain the ranking in total industrial production in the manufacture of textiles and other consumer goods. It is second in total industrial output and its production of chemicals, electric power, machinery and equipment, and iron and steel is also

Introduction

large. Much of the region's productive capacity is located in Shanghai, China's largest industrial and commercial metropolis.

North China ranks third in total industrial production, and its major industrial area is located in a triangle formed by the cities of Beijing, Tangshan and Tianjin. The region leads the nation in coal output and ranks high in the production of iron and steel, chemicals, electric power, textiles and paper. Industrial development of the region had been aided by plentiful supplies of local coal and a relatively good railway network.

Central-South China, ranking second after the East in population, is China's largest producer of refined sugar and ranks second in textile and paper production. Light industry is centred in the Guangzhou area, which specializes in sugar, paper, silk textiles and various handicrafts. Heavy industry is concentrated in the middle Yangzi valley at Wuhan and at Loyang in northern Henan. The region continues to be an important producer of raw materials, particularly non-ferrous metals, such as tungsten, manganese and antimony.

The predominantly mountainous and formerly isolated provinces of South-west China have received a modest and diversified industrial buildup under the present government. Mining is important; the region probably leads the nation in tin production and it is also responsible for sizeable outputs of copper and lead. New heavy industrial facilities specializing in electronic equipment and chemicals have been constructed in the Sichuan Basin, where growing industrial areas are centred at Zhongqin and Chengdu.

North-west China, although by far the largest region, is the least industrialized. Practically all industry in this region has been developed since 1949. Apart from the petroleum industry, which is widespread and ranks second to that of the North-east, important industrial facilities are pocketed around the cities of Lanzhou and Xian. Soviet assistance in the industrial development of the region has been considerable, but a substantial part of the growing petro-chemical industry at Lanzhou is being constructed with equipment and complete plants imported from the West.

The year 1980 brought significant changes in the leadership of the People's Republic of China. Deng Xiaoping, the powerful deputy premier, succeeded in removing his rivals and placing his trusted associates in key positions. With the appointment of his protégé Zhao Ziyang to replace Hua Guofeng as Premier, Deng's dominance in the government became indisputable. Important changes were also adopted to advance the economy. The principles of managerial autonomy, material incentives, the development of productive forces, and correlation between production and market demands were applied to both industry and agriculture. Fear of Soviet expansion remained the central element in China's foreign policy. Greater cooperation with the United States, friendship with Japan, and confrontation with Vietnam were the result of Soviet expansionism.

Mao Zedong, the late Party chairman, was subjected to more and more direct attacks as the Deng group rose to power. They called Mao's paternal type of rule a remnant of feudalism and regarded the Cultural Revolution as an appalling calamity. Mao's economic policies were denounced as unsuitable to modern times. The Dazhai Agricultural Brigade in Shanxi province, which has been regarded by Mao as a model for agricultural production, was pronounced a failure. The Gang of Four and six other defendants went on trial on 20 November 1980 in Beijing. On 25 January 1981, after more than 2 months, the court reached its verdict. All 10 defendants were found guilty of counter-revolutionary crimes. Jiang Qing (Mao's wife) received a death sentence, which was suspended for 2 years. If, after that period, Jiang showed signs of repentance, the sentence would be commuted to life imprisonment. If not, the court would then order her execution. Zhang Chunqiao received the same sentence, while Yao Wenyuan was sentenced to 20 years and Wang Hongwen to life imprisonment. The other defendants — Chen Boda and the five military leaders — were given prison sentences ranging from 16 to 18 years. Jiang's suspended death sentence was a compromise reached in the Politburo to avoid opposition from any remaining Maoists. The trial was, in fact, a political struggle in legal disguise, but it was necessary as a prelude to the formal assessment of Mao's place in history.

On 30 June 1981, the Central Committee made public a formal evaluation of Mao Zedong — the resolution of 'Certain questions in the History of our Party'. Surveying the 60-year history of the Party, the 35,000-word statement focused its criticism on the Cultural Revolution, which, it said, 'was responsible for the most severe setback and heaviest losses suffered by the Party, the state, and the people since the founding of the Party'. The Cultural Revolution, it went on, 'was initiated and led by Comrade Mao Zedong,' who acted on the basis of 'erroneous left theses.' During the period, he 'confused right with wrong, and the people with the enemy'. He acted 'more and more arbitrarily and subjectively, and increasingly put himself above the Central Committee of the Party'. However, conceded the resolution, Mao in his later years remained alert in the defence of the country's security, stood up to the pressure of 'Soviet imperialism', and pursued a 'correct foreign policy'. For these reasons, and 'particularly for his vital contributions to the cause of the revolution over the years', the Chinese people 'have always regarded Comrade Mao Zedong as their respected and beloved great leader and teacher'. Finally, the resolution stated that 'if we judge his activities as a whole, his contributions to the Chinese revolution outweigh his mistakes'.

The assessment was plainly a compromise between the Deng group and remnant Maoists. Moreover, to strike too hard at Mao, a symbol of Chinese communism for so long, might shake the Communist system too deeply. Nevertheless, Deng achieved his objective of demolishing the image of Mao as an infallible demigod.

The 12th National Party Congress of the Chinese Communist Party was held 1 to 11 September 1982 in Beijing, where a new Party constitution was adopted, which eliminated the posts of chairman and deputy chairman, created a special advisory commission, and expanded the power of the secretariat. The constitutional changes represented a breaking away from a structure that was closely identified with Mao Zedong. The new constitution also called for re-examination of the qualifications of 39 million Party members. The plan was aimed at weeding out leftists and incompetents and ensuring the loyalty of the Party's rank and file. The Congress affirmed the paramount position of Deng Ziaoping in the Party. It elected him chairman of the new Central Advisory Committee and re-elected him Chairman of the Party's Military Commission. It endorsed his constitutional proposals, elected his protégé (Hu Yaobang) to the top leadership, and dropped Hua Guofeng, Mao's chosen successor, from the Politburo. Denouncing Mao's dogmatism and personality cult, the Congress endorsed Deng's pragmatic line and modernization programme.

Earlier, in March 1982, Beijing launched an extensive administrative overhaul to streamline its unwieldy and inefficient bureaucracy. The number of deputy prime ministers was reduced from 13 to 2, while 98 ministries and commissions were consolidated into 52. Each ministry was allowed a minister and only 2 to 4 deputy ministers, whereas previously there could have been 8 or more. The plan would trim the 600,000 administrative staff of the Central Government by 200,000, and replace aged, incompetent workers with younger ones trained in modern technology.

In late November and early December, the annual meeting of the National People's Congress (Parliament) brought other important changes. A new 138-article national constitution, the 4th of the Communist régime, was ratified. During the session, Prime Minister Zhao Ziyang unveiled a new 5-year economic plan (1981-85). The new plan – China's 6th – called for a continuation of general 'economic readjustments'. Emphasis would be given to increased productivity, higher profitability, and 'real growth' – projected at a moderate 4-5% annually. Increased exports and foreign capital would help spur overall economic expansion. Collective and individual enterprises were to supplement state undertakings, and individual incentives would be increased to create more markets for Chinese products and to bring in advanced technology for China's industrial development. Beijing began to phase out the commune system, which had been established in 1958 as the shortcut to 'pure' communism. Communes gave way to *xiang* (rural townships), and production brigades to villages, as units of local government. The economic functions of such units were assigned to agricultural-industrial-commercial companies expressly responsible for rural output.

While China's modernization programme requires economic and technical exchanges with capitalist countries, these may bring foreign influences that threaten the Communist way of life. 'It is therefore necessary', said Hu Yaobang, 'to guard against, and firmly resist, the corrosion by capitalist ideas and to combat any worship of things foreign or fawning on foreigners'. The official press launched a concerted attack on the 'poisoning' effect of capitalist ideology and the 'pollution' it produces. The government forbade unauthorized contacts with foreigners and banned social dancing, western rock music, and racier videotapes and books.

Yet, dedicated to modernization, the new leadership in the 1980s took a more liberal position regarding social life and cultural trends. American television programmes were shown, and western classical music was played in big cities. While items of beauty were condemned as bourgeois during the Cultural Revolution, they were now displayed without fear of official censure. Flowers, paintings and vases reappeared in Chinese homes and women's clothing became colourful again. Artistic and literary freedom, however, was still remote. Deng Xiaoping personally directed a campaign against 'bourgeois liberalism' among Chinese writers and artists whose work he said propagated 'opposition to the leadership of the Party.' He insisted that the main task of art and literature is to heighten people's enthusiasm for socialism.

Beijing made the Taiwan question a test of its relations with the United States. In April 1982, when the Reagan administration was ready to proceed with a $60 million sale of military equipment to Taiwan, China protested loudly, contending that in the Shanghai Communiqué of 1972, the United States acknowledged only one China and that Taiwan was an integral part of it. Consequently, said Beijing, arms sales to Taiwan constituted an interference in China's internal affairs and an infringement of its sovereignty over Taiwan. Deng

Introduction

Xiaoping warned that his country was 'well prepared' to downgrade diplomatic relations with the United States if no agreement could be reached over the Taiwan problem. On 17 August, after much delicate negotiation, the two nations issued a joint communiqué in which China stated that its message to Taiwan on 1 January 1979 'promulgated a fundamental policy of striving for peaceful reunification of the mother-land' and that the plan put forward on 30 September 1981 'represented a further major effort under this fundamental policy to strive for a peaceful solution to the Taiwan question'. For its part, the United States stated that the arms sales to Taiwan 'will not exceed, either in qualitative or in quantitative terms, the level of those supplied in recent years', and that it 'intends to reduce gradually its sales of arms to Taiwan, leading over a period of time to a final resolution'. Beyond the Taiwan question, China and the United States made good progress in the expansion of economic and technical cooperation. As Washington liberalized its export policy towards Beijing, trade between the two countries rose sharply, with China becoming the 14th largest trading partner of the United States.

The future of Hong Kong was the major subject of discussion when the British Prime Minister Margaret Thatcher visited Beijing, 22-26 September 1982. China made it clear that it planned to regain sovereignty over Hong Kong, although it assured island residents that they had no cause for concern. On 24 September, after a lengthy conference with Deng Xiaoping, Prime Minister Thatcher read a joint statement announcing that China and Great Britain agreed to enter talks through diplomatic channels 'with the common aims of maintaining the stability and prosperity of Hong Kong'. No details were given as to their respective positions.

On 24 March 1982, Soviet President Leonid Brezhnev proposed that Moscow and Beijing resume border talks, which had been suspended since 1978, to discuss measures to improve relations. China's response was cautious. When Brezhnev, on 26 September, appealed for 'a normalization, a gradual improvement of relations', Beijing finally agreed to increase contacts. On 5 October, talks were resumed in Beijing. Foreign Minister Huang Hua led the Chinese delegation to Brezhnev's funeral on 15 November. The next day Huang met with his Soviet counterpart, Andrei Gromyko, in the first high-level talks between the two powers in 13 years. One week later, in his first major policy speech, new Soviet chief Yuri Andropov promised to seek improved relations with China.

On 26 September 1982 Japanese Prime Minister Zenko Suzuki arrived in Beijing on an official visit to commemorate the 10th anniversary of the normalization of relations between the two countries. In his talks with Chinese leaders, Suzuki agreed to increase Japanese investment in offshore oil exploration by $400 million to a total of $600 million.

In other parts of Asia, China played an instrumental role in the formation of a Cambodian guerrilla coalition when that country's three major resistance leaders signed a declaration to join forces in the struggle against Vietnamese occupation. Numerous conflicts occurred along the Chinese-Vietnamese border during 1982, with many Chinese peasants reported killed or wounded.

China and India held talks in May 1982 on the 20-year-old border dispute that had been the obstacle to normal relations between the two countries. Beijing proposed that the discussions be extended to include economic relations, technological cooperation and cultural exchanges. No accord was reported, but the two sides agreed to meet again. Over protests from New Delhi, China and Pakistan opened the Khunjerab Pass on 27 August 1982. Situated at the end of a highway from Xinjiang into Pakistan, the pass links the two countries along the ancient Silk Road. Finally, on 20 December Prime Minister Zhao Ziyang set out on a month-long, 10-nation tour of Africa to strengthen ties with the Third World.

Nature and Form of this Bibliography

In accordance with series style, first priority in selection was given to works which can be expected to be found in the larger public and university libraries. Many of the books listed are still in print. Works cited are in the English language, mainly published by American and British publishers between 1970 and 1982. Thousands of books on China have been published since 1970, along with many thousands of articles published by hundreds of periodicals. It was necessary to omit all periodical articles and to focus on complete books.

The subject classification carries 31 category titles, based on previous volumes in the series and within each section, the annotations are listed alphabetically by author. Each annotation gives a brief description about each book in a factual and objective way. Although I have been able to see all 1,470 works in one of the following three libraries — University of Nebraska-Lincoln, Yenching Library at Harvard University and the Hoover Institute at Stanford University — I was not able to read all in full. As a result, the annotations were written with the help of such sources as book review digests, review articles in periodicals, and by scanning the contents of the work.

Introduction

In 1958 a phonetic alphabet was officially introduced to transcribe Chinese characters for texts in the Roman alphabet. The widespread use of *Pinyin* has led to a gradual suppression of the Wade transliteration system formerly widely used in English-language works. In this bibliography, names are given largely according to the *Pinyin* system. However, wherever possible, particularly in the annotations (but also as cross-references in the index), reference is given to Wade-Giles forms.

Sources and Acknowledgements
The sources used in compiling this volume are various, including libraries, bibliographies, periodicals (*China Quarterly, Journal of Asian Studies, Foreign Affairs, Pacific Affairs,* etc.), publishers' lists, newsletters from various professional organizations and book exhibits at these organizations' annual meetings. I acknowledge with gratitude the excellent services of the staffs of the libraries of the University of Nebraska-Lincoln; Yenching Library, Harvard University; and the Hoover Institute, Stanford University. I am grateful to the Research Council and the Department of Political Science at the University of Nebraska for granting me a semester-leave with a Faculty Development Fund enabling me to complete primary research at Harvard and Stanford. Many thanks go to my lovely wife, Nelly, and three daughters, Margaret, Elizabeth and Patricia, for their proof-reading and above all for their support. Without their encouragement and participation, this book may not have been published. Since the book is not exhaustive, critics will notice some omissions and shortcomings, or disagree with some of my choices. For all these I shall be entirely responsible. Finally, I hope that this volume can serve the purposes that the *World Bibliographical Series* was originally set up to fulfill.

Lincoln, Nebraska
1983

The Country and Its People

1 The official guidebook of China.
Beijing: China Travel and Tour Press, 1981. 352p. maps.
This book accompanies the reader through China from Beijing (Peking) to
Shenyang - through cities and towns both well-known and practically unknown.
The book is filled with details about temples and palaces, public buildings, monu-
ments and art treasures, historic sites, parks and recreation areas in more than
seventy-one regions and cities. Thirty maps and site plans are included.

2 China.
New York: McGraw-Hill, 1980. 288p. photos.
This book paints a vivid portrait of contemporary Chinese life, written by top
Chinese authorities in their specialized fields. It also includes 295 illustrations
(most in full colour) photographed especially for this project by a team of young
photographers.

3 China: land of charm and beauty.
Shanghai, China: Shanghai People's Publishing House, 1976.
258p.
This book has 232 quality photographs with brief captions in English and Chinese
to show the magnificent scenery, historic sites of ancient and new China, and the
changing scene in agriculture and industrial construction. It is a perfect gift for a
friend who did not make the trip or for yourself when you get home.

**4 China and the search for happiness: recurring themes in four
thousand years of Chinese cultural history.**
Wolfgang Bauer, translated from the German by Michael
Shaw.   New York: Seabury Press, 1976. 502p.
One of the major 20th-century works in sinology, this book studies in rich detail
the recurring themes in some four thousand years of Chinese intellectual history.

The Country and Its People

Bauer describes the ways in which Chinese individuals might discover ultimate goodness and achieve happiness.

5 **Festivals in classical China: New Year and other annual observances during the Han dynasty 206 BC-AD 220.**
   Derk Bodde.   Princeton, New Jersey: Princeton University Press, 1975. 435p.
Bodde brings together hundreds of references to festivals in Chinese literature and presents a spectrum of the cosmological concepts, religious and magical beliefs, court life and folk practices of the classical Chinese. The core of this volume is basically a copiously-annotated, partial translation of the 'Treatises on rituals' of the *Hou-Han-Shu*.

6 **The Chinese.**
   David Bonavia.   New York: Lippincott, 1980. 288p.
This portrait of life in China today concerns peasants and city dwellers - their jobs and attitudes; problems and joys; their roles as men and women, parents and children; their increasing numbers; their medicines; their officials and laws; their competition for education and its privileges; their new consumerism and their changing language. In addition the new relationship with the United States is weighed against China's mounting conflict with the Soviet Union.

7 **China, 1949-1976.**
   Colin Brown.   London: Heinemann, 1977. 200p.
Relying heavily on contemporary documents, this book contains an analysis of the transformation of China's world role since the Communist Revolution and of the changes in the country's internal policies and social and economic organization. It also has a postscript on the fall of Teng Hsiao-ping (Deng Xiaoping) and the death of Mao Tse-tung (Mao Zedong).

8 **China: a second look.**
   Claudie Broyelle, Jacques Broyelle, Evelyne Tschirhart.   Atlantic Highlands, New Jersey: Humanities Press, 1980. 308p.
Eye-witness accounts by three French Marxists of the control exercised by the Communist Party bureaucracy in the early 1970s.

9 **China since the Gang of Four.**
   Edited by William Brugger.   New York: St. Martin's Press, 1980. 288p.
In seven specially-commissioned essays, this book explores the dramatic changes that have occurred in China since the death of Chairman Mao and the arrest of the Gang of Four in late 1976. The contributors consider the crucial questions of how far Mao's policies have been abandoned or modified and the reactions of the Gang of Four in their attempt to identify the broad significance of the recent Chinese experience.

10 **China.**
Keith Buchanan, Charles P. Fitzgerald, Colin A.
Ronan. Boston, Massachusetts: Little, Brown, 1981. 520p.
maps. photos. illus.

Uniquely organized into three fundamental areas - the land and its people; history and culture; science and technology - this volume presents a complete picture of Chinese civilization, capturing in brilliant colour photographs and cogent text, the splendour and fervour of everyday life in China today. Includes over 600 photographs and illustrations and numerous maps, charts and diagrams.

11 **China: alive in the bitter sea.**
Fox Butterfield. New York: Times Books, 1982. 468p.

For three decades China has been a closed society. Now, Fox Butterfield, the first *New York Times* correspondent permitted to live in Beijing (Peking) since 1949, presents a brilliantly original work that reveals the Chinese as only they know themselves. With the incomparable advantage of speaking the language, and with daily and relentless observation, he gives readers a unique report of the present state of China in this overwhelming book.

12 **Twentieth century China.**
O. Edmund Clubb. New York: Columbia University Press, 1978. 3rd ed. 312p.

This book, written by a former American diplomat, is brisk and pungent in style and its keynote is realism. This new edition includes chapters on Mao's final years and the beginning of the pragmatist régime.

13 **China's civilization: a survey of its history, arts, and technology.**
Arthur Cotterell, David Morgan. New York: Praeger, 1975. 320p. maps. photos.

For each of the main historical periods, there are sections on such topics as economics and society, science and technology, political changes, and artistic achievements. Numerous maps, photographs, and reproductions from classical Chinese work together with accounts written by contemporary Western travellers in China combine to make this work a unique introduction to Chinese civilization.

14 **The Chinese experience.**
Raymond Dawson. London: Weidenfeld & Nicolson, 1978. 318p.

This book attempts to explain the constant and essential features of Chinese civilization and history under four major headings: political; philosophical; socioeconomic; and aesthetic. In essence, it is an advanced text that treats and interprets the civilization of China from ancient times to the 1970s in topical order.

The Country and Its People

15 **China: the land and its people.**
R. R. C. De Crespigny. New York: St. Martin's Press,
1971. 235p.
Beginning with a general overview, the author proceeds with an analysis of the climate, geology and land reforms, soils, agriculture and industry, population, etc. by geographical region.

16 **China's civilization and society: a source book.**
Edited by Patricia Buckley Ebrey. New York: Free Press,
1981. 429p.
This is a book of primary source materials covering Chinese history from the classical period (1766 BC) to the 20th century (1979). It includes letters, diaries, stories, folk-tales, newspaper articles, essays and excerpts from handbooks and histories. These translations, arranged chronologically, by major period, are intended to introduce the reader to Chinese civilization.

17 **East Asia: tradition and transformation.**
John K. Fairbank, Edwin O. Reischauer, Albert M.
Craig. Boston, Massachusetts: Houghton Mifflin, 1978. 2nd
ed. 982p.
This book is a comprehensive, one-volume history of Chinese, Japanese, Korean and Vietnamese civilizations. The authors place particular emphasis on distinctive intellectual and aesthetic achievements. They also include up-to-date interpretations, with special attention to the Vietnam war, Korea, and recent transformations in Japanese and Chinese societies. The work covers the period from 1500 BC to 1978. Particularly interesting is the comparative material which not only juxtaposes Chinese and Japanese history but also often compares with the Western experience and poses useful and provocative questions.

18 **China: old and new.**
John K. Fairbank. Cambridge, Massachusetts: Audiovisual
Division, Harvard University Press, 1977.
China: Old and New is many Chinas. We see China in dynastic times, China under Western domination, China in upheaval, and China today. Fairbank's analysis is sympathetic and scholarly. In a series of fifteen colour film-strips that form a masterful introduction to China, he shows readers all of China: its people, history and culture.

19 **China Handbuch.** (Handbook of China.)
Edited by Wolfgang Franke, Brunhild Staiger. Dusseldorf,
GFR: Bertelsmann, 1974. 1,767p.
This handbook covers the period from 1840 to the present. It contains in alphabetical order over 300 items written by some 130 authors, selected under headings such as geography, history, society and economy, with close on 50 items in each section. The remaining third of the volume covers such wide-ranging aspects of Chinese affairs as constitutions, institutions, law, education, communications, religion, historiography, language, literature, the arts, and last, but not least, China's international relations.

20 **Mao's people: sixteen portraits of life in revolutionary China.**
B. Michael Frolic. Cambridge, Massachusetts: Harvard
University Press, 1980. 278p.

In 16 vignettes culled from interviews with over 200 Chinese refugees, the author
offers a panorama of contemporary life in the People's Republic of China. His
informants are from all over China. They include peasants, workers, soldiers,
students, housewives, technicians, translators, even criminals. The wide demographic, geographic, and occupational range provided by the 16 narrators make
this a unique account of everyday life in China.

21 **A history of Chinese civilization.**
Jacques Gemet, translated from the French by J. R.
Foster. Boulder, Colorado: Westview Press, 1980. 750p.

The book, first published in France in 1974 as *Le Monde Chinois*, is finally
available in English. Reviewed in France as the most comprehensive single-volume
history - social, political, economic, technological, religious and intellectual - of
China, from the earliest times to the present day, it will be an equally invaluable
introduction for the English-speaking world. The author has updated this edition
to include the fall of the Gang of Four and has revised earlier parts of the text in
the light of recent scholarship.

22 **The People's Republic of China: a handbook.**
Edited by Harold C. Hinton. Boulder, Colorado: Westview
Press, 1979. 450p.

In this volume, 11 specialists have contributed articles to inform the general
reader about the People's Republic. Each piece discusses issues such as population, the political system, geography, history, agriculture, industry, social affairs,
culture, foreign policy, education, society, technology and military affairs. General
readers can use the book to obtain up-to-date and accurate information about
China.

23 **The People's Republic of China: an overview.**
Edited by Joyce K. Kallgren. Berkeley, California: Center
for Chinese Studies, University of California, 1979. 122p.

The essays can be grouped in three categories: those dealing with the development
of political institutions since 1949; secondly, those which consider economic policy
and achievements; thirdly, essays on domestic policy and foreign relations.

24 **Encyclopedia of China today.**
Frederic M. Kaplan, Julian N. Sobin, Stephen Andors,
introduction by John Service. New York: Macmillan, 1979.
336p. maps. bibliog. charts. tables. glossary.

This encyclopaedia sets out, in clear, concise prose and in short sections unim-
peded by footnotes, a mass of information on China's geography, politics, economy, industry, agriculture, health care, education, culture, travel and services in
an easy-to-read, indexed format, buttressed by 55 tables, 3 chronologies and 14
maps and charts, as well as a glossary and annotated bibliography.

25 Mao and China: from revolution to revolution.
Stanley Karnow. New York: Viking Press, 1972. 592p.

The author offers a compelling and brilliant account of the events that changed the face of China in the 1960s - and gives us some important and well-founded answers to many of our questions about this extraordinary country today and in the future. He makes Mao and his antagonists speak out in the heat of their struggle as no one has done before. His book is a bold attempt to describe the course of the Cultural Revolution, the debate and struggles among Chinese leaders which led up to it, and Mao's central role.

26 Modern China: an interpretative anthology.
Edited by Joseph R. Levenson. New York: Macmillan, 1971. 236p.

A collection of essays by distinguished historians, linked together by the cryptic and aphoristic comments of the editor. This book deals with the question of how the Chinese have tried to define China and its history, the role of the past and feelings about the past in these definitions, what threatened the old order and why people felt the need to threaten it, and the goals of those who constituted the threat.

27 Chinese shadow.
Simon Leys. New York: Viking Press, 1977. 220p.

Leys, a Belgian art historian, presents a critical assessment of contemporary Chinese cultural values. As he sees it, the rulers of China have displaced a rich literary heritage with a monotony of Maoist propaganda, turned temples into warehouses and barracks and suppressed compassionate human relations in the name of class.

28 Traditional China.
Edited by James T. C. Liu, Du Weiming. New York: Prentice-Hall, 1970. 179p.

A collection of essays by James Liu and Tu Wei-ming (Du Weiming) which discuss topics such as geographical isolation the urban-rural continuum, state monopolies and capitalism, the closed society, civil service systems, peasant rebellions, law and property, and the philosophic teachings of Confucianism, Taoism, and Buddhism before the dawn of China's modern period. This work offers a good background to the cultural legacy of modern China.

29 The Chinese way: life in the People's Republic of China.
Gil Loescher. New York: Harcourt, 1974. 206p.

Covering the major historical events in two chapters, the authors then discuss topics like the People's Liberation Army and its relation to the public, the use of dance for communicating political ideas, the changes in the Chinese language to improve literacy, and the role of women in pre-and-post revolution China.

30 Mao's China: a history of the People's Republic.
Maurice Meisner. New York: Free Press, 1977. 512p.

Part of this book is a general inquiry into the Chinese historical environment from which Chinese Marxist revolutionaries emerged and an account of the conditions they encountered and transformed. Parts two to five attempt to relate and assess the history of what now can be called the Maoist era from the time Mao Tse-tung (Mao Zedong) announced the birth of the new state in 1949 to his death on 9 September 1976. This book approaches its subject from a basically theoretical perspective. There is a lot of Marx as well as Mao.

31 An introduction to Chinese civilization.
Edited by John Meskill, J. Mason Gentzler. New York: Columbia University Press, 1973. 699p.
This book consists of a history of China, followed by ten essays on aspects of Chinese civilization - anthropology, archaeology, art, the economy of traditional and modern China, geography, political institutions, language, literature and religion. Portions of the book were prepared under contract to the US Office of Education and were tested as teaching material at Columbia University before being expanded into the book.

32 Mao's people.
B. Michael Frolic. Cambridge, Massachusetts: Harvard University Press, 1980. 278p.
This book contains firsthand accounts of what daily life is really like in China. Drawn from hundreds of interviews, these engrossing vignettes range from the totally corrupt man who loved dog meat to life among the Tibetans.

33 China: tradition and revolution.
Peter H. Mitchell. Toronto: Macmillan, 1977. 234p.
The author argues that understanding can only come through approaching contemporary China in terms of China's own past. In the opening chapters, he sketches the geographical background, the condition of the peasantry and the intellectual and imperial framework of the state superstructure. He then discusses extensively the impact of the outside world, and shows both the internal and external causes of the breakdown of the traditional system. The Communists' success is seen largely as the result of their leadership of the peasantry who are the time-honoured force for change in China. The book concludes by looking at the new China and sees it as relatively successful in solving the traditional internal problems of poverty.

34 China: its history and culture.
W. Scott Morton. New York: McGraw-Hill, 1980. 276p. illus.
This book is a concise study of China's history and culture from ancient times to the present, by a well-known sinologist. Filled with photographs, maps, paintings, and drawings, this book gives approximately equal treatment to all periods.

35 China: revolution continued.
Jan Myrdal, Gun Kessle, translated from the revised Swedish edition by Paul Britten Austin. New York: Pantheon Books, 1971. 224p. photos.
After seven years, the authors of *Report from a Chinese Village* returned to the village of Liu Ling in Northern Shensi province. They interviewed the villagers and reported on the nature of China's Cultural Revolution at the village level and its effect on the structure of local government, finance and investment, the roles

of various groups within the community, and women's liberation. Gun Kessle furnishes amazing photographs, primarily of the 'common people'.

36 China briefing, 1980.
Edited by Robert B. Oxnam, Richard C. Bush. Boulder, Colorado: Westview Press, 1980. 126p.

Since the death of Mao Zedong (Mao Tse-tung) in September 1976, China has made breath-taking changes in all areas - politics, economics, foreign policy, culture, and so on. Simultaneously, the island of Taiwan has been undergoing a political evolution in the wake of the termination of formal relations with the United States. This book charts the many changes that have occurred since late 1978.

37 The Chinese: portrait of a people.
Alain Peyrefitte, translated from the French by Graham Webb. New York: Bobbs-Merrill, 1977. 419p.

A report by a former French diplomat who, travelling in China in 1971, had discussions with Chou En-lai (Zhou Enlai) and lesser dignitaries, observed the use of acupuncture as anaesthesia, visited steel mills and collective farms, saw museums and plays, explored big cities, admired newly-tamed great rivers, talked to students and teachers from kindergarten to college level. His generally favourable fascination is balanced by a realistic appraisal of the régime's shortcomings.

38 China: an introduction.
Lucian W. Pye. Boston, Massachusetts: Little, Brown, 1978. 2nd ed. 384p. maps. tables.

This book covers the general history of Chinese civilization from the early beginnings of Chinese history to the late 1970s. It provides the interested reader with an excellent general background. The Communist régime is treated at great length. For an additional aid to the reader, tables on such subjects as Chinese language, population and the dynasties, as well as maps of China, are featured throughout the book.

39 China: a general survey.
Qi Wen. Beijing: Foreign Language Press, 1979. 252p.

This book by Ch'i Wen (Qi Wen) is an official publication. The five chapters are entitled geography, history, politics, economy and culture, respectively, and each has a number of sections - for education, science, technology, medicine and health care, sport, literature, art, and news and publications. Readers are likely to find this book useful as a brief résumé of the present state of official thinking and practice.

40 Mao's way.
Edward E. Rice. Berkeley, California: University of California Press, 1972. 569p.

This book follows Mao Tse-tung's (Mao Zedong) career from his birth in 1893 up to and including 1971 and traces the course of Mao's Cultural Revolution from the cool vantage point of an analyst of political tactics. The author uses an enormous number of primary and secondary sources to describe in a systematic and chronological fashion the contending groups in this upheaval in China.

41 The mind of China: the culture, customs, and beliefs of traditional China.

Ben-Ami Scharfstein. New York: Basic Books; Dell, 1974. 181p.

The five parts of this book examine various facets of the world of the Chinese literati. In the first, their mode of life and upbringing has been recreated. Part two is a consideration of the Chinese character as seen in the careers and work of poets and painters. The remainder of the book deals in succession with the Chinese consciousness of the historical process, views about the universe, and the role of language and philosophy in shaping the Chinese mind.

42 China: facts and figures annual. Volume iv.

Edited by John L. Scherer. Florida: Academic International Press, 1981. 422p.

This volume is an impressive compendium of information on China. It presents its materials in lists or tables, occasionally accompanied by brief prose commentaries. It draws heavily on recent US government publications, but also cites various Chinese published sources and a variety of other Western materials. The data is organized into 12 main categories: government, Communist party, armed forces, demography, economy, agriculture, trade and foreign aid, transportation, communications, institutions, health, education and welfare, and special topics.

43 The China reader, volume i, ii, iii and iv.

Edited by Franz Schurmann, Orville Schell (for volumes i-iii), David Milton, Nancy Milton, Franz Schurmann (for volume iv). New York: Random House, 1970. 1974.

This comprehensive history covers the years from the Manchu dynasty to the Cultural Revolution and the reopening of communications with the West in the 1970s. Among the political leaders, literary men, scholars, and journalists contributing to the volumes are Anna Louise Strong, Joan Robinson, Mao Tse-tung (Mao Zedong), Louis Kraar, James Reston, Joseph Alsop and Edgar Snow.

44 The gate of heavenly peace: the Chinese and their revolution, 1895-1980.

Jonathan D. Spence. New York: Viking Press, 1981. 465p.

Spence has brought the past 100 years of the Chinese revolution to life with a novelist's flair and an historian's analytical facility. This is intellectual history of the first order. It weaves together the lives of three Chinese intellectuals - the utopian theorist Kang Youwei (K'ang Yu-wei), the writer Lu Xun (Lu Hsun), and the feminist and writer Ding Ling (Ting Ling) - to capture the meaning of the passage from Imperial to Communist China.

45 The China difference.

Edited by Ross Terrill. New York: Harper, 1979. 335p.

This book examines Chinese social and cultural life, covering such topics as Chinese ideas of public and private life, religion (both theistic and political), popular attitudes towards politics and work, law and human rights and the arts. The contributors, with actual living or travelling experience in the People's Republic tell readers what China is like and how it differs from the rest of the world.

The Country and Its People

China: a country study.
See item no. 1240.

China yesterday and today.
See item no. 1242.

China: A Handbook.
See item no. 1262.

China image.
See item no. 1264.

Geography

General

46 The transformation of the Chinese earth: aspects of the evaluation of the Chinese earth from earliest times to Mao Tse-tung.
Keith Buchanan.   New York: Praeger, 1970. 336p.
The author has presented an interdisciplinary study of the transformation of the Chinese earth based upon works in geography, history, economics, ethnology, demography, politics, literature and traditional social structure. While examining this transformation in its historical and global context, he emphasizes the human significance, particularly the role of the peasants in the last two decades.

47 The Sinkiang story.
Jack Chen.   New York: Macmillan, 1977. 386p.
The first 270 pages are a monotonous summary of anthropology, geography, and history from about 3,000 BC until the founding of the People's Republic of China in 1949. The remaining 100 pages are based on notes made by the author Jack Chen (Ch'en) when he was in Sinkiang in 1957. The book contains a useful glossary of geographical, people's and tribes' names.

48 An outline of Chinese geography.
Chung Chi.   Beijing: Foreign Language Press, 1978. 186p. maps. photos.
The author Chung Chi provides a concise guide to China's various regions, climates, vegetation, animals and birds with maps, photographs, and colour fold-out maps.

49 China charts the world: Hsu Chi-yu and his geography of 1848.

Fred W. Drake. Cambridge, Massachusetts: East Asian Research Center, Harvard University, 1975. 272p.

This book is an account of the life and writings of Hsu Chi-yu (Xu Qiyou), Governor of Fukien. After the Chinese defeat in the 1839 Opium War, Hsu (Xu) attempted to present to the Chinese literati a basic picture of the earth's geography and a view of a pluralistic world of competing states. He published the first Chinese scientific geography of the non-Chinese world entitled *Ying Huan Chih-lueh (Ying Huan Zhilue) (A short account of the maritime circuit)*. Compiled from atlases and materials made available to Hsu (Xu) mostly from missionaries, the book was filled with inventories of resources, economic systems and cultural patterns of the Western world.

50 The Great Wall of China.

Jonathan Fryer. New York: Barnes, 1978. 207p.

The author covers the whole of China's long history as he traces the Great Wall from its beginnings to the present in an entertaining account, embellished by legends and anecdotes, presented with literary verve and charm.

51 Peking.

Felix Greene. New York: Mayflower, 1978. 162p. photos.

The author views the capital city of China with a critical but affectionate eye, sensitive to its beauty and responsive to its history and people. His interviews tap the inner life of its citizens, their home and work problems. His colour photography is superb.

52 Water management in the Yellow River basin of China.

Charles Greer. Austin, Texas; London: University of Texas Press, 1979. 174p.

The Yellow River, China's Sorrow! This book deals with the river and the human efforts to cope with its whims and to manage it. Greer, a geographer, provides geomorphological and climatic detail, and a longer, though still brief, historical view of farmers, managers and their approaches to river management.

53 The Great Wall.

Luo Zewen, Dick Wilson, Jean-Pierre Drege, Hubert Delahaye. London: Michael Joseph, 1982. 124p.

A team of researchers, historians, graphic experts and photographers from both East and West have been granted access to all the archives and to the Wall itself to produce the definitive one-volume portrait. The text answers questions concerning the exact route of the Wall, its history, its military role and its survival and describes artistic and architectural features and archaeological discoveries including the recent exhumation of the tomb of China's first emperor with its life-size statues of thousands of soldiers.

54 The idea of China: myth and theory in geographic thought.

Andrew J. March. New York: Praeger, 1974. 167p.

The author argues that the standard image of China in the European mind owes more to the Western need for a contrasting backdrop to define the European identity than to Chinese reality. He believes that the role of geography is best understood as secondary to the roles of human dynamism and class struggle.

55 **China geographer. No. 11, agriculture.**
Edited by Clifton W. Pannell, Christopher L. Salter. Boulder, Colorado: Westview Press, 1981. 144p.

Previously appearing in journal format three times a year, the *China Geographer* is now published by Westview Press as a hard cover annual. Each volume will focus on a special aspect of China's physical or human geography and will contain, along with original articles based on primary data, book reviews and other materials of interest to geographers of China. The first volume in the new format, number 11, examines agriculture and forestry in the People's Republic.

56 **China and Inner Asia: from 1368 to the present day.**
Morris Rossabi. New York: Pica Press, 1975. 320p.

Rossabi's work combines chronological and geographical approaches to survey political and economic relations between China and the areas to her north and west including Manchuria, Mongolia, Sinkiang (Xinjiang), and parts of Soviet Central Asia. Part I details Ming China's relations with Inner Asia; part II focuses on the Russian advance across Siberia and the decline of Inner Asia; and part III concerns Inner Asia in the 20th century.

57 **China's changing map: national and regional development, 1949-71.**
Theodore Shabad. New York: Praeger, 1972. 370p.

The author updates his earlier work, making this an indispensable geographical and economic reference tool for the student of Chinese affairs.

58 **China: a geographical survey.**
T. R. Tregear. Sevenoaks, England: Hodder & Stoughton, 1980. 352p. photos.

This volume is newly published, but it is not a new book. It is essentially a reprint within one cover of materials from the author's *Geography of China* (1965) and *Economic Geography of China* (1970). Most of the photographs are more recent than the text, and the book is attractively presented. The author draws his information from first-hand experience of the country and constant monitoring of Chinese newspapers, magazines and reports.

59 **Readings in Chinese geography.**
Jack F. Williams, Yong Deng Jiaye. Honolulu: University Press of Hawaii, 1970. 172p.

The authors Jack Williams and Yung Teng Chia-yee (Yong Deng Jiaye) progressively introduce advanced students to place-names and geographical terms necessary to enable the use of primary source materials in Chinese.

60 **China: all provinces and autonomous regions.**
Zheng Shifeng, designed by Massino Vignell. New York:
McGraw-Hill, 1980. 285p.

The captioned photographs are divided by the author Cheng Shih-feng (Zheng Shifeng) into an introduction and seven regional chapters. The seven regional chapters group the provinces in China proper and the former empire's subject dependencies, from Manchuria to Taiwan and Tibet. The location of each region is shown at the beginning of its chapter on the outline map of China as a whole.

61 **China city brief.**
United States Central Intelligence Agency. Washington,
DC: US Government Printing Office, 1975. 167p.

This book gives descriptive information on the following 13 cities: Anshan, Changsha (Zhangsha), Changchow (Zhangzhou), Chungching (Zhongqing), Hangchou (Hangzhou), Canton (Guangzhou), Kueilin (Guilin), Kunming (Gunming), Peking (Beijing), Shanghai, Suchou (Suzhou), Tientsin (Tianjin) and Wuhan. A separate part summarizes weather conditions and new street maps for each city complete this unique reference work.

62 **Karst in China.**
Beijing: Foreign Language Press, 1976. 143p. photos.

This book has striking photographs of limestones, particularly in the area of Guilin (Kuei-lin) and southern China, including caves and mountain scenery.

Maps and atlases

63 **A map history of modern China.**
Brian Catchpole. London: Heinemann, 1976. 152p.

The author has put the main events of the 20th century into the context of Chinese history. Students in Chinese history, Asian studies and world civilization will find the book an enjoyable and helpful textbook.

64 **The Times atlas of China.**
Edited by P. J. M. Geelan, D. C. Twitchett. London: Times
Books, 1974. 144p.

In addition to full-page maps of all twenty-nine provinces and major autonomous regions, with associated notes and a list of all place-names with their Chinese ideographs, the atlas contains seventeen historical maps of various aspects of modern China (such as population, national minorities, climate, agriculture, roads, waterways, railroads, minerals, energy, trade, industry, administrative divisions, and China's international frontiers), five physical maps, and thirty-two city plans. There is also a glossary, and an index which gives the place-names according to the Wade-Giles romanization system.

65 **Atlas of China.**
Hsieh Chiao-min, edited by Christopher L. Salter   New
York: McGraw-Hill, 1973. 282p.
The author Hsieh Chiao-min has packed this volume with factual information to
delight China buffs. Altogether the atlas includes 273 maps, divided into four sections:
physical geography; cultural patterns; economic geography (divided into regions); and
historical geography (beginning with the Chun-Chiu (Zhun-Jiu) period).

66 **China in maps, 1890-1960: a selective and annotated
cartobibliography.**
Jack F. Williams.   East Lansing, Michigan: Michigan State
University Press, 1974. 365p.
A cartobibliography is a bibliography of maps, including only official sheets
published during the period indicated by the governments of China, France, Great
Britain, Germany, Japan, the Soviet Union and the United States.

67 **People's Republic of China: administrative atlas.**
United States Central Intelligence Agency.   Washington,
DC: US Government Printing Office, 1976. 68p.
The atlas contains maps of each province broken down into sub-provinces and
hsien (xian). It has a table of conversion from the Wade-Giles transliteration
system to Pinyin.

68 **People's Republic of China: atlas.**
United States Central Intelligence Agency.   Washington,
DC: US Government Printing Office, 1971. 82p.
The atlas contains maps of China by area and other useful maps of resources,
ethnic groups, railroads, waterways, precipitation, agriculture, fuels and power,
industry, agriculture etc.

69 **Rand McNally illustrated atlas of China.**
New York: Rand McNally, 1972. 80p.
This atlas has been prepared under the auspices of the US Government. China is
divided into six regional sections: the Northeast, the North, the South, the South-
west, the Tibetan (Xizang) Highlands, and the Sinkiang (Xinjiang) region. Each
section in turn is described, illustrated with photographs, and mapped. The geographic section is followed by information on specific aspects of the country -
administrative divisions, population, ethnic and linguistic groups, railways, fuels
and power, industry and human resources, roads and waterways, climate, agriculture, minerals and metals and economy.

Tourism and
Travellers' Accounts

General

70 Prisoner of Mao.
Bao Ruo-Wang, Rudolph Chelminski.   New York: Coward,
McCann & Geoghegan, 1973. 318p.

The author, Bao Ruo-Wang (Pao Jo-wang) or Jean Pasqualini, son of a Corsican
(therefore French national) father and a Chinese mother, spent seven years in
Chinese prisons from 1957 to his release in 1964 on the occasion of Gaullist
France's recognition of China. He was employed during the period from 1945 to
1954 by various embassies in China doing translation and other work. Eventually,
he was imprisoned for assisting the imperialists. This book is the narrative of his
life in the prison camp.

71 To China and back.
Jan Bredsdorf, translated from Danish by Alice
Roughton.   New York: Pantheon, 1980. 207p.

The author describes his experience 1976-77 as a teacher of English to students
in Peking (Beijing) who were in their early or mid-twenties, comparing it with his
earlier stay from 1965-68. He prefers the bureaucratic chaos of the Cultural
Revolution to the bureaucratic legality which replaced it.

72 China: the quality of life.
Wilfred Burchett, Rewi Alley.   New York: Penguin Books,
1976. 312p.

This is a unique report which grew out of the authors' travels across China, in
which they try to measure the changes that have occurred in recent years in
China and set them in perspective against the old China. There are chapters on
communes, health, minorities, the concept of 'Serve the People' and Chinese

attitudes and policies towards history and youth. Particularly useful are chapters on Taching, Tachai and Taoyuan (Tajing, Dazhai, Daoyuan).

73 Barbarians and mandarins: thirteen centuries of western travellers in China.
Nigel Cameron. London: Phoenix, 1970. 443p.

This is a history of some of the Western travellers to China, most of whom paid extended visits, some of whom were on official missions. The book describes the adventures and achievements of individual travellers. It contains competent maps, a detailed index of considerable value and a full bibliography.

74 The face of China as seen by photographers and travellers, 1860-1912.
Prefaced by L. Carrington Goodrich, historical commentary by Nigel Cameron. New York: Aperture, 1978. 159p.

This is a catalogue for an exhibition of photographs from the archives of Harvard University, presented by the Philadelphia Museum of Art in the spring of 1978. This volume contains photographs of the land and people of China taken by little known, or in some cases by completely unknown, photographers who visited China in the last decade of the Ch'ing (Qing) dynasty.

75 China today and her ancient treasures.
Joan Lebold Cohen, Jerome Alan Cohen. New York: Abrams, 1974. 399p. photos.

Introducing his wife's photographs in their lavishly-produced volume, Jerome Cohen stresses the importance of actually seeing China, if only through pictures. The Cohens have used photographs and an accompanying text to tell the history of China from the earliest times to the present day. To do this, they have made ingenious use of the material available on a fairly well-worn route which included Canton (Guangzhou), Peking (Beijing), Shanghai, Loyang (Luoyang), and Sian. They contrast modern and ancient Chinese artistic expression and discuss the political and social evolution of contemporary China.

76 Behind the Great Wall: a photographic essay on China.
Mary Cross, Theodore Cross. New York: Atheneum, 1979. 108p. photos.

The authors seek to share, through photographs and commentary, scenes of China, which they toured in 1978. There are approximately one hundred photographs, mostly of urban life, pictures of the young, the old, soldiers, street scenes and waterways. The authors broke away from the organized tour group wherever possible to find aspects of Chinese life that many Western visitors might not ordinarily witness.

77 A Peking diary: a personal account of modern China.
Lois Fisher. New York: St. Martin's Press, 1979. 256p.

From 1973-1976, Fisher, an American, lived in Peking (Beijing) with her journalist husband. This book recounts her adjustments to China and her observations of the people in Peking (Beijing) and other Chinese locals. Although always regarded as an outsider, she deliberately shunned services designed for foreigners, choosing instead to mingle with ordinary citizens, to frequent their shops and restaurants, and to travel by bicycle exploring the back alleys and out of the way corners of Peking (Beijing). Here she focuses on the details of daily life rather than larger issues of history, politics or economics.

78 China: a world so changed.
C. P. Fitzgerald. London: Heinemann, 1973. 243p. photos.

The book, designed for Western readers, is a combination of a coffee table collection of pictures and a simple history of China. It is for the putative tourist rather than the academic.

79 Faces of China: tomorrow, today, yesterday.
Pat Fok, Ross Terrill. London: Michael Joseph, 1974. 190p.

Mrs Fok's photographs have much charm and capture in many cases the still leisurely pace of life in China. The narrative is straightforward and informative about Chinese daily life and the country's recent achievements.

80 Report from Peking: observations of a Western diplomat on Cultural Revolution.
D. M. Fokkema. London: Hurst, 1972. 174p.

The author sees China mostly from Peking (Beijing), as Embassy Secretary and then Chargé d'Affaires for the Office of Netherlands Chargé d'Affaires. He takes trips to Shansi, Hangchou (Hangzhou) and Shanghai. The narrative runs up to the Ninth Party Congress, a year after he had left China. He concentrates on tracing the shifts in mood of the citizenry as the political turbulence rises and falls.

81 The Chinese: portrait of a people.
John Fraser. New York: Summit Books, 1980. 463p.

The author, dance and theatre critic for the *Toronto Globe and Mail*, was posted to China by his newspaper for two years beginning in late 1977. His arrival after the fall of the Gang of Four, meant that he was witness to important political changes in China, as the pragmatists solidified their hold over a country once in the grip of Maoist radical ideology. His narrative climaxes in an account of the move for liberation represented by the dazibao (Ta Tzu Pao) wall poster flurry at Xian (Hsi An) Democracy Wall - in which the author played a part.

82 Last moments of a world.
Margaret Gaan. New York: Norton, 1978. 273p.

The author, standing apart from both the Kuomingtang (Guomindang) and the Communists, sees the beggary, the peasants' heavy tax burden, the ballooning inflation, and the pervasive Kuomingtang (Guomindang) corruption or squeeze with striking candour. The autobiographical and historical reflections merge to explain clearly why the Communist revolution succeeded. She views the Communist victory with a mixture of relief for China and sadness for her own loss and exile.

83 A China passage.
John Kenneth Galbraith. London: Deutsch, 1973. 143p.

His contribution to the knowledge of China is presented in the form of a day-to-day account of his three weeks away from Harvard. He concludes that there can be no serious doubt that China is devising a highly effective and relatively flexible economic system and he offers a provocative appraisal of the nature of work in China, such as the manner in which production decisions are made and the efforts to eliminate hierarchy and class structure in organizations.

84 Daily life in People's China.
Arthur W. Galston, Jean Savage. New York: Crowell, 1973. 255p.

This book is based on the travel diaries of an American scientist who visited China in 1971. He was the first scientist from the United States to visit China since 1949. He spent a short time visiting universities and research institutes during his 1971 visit, and then returned with his wife and daughter for a longer stay in 1972. During the second visit, the Galston family spent two weeks living and working at the Marco Polo Bridge Commune near Peking (Beijing). The book has a great deal of detail concerning horticulture, the working of the farm folk, the devotion and ingenuity of factory labourers, and the continued emphasis on superb manners of the Chinese toward their guests. Most striking is his praise for the revamping of medical education and the marked improvement in the health of the people.

85 Freedom is a world.
Eric Gordon. London: Hodder & Stoughton, 1971. 351p.

Eric Gordon is a British left-wing journalist who, along with his wife, Marie, and son, Kim, was placed under two years' 'hotel arrest' in China during 1967-69. He had attempted to smuggle out of the country certain publications which were not to be exported. Gordon's attempt failed and his two years' detention was the result. The book is mostly a chronicle of those two years in a Peking (Beijing) hotel room.

86 Hsiang-Ya journal.
Ruth Altman Greene. Hamden, Connecticut: Archer Books, 1977. 171p.

The Greenes were astute, empathetic observers of the passing scene, and they wrote rich, marvellously detailed letters to family, friends and business associates. With these as a basis, Ruth Greene has written a fascinating memoir, the *Hsiang-Ya (Xiangya) Journal*, providing intimate vignettes of life in China during the 1920s to the 1940s.

87 Captivity: 44 months in Red China.
Mary Ann Harbert. London: Delacorte Press, 1973. 319p.

This is an account of the author's detention in China between 1968 and 1971. Captured with her sailing companion, Jerry McLaughlin, in the South China Sea, they were accused of trespassing in Chinese waters and detained in a series of make-shift prisons.

88 China: day by day.
Eileen Xu-Balzer, Richard J. Balzer, Francis Xu. New Haven, Connecticut: Yale University Press, 1974. 111p. photos.

The authors, Eileen Hsu-Balzer, Richard Balzer and Francis Hsu (Xu), visited China in the summer of 1972 and as a result have produced this competent pictorial travelogue. Like many tourists since the Cultural Revolution they visited the customary round of factories, communes and sights. However, unlike most other tourists they had the advantage of being able to visit and talk to Chinese relatives. The result is an interesting, and sometimes extremely detailed, introduction to contemporary China.

89 Letters from China.
Maureen Hynes. New York: Women's Press, 1981. 253p.

In the spring of 1980, the author was selected by the Canadian External Affairs Department to teach at Szuchuan (Sizhuan) University in China. This collection of letters to friends, family and colleagues offers insight into China's male/female relationships, the Cultural Revolution and the bewildering, intoxicating reality of living abroad. The book is highly recommended for potential China-bound teachers and scholars.

90 China revisited: after forty-two years.
Jiang Ye. New York: Norton, 1977. 180p.

In 1933, Chiang Yee (Jiang Ye), then the governor of a district in China, was forced to leave his homeland after an argument with a warlord. In 1975, after an absence of forty-two years, he returned to China. In this book, he tells of his travels and records his impressions of the new China compared to the China he remembered. His reunion with his family provided an occasion to admire the industrial progress, educational gains, and sense of purpose and unity of the Chinese. His observations on art, historic treasures, and agriculture are likewise uniformly favourable.

91 The Chinese difference.
Joseph Kraft. New York: Saturday Review Press, 1973. 113p.

The author remained in China after President Nixon's visit. He describes the new bridge over the Yangze (Yangzi) at Nanking, steel factories, a May 7th Cadre School, rural peasants on communes and at home, numerous Communist officials, and interviews a leading nuclear physicist, Chien (Jian), and China's best-selling novelist Han Jan (Han Ran). Kraft seeks to portray the ways in which the new society is different from the West. He seeks to assay the difference in foreign policy and in the central domestic issue of the relation between agriculture and industry. Almost half of his book is devoted to Nixon's visit to Peking (Beijing).

92 The 3 Chinas, up close coming home - to China.
Creighton Lacy. Philadelphia: The Westminster Press, 1978. 216p.

What is life like in China today? How does it compare to life under previous régimes? Here, in one book, are revealing new insights into old China, Chiang Kai-shek's (Jiang Jieshi) China, and contemporary China - as seen through the eyes of a former missionary who has known all three Chinas intimately.

93 Marco Polo in China.
Li Mankin. New York: Kingsway, 1982. 112p. maps. photos.

Filled with maps, photographs, drawings and over 75 colour plates, this book follows Marco Polo's journey from Venice along the Silk Road to China's capital, south through central China, and finally, his perilous and circuitous route back to Europe via the Persian Gulf. The book includes diagrams and descriptions of the set-building and filming inside China of the historic NBC mini-series for US television.

94 In the eye of the typhoon.

Ruth Earnshaw Lo, Katherine S. Kinderman, introduced by John K. Fairbank. New York: Harcourt Brace, 1980. 289p.

Midnight raids, loss of work and friends, forced re-education programmes and sharing of one's home were some of the burdens to be borne by middle-class victims of China's Cultural Revolution. Ruth Earnshaw Lo (Luo), an American woman, and her Chinese husband, a professor, lived through the Revolution. The book describes the Lo family's life at Zhong Shang (Chung Shang) University, near Canton (Guangzhou) from 1966 to 1978.

95 Daily life in revolutionary China.

Maria Antonietta Macciochi. New York: Monthly Review, 1972. 506p.

This book is an account of a two-month visit to China in the autumn of 1970 for the purpose of reporting on life in China after the Cultural Revolution. The author previously visited China in 1954. The merit of the book is the ability of the author, herself a leading member of the Italian Communist Party, to place the confusing events of, and reasons for, the Cultural Revolution in the broader context of the Marxist-Leninist theory of revolution and the nature of the state under socialism.

96 Inside China.

Malcolm MacDonald. Boston, Massachusetts: Little, Brown, 1981. 208p.

MacDonald, a British diplomat, writes mainly of Chinese internal development and foreign policy since the 1960s. From his friendship with Premier Chou En-lai (Zhou Enlai) and Marshal Chen Yi (Zhen Yi), he gained rare insights into China's goals of modernization of agriculture, industry and in defense. He discusses the Chinese perception of the threat of Russian hegemony and their changing views of the United States. He also covers living standards, art and fashion.

97 Stranger in China.

Colin McCullough. New York: Morrow, 1973. 292p.

The book is an account of the sojourn, 1968-70, in China of a correspondent for the *Toronto Globe and Mail*. McCullough, his wife and small daughter arrived in Peking (Beijing) in the spring of 1968 during the last phases of the Cultural Revolution. He presents a very loosely organized and yet extremely interesting picture of life in Peking (Beijing).

98 China returns.

Translated from the German by Klaus Mehnert. New York: Dutton, 1972. 322p.

Mehnert toured China in 1971 at the invitation of Cambodia's exiled prince, Norodom Sihanouk. The first section of the book records what the author saw and heard in 1971 on his fourth visit to China. The second section offers some conclusions on his observations. The third section fills in the background with information on the Cultural Revolution. He describes flood control systems, communes, factory-universities and theatrical productions, as well as the Mao cult and the changes wrought by the revolution.

99 Chinese encounters.
Inge Morath, Arthur Miller. New York: Farrar, Straus & Giroux, 1979. 252p. photos.

The husband-and-wife team contribute, respectively, text and photographs on China as it appeared during their visit of late 1978. Miller, focusing on the present, saw a country only recently emerging from 12 years of Cultural Revolution, during which many actors and dramatists were imprisoned. He places the blame beyond the Gang of Four by implicating Mao himself. Morath centres on the timelessness of the Chinese landscape and architecture, and also includes portraits of the people. The book is a perceptive, balanced view of China, present and past.

100 China, a visual adventure.
Carl Mydans, Michael Demarest. New York: Simon & Schuster, 1979. 160p.

Carl Mydans, a photographer for *Life* magazine who returned to China after many years, and Michael Demarest, a veteran journalist, combined their talents to produce a fascinating overview of China's urban and rural life.

101 China notebook, 1975-1978.
Translated from Swedish by Jan Myrdal. New York: Liberator Press, 1979. 160p.

A longtime observer of China discusses changes in the village of Liu Ling since his first visit in the 1950s, the exposure of the Gang of Four and China on the eve of a new millenium.

102 The Silk Road.
Jan Myrdal. New York: Pantheon, 1981. 272p.

In 1979, writer Jan Myrdal and photographer Gun Kessel toured portions of the Silk Road, the pivot of Asia - the Chinese Pamir where China meets Russian Central Asia and Afghanistan. Myrdal believes that Russia is still attempting to extend her power in Asia but that the United States is no longer interested in an Asian involvement. There are valuable insights into the historical background of the cold war in Asia between Russia and China.

103 The New York Times report from Red China.
James Reston, Tillman Durdin, Seymour Topping, with photos and additional articles by Audrey Topping, edited and introduced by Frank Jing. New York: Quadrangle Books, 1972. 367p.

These articles by correspondents of the first American newspaper permitted to cover life inside the People's Republic deal with foreign policy, the transformation of Chinese society, everyday life, government, education and child rearing, science and medicine and culture. The high point of the book is a long interview between Reston and Premier Chou En-lai (Zhou Enlai) on the Chinese negotiating position with respect to the United States and general Chinese views on the outside world.

104 Reports from China: 1953-1976.
Joan Robinson. London: Anglo-Chinese Education Institute, 1977. 131p.

This book contains nine articles originally written by the author between 1953 and 1976. She has visited China on six occasions and her attitude throughout towards the Chinese and their revolutionary struggle and experiments is principally favourable, though not entirely uncritical.

105 Vision of China: Photographs by Marc Riboud, 1957-1980.
Marc Riboud. New York: Pantheon, 1981. 116p.

In 1957, Riboud was one of the first European photographers permitted to enter China and he returned in 1965, 1971, and 1980 to continue to document this land for books and magazines. His subject is people at work in agriculture and industry or carrying on their everyday activities.

106 Beyond the crimson morning: reflections from a journey through contemporary China.
George Ryga. New York: Doubleday, 1979. 204p.

In 1977 the author led a group of Canadian tourists on a tour of the People's Republic. In this book, Ryga, who is a Canadian playwright and novelist, reflects on the phenomenon of modern China. He examines the struggle of the Chinese people to update their backward technology and reshape it to fit the needs of today's society. He looks at everything with a thoughtful eye: he constantly analyzes, reflects and compares.

107 China diary.
Charlotte Y. Salisbury. New York: Walkers, 1973. 210p.

For the reader seeking an impressionistic, people-orientated introduction to contemporary Chinese life or for the prospective tourist eager to preview the experience of travel in the People's Republic, this book is a real find. Mrs Salisbury's deep personal concern with problems plaguing modern America - drugs, crime, pollution, day-care centres, the old - and her attempt to understand the Chinese solution to similar social phenomena, constitute her principal field of interest.

108 To Peking - and beyond: a report on the new Asia.
Harrison E. Salisbury. New York: Quadrangle Books, 1977. 308p.

In the early part of May 1972, Salisbury, associate editor of the *New York Times*, spent two weeks visiting the Democratic People's Republic of Korea, and then joined his wife Charlotte in Peking (Beijing) for a six-week trip through China. He reports on Sino-Soviet relations, the new Chinese man, and the Chinese population problem and describes interviews with Chou En-lai (Zhou Enlai), Prince Norodom Sihanouk, and Premier Kim Il-Soong of North Korea as well as with other people in many walks of life.

109 Watch out for the foreign guests! China encounters the West.
Orville Schell. New York: Pantheon Books, 1981. 178p.

Schell's thoughtful, yet entertaining travel journal, *In the People's Republic*, which came out four years ago, records his first trip to China. He has since returned to China twice and *Watch out for the foreign guests!* continues the account of his travels. On his second trip to China, Schell felt he was entering a different country, and by the time he returned yet again in 1979 the pace of change had accelerated beyond anything he could have thought possible even a few months earlier.

110 In the People's Republic: an American's firsthand view of living and working in China.
Orville Schell. New York: Random House, 1977. 271p.

In 1976 Schell worked as part of an American youth delegation in the Shanghai Electrical Machinery Factory and on the Tachai (Dazhai) commune. This light, personal account of his experiences is written in the style of a standard travel report. His description of the emotional enjoyments and the intellectual frustrations he experienced during his visit is thought-provoking.

111 China: its history and culture.
Morton W. Scott. New York: Lippincott, 1981. 276p.

Written as an introduction to China for those who might travel there or have just returned, the book discusses the development of China from the earliest times to the present. It is a concise, scholarly and quite readable introduction to the world's oldest continuous civilization.

112 An American in China.
Sidney Shapiro. New York: American Library, 1980. 282p.

Arriving in China in 1947, Shapiro stayed, married and became a citizen. For thirty years he has lived and worked among the Chinese as a distinguished translator of foreign fiction, and his account of those years provides unique insights into China's politics, economy, culture, and the daily lives and deepest feelings of her people. It is one of the most vivid and knowledgeable accounts to have reached the West.

113 Families of Fengsheng: urban life in China.
Ruth Sidel. Baltimore, Maryland: Penguin Books, 1974. 166p.

This is a direct report on neighbourhood life in China's cities since the Cultural Revolution. The author describes neighbourhood committees, locally-managed factories, labour relations, health care and the role of women and senior citizens in a collective society.

114 China on stage: an American actress in the People's Republic.
Lois Wheeler Snow. New York: Random House, 1972. 328p.

Mrs Snow visited China for the first time, with her husband, in July 1970. On her return, she wrote about her findings. However, the book is no travelogue. For most of her life, Mrs Snow has been an actress, and consequently it was the

Chinese theatre that interested her most. The result is an explanation of Maoist life in literature and art, with special reference to, and detailed discussion of Chiang Ch'ing's (Jiang Qing) revolutionary model operas and ballets. She travelled widely and saw plays in schools and in the countryside as well as Peking (Beijing) and other major cities. Her book includes the full text of three revolutionary operas - *Taking mountain by strategy*, *Shachiapang*, and *The red lantern*; and one ballet, *Red detachment of women*.

115 Broken bits of old China: glimpses of China, 1912-1923.
Marjorie Rankin Steurt.   New York: Nelson, 1973. 152p.
This book contains reminiscences of the author's experiences as a teacher/missionary in a Chinese girls' school, 1912-1923. The narrative describes incidents in the everyday life of the Shantung (Shandong) Chinese and the situation of a foreigner living in their midst. There are interesting descriptions of treks through the countryside, a typical peasant wedding, Chinese food, clothing, customs and attitudes, a funeral and festivals.

116 Eight hundred million: the real China.
Ross Terrill.   Boston, Massachusetts: Little, Brown, 1972. 235p.
Terrill, an Australian journalist and Harvard scholar, distills his 1971 travel notes into a remarkably vivid picture of the flavour of life in the China of the table tennis era. The author, a previous resident of Hong Kong, had travelled in China in 1964. He describes the changes since the Cultural Revolution and reports on interviews with Premier Chou En-lai (Zhou Enlai), Prince Norodom Sihanouk and other high officials as well as meetings and interviews at six major universities and sessions with Chinese diplomats, journalists and factory workers. His reflections on the shaping of Chinese diplomacy and on the tensions in Chinese intellectual life are particularly instructive and perceptive.

117 Flowers on an iron tree: five cities of China.
Ross Terrill.   Boston, Massachusetts: Atlantic; Little, Brown, 1975. 423p.
This book covers Terrill's 1973 visit to Shanghai, Dairen (Dalian), Hangchow (Hangzhou), Wuhan, and Peking (Beijing). He deals with the ways that ordinary Chinese people live. He offers interesting reflections on how things have changed and how they have remained the same in China.

118 Dawn wakes in the East.
Audrey Topping.   New York: Harper, 1973. 162p.
The author blends personal experience, including past familial association with China and recent festive receptions by Premier Chou En-lai (Zhou Enlai), with descriptions of living conditions and their historical background. Impressions most vividly conveyed are that: China has been remarkably transformed into a just and rapidly developing society; Chinese are today happy, hard-working, and altruistically motivated.

119 Journey between two Chinas.
Seymour Topping.   New York: Harper, 1972. 459p.
The author revisited China in 1971 after a twenty-two year absence. He travelled for five weeks on the mainland, talking with peasants, students, urban workers,

and government officials of every rank. His trip ended with an interview with Premier Chou En-lai (Zhou Enlai).

120 Living in China.
Andrew Watson. Totowa, New Jersey: Rowman & Littlefield, 1975. 192p.

The author, a British sinologist, taught English for two years at the Sian (Xian) Foreign Language Institute in the late 1960s. His basic aim is to describe as accurately as possible the life of the ordinary man in China. The book contains basic information on all aspects of modern Chinese life: social values and institutions; political leadership and organizations; rural and urban institutional structures and patterns of life; brief historical surveys of industrial and agricultural policy; detailed descriptions of the everyday life of worker and peasant families; education and the arts; the medical system; science; religion and national minorities.

121 China 'spy'.
George Watt. London: Johnson, 1972. 208p.

The author worked in China as an engineer helping to construct a polypropylene plant at Lanchow (Lanzhou) during the Cultural Revolution. This is the story of the vicissitudes he and his colleagues suffered as the Cultural Revolution disrupted their work and lives, culminating in Watt's arrest for alleged spying, his imprisonment and his release in 1970 when the political climate changed.

122 Inside China.
Peter Worsley. Totowa, New Jersey: Rowman & Littlefield, 1975. 270p.

This book is another traveller's report from China, by a British sociologist, but worth reading for the author's sensitivity to social details. His frankly partisan vision does not exclude acute analysis and occasional criticism.

123 China: the dream of man?
Tove Zetterholm. Stanford, Connecticut: Ridgeway, 1978. 293p. photos.

This book contains 237 pages filled with fascinating colour photographs of all kinds of people and places, from the four corners of China. It has wondrous reports about the miracle of China today.

Guidebooks

124 China companion.
Evelyne Garside. New York: Farrar, Strauss & Giroux, 1982. 275p.

This book is a practical guide to over 100 cities and places of interest in China. It is organized geographically. The author lived for many years in Peking (Beijing) and travelled extensively throughout China.

Tourism and Travellers' Accounts. Guidebooks

125 China Guidebook.
Frederic M. Kaplan, Arne de Keijzer. New York:
Houghton Mifflin, 1982. 528p.

Intended as a book for both the general tourist and the traveller with business or professional interests, the authors have included most of the information which any traveller would need on the formalities of getting to China - visa applications, modes of travel, advice on costs, currency, customs restrictions, health questions and social mores. The book covers 80 cities and towns in China, discussing the history and highlights of each city, hotel accommodation, shopping and other useful aspects.

126 Travel guide to the People's Republic of China.
Ruth Lor Malloy. New York: Morrow, 1975. 190p.

The author describes how to obtain a visa, when to go, where to go, what to take and what to see, plus information about hotels, food, costs, etiquette, emergencies, transport and shopping. The book also includes a résumé of Chinese history, explanations of special terminology and words to popular songs.

127 Nagel's encyclopedia-guide: China.
New York: Cowles, 1979. 1,568p.

This volume is the most comprehensive one-volume guide available in English for library, reference, or travel. It was first published in French in 1967. It includes a comprehensive survey of China's civilization, geography, language, history, literature and art and popular culture. It also contains a region-by-region guide and city plans.

Flora and Fauna

128 **Wheat in the People's Republic of China.**
Edited by Virgil A. Johnson, Halsey L. Beemer,
Jr. Washington DC: National Academy of Sciences, 1977.
190p.

This is the report of the US Wheat Research Delegation that visited China in May and June 1976. The delegation visited the wheat growing areas in China to see communes and research institutions. The information the delegation obtained deals with land, water resources, management, wheat cropping systems, plant protection, plant breeding and double cropping systems.

129 **Chinese herbs: their botany, chemistry and pharmacodynamics with special sections on mineral drugs, drugs of animal origin, 300 Chinese prescriptions, toxic herbs.**
John D. Keys. New York: Tuttle, 1976. 388p.

More than 250 entries of plants are arranged by botanical classification, giving for each the Latin botanical name, common English name, complete botanical vocabulary, a brief pharmaceutical description of the drug (including pharmacodynamic investigations, together with any related use of the drug given in other pharmacopoeias as well as references to related plants).

130 **Vegetable marketing systems in the People's Republic of China.**
Edited by Donald Plunknett, Halsey L. Beemer,
Jr. Boulder, Colorado: Westview Press, 1981. 386p.

This is the report of the US Vegetable Farming System Delegation that visited China in June and July 1977. The delegation visited communes, research institutes, agricultural colleges, and universities in many cities to obtain their information, the bulk of which concerns areas adjacent to cities rather than rural areas, such as land and water resources and management, vegetable cropping systems, environmental control structures, plant protection, plant breeding, seed production and maintenance, supply and marketing in cities, and the economics of municipal vegetable supply in China.

131 **Plant studies in the People's Republic of China: a trip report of the American Plant Studies Delegation.**
Washington, DC: National Academy of Sciences, 1975.
205p.
This is a report of a delegation of American agronomists who visited the People's Republic of China for three weeks in August, 1974. The summary in the book offers highly valuable insights into Chinese agriculture.

132 **Rice research and production in China: an IRRI team's view.**
Manila: International Rice Research Institute, 1978. 118p.
The Team of the International Rice Research Institute visited China in 1977. The team found China's fraternity of scientists out of touch with the mainstream of international scientific activity and it saw little evidence of basic research in genetics, physiology, entomology, pathology and related disciplines. The report states that 'further gains in grain production will depend almost completely on the development and application of the new crop technology'.

Insect control in the People's Republic of China.
See item no. 1023.

Rice Improvement in China and other Asian countries.
See item no. 1024.

Prehistory and
Archaeology

133 **The Art and Archaeology in China.**
Edmund Capon. Cambridge, Massachusetts: MIT Press,
1977. 192p. illus.
This book contains beautiful illustrations of ancient art objects recently unearthed
in China. Based on the *Exhibition of Archaeological Finds from China* which
travelled to Europe, the United States and Australia, the book provides historical
and social background as well as a commentary on what these treasures mean to
the Chinese people today.

134 **Toward a people's anthropology.**
Fei Xiaotong. New York: New World Press, 1981. 121p.
The book contains six articles chronicling the remarkable career and life of
China's most famous anthropologist, Fei Xiaotong (Fei Hsiao-tong), including his
acceptance speech for the 1980 Malinowski Award and important pioneering
articles in the field of ethnic anthropology in China. The reader will treasure
these rare glimpses into minority life in China.

135 **Ancient China.**
John Hay. New York: Walck, H. Z., 1974. 128p. photos.
figs.
The author presents an account of the country's history from 6,000 BC to the
present People's Republic of China. He discusses important archaeological discoveries, from the remains of *homo erectus* at Choukoutien (*sinanthropus
pekinensis*/Peking man) and of Neolithic, Bronze and Iron Age cultures to those
of the T'ang (Tang) dynasty. Throughout the book, there are frequent comparisons which help readers relate the material to Western history and achievements,
and many good photographs (some in colour) and drawings elucidate the text.

136 **The cradle of the East: an inquiry into the indigenous origins of techniques and ideas of Neolithic and early historic China, 5,000-1,000 BC.**
He Bingdi. Chicago: University of Chicago Press, 1976. 440p.

Whether Chinese civilization received external stimuli at various times in its early development is always an interesting and important question - to which Ho Ping-ti (He Bingdi) attempts to give a uniformly negative answer. He sets out to provide a new picture of the origins of Chinese civilization and concludes that China is a cradle of civilization no less worthy of the name than those acknowledged by most scholars: Mesopotamia and Central/South America.

137 **Sources of Shang history: the oracle-bone inscriptions of Bronze Age China.**
David N. Keightly. Berkeley, California: University of California Press, 1978. 281p.

The author discusses the nature of oracle-bone inscription, shows how they may be deciphered and dated and suggests the historical information which may be inferred from them. He considers types of bones used, techniques of preparation, divination procedures, writing methods, characteristic types of inscriptions, authentification of dates and reading of inscriptions. He gives an appreciation of the Shang texts as historical sources. Notes refer the reader to previous literature on the subject and indicate current controversies and future areas of research.

138 **An Yang.**
Li Qi. Seattle, Washington: University of Washington Press, 1977. 304p.

Li Chi (Li Qi), born in 1896, educated at Clark University in Massachusetts (BA 1919; MA 1920) and Harvard (PhD 1923), has been associated in various leading capacities with the Institute of History and Philosophy of the Academia Sinica for the last half century. Here he discusses the archaeological evidence uncovered by the Academia Sinica's excavations at An Yang (Anyang), the administrative and cultural centre of the Shang dynasty, which will interest students of both Bronze Age China and 20th-century Chinese intellectual history.

139 **China in antiquity.**
Henri Maspero, foreward by Paul Demieville, translated by Frank A. Kierman, introduction by Denis C. Twitchett, Amherst, Massachusetts: University of Massachusetts Press, 1979. 527p.

When Henri Maspero's masterful history of ancient China to 221 BC *La Chine Antique*, first appeared in 1927, it was unprecedented. It remains unparalleled. No other work offers such a comprehensive, concise, basic, perceptive treatment of pre-imperial China. A revised edition, prepared by Paul Demieville on the basis of Maspero's own marginalia to the original edition, appeared in 1955. This second edition of the book has now been translated into English, by Frank Kierman, and is completed with maps more readable than those in the original and has the welcome addition of an index of romanized Chinese terms together with characters.

Prehistory and Archaeology

140 The imperial Ming tombs.
Ann Paludan, foreword by L. Carrington Goodrich. New Haven, Connecticut: Yale University Press, 1980. 238p.

In a valley just outside Peking (Beijing), thirteen of the eighteen emperors of the Ming dynasty lie buried in one of the largest splendid imperial mausolea in the world. This comprehensive guide to the tombs includes a history of the valley, vivid descriptions of each of the tombs and the emperors buried therein and accounts of the classical Chinese philosophy of death and geomancy and the traditional principles of Chinese architecture.

141 Treasures from China.
Michael Ridley. London: Dolphin Press, 1973. 144p. illus.

This is a book designed to capture the market created by the visit to Europe in 1973 of an exhibition of recent Chinese archaeological finds. It describes some of the discoveries made during the Cultural Revolution and puts these in the context of Chinese history. It is well illustrated.

142 Ancient China: studies in early civilization.
Edited by David T. Roy, Tsuen-Hsuin Tsien. Hong Kong: Chinese University Press, 1978. 370p.

The sixteen chapters of this volume, which is dedicated to Professor Herlee G. Creel, serve to illustrate the extent of his contributions to sinology, whether in archaeology, philosophy, philology, religion, or other fields, for almost all the chapters build directly on his achievements or draw inspiration from his teaching.

143 China: an anthropological perspective.
Leon E. Stover, Takes K. Stover. Pacific Palisades, California: Goodyear, 1975. 244p.

The book is a short general introduction to Chinese culture and society. The intention is to combine the anthropology of folk culture with the sinology of the culture of the ruling class, and to portray the interaction between 'little tradition' and 'great tradition'.

144 The prehistory of China: an archaeological exploration.
Judith M. Treistman. Garden City, New York: Doubleday, 1972. 156p.

This book traces the prehistory of China from the time when the first man-like creature was known to have inhabited Asia and journeys in time to the earliest literate societies, which were recorded in dynatic histories as Shang (1750-1100 BC) and Chou (Zhou) (1100-22 BC). This is the period which encompasses the beginnings of civilization and the development of feudalism and which forms the basis of medieval China. This is an up-to-date account of what has been learned of life in China from Peking Man (Beijing Man) to the time of the written histories of the Greeks.

145 Ancient China: the discoveries of post-liberation archaeology.
William Watson. London: BBC Publications, 1974. 108p.

The occasion for the present edition was the journey the author made to China to produce two programmes for the BBC on archaeological discoveries in post-liberation China, and the programmes were in turn occasioned by the 1973

Burlington House exhibition of Chinese archaeology. The book, just over 100 pages long, contains about 30 pages of text and the rest of illustrations and captions. It tells of archaeological finds relating to every period of Chinese prehistory and history up to the end of the Yuan period in the 14th century.

146 The genius of China.
William Watson.   New York: Barrons, 1973. 159p.
This book is a detailed catalogue with black-and-white illustrations of the 1973 Burlington House exhibition of Chinese archaeology which was also shown in the United States in 1974-75.

147 Shang civilization.
Zhang Kuangzhi.   New Haven, Connecticut: Yale University Press, 1980. 417p.
The author Chang Kwang-chih (Zhang Kuangzhi) provides a description of the Shang period (traditional dates 1766-1122 BC). The author starts from the archaeological evidence and goes on to characterize the Shang state and society. His treatment covers urban forms, kingship, writing, economic activities and social structure. He surveys the chronology of the dynasty and the problems of locating the site of the Shang capital.

148 Early Chinese civilization: anthropological perspectives.
Zhang Kuangzhi.   Cambridge, Massachusetts: Harvard University Press, 1972. 229p.
The author Chang Kwang-chih (Zhang Kuangzhi) in his first two articles traces the development of China's early agriculture and urban life according to recent archaeological evidence. In the remaining pieces, the author focuses on the early urban society of the Shang and Chou (Zhou) dynasties. His major concern is with the relationship of dualistic phenomena, especially lineage systems, and such matters as political organization, the structure of cities, mythological patterns and the preparation and service of food. The book extends beyond the spheres of archaeology and anthropology proper into the domains of literature, epigraphy, palaeography, linguistics and the arts.

149 Food in Chinese culture: anthropological and historical perspectives.
Zhang Kuangzhi.   New Haven, Connecticut: Yale University Press, 1977. 236p.
Each of the contributors to this book, edited by Chang Kwang-chi (Zhang Kuangzhi), covers one of the major periods of Chinese history: ancient, Han, T'ang (Tang), Sung (Song), Yuan-Ming, Ching (Qing) and modern. In each essay, the principal foodstuffs, the methods of preparing and preserving foods, the utensils used and the customs of serving and eating food are described and their effects on Chinese society are analyzed. When the data permit, the authors discuss aspects of Chinese thought - philosophical, religious and medical - that pertain to food.

150 **The archaeology of ancient China.**
Zhang Kuangzhi.   New Haven, Connecticut: Yale
University Press, 1977. 3rd ed. 222p.

In this new and enlarged edition, Chang Kwang-chih (Zhang Kuangzhi) extends his basic thesis of an indigenous development of Chinese civilization and evaluates the latest archaeological information that has become available - in particular, the radio-carbon dates announced since 1972 and important discoveries made outside the nuclear area of North China.

151 **Historical relics unearthed in new China.**
Beijing: Foreign Language Press, 1972. 217p.

This book contains over 200 photographs in colour and monochrome of some of the most outstanding archaeological discoveries during the period of the Cultural Revolution, including the now famous jade burial suits from the Manch'eng tombs. The quality of reproduction is excellent.

History

Pre-20th century

152 **China enters the twentieth century: Chang Chih-tung and the issues of a new age, 1895-1905.**
Daniel H. Bays. Ann Arbor, Michigan: University of Michigan Press, 1978. 295p.

Using the career of Chang Chih-tung (Zhang Zhidong) as the basis of his study, the author carefully weaves into his narrative and analysis many of the most important strands of late 19th-and early 20th-century Chinese history: imperialism, nationalism, anti-manchurianism, provincialism, modernization, rights recovery, the changing role of the traditional élite and, of course, revolution.

153 **Genghis Khan.**
Peter Brent. New York: McGraw-Hill, 1976. 264p.

Brent traces the history of the Mongol conquests from the rise of Genghis Khan in the 12th century to the empires of Khubilai Khan in China, the Ilkan in Persia, the Golden Horde in Russia, and the Chagatai of Turkestan in the 13th and 14th centuries. He gives a careful and convincing estimate of their contribution to history.

154 **Peasant revolts in China, 1840-1949.**
Jean Chesneaux, translated by C. A. Curwen. London: Thames & Hudson, 1973. 180p.

The author considers the role of peasant movements in China's national development. He recounts the historical and social background of traditional Chinese peasant rebellions before moving on to a summary and discussion of the great 19th-century uprisings. This study, covering the period from the Opium War to 1949, provides a synthesis of Chinese peasant rebellions, which evolved into such larger movements as the T'aiping (Taiping) rebellion (1850-64), the Boxer uprising (1900), the republican revolution (1911) and the Chinese Communist movement.

155 China from Opium War to the 1911 revolution.

Jean Chesneaux, Marianne Bastid, Marie-Claire Bergere, translated from French by Anne Dastenay. New York: Pantheon, 1977. 226p.

This work is the first volume of a two-volume reworking of modern Chinese history by a group of French historians. The authors analyze the Second Opium War, deal with rebellions other than the T'aiping (Taiping), discuss foreign involvement in China, and interrelated diverse intellectual and cultural movements.

156 Chinese civilization from the Ming revival to Chairman Mao.

Young Yap Cottevell. New York: St. Martin's Press, 1976. 256p.

This is a history that explores the underlying continuity of Chinese civilization from the close of the Yuan dynasty (1368) to the death of Chairman Mao (1976). The book, although only briefly touching upon such significant topics as the artistic and literary achievements of the Ming and Ch'ing (Qing) dynasties, China's response to the West, the conflict between Communist and Nationalist forces during the Republican years, and the economic and political achievement of the People's Republic under Chairman Mao, provides the general reader with a good overview for understanding the complexities of modern China.

157 The origins of statecraft in China: the western Chou empire.

Herlee G. Creel. Chicago: University of Chicago Press, 1974. 559p.

This is the first volume of a project to study the origins and evolution of China's traditional political institutions. The subject of the present book is the government of the western Chou (Zhou) (traditionally dated from 1122 to 771 BC), the formative period out of which the classical civilization of China emerged in the latter part of the first millennium BC. Creel shows an admirable determination to rid himself of preconceptions based on the traditional views of the Confucian school and modern scholarly dogmas and to concentrate directly on what Chou (Zhou) texts themselves tell us.

158 Conquerors and Confucians: aspects of political change in late Yuan China.

John W. Dardress. New York: Columbia University Press, 1973. 245p.

The author first analyzes the circumstances under which the Yuan dynasty by the 1320s came to sever its connections with the Mongol world empire and to merge fully with the Chinese historical mainstream. He then traces the rise into dominance of Confucian political ideology within the non-Chinese ruling establishment and argues that the processes of Yuan political breakdown are of direct relevance to much of Chinese history in general in that they reflect political and ideological fissures whose origins are Chinese rather than Mongol.

159 **The T'aiping rebellion and the western powers: a comprehensive survey.**
S. Y. Deng. New York: Oxford University Press, 1971. 327p.

The T'aiping (Taiping) rebellion (1850-1864) cost the lives of millions of Chinese, severely weakened the dying Manchu dynasty, and opened the country to increasing Western influence. The author, S. Y. Teng (Deng), devotes his attention to complex historical problems including the extent of missionary influence and the importance of General Gordon and other Western personalities.

160 **The Pigtail War: American involvement in the Sino-Japanese war of 1894-95.**
Jeffrey Dorwart. Amherst, Massachusetts: University of Massachusetts Press, 1975. 168p.

The author provides interesting details on US involvement in the Sino-Japanese war of 1894-95. It is written from the dated approach of reporting what one diplomatic clerk said to another diplomatic clerk. The author concludes that President Cleveland and Secretary of State Gresham were ideological leaders who became entangled more deeply than they had planned.

161 **Early Ming China: a political history, 1355-1435.**
Edward L. Dreyer. Stanford, California: Stanford University Press, 1981. 347p.

This is the first modern history, in any language, of the very late Yuan and early Ming period of China, a time of momentous changes whose impact on China's subsequent history is not perfectly understood. Among these changes were the moving of the capital to Peking (Beijing), and the launching of an ambitious naval programme that took Chinese ships as far as the coast of Africa.

162 **Cultures in collision: the Boxer rebellion.**
William J. Dyiker. San Rafael, California: Presidio Press, 1978. 226p.

The significance of the book is in providing a balanced and comprehensive account of the whole crisis. According to the author, the Boxer rebellion is the strength of two cultures on a collision course: the expanding West, vigorous, vital, self-confident, clashing with an introverted China, tradition-bound, arrogant in its self-sufficiency.

163 **A history of China.**
Wolfram Eberhard. Berkeley, California: University of California Press, 1976. 4th ed. 380p.

The author stresses the main lines of development of the Chinese social structure from earliest times to the present. First published in 1950, this completely revised edition of his *History* incorporates much new material, including a review of recent Chinese foreign policy. The book contains analyses of the rise and fall of dynasties with special emphasis on the impact of nomadic peoples on internal developments. He concentrates on showing the main lines of China's social and cultural development to the present.

164 **The Cambridge history of China: late Ch'ing 1800-1911, part I.**
John K. Fairbank, D. C. Twitchett. New York: Cambridge University Press, 1978. 713p.

This is the first fruits of a project begun in 1966, which will eventually result in an 11-volume compendium on Chinese history. In this volume Fairbank and seven scholars contribute 11 essays treating Ch'ing (Qing) dynastic decline, the mid-century rebellions, Western impact on China and China's restoration.

165 **The Cambridge history of China: late Ch'ing 1800-1911, part II.**
Edited by John K. Fairbank, Kuangqing Liu. New York: Cambridge University Press, 1980. 658p.

In this volume, contributors focus on commercial and technological growth, foreign relations, the stimulation of Chinese intellectual life by the outside world and military triumphs and disasters.

166 **The Opium War, 1840-1842.**
Peter Ward Fay. Chapel Hill, North Carolina: University of North Carolina Press, 1975. 406p.

This book is richly narrative with metaphors, anecdotes and a lyrical style. The author begins with a discourse on the production and use of opium in the early 19th century and he then describes the India-to-China opium trade carried on by English traders, the life-styles of the traders and of the missionaries who followed them to the China coast and the growing tension. He recounts the series of expeditions and battles in which the British forced the opening of China to the West.

167 **A century of Chinese revolution 1851-1949.**
Wolfgang Franke. New York: Harper, 1971. 348p.

Beginning with a discussion of the importance of the idea of revolution in Chinese historical perspective, the author describes briefly but competently the T'aiping (Taiping) rebellion (1850-64), the reform movement (1898), the Boxer uprising (1900), the republican revolution (1911), the May 4th movement of 1919, the victory and collapse of the Kuomingtang (Guomindang), and the victory of the Chinese Communists. There are excellent chapter by chapter bibliographies, including the best of recent scholarly publications.

168 **A modern China and a new world: K'ang Yu-wei, reformer and utopian, 1858-1927.**
Gongzhuan Xiao. Seattle, Washington: University of Washington Press, 1975. 669p.

Kung-chuan Hsiao (Gonzhuan Xiao) divides K'ang Yu-wei's (Kang Youwei) life and thought into two major stages. During the first, which lasted through the early 1900s, K'ang (Kang) believed in a benevolent cosmos - a place of universal 'soul substance' which partook of primal good, and where it was the duty of the enlightened to reform the world. In the second phase, which began around 1910 and lasted until his death in 1927, he ceased to believe in meliorism and detached himself from the world, directing his inner energies beyond the planet itself to a kind of higher state of apoliticial cultivation. According to the author, the two phases of the philosopher's life were discrete, even contradictory.

169 The China station, war and diplomacy, 1830-1860.
Gerald S. Graham. New York: Oxford University Press, 1978. 472p.

The author analyzes in detail how China was opened to Western powers by the British Royal Navy. In addition, the author considers the conflict of personalities, the frustrations, the irritations, and the bewilderment of the men who tried to come to terms with the mysterious Middle Kingdom, whose customs, laws, and moral standards baffled and provoked them to no end. The author includes accounts of the major naval actions in south, central and north China. He traces the interaction among naval and civilian authorities in London, Calcutta, Trincomalee, Hong Kong, Shanghai and many other stations.

170 Intellectuals and the state in modern China, a narrative history.
Jerome B. Grieder. New York: Free Press, 1981. 395p.

The book deals with the important role of the intellectuals in modern China. The author begins with the Ming loyalists and avoids reducing all intellectual ferment in China since the late 19th century to a one-way response to western challenges. The People's Republic does not fall within the scope of the book, but in an epilogue a few questions are broached.

171 The dragon wakes: China and the West, 1793-1911.
Christopher Hibbert. New York: Harper, 1970. 427p.

This book is an account of Anglo-Chinese (rather than Western-Chinese) relations during the period. The author gives the British version of the Macartney and Amherst missions to China, the opium trade and the Opium War, the Anglo-French war with China, the T'aiping (Taiping) rebellion and the like. He relies heavily upon diaries and journals of those who visited China (in official, semi-official or private capacities) and also cites Chinese sources. Many of his sources, never published before, are manuscript diaries, letters, papers and notebooks, many of which have not previously been translated from Chinese.

172 A short history of China.
Hilda Hookham. New York: St. Martin's Press, 1971. 240p.

The author traces the continuity of China's civilization from prehistory. She takes as the framework for the book a policital account of all the major dynasties from Chou (Zhou) to Ch'ing (Qing), but also describes the frequent periods of disunity when warlords ruled separate regions of the country. There is also an account of China's two republics of recent times, the first which ended in 1949, and the People's Republic of China. At each stage the social and cultural life of the Chinese people is described against the background of political events.

173 **Autocracy at work: a study of the Yung-cheng period, 1723-1735.**
Huang Bei. Bloomington, Indiana: Indiana University Press, 1974. 500p.

The Emperor Yung-cheng (Yong Zheng), characterized by generations of Chinese historians as ruthless and oppressive, is increasingly emerging as perhaps the major institutional consolidator and reformer among the Ch'ing (Qing) emperors. Relying on the major official and semi-official sources for the period and building on the research of the Kyoto historians as well as of contemporary Chinese and Western scholars, Huang Pei (Huang Bei) has brought a wide range of issues to the attention of a Western audience for the first time.

174 **China's imperial past: an introduction to Chinese history and culture.**
Charles O. Hucker. Stanford, California: Stanford University Press, 1975. 474p.

It is a sober, solid and eminently reliable introduction to traditional China. Adopting a tripartite periodization, the author first introduces the reader to the general history of each period and then in separate chapters analyzes major developments in political, social and economic history, in the history of ideas and in literature and the arts.

175 **China to 1850.**
Charles O. Hucker. Stanford, California: Stanford University Press, 1978. 259p.

The book is a distillation of what every general reader and student beginning a study of China should know about the history of traditional Chinese civilization. It touches on all aspects of Chinese life and culture, broadly surveying general history, socio-economic organization, political institutions, religion and philosophy, and literature. The result is a concise overview that is both absorbing in itself and basic to a more detailed study of China's long and complex evolution.

176 **The Ming dynasty: its origins and evolving institutions.**
Charles O. Hucker. Ann Arbor, Michigan: University of Michigan, Center for Chinese Studies, 1978. 105p.

As the title indicates, this book is not a survey of Ming history. The author outlines the decline of Mongol power in China, the rise of Chinese rebel forces and the warfare among them, and the victory and consolidation of the Ming government.

177 **The medieval Chinese oligarchy.**
David G. Johnson. Boulder, Colorado: Westview Press, 1977. 281p.

The author discusses in detail medieval definitions of the social élite, and, with the help of several manuscripts of the 9th century identifies the families that belonged to that class. He explains the demise of the oligarchy largely in terms of the nature of the clan itself, and he further suggests that the emergence of a new ruling élite in Sung (Song) times was directly connected to the emergence of new kinship institutions and ideology.

178 **K'ang-hsi and the consolidation of Ch'ing rule, 1661-1684.**
Lawrence D. Kessler. Chicago: University of Chicago Press, 1976. 251p.

As the first book to deal with the complexities of imperial power at the time when the K'ang-hsi (Kangxi) emperor took the helm, it is worth a look. The study provides a detailed narrative of how this emperor put down the remaining dissidents in the empire, countered Russian encroachment into north China, and wooed and won the Confucian scholar-élite to his service.

179 **Monarchy in the emperor's eyes: image and reality in the Ch'ien-lung reign.**
Harold L. Khan. Cambridge, Massachusetts: Harvard University Press, 1971. 314p.

The author begins with a description of the emperor's persona, the image created by Chinese official historiography. He then concentrates on Ch'ien-lung's (Qianlong) own career. He draws distinctions between the various interpretations of Ch'ien-lung (Qianlong) that have come down to us. He is critical of the emperor, especially with respect to the last years of his reign, seen as a magnificent façade covering internal decay and decline.

180 **Chinese ways in warfare.**
Frank A. Kierman, Jr., John K. Fairbank. Cambridge, Massachusetts: Harvard University Press, 1974. 401p.

The contributors indicate that they merely seek to examine the extensive documentation of Chinese military history that has been known about but little used. The volume covers the pre-Han era down to the late Ming. In a brief introduction, Professor Fairbank makes clear that what is needed is an effort to see Chinese military history as an aspect of China's culture as a whole.

181 **The Manchurian frontier in Ch'ing history.**
Robert H. G. Lee. Cambridge, Massachusetts: Harvard University Press, 1970. 318p.

The aim of this study is to show that the late 19th-century political changes in the Manchurian frontier zone were not only the result of Chinese economic and political developments, but also of changes in Manchuria itself, in which Chinese immigration was most important in saving Manchuria from permanent annexation by Russia or Japan.

182 **China: an interpretive history: from the beginnings to the fall of Han.**
Joseph R. Levenson, Franz Schurmann. Berkeley, California: University of California Press, 1971. 152p.

The authors take the story of China to the fall of Han, pointing out those problems of interpretation which have occupied historians. With admirable brevity they have been brilliant in highlighting the facts, the problems and in offering interpretations.

183 The ageless Chinese: a history.
Dun J. Li. New York: Scribner, 1970. 2nd ed. 591p.

In this second edition, the author tells the story of China from earliest times to the present, discusses traditional Chinese society and the Western impact in the modern period and explains national customs, thought and language as aids to a comprehension of China's political and economic life. He edited and translated a series of supplementary readings in the succeeding years: *The road to Communism: China since 1912* (1971); *The civilization of China: from the formative period to the coming of the West* (1975); and *Modern China: from mandarin to commissar* (1978).

184 The first emperor of China: the politics of historiography.
Li Youming. White Plains, New York: International Arts and Sciences Press, 1975. 356p.

Since 1972 there has been a dramatic effort to revalue the political methods of the Ch'in (Qin) unification of China in the third century BC - not merely to reverse symbols but also to argue new criteria for political judgement. Li Yuming's (Li Youming) anthology of well-translated Communist publications and her introductory essays make it possible to watch this effort unfold and to appreciate its broad implications.

185 Shang Yang's reforms and state control in China.
Li Youming. New York: Sharp, 1977. 270p.

An important work which accorded with the anti-Confucian line of the mid-1970s was Yang Kuan's (Yang Guan) *Shang Yang P'ien-fa* (*Shang Yang Pianfa*), originally published in 1959 but reissued in nearly two million copies in 1973-74. Li has ably translated this book to illustrate traditional and contemporary Chinese views of Shang Yang and his policies.

186 Crisis and conflict in Han China 104 BC to AD 9.
Michael Loewe. London: Allen & Unwin, 1974. 340p.

This book contains nice case studies of crisis and conflict in the second half of the Former Han dynasty. The author combines the chronological and the topical approaches in arranging the cases and in his treatment of each case. Detailed description of events at the court is supplemented by summary statements on the background and by topical essays analyzing the intellectual or institutional context in which the events took place.

187 The heathen Chinese: a study of American attitudes toward China, 1890-1905.
Robert McClellan. Columbus, Ohio: Ohio State University Press, 1970. 272p.

This is a study of changing American attitudes toward China -from appreciation of the Chinese labourer for his work on the transcontinental railway to resentment and hostility. The author, through quotations from books, manuscripts, government publications, newspapers, magazine articles and excerpts from the letters and papers of prominent American historical figures, demonstrates the early bias against the Chinese.

188 **Modern China: a chronology from 1841 to the present.**
Colin P. Mackerras, with the assistance of Robert
Zhan. London: Thames & Hudson, 1981. 528p.

This volume encompasses every aspect of Chinese history since 1842 - the year of
the first of the so-called unequal treaties between China and the Western powers.
It provides the salient facts in events ranging from the appearance of the first
Chinese-language daily newspaper (in 1858) to the announcement by the Chairman of Coca-Cola Company of the agreement to open a bottling plant in Shanghai (in 1978). The range of sources is vast, spanning both Asian and European
languages and including both primary material and documentary studies, as well
as standard works. Pinyin romanization has been used throughout for Chinese
names, except in very special cases where confusion might have resulted. Glossaries of names and terms and full indices, all with Chinese characters, are also
included.

189 **Village and bureaucracy in southern Sung China.**
Brian E. McKnight. Chicago: University of Chicago Press,
1972. 219p.

The author explores the institutions which were operative in the processes of local
government in the 12th and 13th centuries and the shifts in the burden of
obligations to serve borne by those who stood between the rulers and the ruled.
He concludes that those persons obliged to assist the local officials were drawn
from the assertive market-oriented rural estate owners, a group which came into
existence in the 8th century and was transformed into a literati-dominated gentry
society after the 14th century.

190 **Science in traditional China.**
Joseph Needham. Cambridge, Massachusetts: Harvard
University Press, 1981. 256p.

The author examines the philosophy, social structure, arts, crafts and even military strategies of China and makes instructive comparisons with similar elements
in Indian, Hellenistic and Arabic cultures.

191 **The spirit soldiers: a historical narrative of the Boxer
rebellion.**
Richard O'Connor. New York: Putnam, 1973. 379p.

The author has put together an interesting narrative of the turmoil which
engulfed Peking (Beijing), Tientsin (Tianjin) and many other places in China in
1900. The narrative is apparently based on the firsthand evidence now available,
including files of some London and New York, Shanghai and Peking (Beijing)
newspapers and many memoirs. The author attempts a history of the Boxer
rebellion from the Chinese point of view as well as from that of the West.

192 **Ruling from horseback: Manchu politics in the Oboi regency,
1661-1669.**
Robert B. Oxnam. Chicago: University of Chicago Press,
1975. 250p.

This book examines the clash of Manchu and Chinese political traditions during
an important period of early Ch'ing (Qing) history, the first nine years of the
K'ang-hsi (Kangxi) reign. The author has gathered together information and

biographies to present institutions and events of the regency under his various categories.

193 Rebels and revolutionaries in north China, 1845-1945.
Elizabeth J. Perry. Stanford, California: Stanford University Press, 1980. 318p.

Why do peasants rebel? In particular, why do some peasants rebel and not others? Starting from the premise that rebellion recurred persistently only in certain geographical areas, the author examines three notable movements in the region of Huai-pei (Huaibei): the Nien (Nian) rebels of the 1850s and 1860s, the Red Spear Society of the Republican era and the movement of the 1930s and 1940s. The author also throws new light on the role of secret societies in peasant protest, and offers a fresh interpretation of the relationship between rebellion and revolution.

194 The military establishment of the Yuan dynasty.
Qijing Xiao. Cambridge, Massachusetts: Harvard University Press, 1978. 314p.

The author Ch'i-ching Hsiao (Qijing Xiao) proposes that the military institution of the Yuan dynasty offers an important key to understanding China's social evolution. The author examines the military system, the imperial guard and the garrison to provide a basic research tool for the study of Chinese institutional history.

195 The T'aiping revolutionary movement.
Ren Yuwen. New Haven, Connecticut: Yale University Press, 1973. 616p.

The T'aiping (Taiping) revolutionary movement, 1851-1866, was one of the cataclysmic events of history. Reconstructing the details of titanic struggles with painstaking care, Jen Yu-wen (Ren Yuwen) gives readers a comprehensive picture of the entire movement, presenting a wealth of new information and insights on its origins and on the motives and actions of its leaders.

196 China's republican revolution: the case of Kwangtung 1895-1913.
Edward J. M. Rhoads. Cambridge, Massachusetts: Harvard University Press, 1975. 365p.

Rhoads' regional focus permits careful attention to the social context. His careful chronology, distinguishing between the early, middle and last phases of the post-Boxer years, allows the interweaving of the various contemporaneous strands of reform and revolution. He avoids the sense - destructive to investigation - that all roads lead to 1911. He traces the social, political and economic history of the republican revolution. He contends that, contrary to traditional accounts, Sun Yat-sen (Sun Yixian) and his Revolutionary Alliance did not move easily from success to success; and that on the eve of the 1911 Revolution, the movement was disorganized and demoralized.

197 **Dissent in early modern China: Ju-lin Wai-Shih and Ch'ing social criticism.**
Paul S. Ropp. Ann Arbor, Michigan: University of Michigan Press, 1979. 329p.

This is a study of intellectual ferment - dissent, change and social criticism - in 18th-century China, as seen through the life of Wu Ching-tzu (Wu Qingzi), author of China's greatest pre-20th-century satirical novel, *Ju-lin Wai-shih* (*Rulin Waishi*). Ropp illuminates the 18th century as an era of both decline and renewal and one whose social criticism foreshadowed similar dissent which culminated in reformist and revolutionary movements in the 20th century.

198 **Modern China: the story of a revolution.**
Orville Schell, Joseph Esherick. New York: Knopf, 1972. 149p.

In their recounting of China's modern history from the Opium War up to and including Communist Revolution, the authors attempt to show how war, famine and social change affected the traditional way of life of the peasant. The authors relate events in China to the American scene in a way that students can identify with. This book presents information in a readable and understandable manner - the authors are concerned with the causes of events rather than with their factual presentation.

199 **Ku Chieh-kang and China's new history: nationalism and the quest for alternative tradition.**
Laurence A. Schneider. Berkeley, California: University of California Press, 1971. 276p.

The book consists of an analysis of Ku Chieh-kang's (Ku Qiegang) re-evaluation of the nation's heritage, and a discussion of Ku's own concept of the classics as history, in which context the original creation of Confucian orthodoxy is seen as the work of Ch'in (Qin) and Han scholars preoccupied with the political issues of their own time. Ku found in China's own intellectual heritage a heterodoxy. And in that same heritage, Ku also found the basis for China's new culture which, according to his historical arguments, should be a culture of the people.

200 **The T'aiping ideology: its sources, interpretations, and influences.**
Vincent Y. C. Shi. Seattle, Washington: University of Washington Press, 1973. 576p.

The author's philosophically-oriented study transcends many of the limitations which hampered prior inquiries. In three tightly-knit sections, he explores the principal elements of T'aiping (Taiping) ideology, probes its underlying historical and cultural roots and evaluates the numerous interpretations adduced since the upheaval itself.

201 Mercenaries and mandarins: the ever victorious army in nineteenth century China.

Richard J. Smith. Millwood, New York: Kraus, 1978. 271p.

The author examines the activity and significance of the small foreign-trained forces led by the mercenaries Frederick Ward and Charles Gordon in the suppression of the great T'aiping (Taiping) rebellion in the 1860s. He presents the background to the episode, discusses comparable sino-western enterprises such as the imperial maritime customs service and analyzes the consequences.

202 To change China: western advisers in China, 1620-1960.

Jonathan D. Spence. Boston, Massachusetts: Little, Brown, 1970. 335p.

From the beginning of the 17th century to our own decade, we follow the rising then ebbing fortunes of a wide variety of individuals who went to China for almost every sort of reason and generally ended their careers disheartened.

203 Emperor of China: self-portrait of K'ang-hsi.

Jonathan D. Spence. New York: Random House, 1974. 217p.

The author created this autobiography by linking together segments from the public and private papers of the Kang-hsi (Kangxi) emperor, who reigned from 1661 to 1722. The Emperor's thoughts are arranged under five headings: 'In motion', 'Ruling', 'Thinking', 'Growing old' and 'Sons'.

204 The Cambridge history of China: Sui and T'ang China, 589-906.

Dennis C. Twitchett. London: Cambridge University Press, 1979. 850p. Part I.

This volume is the first of two devoted to the Sui and T'ang (Tang) dynasties (581-907). It presents a narrative account of this period, during which China underwent far-reaching changes in political institutions, in her relations with the neighbouring countries, social organization, in the economy and every sphere of intellectual, religious and artistic life.

205 The fall of imperial China.

Frederic Wakeman, Jr. Berkeley, California: University of California Press, 1975. 276p.

A social history of China from the Ming dynasty to the death of Yuan Shi-kai (Yuan Shigai). Wakeman begins with an analysis of three social classes in China: peasants, merchants and gentry. He then examines the dynastic cycle in reaction to forces generated by social change and class dissatisfaction. The nadir of the cycle - the withdrawal of Heaven's Mandate - is discussed in the context of the fall of the Ming dynasty in the 17th century and then the collapse of the Ch'ing (Qing) in the early 20th century. He also describes the foundations laid for a new political system and offers preliminary reasons for the failure of the republic based on the problems which predated their creation.

206 **Conflict and control in late imperial China.**
Edited by Frederic Wakeman, Jr., Carolyn
Grant.   Berkeley, California: University of California Press,
1975. 352p.

The nine essays in this volume expose the social forces within China that governed historical change long before the Opium War began. Instead of focusing on the response to the West in the 19th century, the authors treat the period from the late Ming period to the early republic as an integral whole.

207 **The dragon empress: the life and times of Tsu-hsi Empress Dowager of China 1835-1908.**
Mariana Warner.   New York: Macmillan, 1972. 271p.

This volume recounts the decline of the Chinese empire and the fall of the Ch'ing (Qing) dynasty. It describes the personality of Tsu-hsi (Zuxi), the woman: her passion for power and intrigue; her obsession with ritual and ceremony; her love of gardens, painting, and the theatre; her excessive vanity and extravagance; her corruption and cruelty; and her legacy - a China torn from more than two thousand years of dynastic rule and tradition, facing a precarious future fraught with revolution.

208 **The district magistrate in late imperial China.**
John R. Watt.   New York: Columbia University Press,
1972. 340p.

The focus of this study is government administration at its lowest level, the level at which it most directly affected the lives of the people: the office of the local magistrate. The author traces the development of this office and its changing image throughout China's early modern history. His conclusion is that the Ming founder's rural control system, usually characterized as tyrannical, was actually an attempt to strengthen both popular autonomy and the central authority at the expense of local officials.

209 **Introduction to Chinese history: from ancient times to 1912.**
Bodo Wiethoff, translated by Mary Whittall.   Boulder,
Colorado: Westview Press, 1975. 190p.

This book was first published in German (1971). The first section deals with historiography. It briefly summarizes the history of European views of Chinese history. The following sections cover geography and demography, while the bulk of the book is devoted to 'polarities and tensions'. The three polarities he chooses to deal with are: centre and periphery; the rulers and the ruled; and China and the outside world. It is the author's theme that European concepts of China have rarely reflected Chinese reality, but have first and foremost been the response to European needs.

210 **Perspectives on the T'ang.**
Edited by Arthur Wright, Dennis C. Twitchett.   New
Haven, Connecticut: Yale University Press, 1973. 458p.

In addition to a long introduction by the editors, there are five articles on 'Institutions and politics', three on 'Thought and religion' and three on poetry. Those who are interested in Chinese social structure, population studies, Buddhism, or literary criticism should take note of this book.

211 The Sui dynasty: the unification of China, AD 581-617.
Arthur Wright. New York: Knopf, 1978. 237p.

Observers have long marvelled at the political unity of imperial China, which was sustained for centuries at a time and repeatedly restored after temporary break-downs. The author argues that this unity was not intrinsic to Chinese civilization. In the 6th century, when China had been divided into north and south for two centuries, the policies and talents of the Sui leaders enabled them to bring about reunification. Had they failed, the Chinese world thereafter might have remained divided into separate states.

212 Passage to power: K'ang-hsi and his heir apparent, 1661-1722.
Silas Wu. Cambridge, Massachusetts: Harvard University Press, 1979. 252p.

In this book the author has performed a service not only for specialists in the early Ch'ing (Qing) period, but also for those interested in the K'ang-hsi (Kangxi) period and in the relationship between personality, consanguinity, institutions and political power. He recreates the conflict and intrigue that marked the struggle for succession to the throne of China during the reign of Emperor K'ang-hsi (Kangxi). K'ang-hsi (Kangxi) is depicted here as a psychologi-cally complex individual.

213 The rise of modern China.
Immanuel C. Y. Xu. New York: Oxford University Press, 1970. 830p.

The book is a masterful work of scholarship in which the author Hsu (Xu) traces the political, intellectual, social and economic changes that have affected every phase of Chinese life from 1600 to the present and how they were precipitated, to a large degree, by foreign influence.

214 Readings in modern Chinese history.
Edited by Immanuel C. Y. Xu. New York: Oxford University Press, 1971. 701p.

This book of readings is designed as a companion volume to the author's *The rise of modern China*. The strength of Hsu's (Xu) reader lies in its first four parts covering pre-Communist China and especially in the second part 'Confrontation with the outside world, 1800-1900'. The editor's selections are well-balanced rather than provocative.

215 The comprador in nineteenth century China: bridge between East and West.
Yanping Hao. Cambridge, Massachusetts: Harvard University Press, 1971. 315p.

Using many materials published here for the first time, Yen P'ing Hao (Yanping Hao) examines the comprador's prominent role in affecting modern China's social change, economic development (especially the early industrialization), intellectual outlook, and acculturation. The most important conclusion appears to be that in many respects the comprador played a significant role in modern China's eco-nomic development - a role that stemmed from his position as an economic middleman between East and West.

The Chinese Opium Wars.
See item no. 1238.

Chinese socialism to 1907.
See item no. 1239.

Memories of Loyang: Yang Hsuan-chih and the lost capital (493-534).
See item no. 1246.

Marco Polo.
See item no. 1252.

Selections from records of the historian.
See item no. 1258.

The first revolution in China: a theory.
See item no. 1265.

The travels of Marco Polo.
See item no. 1267.

1900-1949

216 **Marshall in China.**
John Robinson Beal. New York: Doubleday, 1971. 385p.
The official record of the Marshall mission is contained in documents already published in 1949 in the white paper on American policy towards China. This record has, however, been supplemented by reminiscences of various individuals who were involved in the events of the period and Beal's book can claim to be among the most valuable of such memoirs. He was present in Chungking (Zhongqing) and afterwards in Nanking (Nanjing). He was in China in an official capacity and had a good opportunity to observe what went on in connection with Marshall's mission.

217 **Origins of the Chinese revolution, 1915-1949.**
Lucian Bianco, translated from French by Muriel
Bell. Stanford, California: Stanford University Press, 1971.
238p.
This book deals with the major questions of the Chinese revolution: Why did it occur and why did it take the form it did? Bianco's answers are delivered by means of one of the most compact and vivid descriptions of the Chinese revolution available. He examines the intellectual origins of the Chinese revolution, the early years of the Communist Party, the social causes of the revolution and the relationship of the Red Army with the Communist Party.

218 **Yenan in June 1937: talks with the Communist leaders.**
T. A. Bisson. Berkeley, California: University of California
Press, 1973. 267p.
Mao's interviews with Edgar Snow are well known; those a year later with T. A. Bisson, Mr and Mrs Philip Jaffe and Owen Lattimore less so, and of these only one has been available before in Nym Wales' mimeographed Yenan (Yanan)

notebooks. Bisson has now resurrected his own notebooks to provide a revealing glimpse of Mao's view of the world and of China's ability to exploit its semi-colonial contradictions.

219 A short history of nationalist China, 1919-1949.
George F. A. Botjer.   New York: Putnam, 1980. 312p.

This account of the Nationalist government's growth and decline follows the May 4th Movement to the Three People's Principles, the rise of Sun Yat-sen (Sun Yixian) and later Chiang Kai-shek (Jiang Jieshi), the Sino-Japanese War, and the final civil war, which drove the Nationalists to Taiwan. The book includes portraits of the principal personalities and the political and philosophical beliefs that shaped their actions. The study stresses that the Nationalists never controlled a united China.

220 The peace conspiracy: Wang Ching-wei and the China war, 1937-1941.
Gerald E. Bunker.   Cambridge, Massachusetts: Harvard University Press, 1972. 327p.

Bunker describes the cautious attempts by some Chinese and Japanese to halt the Chinese war, Wang Ching-wei's (Wang Jingwei) flight first to Hanoi and then to Shanghai and his actions there as the chief of state of the puppet régime in occupied China. The strongest point of the book is its accurate accounting of men and events during those seven years. The book offers an interpretation of Wang's intention at the time of his defection.

221 The Japanese siege of Tsingtau.
Charles B. Burdick.   Hamden, Connecticut: Archon Books, 1976. 274p.

Most historians of East Asia mention that Japan declared war on Germany in 1914 under the terms of the Anglo-Japanese alliance of 1902 and proceeded to capture the German-leased territory Tsingtau (Qingdau) and to take over the rights which the Germans had acquired in Shangtung (Shandong), but few give any details. This book gives detailed accounts of the military operations based on unpublished materials from German, Japanese, Australian, British and American archives, on diaries, memoirs and correspondence and on a wide selection of published books and articles.

222 China in the 1920s: nationalism and revolution.
Edited by Gilbert F. Chan, Thomas H. Etzold.   New York: New Viewpoints, 1976. 249p.

This book, the first of a planned three-volume series covering Chinese political history to 1925, consists of ten short articles especially written for this collection. Four of the articles deal with the revitalized centre of Chinese nationalism and revolution in Canton (Guangzhou) under the direction of Sun Yat-sen (Sun Yixian), while most of the others explore the response of the Chinese warlords, the student movement and the foreign powers to the nationalist movement.

223 **China at the crossroads: nationalists and communists, 1927-1949.**
Edited by Gilbert F. Chan. Boulder, Colorado: Westview Press, 1980. 288p.

Concentrating on a transitional epoch, 1927-1949, when China was at the crossroads of revolution, the contributors analyze the Kuomintang's (Guomindang) inherent weakness as a revolutionary force and the Communists' success in the quest for new formulas to guide the modernization movement. Rejecting the suggestion that external factors determined the outcome of the Kuomintang-Communist (Guomindang-Communist) conflict, they stress instead the more fundamental issues of the Chinese revolution, pointing to problems such as factionalism in Nanking (Nanjing), the weakness of the New Life Movement as an experiment in propaganda and mass mobilization, the failure of land reform, and the ineffectiveness of the anti-Japanese boycott of 1931-32.

224 **Historiography of the Chinese labor movement.**
Ming Chan. Stanford, California: Stanford University Press, 1981. 350p.

The book provides a critical survey of over 700 titles of major Chinese works that are useful for serious study of the Chinese labour movement, a long-neglected subject.

225 **Dilemma in China: America's policy debate, 1945.**
Kenneth S. Chern. Hamden, Connecticut: Shoe String Press, 1979. 277p.

The book makes a detailed analysis of the debate over China conducted in 1945 by the Senate Foreign Relations Committee led by such figures as Tom Connally and Arthur Vandenberg, both continuing the wartime assumptions of a bipartisan foreign policy. The debate reached its climax at the end of the year, dramatized in November by Patrick Hurley's public charges against the State Department's China specialists and his own resignation as ambassador to China.

226 **China from the 1911 revolution to liberation.**
Jean Chesneaux, Francis Le Barbier, Marie-Claire Bergere, translated from the French by Paul Auster, Lydia Davis. New York: Pantheon, 1978. 469p.

This is the second volume of the English translation of a major French text on modern Chinese history. The book covers politics, economics, social and cultural changes and foreign affairs. Its Marxist interpretative framework leads to bold generalizations about the bourgeoisie or the peasants that, to cautiously empirical Americans, will seem stimulating but not definitive.

227 **The Shanghai capitalists and the nationalist government, 1927-1937.**
Park M. Coble. Cambridge, Massachusetts: Harvard University Press, 1980. 346p.

A common generalization about the Nationalist government in China during the decade 1927-1937, has been that Chiang Kai-shek's (Jiang Jieshi) régime was closely allied with the capitalists in Shanghai. This book paints a different picture

- that Nanking (Nanjing) sought to control the capitalists politically and economically.

228 The connection: Roger S. Greene, Thomas W. Lamont, George E. Sokolsky and American-East Asian relations.
Warren I. Cohen. New York: Columbia University Press, 1978. 320p.

This is a very readable account of American attitudes toward East Asia in the first half of this century, based on the stories of three Americans - Roger S. Greene, Thomas W. Lamont and George E. Sokolsky - who played key roles in shaping American opinion about the Far East. The author seeks to reveal the limits of such attempts at influence as well as the impact of Sokolsky's attacks on the Truman administration for the hardening of US attitudes to Mao's China.

229 The dream and the destiny.
Alexander Cordell. London: Hodder & Stoughton, 1975. 445p.

In 1938, Edgar Snow published the first English account of the Long March in *Red star over China.* Snow's prose was matter-of-fact; the drama of the March lay in the story he told, not in the way in which he wrote it. Other accounts have followed, which have provided detail, but none have tried to dramatize the drama, as this book does.

230 China: this century.
R. R. C. De Crespigny. New York: St. Martin's Press, 1975. 299p.

For the teacher in search of a concise introduction to modern Chinese political history suitable for college students, this book can be highly recommended. It has all the features one looks for in a fine textbook. It is written in a lucid, engaging style. Major issues and personalities are discussed with just enough details and anecdotes to clarify them but not so many as to swamp the reader.

231 Revolution and history: origins of Marxist historiography in China: 1919-1937.
Arit Dirlik. Berkeley, California: University of California Press, 1978. 309p.

Dirlik examines the application of the materialist connection of history to the analysis of Chinese history in a period when Marxist ideas first gained currency in Chinese intellectual circles. He gives the historical analyses of major Marxist historians of the period in detail and relates them to trends in contemporary politics, thought and historiography.

232 The memoirs of Li Tsung-jen.
T. K. Dong, Li Zongren. Boulder, Colorado: Westview Press, 1979. 642p.

For over a quarter of a century, Li Tsung-jen (Li Zongren) was Chiang Kai-shek's (Jiang Jieshi) major collaborator as well as his principal political rival. His memoirs, presented here by T. K. Tong (Dong) and Li Tsung-Jen (Li Zongren) encompass not only the life story of a top militarist-politician in Republican China, but also the entire political history of the Nationalist régime.

233 The abortive revolution: China under nationalist rule, 1927-37.
Lloyd E. Eastman.   Cambridge, Massachusetts: Harvard University Press, 1974. 398p.

In this fine study, Eastman explores, in depth, selected aspects of Chinese history of the Nanking (Nanjing) decade, to isolate the forces that prevented the recreation of national unity and vitality under the Kuomintang (Guomindang) government. He attempts to discover what forces prevented the Kuomingtang (Guomindang) from achieving a viable political system. He concludes that, in the main, the Kuomintang (Guomindang) officials were not dedicated to the welfare of society and political forces outside the régime were not strong enough to impose accountability upon it.

234 Lost chance in China: the World War II dispatches of John S. Service.
Edited by Joseph Esherick.   New York: Random House, 1974. 409p.

These dispatches to the US Foreign Service cover the period from October 1941 to April 1945. The subjects range from the hardships of peasant life to the gossip of Chungking (Zhongqing), and from the politics and economy of the Communist border region to statements by Mao Tse-tung (Mao Zedong) on Communist policy, and his hopes for the future of Sino-American relations.

235 Chinese-American interactions: a historical summary.
John K. Fairbank.   New Brunswick, New Jersey: Rutgers University Press, 1975. 90p.

In the first essay, Fairbank discusses the American interest in China trade and concludes that the turning inward of American capital investment after the civil war ended the close connection between the wealthy New England commercial class and the Orient. In his second essay, he surveys the accomplishments of missionary education from the 1870s to the 1930s. Finally he takes up the question of diplomacy. He contends that the US generally followed British policy in China and consequently the American government suffered in the 1940s from a lack of national tradition and experience in defining the strategic power interests of the US in China.

236 Backward toward revolution: the Chinese revolutionary party.
Edward Friedman.   Berkeley, California: University of California Press, 1974. 356p.

In the first part of this book, the author looks at the revolutionary experience of the Sun Yat-sen (Sun Yixian) faction in the decade prior to the establishment of the Chinese Revolutionary Party in 1914, and focuses on the relationship of political programme to political party. The meaning and purpose of an exclusivist, revolutionary single-party organization is analyzed. Part two examines the process by which the Chinese Revolutionary Party was formed and its political ideology. Part three examines the attempts of revolutionary intellectuals to unite with armed rural rebels. In the final section, part four, the revolutionary movement is viewed in the context of larger changes occurring in China and on the international scene.

237 The Chinese communist treatment of counter revolutionaries, 1924-1949.
Patricia E. Griffin.   Princeton, New Jersey: Princeton University Press, 1976. 256p.

This book is divided into three phases: the Kiangsi (Jiangxi) Soviet; Yenan (Yanan); and the Civil War 1945-1949. In the first segment, the author explains to whom the term counterrevolutionary was applied during the Kiangsi (Jiangxi) Soviet and attempts to analyze statistically the punishments meted out to these individuals. The subsequent sections trace the changes that were made in definitions and punishments during the Yenan (Yanan) and Civil War periods.

238 Ch'en Tu-hsiu (1879-1942) and the Chinese communist movement.
Thomas C. Guo.   South Orange, New Jersey: Seton Hall University Press, 1975. 428p.

The author Thomas Kuo (Guo) provides readers with a systematic chronology of Ch'en Tu-hsiu's (Chen Duxiu) life and an extensive selection from his writings. The author also places the blame for Ch'en's (Chen) failure on his personality (and the Soviet advisor Borodin) rather than on the Nationalists or the Chinese Communists.

239 The Long March to power: a history of the Chinese Communist Party, 1921-72.
James P. Harrison.   New York: Macmillan, 1973. 369p.

This carefully documented study traces the Communist Party's fortunes from the first appearance of Marxism in China through the revolutionary struggle of 1949 to 1972 and looks forward to the problems of the future. Harrison claims that his view of the history of Chinese Communism is dominated by two interlocking themes: the ability of the Communists to capture the spirit of revolutionary nationalism in modern China, and their skill in organizing the masses.

240 Progressivism and the open door, America and China, 1905-1921.
Jerry Israel.   Pittsburgh, Pennsylvania: University of Pittsburgh Press, 1971. 222p.

After research in published and unpublished materials, the author has concluded that Americans concerned with China were divided by the tensions between the competitive and cooperative attempts to achieve the goals of the Open Door policy. Altering the term from its earlier sense of equal opportunity for all to trade with the Chinese, he defines Open Door after 1905 as a basic plan or system for the opening of the Chinese markets and mind to American products, money and ideas.

241 **The northern expedition: the Chinese national revolution 1926-28.**
Donald A. Jordan.   Honolulu: University Press of Hawaii, 1976. 341p.

This book provides a detailed chronological description of the Northern Expedition, the 1926-28 military campaign to eliminate warlord power and unite China. The volume is divided into five sections. The first of its five parts details political activities from 1926-28 at the revolutionary base at Canton (Guangzhou). It is followed by an account of the military events of the Northern Expedition. Part three deals with the role of the masses during the campaign and part four examines the actions of the political arm of the Northern Expedition Armies. The final section describes how warlords were enticed to defect to the revolutionaries.

242 **The China hands: America's foreign service officers and what befell them.**
E. J. Kahn.   New York: Viking, 1975. 337p.

Between 1951 and 1954, many of the most talented Foreign Service officers who specialized in China were forced out of their jobs because of alleged 'loyalty' shortcomings. Kahn is deeply sympathetic to the beleaguered Foreign Service officers. The 13 men - among them John Stewart Service, John Carter Vincent and John Paton Davies - were blamed for the loss of China to Mao Tse-tung (Mao Zedong) due to their reports of the Chinese situation during and immediately after the Second World War.

243 **Along alien roads: the memoirs of a soviet military advisor in China, 1938-1939.**
Aleksandr Ia. Kalyagin, translated and edited by Steven L. Levine.   New York: East Asian Institute, Columbia University, 1982. 287p.

This is an abridged translation of the reminiscences of Aleksandr Kalyagin, Soviet military specialist and senior advisor to the head of the Chinese Army Engineers from 1938-1939. He provides first-hand information about a period when Soviet Russia was the only foreign country giving China substantial military assistance. His perceptive observations make a unique contribution to our understanding of the anti-Japanese war period.

244 **Resistance and revolution in China, the communists and the second united front.**
Tetsuya Kataoka.   Berkeley, California: University of California Press, 1974. 320p.

The author considers how the Chinese Communist Party laid the foundation for victory in the period of the Second United Front from 1935-1941, or the extent to which the war of resistance against Japan was also a revolutionary war. He agrees with the prevailing opinion that the Long March was a disaster for the Communist Movement and Mao. Henceforth, the Communist movement was transformed into an anti-Japanese resistance during which the Party could carry on with the revolution and the ideological struggle.

245 The crisis of Chinese consciousness: radical anti-traditionalism in the May Fourth era.
Lin Yusheng. Madison, Wisconsin: University of Wisconsin Press, 1979. 201p.

How does the author Lin Yu-sheng (Yusheng) account for the existence of the extraordinary iconoclastic attitude toward the cultural heritage of the Chinese past? He has, quite logically, tried to explain a unique modern phenomenon by seeking unique qualities in Chinese tradition. From his analysis of the May 4th Movement (1915-27) the author seeks to show the origins, nature and implications of anti-traditionalism in 20th-century China. In explicating his thesis he examines the ideas of Ch'en Tu-hsiu (Chen Duxiu), Hu Shi and Lu Hsun (Lu Xun), leaders of the May 4th intelligentsia.

246 Chinese communism 1931-1934: experience in civil government.
Trygve Lotveit. Stockholm: Scandinavian Institute of Asian Studies, 1973. 290p.

The first half of the book is devoted to a detailed description of the structure and function of the soviet on different levels, from the Hsiang (Xiang) Soviet, through the intermediate soviets, to the central government of the Chinese Soviet Republic. The second half deals more specifically with the evolution of the policy adopted by the Chinese Communists towards justice, class and finances during the period.

247 Chinese exclusion versus the Open Door policy, 1900-1906.
Delber McKee. Detroit, Michigan: Wayne State University Press, 1977. 292p.

The purpose of this book is to expose what the author calls the 'second policy' of the United States toward China, early in this century. In 1900, the United States proclaimed an Open Door policy of urging equal access for all nations to China for missionary work and commerce. Yet, the United States simultaneously continued the internal policy of denying entry to Asians on a purely racial basis. Thus America remained a closed door to Chinese and Japanese not only for immigrants but also for tourists, businessmen and students.

248 Otto Braun: Comintern agent in China, 1932-1939.
Jeanne Moore. London: Hurst, 1980. 320p.

Otto Braun (1902-74), after a sensational escape from a Berlin prison and military training in Moscow, was sent to China in 1932 as the Comintern's military advisor to the Central Committee of the Chinese Communist Party, and for some years was in close touch with the leading figures of the revolution, and exerted considerable influence. He was the only foreigner to take part in the Long March. This book is of unique value, for its description of momentous events and of the relationships between and the characters of leading participants in the revolution.

249 **Duel for the middle kingdom: the struggle between Chiang Kai-shek and Mao Tse-tung for control of China.**
William Morwood. New York: Everest House, 1980. 424p.

Morwood's account of China between 1911 and 1949 argues that the upheaval took the form of an unrelenting duel between two giants: Chiang Kai-shek (Jiang Jieshi), champion of the old values, and Mao Tse-tung (Mao Zedong), representative of the Chinese Communist Party, the prophet of the future. This book analyzes the personalities and individual actions of the major leaders more than the underlying social and economic forces.

250 **The fall of Shanghai.**
Barber Noel. New York: Coward, McCann & Geoghegan, 1979. 287p.

Despite the struggle for power in China between Chiang Kai-shek (Jiang Jieshi) and Mao Tse-tung (Mao Zedong), the international city of Shanghai, with its foreign residents, continued to prosper until 1949, when the Communists crossed the Yangtze (Yangzi) and Shanghai fell to Mao Tse-tung (Mao Zedong). This book deals with that period - the Communist takeover of the city. It is a book about people - the inhabitants of Shanghai, and their experiences prior to, during, and after the Communist takeover.

251 **Civil war in China, the political struggle, 1945-1949.**
Suzanne Pepper. Berkeley, California: University of California Press, 1980. 258p.

This is an account of the political conflict between the Nationalists and Communists during China's civil war of 1945-49. In this study, Pepper reconsiders the question of whether the Kuomintang (Guomindang) lost control, 1945-49 through their own failings, or whether the Communists gained power because of the strength of their political programme. The conclusions she reaches emphasize the Kuomintang's (Guomindang) lack of a rural programme and its mismanagement of urban areas. She argues that the Communists had a good rural strategy, especially in north China.

252 **Early Chinese revolutionaries, radical intellectuals in Shanghai and Chekiang, 1902-1911.**
Mary Bakus Rankin. Cambridge, Massachusetts: Harvard University Press, 1971. 340p.

Mrs Rankin's interest lies in radical student politics in Shanghai and Chekiang (Zhejiang) in the opening decade of the century. Her first underlying assumption is that the basic aim of the 1911 Revolution was modernization, closely tied to nationalistic attitudes. Her second assumption is that students and intellectuals formed the core of the revolutionary movement, which was a political phenomenon distinguished from the Revolution itself. She describes the progressive alienation of a young generation of upper-class intellectuals from the Confucian tradition, and their growing opposition to the Manchu imperial house.

253 **The forgotten ambassador: the reports of John Leighton Stuart, 1946-1949.**
Edited by Kenneth Rea, John C. Brewer. Boulder, Colorado: Westview Press, 1981. 350p.

The main theme in Stuart's dispatches to the State Department is the Chinese request for US aid as a precondition for reform and the US response that aid would be useless until reform took place. Thus, Stuart's reports, which become tinged with sadness, reflect the dilemma of a man who believed the Nationalist government could defeat the Communists, but who also realized that his ideas were not apt to be adopted.

254 **Yenan and the Great Powers: the origins of Chinese Communist foreign policy, 1944-46.**
James Reardon-Anderson. New York: Columbia University Press, 1980. 240p.

Drawing on the accounts of American observers in China, on reports and opinions in the Chinese press, and on a variety of other Chinese and English sources, the author presents a challenging argument that military and political factors, and not ideology, guided Chinese Communist foreign policy at the end of the Second World War.

255 **The Communist conquest of Shanghai: a warning to the West.**
Paolo Rossi. Arlington, Viginia: Crestwood Books, 1970. 170p.

Paolo Rossi was Italian Consul-General in Shanghai from 1948 until he closed the Consulate in 1952. He died in 1969 and the manuscript for this book appears to have been prepared from notes after his death by Anthony Kubek, who also provides an introduction and epilogue.

256 **The Yenan way in revolutionary China.**
Mark Selden. Cambridge, Massachusetts: Harvard University Press, 1971. 311p.

This is a vivid history of the Chinese Communist areas during the war years. It suggests that rural revolution succeeds in areas not yet modernized; that concrete economic and political democracy can be a deeper and more enduring motive than nationalism; that the Yenan (Yanan) experience gave the later rulers of China a unique education in, and model for, government.

257 **China in disintegration: the republican era in Chinese history, 1912-1949.**
James E. Sheridan. New York: Free Press, 1975. 338p.

The book is concerned with the forces of national integration which surmounted the collapse of domestic order, after the revolution of 1911. It seeks to show why the Kuomintang (Guomindang) failed and the Communists succeeded in reintegrating the Chinese nation. The author discusses warlords and warlordism, the republican revolution, the May 4th intellectual movement, the Nanking (Nanjing) decade of Kuomintang (Guomindang) rule and the origins of the Chinese Communist Party.

258 American and Chinese Communists: 1927-1945, a persuading encounter.
Kenneth R. Shewmaker. Ithaca, New York: Cornell University Press, 1971. 340p.

Focusing on the writings and experiences of Americans who travelled in China from 1937 to 1945, this book describes and analyzes their almost unanimously favourable reactions to Chinese Communists. A major aim of the book is to show that the conspiracy thesis is wholly inadequate to deal with the complexities of Sino-American contacts. On the other hand, the author criticizes as oversimple the image of the Communists as 'agrarian reformers' that was prevalent among American observers during the 1930s and 1940s.

259 Edgar Snow's China.
Lois Wheeler Snow. New York: Random House, 1981. 279p.

No Westerner since Marco Polo has so profoundly influenced our attitudes toward China as the late Edgar Snow. This personal account by his wife gives a splendid introduction to Snow's writings and reproduces many of the photographs he took while covering China for a number of US publications.

260 While China faced West: American reformers in Nationalist China, 1928-1937.
James C. Thomson, Jr. Cambridge, Massachusetts: Harvard University Press, 1974. 310p.

Thomson was raised in China by missionary parents. He uses his experience as a China-watcher in Washington to expose the ambiguities of what he calls the 'export of benevolence'. While he relies on Western sources, he gives a shrewd but sympathetic picture of his protagonists.

261 Stilwell and the American experience in China 1911-1945.
Barbara Tuchman. New York: Macmillan, 1971. 621p.

Mrs Tuchman, who was a China news correspondent in the 1930s and who won a Pulitzer prize in 1962, makes a fascinating copy out of Joseph Stilwell's many journeys in China. Stilwell combined a career focused on China with a background that was quintessentially American. His connection with China spanned the formative period from the year of the Revolution to the decline of the Nationalist government.

262 The extraterritorial system in China: final phase.
John Carter Vincent. Cambridge, Massachusetts: Harvard University Press, 1970. 297p.

In the period between the two world wars, constant pressures were exerted by the Kuomintang (Guomindang) government to undermine the extraterritorial system founded by the 'unequal treaties'. The author has prepared a series of case histories describing the difficulties of interpreting and maintaining American rights granted by treaty in the face of Chinese antagonism.

263 The Vladimirov diaries: Yenan China, 1942-1945.
Peter Vladimirov. New York: Doubleday, 1975. 538p.

The account of events and personalities kept by Vladimirov, *Tass* correspondent and Comintern agent. He was sent to Mao Tse-tung's (Mao Zedong) Communist strongholds in Yenan (Yanan) during World War II, when the Chinese Communists were split over the issue of cooperation with Chiang Kai-shek (Jiang Jieshi) in the fight against the Japanese invaders.

264 The Kiangsi Soviet Republic: Mao and the National Congress of 1931 and 1934.
Derek J. Waller. Berkeley, California: Center for Chinese Studies, University of California, 1973. 116p.

Waller focuses on one of the institutions of the Republic's central government, the National Soviet Congress, which was convened only twice, and for rather brief sessions, in November 1931 and January-February 1934. He also surveys the election movements leading up to the two Congresses, and to some extent, he deals with other central government organs and with the organization of local government. The book, which is carefully documented, is based on a number of important laws, regulations, speeches and authoritative articles of the period.

265 Mao's betrayal.
Wang Ming. Moscow: Progressive Publishers, 1979. 278p.

This book has some historical value. It is the account of two crucial but still obscure political events in the political history of the Chinese Communist Party: the Kao Kang (Gao Gang) affair and the Emergence Salvation Campaign of 1943.

266 The Long March 1935: the epic of Chinese communism's survival.
Dick Wilson. New York: Viking, 1972. 231p.

A journalist and long-time Asian expert combines painstaking research and vivid style to present a picture both sympathetic and skeptical of the mythic-historic key points in the Communist Chinese Revolution. This is an account of the 6,000 mile march of the Chinese Communist Army. Wilson also treats the political events of the Long March in the greatest detail.

267 The Sian incident: a pivotal point in modern Chinese history.
Wu Dianwei. Ann Arbor, Michigan: Center for Chinese Studies, 1976. 285p.

Wu Tien-wei (Wu Dianwei) has assembled, through interviews and an exhaustive combination of Chinese and English sources, an impressive collection of 'crucial details' of the Sian Incident. They are sufficient to support well-balanced and convincing exposition of the background causes that led to the kidnapping, the details of the event itself, the dissolution of the affair and the aftermath. He ends his study with a recapitulatory chapter on the historical significance of the Sian coup and settlement.

268 **The rise of the Chinese Communist Party: autobiography of Chang Kuo-tao, Volume I, 1921-1927; Volume II, 1928-1938.**
Zhang Guodao. Lawrence, Kansas: University of Kansas Press, 1971-72. 2 vols. 756+689p.

The two volumes that Chang Kuo-tao (Zhang Guodao) has devoted to the history of the Chinese Communist Party from 1921 to 1938, by way of his own autobiography. He was one of its founders, as a member of its First Congress and one of its most important figures until the flight from Yenan (Yanan) in April 1938. He provides important, and sometimes new, insights, into the manner in which the Chinese Communist Party formulated its political policies, strategies and tactics and the heated debate that often went on behind the scenes.

269 **The military-gentry coalition: China under the warlords.**
Jerome Zhen. Toronto: University of Toronto-York University Joint Center for Modern East Asia, 1979. 201p.

According to the author, Jerome Chen (Zhen), during the warlord period China was in the grip of a coalition of warlords and rural gentry. From 1860 to 1895, power in China was concentrated in the hands of a gentry-military coalition, but after 1895 the military played the dominant role in the coalition. Both coalitions shared certain characteristics: both the gentry and the military were primarily interested in maintaining and enhancing their own positions of authority, rather than working for any social, ideological or political goals; both were willing to use the resources immediately to hand - the wealth of the land, the labour of the people and the taxes of the populace - to achieve their goals; and both were extremely conservative and strongly opposed to anything that hinted of altering the status quo.

China called me: my life inside the Chinese revolution.
See item no. 1241.

America's cultural experiment in China, 1942-49.
See item no. 1244.

The unknown war: North China 1937-1945.
See item no. 1248.

China scapegoat: the diplomatic ordeal of John Carter Vincent.
See item no. 1250.

Tigers over Asia.
See item no. 1253.

China historiography on the revolution of 1911: a critical survey and a selective bibliography.
See item no. 1452.

Post 1949

270 Uncertain passage: China's transition to the post-Mao era.
A. Doak Barnett. Washington, DC: Brookings, 1974. 387p.

The author discusses the issues confronting China in 1974 - achieving ideological consensus and institutional stability, defining the political role of the military, and improving the country's economic performance and development strategies. He also examines critical problems related to leadership, authority and the succession process itself. Finally, he analyzes China's interaction with the outside world and comments on the implications of trends in China for US policy.

271 China in ferment: perspectives on the Cultural Revolution.
Edited by Richard Baum, Louis B. Bennet. Englewood Cliffs, New Jersey: Prentice-Hall, 1971. 246p.

In this volume, the editors have collected writings by political scientists, government leaders and scholars from both China and the United States which probe the events leading up to the revolution and which seek to assess its impact on the political, economic and social life of China. The essays discuss the strengths and weaknesses of Mao's influence on the Red Guards, the need for army interference to keep the revolution under control and the effect the revolution could have on future Chinese political and military behaviour.

272 China since Mao.
Charles Bethelheim, Neil G. Burton. New York: Monthly Review Press, 1978. 130p.

Two Marxist intellectuals, one, a French theoretician, and the other, a Canadian living and working in China, argue about the significance of the changes that have taken place in China since the death of Mao. Essentially, the authors are debating whether the present leaders of the People's Republic of China have ended the Chinese Revolution and betrayed their Maoist heritage, or whether they are building on but moving beyond it.

273 Contemporary China.
Bill Brugger. London: Croom Helm, 1977. 451p.

This is a history of the People's Republic of China from its founding in October 1949 to the 10th Party Congress in 1973. The author emphasizes in particular the dialectical interaction between central leadership and mass initiative as providing the clue to the understanding of developments. He borrows from the terminology of the social sciences to divide the history into nine cycles up to August 1973. It is filled with information, well documented, clearly organized and occasionally quite perceptive.

274 China: the impact of the Cultural Revolution.
Bill Brugger. New York: Barnes & Noble, 1978. 300p.

The book consists of seven chapters, plus an introduction and conclusion, each focused on the ideological and policy implications of the Cultural Revolution. In the conclusion, the author attempts to put the political development from the Lin Piao (Lin Biao) incident to the fall of Chiang Ching (Jiang Qing) into perspective, raising some of the fundamental contradictions that face the new leadership.

275 **China since the Gang of Four.**
Edited by Bill Brugger. New York: St Martin's Press, 1980. 288p.

In seven specially commissioned essays, this book explores the dramatic changes that have occurred in China since the death of Chairman Mao and the arrest of the 'Gang of Four' in late 1976. The contributors consider crucial questions about the extent to which Mao's policies have been abandoned or modified and the reactions to the 'Gang' in their attempt to identify the broad significance of the recent Chinese experience.

276 **China: radicalism to revisionism 1962-1979.**
Bill Brugger. New York: Barnes & Noble, 1981. 275p.

Although the Chinese celebrated the 30th anniversary of the founding of the People's Republic of China with considerably less fanfare than expected, the event did provide Western scholars with a good opportunity to assess the country's achievements to date.

277 **China: liberation and transformation 1942-1962.**
Bill Brugger. New York: Barnes & Noble, 1981. 275p.

This book is a rewrite and an update of his earlier book, *Contemporary China*, with new materials on the Kao Kang (Gao Gang) and Peng Te-huai (Peng Duhuai) affairs.

278 **China: the People's Republic, 1949-1976.**
Jean Chesneaux, with the assistance of J. Bollassen, A. M. Dubois, F. Le Barbier, J. F. Oliver, J.-P. Peeman, N. Wang, translated from the French by Paul Auster, Lydia Davis. New York: Pantheon, 1979. 693p.

This is the third and final volume in a series by French scholars on China's recent past. Chesneaux offers a highly perceptive and generally sympathetic narrative history of the Cultural Revolution. He sees it as the true revolution for the people: anti-Stalinist. He discusses the issues such as the role of the bourgeoisie, the problems of the Chinese working class, the conflict between the policy lines advocated by Mao Tse-tung (Mao Zedong) and Liu Shao-chi (Liu Shaoqi).

279 **China's socialist revolution.**
John Collier, Elise Collier. New York: Monthly Review Press, 1973. 270p.

The authors recount their experiences as teachers and workers in China at the height of the Cultural Revolution from 1966-1968. The Colliers were among the first foreigners allowed to participate in the movement on an equal footing with Chinese and they travelled widely through the countryside, visiting factories, farms and schools, doing manual labour and taking sides in political struggles and demonstrations.

280 **A history of the Chinese Cultural Revolution.**
Jean Daubler, translated from the French by Richard
Seaver, with a preface by Han Suyin.   New York: Vintage
Books, 1974. 219p.

A French Marxist who participated in the Cultural Revolution presents an eye-witness account of the events and examines their consequences for China's Marxist régime. This is the first book on the Cultural Revolution to take the ideology behind it seriously. Daubler's own personal experience of the Cultural Revolution adds an extra dimension to the records.

281 **Mao's great revolution.**
Robert S. Elegant.   New York: World Publishing, 1971.
478p.

This is a report on the machinations of the inner circle of the Chinese Communist Party before, during and after the Red Guard upheaval. The author details the cross-currents that led to the Red Guard uprisings and to the crushing of the Mao-inspired movement. He relates how, ultimately, the army re-established some degree of effective rule while Mao was relegated to a weakened position. He concludes that the actors were motivated solely by power considerations and not at all by ideology or patriotism.

282 **The Chinese Cultural Revolution.**
Jean Esmein.   New York: Doubleday, 1973. 346p.

The French version of this book, *La Revolution Culturelle Chinoise*, by a former press attaché at the French Embassy in Peking (Beijing), was first published in 1970. The book describes the Cultural Revolution on the basis of the official press, the Red Guard press reports and personal observations in terms of the different groups involved. The cut-off date was the Ninth Party Congress in April 1969.

283 **China perceived: images and policies in Chinese-American
relations.**
John K. Fairbank.   New York: Knopf, 1974. 245p.

This volume is primarily a collection of previously published essays and lectures by the author. He looks at China's history, its involvement with the US and the permutations in its foreign policy. In his mind, there is a definite causal connection between American ignorance and the misuse of American power in the region.

284 **The United States and China.**
John K. Fairbank.   Cambridge, Massachusetts: Harvard
University Press, 1979. 512p.

The new edition, like the earlier ones, contains a history of China, an analysis of Chinese society, and an account of Sino-American relations. There are new sections on the last decade's historic events, including US recognition of China in December 1978. For the first time, illustrations have been included in the book. The comprehensive bibliography has been completely revised and updated.

285 Chinabound: a fifty-year memoir.
John K. Fairbank. New York: Harper, 1982. 416p.

The memoir records Fairbank's fifty-year experience with the East. He describes the growth of the Left in China, his distaste for McCarthyism and official US ignorance of Asia, which deepened his commitment to establish centres of learning not only at Harvard but also across the country. The book is a record of US relations with China and the story of the man who bridged the gap in the understanding of that part of the world.

286 Coming alive: China after Mao.
Roger Garside. New York: McGraw-Hill, 1981. 458p.

Garside was the First Secretary in the British Embassy in Peking (Beijing) from the time of the death of Premier Chou En-lai (Zhou Enlai) in January 1976 until the upsurge of the democratic movement in the winter of 1978-79. He was in the Tien An Men (Diananmen) Square when angry crowds rioted in April 1976 and spent hours at Democracy Wall in 1978-79, when young Chinese felt free to speak their minds. He talked with Wei Ching-sheng (Wei Jingsheng) and other leaders of the movement for democracy and human rights. He observed Chairman Hua Kuo-feng (Hua Guofeng) and Vice Chairman Ten Hsiao-ping (Deng Xiaoping) at close quarters and followed changes in various fields of policy.

287 The mandate of heaven: Marx and Mao in modern China.
Nigel Harris. New York: Quartet Books, 1978. 307p.

Harris attempts to show that China under the Communists is not and never has been the democratic, egalitarian society some would have us believe. He sees it as a bureaucratic, nationalist state not unlike the USSR, driven by the urge to accumulate capital for economic development.

288 Hundred day war: the Cultural Revolution at Tsinghua University.
William Hinton. New York: Monthly Review, 1972. 288p.

The author tells the story of student factional struggles at Tsinghua (Qinghua) University during the Cultural Revolution. The account is based on three weeks of interviews conducted at Tsinghua (Qinghua) in 1971. As an account of one episode in the Cultural Revolution, this is a rich and important book with significant glimpses into Chinese society and politics.

289 Turning point in China: an essay on Cultural Revolution.
William Hinton. New York: Monthly Review, 1972. 112p.

This book outlines the Maoist interpretation of the Cultural Revolution. Hinton challenges the interpretation put forward by most Western students of China. He argues that the Cultural Revolution, far from being a single leadership struggle between different personalities, was precisely what Mao said it was - a struggle between working-class revolutionaries and Party members in power taking the capitalist road.

290 A short history of Chinese communism.
Franklin W. Hou. Englewood Cliffs, New Jersey:
Prentice-Hall, 1973. 2nd ed. 278p.

Closely tracing the Chinese Communist Party's revolution from a small Soviet-directed movement to an independent and successful force, the author discusses the social and cultural factors behind the birth of the Chinese Communist ideology, as well as the industrial and social progress brought about by the Party since the establishment of the People's Republic of China in 1949. The changing strategies and foreign policies are examined, as is its internal structure, power struggles, and revolutionary adaptations of orthodox Marxism. The new edition includes a chapter on the Cultural Revolution.

291 The second Chinese revolution.
K. S. Karol, translated from French by Mervyn
Jones. New York: Hill & Wang, 1974. 427p.

Based on the author's return trip to China in 1971, this book seeks to come to grips with the many fundamental problems, puzzles and paradoxes posed by China's Great Proletarian Cultural Revolution. Was the Cultural Revolution really necessary? Did it succeed in futhering Maoist objectives? And what is its legacy both within China and vis-à-vis the outside world? While these questions are not original, the author succeeds in bringing a rather fresh perspective to the twin tasks of analysis and evaluation.

292 Revolution and cosmopolitanism: the Western stage and the Chinese stage.
Joseph R. Levenson. Berkeley, California: University of
California Press, 1971. 238p.

Based upon a careful analysis of a wide selection of Western plays translated into Chinese during the 20th century, this study tries to place the Communist Cultural Revolution into a new historical perspective. Beginning with the demise of Confucian China which 'New Youth' intellectuals found too provincial, the author shows how these same cosmopolitans became in turn too bourgeois to alter Maoist tastes. This is an attempt to put the Cultural Revolution into historical perspective as the latest stage in modern China's turbulent transition from insularity to internationalism.

293 Revolution and tradition in Tientsin, 1949-1952.
Kenneth Lieberthal. Stanford, California: Stanford
University Press, 1980. 397p.

Tientsin (Tianjin), China's second-largest industrial and commercial centre, was the first of the major treaty ports to come under Communist rule in 1949. With its mixture of traditional China and modern Western ideas, it represented a complex challenge to the new régime. This book uses an analysis of how the Communists expanded and consolidated their power in Tientsin (Tianjin) to illuminate several fundamental issues confronting the People's Republic of China then and now. How is political consciousness shaped? What are the social bases of anti-Communism in urban China? And most important, can mass mobilization be used more effectively than organizational control to produce lasting changes in attitudes and social practices?

294 The coming decline of the Chinese empire.
Victor Louis. New York: Times Books, 1979. 198p.

A Soviet journalist long known for his KGB connections, paints a picture of a consistently expansionist, exploitative China sitting on the backs of its repressed minorities and itching to conquer the Soviet Far East, Siberia and Central Asia. Salisbury E. Harrison points out in a useful introduction, that the alarming point about this book is that Louis seems to be trying to lay a foundation for a Soviet preemptive strike against China.

295 The origins of the Cultural Revolution: contradictions among the people, 1956-59.
Roderic MacFarquhar. New York: Columbia University Press, 1974. 439p.

In the first book of his projected three volume study of 1956-66 the decade that preceeded the Cultural Revolution in China, MacFarquhar examines 1956-59. He contends that it was during this crucial period that Mao-Tse-tung's (Mao Zedong) thoughts and actions set in motion a chain of events that were to lead inexorably to the upheavals of 1966.

296 China: the impacts of revolution.
Edited by Colin P. Mackerras. New York: Longman, 1976. 273p.

This book is a collaborative effort of six Australian scholars. The authors state in their preface that the purpose of the book is to trace China's development from 1911 to 1974. The account is thematic and chronological, as well as informative and interpretative.

297 Army and masses in China: a Marxist interpretation of the Cultural Revolution and its aftermath.
Livio Maitan, translated from Italian by Gregor Benton, Marie Colliti. London: Humanities Press, 1976. 373p.

Maitan has written one of the most astute and penetrating analyses of the internal and external politics of the Cultural Revolution. The Marxist technique he uses affords him a powerful tool to trace the triumph of bureaucratization in both Marxist superstates, China and Russia. The theme of the book is that China's popular revolution was paradoxically made by the Communist Party and Red Army whose structures were themselves essentially authoritarian. After the liberation, popular support for the new régime was thus never permitted to develop into a socialist democracy in which the masses could check and control the leaders of Party and state.

298 The wind will not subside: years in revolutionary China, 1964-69.
David Milton, Nancy Milton. New York: Pantheon, 1976. 397p.

This is a vivid picture of the Cultural Revolution painted by two eye witnesses; teachers at the First Foreign Languages Institute in Peking (Beijing). This book gives Mao a heroic role while acknowledging that his revolution from above was a mixed kettle of fish. The narrative gives the detailed subtleties of Chinese political behaviour.

299 **The Cultural Revolution in China.**
Edited by Thomas W. Robinson. Berkeley, California:
University of California Press, 1971. 476p.

This book offers five case studies of central features of the Cultural Revolution.
The China scholars associated with the Rand Corporation assess the effects of the
Cultural Revolution on China's political development and foreign policy. The
essay by Harry Harding Jr. provides a stimulating analysis of the points of
difference between Mao and his opponents over principles of policy-making and
organizational structure.

300 **The People's Republic of China: a documentary history of revolutionary changes.**
Edited by Mark Selden, Patti Eggleston. New York:
Monthly Review Press, 1979. 718p.

This is a collection of documents on the Chinese revolution from 1946 to the
present. The focus of attention is on the relationship between socialism and economic development. The editor is thoroughly sympathetic with his subject.

301 **The Long Revolution.**
Edgar Snow. New York: Random House, 1972. 269p.

Snow describes his last six-month visit to China in 1970-71. He surveys the
changes in the lives of common people. He describes the barefoot doctors, the
May 7th Cadre Schools, and food costs; how acupuncture is tested and used as a
cure and an aesthetic, sex, marriage, birth control, abortion, communes, the
People's Liberation Army and the Cultural Revolution.

302 **Half the world: the history and culture of China and Japan.**
Edited by Arnold Toynbee. London: Thames & Hudson,
1973. 359p.

In this book, readers will find selections on Chinese and Japanese history and
culture presented by some of the best scholars in the field. Each chapter has
many fine illustrations and photographs and reveals the salient features of the
grand traditions.

303 **Communist China, 1949-1969: a twenty-year appraisal.**
Edited by Frank N. Trager, William Henderson. New
York: New York University Press, 1970. 356p.

The book consists of fourteen articles surveying and analyzing the first two
decades of Communist rule in China. The authors examine foreign policy, politics,
ideology, military affairs, culture, education, economics and agriculture. They
simply show, with statistics when available, what China looks like after twenty
years.

304 History and will: philosophical perspectives of Mao Tse-tung's thought.
Frederic Wakeman, Jr.   Berkeley, California: University of California Press, 1973. 392p.

In this analysis of Mao's thought, the author deals with a variety of historical and philosophical subjects which provide the intellectual background of Maoism. The central theme of the book is the contradiction between objective history and subjective will, which converge, according to the author, in the single focus of the Cultural Revolution.

305 The Chinese Cultural Revolution.
Adrian Xia.   New York: Seabury, 1972. 254p.

Based on many previously inaccessible or little known Chinese publications and documents, the author, Adrian Hsia (Xia), gives a thorough analysis and critique of the turmoil that existed in China during the mid-1960s. He examines modern trends in various strata of Chinese society - youth, intellectuals, peasants, workers, as well as the Party and the army - and then focuses on the contradictions and stresses in Chinese society both before and after the Cultural Revolution.

306 Radicals and radical ideology in China's Cultural Revolution.
Parris H. Zhang.   New York: Research Institute on Communist Affairs, Columbia University, 1973. 103p.

As the title indicates, it is upon the 'radicals' that the author, Parris Chang (Zhang), has focused his attention, but they were after all the stars of the Cultural Revolution, and it is a legitimate slant. He concludes that the potential for radical revival will continue to exist unless the Chinese leadership can reduce the grievances and accommodate the aspirations of the young and the large underprivileged sections of the Chinese population.

307 Inside the Cultural Revolution.
Jack Chen.   London: Sheldon, 1976. 483p.

The author, Jack Ch'en (Chen), seeks to present a personal account of what the Cultural Revolution has meant in human terms - for the Chinese people and for his own family. He details the involvement of the Chen (Zhen) family with the emergence of modern China over three generations, and offers personal insights into the major and minor figures of the Cultural Revolution.

308 A chronology of the People's Republic of China, 1949-1969.
Peter Zheng.   Totowa, New Jersey: Littlefield & Adams, 1972. 347p.

The author, Peter Cheng (Zheng), covers the daily recorded events concerning the People's Republic of China from the day of its inauguration in 1949 through 1970. This account has been compiled from reports appearing in publications in China, England, France, India, the United States and Japan. With a new era of foreign relations beginning between the People's Republic of China and the United States resulting from President Nixon's visit, this chronology should be in demand.

Biographical Works

Mao Zedong

309 **Mao Tse-tung and Gandhi: perspectives on social transformation.**
Jayantanuja Bandyopadhyaya.   Bombay, India: Allied, 1973. 156p.

This is a short book with a thin analytical framework. It proceeds, after a brief comment on historical backgrounds and ideological perspectives of Gandhi and Mao, to examine complementary themes like 'People's war and satyagraha' and 'mass line and constructive program'. The book concludes with essentials of the respective achievements of the two leaders and the author's formulation of a tentative 'third model' of social and political change.

310 **Mao Tse-tung: a guide to his thought.**
Alain Bouc, translated from the French by Paul Auster, Lydia Davis.   New York: St. Martin's Press, 1977. 230p.

This study seeks to emphasize, through a description of the man himself, the depth and influence of his political thought. What the author has stressed are the larger political problems, the problems of socialism and democracy, violence and dictatorship. There are several pages devoted to the search for a balanced society and the definition of social and individual morality. The book begins by discussing Mao Tse-tung's (Mao Zedong) reflections about his own country.

311 **Mao Tse-tung: an ideological and psychological portrait.**
Fedor Burkatsky.   Moscow: Progress, 1980. 397p.

A prominent Soviet social scientist explores Mao's ideology and psyche. The author sees three choices for China: to restore friendship and cooperation with the USSR and other socialist countries, to follow a path of manoeuvring between the USSR and the United States, or to follow a path of rapproachement with the capitalist West. He concludes that the first choice is the natural way for China to modernize her economy.

312 Mao.
Peter Carter. London: Oxford University Press, 1976. 161p.

This biography recounts Mao Tse-tung's (Mao Zedong) personal life in an historical context - both inside and outside China. Though Carter emphasizes the period prior to Liberation in 1949, the book also covers, although in considerably less detail, the period from the taking of power by the Communists to the death of Mao in 1976.

313 One of the great epics of our century - the rise to power of Mao Tse-tung and the land he led into the 20th century.
Peter Carter. New York: New American Library, 1980. 197p.

The author traces Mao's early life and background, the dramatic events culminating in the establishment of the People's Republic of China - the Long March, the years in the Yenan (Yanan) caves, the war with Japan, the civil war - and Mao's role in the development of the modern state. The newly-updated edition includes an in-depth analysis of Sino-American relations with Mao.

314 Chairman Mao: education of the proletariat.
Chu Don Chean. New York: Philosophical Library, 1980. 478p.

This volume provides an accurate insight into Mao's thoughts and contains a clear statement of his revolutionary ideas and innovative methods in education. The author interprets Mao's ideas and methods as ruralizing, sinicizing and pragmatic in light of social transition in China.

315 Mao.
Philippe Devillers. New York: Schocken, 1970. 317p.

The author takes a historical approach by placing Mao's statements in the context of his life and times and also makes several references to the impact that Mao's essays had at the time they were written. This is a useful introduction to the life and thought of Mao. All of Mao's significant works are dealt with here.

316 Mao Tse-tung and Lin Piao: post-revolutionary writings.
Edited by K. T. Fan. New York: Doubleday, 1973. 437p.

This volume contains some of the most important writings of Mao Tse-tung (Mao Zedong) and Lin Piao (Lin Biao), all written since 1949, which paved the way for China's re-emergence into international politics.

317 Mao Tse-tung and China.
C. P. Fitzgerald. New York: Holmes & Meier, 1976. 166p.

This is not so much a biography of Mao as a brief history of the Chinese Communists from 1949 to 1975. Mao is at the centre of such a study, but the author's interest is less in the man and more in the policies and accomplishments of his régime.

Biographical Works. Mao Zedong

318 Mao Tse-tung, the search for plenty.
Leo Goodstadt. London: Longman, 1972. 266p.

The author seeks to explain the rationale and background of economic development in China. The analysis is based on Chinese materials including newspaper reports of speeches and statements made by leaders at different levels of government. He explains the economic thought of Chairman Mao and examines the extent of its application to Chinese society and the economy.

319 The morning deluge: Mao Tse-tung and the Chinese revolution, 1893-1954.
Han Suyin. Boston, Massachusetts: Little, Brown, 1972. 571p.

This biography takes Mao through the various stages of his career from school in Hunan to his period of early radicalism in Peking (Beijing) in 1919, to Shanghai in 1921, where he founded the Party, into the hills in 1927, through the Long March, the Yenan (Yanan) decade, the battle for China and the founding of the new order up to 1954.

320 Wind in the tower: Mao Tse-tung and the Chinese revolution 1949-75.
Han Suyin. Boston, Massachusetts: Little, Brown, 1976. 376p.

This second volume by Han Suyin completes a massive and sympathetic biography of Mao which is at the same time a penetrating assessment of the complete development of modern Chinese politics. Utilizing press reports, speeches and interviews, the author discusses the Great Leap Forward of 1958-59, the Sino-Soviet split, the Cultural Revolution, Richard Nixon's visit to China and the recent power struggles in China.

321 Mao Tse-tung and the Chinese people.
Roger Howard. New York: Monthly Review Press, 1977. 384p.

This is very much a Party-line chronology of Mao's life, composed in good part of extended quotations from English language accounts and emphasizing military exploits. Howard, in honest sympathy with the Chinese people, has leaned over too far, extending his kindness into the brutal realm of politics.

322 The logic of 'Maoism': critiques and explication.
Edited by James Jie Xiong. New York: Praeger, 1974. 227p.

Four of the articles in this book are revised versions of papers presented at a discussion chaired by James Chieh Hsiung (Jie Xiong) at the 1973 Association of Asian Studies convention. The remaining articles were written for this volume. The strength of the book lies in the material that has been added, particularly in the first article by Bradly Womack on the relationship between theory and practice in Mao's political philosophy.

323 The thought of Mao Tse-tung: form and content.
Steven S. K. Jin. Hong Kong: Center of Asian Studies, University of Hong Kong, 1976. 271p.

Throughout the book, the author, Steven Chin (Jin), not only tries to affirm, obviously quite effectively, that the content of Mao Tse-tung's (Mao Zedong) thought is essentially dialectical materialism or Marxism-Leninism, but also consistently proves that Mao Tse-tung (Mao Zedong), while purging some of the major impurities of dialectical materialism or Marxism-Leninism, makes important contributions to its content.

324 The chairman's new clothes: Mao and the Cultural Revolution.
Simon Leys. New York: St. Martin's Press, 1978. 261p.

This is a translation of the 1971 French publication, *Les habits neufs du Président Mao*. The author, a Belgian specialist in Chinese art, argues that the Chinese Cultural Revolution was a simple power struggle at the top and that there was nothing cultural about it except the name and nothing revolutionary about it except the initial pretext.

325 The early revolutionary activities of comrade Mao Tse-tung.
Li Rui, translated by Anthony M. Sariti, edited by James Jie Xiong, introduction by Stuart Schram. White Plains, New York: Sharp, 1977. 355p.

This is the only book-length biography of Mao published in the People's Republic of China. Although it was written in 1952 and published in 1957, an English translation has not been available until now. The narrative ends in 1927, having emphasized three major phases in Mao's political development: work with the urban intellectuals and the establishment of the Chinese Communist Party (1913-21), struggles in the Hunan labour movement (1921-23), and efforts with the peasant movement (1925-27). The work provides a wealth of otherwise unavailable information. Schram provides an informative introduction which helps to place Li Jui's (Li Rui) opus in perspective.

326 And Mao makes 5: Mao Tse-tung's last great battle.
Edited by Raymond Lotta. Chicago: Banner Press, 1978. 522p.

The 'Gang of Four', according to Lotta, was actually a 'Gang of Five' including and led by Mao himself, because these revolutionaries were Mao's close allies and ardent supporters. In a lengthy introduction, Lotta traces the fierce struggle as it evolved in the years 1973-76, between the Left, led by Mao, who strived to reaffirm and extend the innovations of the Cultural Revolution, and the anti-Mao forces grouped around Chou En-lai (Zhou Enlai) and Teng Hsiao-ping (Deng Xiaoping), who sought to reverse the 'correct verdicts' on the Cultural Revolution. Lotta asserts that Mao's last great battle ended in a right-wing coup barely one month after Mao's death resulting in the ouster of the four most prominent followers of Mao, and that the post-Mao leaders have repudiated Mao's revolutionary line and instituted a revisionist line.

Biographical Works. Mao Zedong

327 **A critique of Soviet economics.**
Mao Zedong, translated by Moss Roberts, annotated by
Richard Levy. New York: Monthly Review Press, 1972.
157p.

This is a translation of notes by Mao on two Soviet books on economic ideology:
Economy: a textbook issued by the Institute of Economics of the Academy of
Sciences of the USSR (1957) and Joseph Stalin's *Economic problems of socialism in the USSR* (1952). Mao's remarks - some approving, some critical - discuss
selected pages in Chinese translations from the Russian edition.

328 **Cult and canon: the origins and development of state
Maoism.**
Helmut Martin. Armonk, New York: Sharpe, 1982. 365p.

This book, a textual analysis of 'state Maoism' and its importance for the Chinese
political system, studies the history of the Mao canon, the apotheosis of Mao in
the 'Little Red Book' by Lin Piao (Lin Biao) during the Cultural Revolution and
the ultimately futile attempt by the 'Gang of Four' to use the Mao texts as a
basis for their legitimacy.

329 **Mao Zedong Text 1949-1976.** (Mao Tse-tung's works,
1949-1976.)
Helmut Martin. Munich, GFR: Carl Hanser-Verlag, 1980.
7 vols.

This work comprises six volumes of text in Chinese, a German translation, an
index and one volume including commentary (approximately 600 pages each).
The publication has been prepared in collaboration with the Mao's writings
project, supervised by Professor Michael Y.M. Kao (Gao) at Brown University.

330 **Mao and the perpetual revolution.**
Franz Michael. Woodbury, New York: Baron, 1977. 320p.

The author has given readers a comprehensive survey of Mao's revolutionary
career, along with a summary of modern Chinese political history and the role of
the Communist Party in the transformation of China. The book is meant to be a
comprehensive assessment of the Chinese leaders in the shaping of events in
China for over half a century.

331 **Mao Tse-tung Chi.** (Collected writings of Mao Tse-tung.)
Compiled by Takeuchi Minoru. Tokyo: Hokubosha, 1970.
vols. 1-7.

The quantity and quality of the editorial work put into this project by Professor
Takeuchi Minoru and his colleagues are such that no individual effort could hope
to compete with their list in accuracy and completeness.

332 **Mao's legacy: lessons for the future?**
Rhoads Murphey. New York: Methuen, 1980. 170p.

What is the impact of Mao's ideology on China today? How much has it been
modified and why? Does China offer a lesson for developing nations in Asia and
elsewhere? The answers emerge in this very readable and objective book which
takes as its point of departure the analysis of urban and rural development in

China from the revolution to the present. Rhoads Murphey also relates China's economic and social achievements to those of India. The comparison of two widely differing political systems leads to surprising conclusions.

333 **Chairman Mao and the Chinese Communist Party.**
Andres D. Onate.   Chicago: Nelson-Hall, 1979. 289p.

The author reviews the political history of China from the downfall of the Manchu empire to the ascent to power of the Communists. The influences of Confucianism on Mao are discussed, the Chairman's early political career and life are described and his most prominent writing critically analyzed. An epilogue describes the struggle for political control after Mao's death.

334 **Mao Tse-tung: the man in the leadership.**
Lucian W. Pye.   New York: Basic Books, 1976. 346p.

This psycho-historical biography associates Mao's concern for contradictions with ambivalence, his generosity toward his enemies with a reaction against aggression, his preference for open debate with narcissism and his difficulties in finding a successor with fear of abandonment. The author probes the links between the private Mao and the revolutionary leader. He considers that the roots of Mao's ability to mobilize emotion, his abandonment of his closest comrades and other salient aspects of his style of leadership lie in his childhood experiences.

335 **Mao Chronik.** (Mao's chronicle.)
Thomas Scharping.   Munich, GFR: Carl Hanser-Verlag, 1976. 235p.

This is a chronicle of the personal and political events in the late Chairman Mao's life, published after his death in September 1976. Based on more than 200 Chinese and Western sources, this pocket-sized book records in chronological order all the important events relating to Mao and his contribution to his era. His political statements are highlighted by brief quotations, documented in each instance.

336 **The political thought of Mao Tse-tung.**
Stuart R. Schram.   New York: Praeger, 1970. rev. 480p.

First published in 1969, this major study has been completely updated and considerably expanded to include many of Mao's little-known but increasingly relevant earlier writings, as well as major new material from the past five years. A skilfully arranged anthology of passages runs from Mao's first appearance in print in 1917, down to his directives on the Cultural Revolution in 1968-69.

337 **Mao Tse-tung unrehearsed: talks and letters, 1956-1971.**
Edited by Stuart R. Schram, translated by John Chinnery.   New York: Pantheon, 1975. 352p.

The documents which deal with political, economical and philosophical problems, consist of 26 statements and speeches from the mass of such material divulged by the Red Guard publication during the Cultural Revolution. In an introduction, Schram highlights Mao's revolutionary concerns and analyzes the reasons for the recent leadership crisis. He elaborates on four important themes in Mao's thought: the Party organization, education and culture, dialectics of development and foreign relations and provides references to where they can be located in the documents.

Biographical Works. Mao Zedong

338 **Continuing the revolution: the political thought of Mao.**
John Bryan Starr. Princeton, New Jersey: Princeton
University Press, 1979. 366p.

Making use of the entire corpus of Mao's writings and speeches available to date,
the author closely examines that aspect of Mao's political thought known as his
'theory of continuing revolution under dictatorship of the proletariat', which has
been treated both by Mao and his successors as the culmination of his theoretical
activity. He investigates the internal logic and evolution of Mao's theory in terms
of various themes. Beginning with a consideration of conflict, the author takes up
the individual concepts of knowledge and action, participation and representation,
political education, history and development.

339 **Post-liberation works of Mao Ze-dong: A bibliography and
index.**
John Bryan Starr, Nancy Anne Dyer. Berkeley, California:
University of California Press, 1976. 222p.

This book is most timely and welcome in the field of contemporary Chinese
studies. It represents a major breakthrough in the development of bibliographical
control and is an important research tool for handling Mao's writings since 1949.

340 **Mao: a biography.**
Ross Terrill. New York: Harper, 1980. 481p.

In this chronological account of the Chinese leader's experiences, Terrill describes
Mao's family background, why he became a rebel, the source of his social and
political ideas, his multiple love affairs, his writings and his acquisition and exercise of power. The author analyzes Mao's flaws and his achievements.

341 **Mao Tse-tung: a critical biography.**
Stephen Uhalley, Jr. New York: Watts, 1975. 233p.

Portraying Mao as 'a simple man of the earth', the author suggests that Mao has,
by combining humanity, intelligence, common sense and determination, developed
political and military strategies which have enabled him to have a greater impact
on more people during his own lifetime than any other individual in history. The
book is well-documented to include up-to-date political analyses of Mao's career
within the context of China's domestic development and foreign relations.

342 **Love and struggle in Mao's thought.**
Raymond Whitehead. New York: Orbis Books, 1978. 166p.

This book helps to demystify Maoism and to clarify, for Western readers, aspects
of the Chinese revolution that have significance for the rest of the world. The
author attempts to analyze the ethics of Maoist thought in terms of class struggle
and in contrast to the perceived sham of Western liberal ethics as a vehicle for
élitist advantage. The book contains basic Maoist theories, their application in
terms of individual transformation and group conflict, present life styles and
contradictions between Maoist thought and liberal values.

343 **The people's emperor: Mao. A biography of Mao Tse-tung.**
Dick Wilson. New York: Doubleday, 1980. 530p.

This book includes excerpts from Mao's writings, speeches, conversations and
poems. The author humanizes Mao with vivid personal anecdotes, some even

revealing his rather prolific sexual activities in the caves of Yenan (Yanan). He concludes that Mao invented for China a complete new system of life, economy and government. But Mao was also a barrack-room philosopher, not able truly to compete with the great thinkers and in the end he failed, largely because he set his goals so high.

344 Mao Tse-tung in the scales of history.
Edited by Dick Wilson.   New York: Cambridge University Press, 1979. 331p.

Some of the best known scholars of China have contributed to this work, written in commemoration of the death of the Chinese leader. The different sides of his complex personality - philosopher, Marxist, teacher, military strategist, politician and economic planner - are well portrayed even if the contributors have limited themselves to a synthesis of ideas expressed elsewhere.

345 The emergence of Maoism: Mao Tse-tung, Ch'en Po-ta and the search for Chinese theory 1935-1945.
Raymond F. Wylie.   Stanford, California: Stanford University Press, 1980. 387p.

This study investigates the political and ideological context of Mao's rise to power in the Chinese Communist Party and in particular the development of the political ideology known as 'Mao Tse-tung (Mao Zedong) thought'. The author's analysis of the complex interplay of élite politics within the Chinese Communist Party falls into two main periods: 1935-40, when the basic ideas behind the Chinese brand of Marxism were worked out by Mao and Ch'en Po-ta (Chen Poda); and 1940-45, when the two men worked to systematize and disseminate Mao's thought as the official guiding doctrine for the Chinese Communist Party.

346 Inside Mao Tse-tung thought.
Ye Qing, edited by Stepan Ban, T. H. Zuan, Ralph Mortensen.   Hicksville, New York: Exposition Press, 1975. 336p.

This is an impassioned catalogue of inconsistencies and dangers in Maoist thought by Yeh Ch'ing (Ye Qing), an ex-colleague who was with Premier Chou (Zhou) in Paris in 1921-24 and with Mao in Hunan in 1927. After his capture by the Kuomintang (Guomindang) forces he became an ideological opponent of Maoism and maintains that posture in this volume.

347 Mao Tse-tung and his China.
Zhang Guoxin.   Exeter, New Hampshire: Heinemann, 1978. 336p.

This is an in-depth assessment of Mao Tse-tung (Mao Zedong) and his politics from the standpoint of Chinese history, philosophy and tradition and in the context of the Cultural Revolution and the Anti-Confucius campaign. Since the People's Republic was established, much of its history has shown a continuous conflict between Marxism and Chinese philosophy. Here the author, Chang Kuo-hsin (Zhang Guoxin) examines this conflict and explains how much of Confucianism is evident in Mao's philosophy.

348 Mao's papers: anthology and bibliography.
Edited by Jerome Zhen. New York: Oxford University Press, 1970. 221p.

This collection of Mao's hitherto untranslated writings affords an invaluable glimpse into the mind of an extraordinary man. The anthology portion contains previously unpublished examples of Mao's written and spoken statements pertaining to the Cultural Revolution (1966-1969). Jerome Chen's (Zhen) translations provide an English-language version of the basic documentation concerning Mao's role in the revolution. The bibliography lists in chronological sequence all of Mao's known writings. The list is given both in English and Chinese.

349 Mao Zedong, a selection of photographs.
Beijing: People's Fine Arts Publishing House, 1978. 200p.

An album of familiar and new colour photographs of the late Chairman Mao.

350 Mao Tse-tung selected works, volume v.
Beijing: Foreign Language Press, 1977. 500p.

In all, the 500 pages of the English edition include approximately 200 pages of new or substantially new material, half of which dates from the period July 1956-December 1957. There is also a substantial number of previously unavailable items from the latter half of 1953.

Mao Zedong 'Talks at the Yanan Conference on Literature and Art': a translation of the 1943 test with commentary.
See item no. 1251.

The adventure of Mao on the Long March.
See item no. 1260.

Others

351 The last Confucian: Liang Shu-ming and the Chinese dilemma of modernity.
Guy S. Alitto. Berkeley, California: University of California Press, 1979. 396p.

This is a history of ideas in action. It should be required reading for every serious student of modern China. No one who reads it will be able again to dismiss Confucian traditionalism as a stereotyped or anachronistic response to the dilemma of modernity. The author possesses the skill that distinguishes the good biographer: the ability to empathize with his subject without sacrificing his own critical sense.

352 Chou En-lai.
Jules Archer. New York: Hawthorn Books, 1973. 188p.

This book describes Premier Chou's (Zhou) life, his up-and-down relationships with Chiang Kai-shek (Jiang Jieshi) and Mao Tse-tung (Mao Zedong). The straightforward and chronological narrative brings out Chou's (Zhou) personal qualities of charm, patience and the ability to compromise.

353 Red Guard: the political biography of Dai Hsiao-ai.
Gordon A. Bennet, Ronald Montaperto. New York: Doubleday, 1971. 267p.

This is an account of the recent Chinese Cultural Revolution. It is the biography of Dai Hsiao-ai (Dai Xiaoai), a Red Guard and student activist leader in the city of Canton (Guangzhou). He traces his initial enthusiasm for Chairman Mao's revolution, his trips across China to mass demonstrations in Peking (Beijing), his growing role as a faction leader and the ultimate disillusionment that led him to leave family and comrades behind and defect to Hong Kong.

354 The last emperor.
Arnold Brachman. New York: Scribner, 1975. 360p.

This is a biography of P'u Yi (Pu Yi), the last Emperor of China, who abdicated the Manchu throne in 1912 at the age of seven, but who, until his death in 1967, could not escape being used as a pawn. P'u Yi (Pu Yi), as the puppet Emperor of Manchukuo, was used by the Japanese expansionists. After the war he was a prisoner of Russia and from 1950-1959 that of China.

355 Hsun Yueh (AD 148-209): the life and reflections of an early medieval Confucian.
Chen Qiyun. Cambridge, England: Cambridge University Press, 1975. 242p.

Hsun Yueh (Xun Yue) has been known chiefly as a Han loyalist who wrote a subsidized dynastic chronicle; so it is important, in a consideration of his work, to know what his historical role was. In addition to analyzing his surviving works, the *Han-chi* and the *Shen-chien* (*Han Ji* and *Shenjian*), the author Ch'en Chi-yun (Chen Qiyun), has outlined those historical events that had an important influence on him and has also discussed the influence which he exerted on the leading men of his own day and upon the events of subsequent ages. In this way, readers can attain a fuller and deeper appreciation both of the intrinsic value of his thought and scholarship and of his individual contribution to China's historiography.

356 Between tradition and modernity: Wang T'ao and reform in late Ch'ing.
Paul A. Cohen. Cambridge, Massachusetts: Harvard University Press, 1974. 276p.

This is a biography of the 19th-century Confucian scholar Wang T'ao (Wang Tau), who was involved in the processes of change in China from tradition to modernity. Spending almost his entire adult life in the fringe world of Shanghai and Hong Kong, Wang, over the course of fifty years, performed an important role as an interculture mediator (helping to translate the Bible into Chinese and the Confucian classics into English). He became a founder of modern Chinese journalism, a promoter of Western learning and an advocate of far-reaching changes in Chinese government and society.

357 **Shen P'u-hai: a Chinese philosopher of the fourth century BC.**
Herlee G. Creel. Chicago: University of Chicago Press, 1975. 341p.

Creel presents thematic discussions of Shen P'u-hai's (Shen Puhai) thought and then traces Shen's relationship with other thinkers of the legalist, Taoist and Confucian traditions. Creel's thesis is that Shen was the first to formulate the theory of administrative techniques which feudal and post-feudal Chinese governments had been evolving for over six hundred years.

358 **Koxinga and Chinese nationalism: history, myth and the hero.**
Ralph C. Crozier. Cambridge, Massachusetts: East Asian Research Centre, Harvard University, 1977. 116p.

The author traces, with subtlety and skill, the twists and turns over time of Cheng Ch'eng-kung's (Zheng Chenggong) symbolic meaning. The purpose of the study is to explore those meanings and the ways in which they have been manipulated by Chinese in different historical situations.

359 **The man who lost China: the first full biography of Chiang Kai-shek.**
Brian Crozier. New York: Scribners, 1976. 430p.

This is a solid, lively and well-written political biography of Chiang Kai-shek (Jiang Jieshi) aimed at the general reader. The author, Brian Crozier, manages to bring out Chiang's (Jiang) virtues as well as his vices. He was very harsh on American China policy in the crucial period from Yalta to the Communist victory.

360 **Hsi-liang and the Chinese nationalist revolution.**
Roger V. Dea Forges. New Haven, Connecticut: Yale University Press, 1973. 274p.

This book traces the career and ideas of the late Ch'ing (Qing) patriot, Hsi-liang (Xiliang) (1853-1917), who was a governor, over the course of a decade, of several major regions of China. In studying late Ch'ing (Qing) political theory, the author emphasizes such crucial issues as the role of tradition, the strong current of anti-imperialism, the development of new state policies and the relations of all these to the collapse in 1911.

361 **Chairman Hua: the new leader of the Chinese Communists.**
Ding Wang, introduction by Jurgen Domes. London: Hurst, 1980. 200p.

Despite his position Hua Kuo-feng (Hua Guofeng) remains a mysterious figure. Official sources in Peking (Beijing) have so far failed to elucidate his background and sudden rise to power from local party cadre to administrator to Mao's successor. Using the widest possible range of sources the author, Ting Wang (Ding Wang), has effectively filled this gap with a full account of Hua's career from the first year of his life to the Cultural Revolution, the death of Mao and the new power structure that has subsequently emerged.

362 Liu Shao-ch'i and the Chinese Cultural Revolution: the politics of mass criticism.
Lowell Dittmer. Berkeley, California: University of California Press, 1975. 400p.

Dittmer illustrates the policy-making process of a revolutionary state creating the diverging exigencies of economic modernization and political development. Liu Shao-ch'i (Liu Shaoqi) emerges as the symbol of a systematic endeavour to combine order with revolution and equality with economic and administrative efficiency. In the end, he was overwhelmed by the sweep and depth of the revolutionary drive in China, as symbolized by Mao Tse-tung (Mao Zedong) and was destroyed politically.

363 Lin Piao: the life and writings of China's new ruler.
Martin Ebon. New York: Stein & Day, 1970. 378p.

This is a brief biographical sketch of Lin Piao (Lin Biao), of the man whom Mao once chose to be his successor. The book also contains twenty of his writings 1940-69 selected to show his military and political views and sketches of the new Politburo members. The author views Madam Mao (Chiang Ching - Jiang Qing) as a potential disputant in post-Mao China.

364 The Soong sisters.
Roby Eunson. New York: Watts, 1975. 136p.

The author has written an interesting book that, in addition to relating the genealogy of these sisters, also provides a glimpse of the political and social turmoil that has characterized China for the past one hundred years.

365 Last moments of a world.
Margaret Gaan. New York: Norton, 1978. 273p.

Gaan, standing apart from both the Kuomintang (Guomindang) and the Communists, sees the beggary, the peasants' heavy tax burden, the ballooning inflation and the pervasive Kuomintang (Guomindang) corruption with striking candour. The autobiographical and historical reflections merge to explain clearly why the Communist revolution succeeded. She views the Communist victory with a mixture of relief for China and sadness for her own loss and exile.

366 The Lin Piao affair: power politics and military coup.
Michael Y. M. Gao. White Plains, New York: International Arts and Science Press, 1975. 591p.

This collection of 73 translated documents, plus Kao's (Gao) introduction, allows interested readers to see all relevant available information: the 1969 official biography; the accused plotters' captured plans and memos; selected attacks in the public press which criticized Lin Piao (Lin Biao) and the Confucius campaigns; and, in Lin's defense, his public addresses and private speeches from the period of the Cultural Revolution when he was riding high.

367 The rise and fall of Lin Piao.
Jaap Van Ginneken, translated from Dutch by D. Adkinson. New York: Avon Books, 1977. 363p.

This study by a Dutch social scientist was first published in Holland in 1974 under the title that translated as *The left current in China*. An epilogue has been added, bringing the account up to December 1976. He analyzes Lin Piao's (Lin Biao) political fortunes from 1958 to 1971. He suggests that Lin may have been dragged into a coup against Mao at the last moment rather than being its principal instigator.

368 Hsiao Hung.
Howard Goldblatt. Boston, Massachusetts: Twayne Publishers, 1976. 161p.

Since her death in January, 1952, at the age of thirty, Hsiao Hung (Xiao Hong) has continued to attract biographical and critical attention. This book is the first systematic examination, in any language, of her literary career. The book includes a chronicle of Hsiao's (Xiao) life as well as discussions of her literary output and her relationships, both personal and literary, with others in the Northeastern group of novelists.

369 Wu Tse-tien and the politics of legitimization of T'ang China.
W. L. Guisso. Dellingham, Washington: Western Washington University Press, 1978. 335p.

The central question in any Wu Tse-tien (Wu Zetian) study must be how a Chinese woman could have gained and maintained such enormous political power for almost fifty years. In attempting to answer this question, the author discusses the social, bureaucratic and religious changes during her era and concludes that basic changes were largely attributable to Wu's special political needs.

370 Li Chih (1527-1602) in contemporary Chinese historiography.
Hok-lam Chan, foreword by Frederick W. Note. White Plains, New York: Sharpe, 1978. 216p.

This is an original and valuable contribution to the study of Chinese history. It constructs a sophisticated bridge between the world of late Ming Confucian scholarship and the world of political and academic struggle in China in the 1970s.

371 Liang Ch'i-ch'ao and modern Chinese liberalism.
Philip C. Huang. Seattle, Washington: University of Washington Press, 1972. 231p.

This book surveys the entire course of Liang's career, with emphasis given to the development of his political ideas. Drawing effectively on primarily Chinese and Japanese sources, Huang casts new light on the shaping of Liang's ideas during his exile in Japan and his ill-fated political enterprises before and after the revolution of 1911.

372 Borodin: Stalin's man in China.
Dan N. Jacobs. Cambridge, Massachusetts: Harvard University Press, 1981. 369p.

This book is an interpretative biography, based on extensive detective work, of Comintern agent in China, Mikhail Markovich Borodin. It has a fine bibliography of Western scholarly works, journalistic accounts, American and British archival collections and Russian reminiscences. The book is a useful addition to the literature on China in the 1920s and on the early years of the Comintern.

373 The story of Genghis Khan.
Charles King.   New York: Roy Publications, 1971. 131p.

This is a biography of the 12th-century Mongolian emperor and it describes how he and his men ruled the area from the Black Sea to Peking (Beijing).

374 Liu Shao-ch'i: Mao's first heir-apparent.
Li Tianmin.   Stanford, California: Hoover Institution, 1975. 223p.

The author, Li Tien-min (Li Tianmin), documents the history of Liu Shao-ch'i (Liu Shaoqi) from his early rise to power to his final downfall and illuminates the power struggles, policy splits and strategy conflicts that are an essential part of Chinese Communist Party politics.

375 General Stilwell in China, 1942-1944: the full story.
Liang Jindong.   New York: St John's University Press, 1972. 321p.

Using new sources from the archives in Taiwan, the author, Liang Chin-tun (Liang Jindong), provides a version of Chiang K'ai-shek's relationship with General Joseph Stilwell which is somewhat different from the more familiar accounts.

376 Struggle for democracy: Sung Ch'iao-jen and the 1911 revolution.
Liew Ki Siong.   Berkeley, California: University of California Press, 1971. 288p.

This is a biography of the political leader who played a leading role in the 1911 Revolution, became the foremost advocate of parliamentary government in opposition to President Yuan Shi-kai (Yuan Shikai) and was assassinated by an agent of Yuan, just as he was about to become Premier. With his death, the Kuomintang, which he had organized, collapsed and the drive for democracy came to an end.

377 The early Chiang Kai-shek: a study of his personality and politics: 1887-1924.
Pichon P. Y. Loh.   New York: Columbia University Press, 1971. 216p.

This is a biographical study which will add to our understanding of the young Chiang (Jiang). The author avoids explaining his subject in terms of Chinese culture and instead employs Erik Erikson's idea about personality formation in a detailed analysis of the Nationalist ruler's first 39 years. His view is that, as a child, Chiang developed a personality incapable of responding normally to a wide range of emotional situations, but able to be challenged and fulfilled when confronted with a crisis which called upon his strength of purpose and leadership ability.

378 Man's fate.
André Malraux.   New York: Random House, 1970. 338p.

This is a novel about the Chinese Revolution and Premier Chou En-lai (Zhou Enlai). As one of the recognized masterpieces of the 20th century, the book also provides political documents of enduring significance.

379 Chang Tso-lin in northeast China, 1911-1928: China, Japan, and the Manchurian idea.

G. McCormack. Stanford, California: Stanford University Press, 1977. 334p.

This account of the career of Chang Tso-lin (Zhang Zuolin), the most powerful Chinese warlord of his time focuses on Chang's struggle with Japan for control over the military, social and industrial development of northeast China. From Japan, Chang enjoyed guarantees of his security against rival warlords; from Chang, Japan obtained the necessary political stability for its agricultural and industrial projects.

380 Fei Hsiao-tung: the dilemma of a Chinese intellectual.

Selected and translated by James P. McGough. White Plains, New York: Sharpe, 1979. 257p.

This collection of essays, by and about Fei Hsiao-tung (Fei Xiaotong), translated from Chinese by James P. McGough, makes an important contribution to our understanding of the social and political background of the present revival of social science in the People's Republic of China. McGough's introduction provides an excellent overview of the intellectual scene surrounding the Hundred Flowers period.

381 Chou: an informal biography of China's legendary Chou En-lai.

John McCook Roots. New York: Doubleday, 1978. 220p.

This is a biography of the former Premier of the People's Republic of China, Chou En-lai (Zhou Enlai). Roots brings a rich background to his subject - born in China, one-time Far Eastern correspondent of the *New York Times* and with a missionary father in whose home Chou was a frequent guest. Yet he maintains a balance between his own material and other sources.

382 Kuo Mo-jo: the early years.

David Tod Roy. Cambridge, Massachusetts: Harvard University Press, 1971. 244p.

Kuo Mo-jo (Guo Muruo) (1892-1979), a founder of the Communist movement in literature during the May 4th Movement and later one of the most industrious and durable of China's Marxist literary men, is the subject of this short biographical study. The author is much more interested in the early rebel poet than in the older rebel Communist author, official and historian.

383 Sun Yat-sen: frustrated patriot.

C. Martin Wilbur. New York: Columbia University Press, 1976. 413p.

This is a solid, detailed analysis of limited but important aspects of Sun Yat-sen's (Sun Yixian) revolutionary career. Drawing from available archival materials in Taiwan, diplomatic documents in various countries, contemporary newspaper reports and observations of those who knew Sun, as well as on works in Chinese and other languages, Wilbur has tried to piece together a picture of Sun Yat-sen.

384 Comrade Chiang Ch'ing.
Roxanne Witke. Boston, Massachusetts: Little, Brown, 1977. 549p.

The value of the book lies not in its pretensions to history but in Chiang Ching's (Jiang Qing) revelations, including those about her early years as an actress, her kidnapping by the Kuomintang and her rivalry with Lin Piao (Lin Biao). The book spans the years from Chiang's girlhood to her overthrow as doyenne of the Cultural Revolution.

385 Yeh Ming-chen: Viceroy of Liang-Kuang, 1852-1858.
J. Y. Wong. Cambridge, Massachusetts: Cambridge University Press, 1976. 260p.

Yeh Ming-chen (Ye Mingzhen), Viceroy of Liang-Kuang (Liang-Guang), 1852-1858, is best known to foreign historians of China as a case in point for the argument that 19th-century Chinese provincial administrators did not have a realistic option of cooperating with the foreign powers. From this point of view, those who offered resistence, as did Yeh, could not have acted out of any enlightened sense of priorities. It is the author's intention to challenge this judgement. Although the primary purpose of the study is to change Yeh's image, many will find it equally valuable for its explanations of the complex Ch'ing (Qing) provincial administrative system.

386 Militarism in modern China: the career of Wu Peifu, 1916-39.
Odoric Y. K. Wou. Folkestone, Kentucky: Dawson, 1978. 341p.

Wou's study of Wu Peifu (Wu Pei-fu), the leading general of the Chihli (Zhili) clique, is a biography, a study of militarism and an examination of 'sub-national foreign relations'. His work contributes to our understanding of each of these aspects of the warlord period. Wu was the mainstay of the Chihli (Zhili) clique that controlled the Peking (Beijing) government from 1920 to 1924. He reached the zenith of personal power and prestige in 1922 when he set out to unify the country by force. Two years later, defeat by a Manchurian General, Chang Tso-lin (Zhang Zuolin), sent him skidding downwards. Chiang Kai-shek's (Jiang Jieshi) Northern Expedition (1926-27) finished his career.

387 The Presidency of Yuan Shih-k'ai: liberalism and dictatorship in early republican China.
Ernest P. Young. Ann Arbor, Michigan: University of Michigan Press, 1977. 347p.

This is a descriptive and extremely thorough study of early republican China. The author analyzes the period between the 1911 revolution and warlordism. He sees the fulfillment of the trends toward decentralization emerging from 1911 to 1913 and considers these the most liberal years in Chinese history. Yuan lost the crucial support of the social élite to pave the way for eventual warlordism.

388 **Liang Ch'i-ch'ao and intellectual transition in China, 1890-1907.**
Zhang Hao. Cambridge, Massachusetts: Harvard University Press, 1971. 342p.

The author, Chang Hao (Zhang Hao), seeks to demonstrate, through an examination of Liang's writings, the intellectual transition from Confucian culturalism to modern nationalism that took place in China in the late 19th and early 20th centuries. The author finds no conflict in Liang's mind over the repudiation of the Chinese tradition.

Ch'en Tu-hsiu (1879-1942) and the Chinese communist movement.
See item no. 238.

Resistance and revolution in China, the communists and the second united front.
See item no. 244.

Who's Who

389 **Who's who in the People's Republic of China.**
Wolfgang Bartke. White Plains, New York: Sharpe, 1981. 729p.

The major part of this work is an alphabetical listing of individuals' biographies. Individuals were chosen for inclusion not in terms of their own profile or standing in the national media, but as occupants of specific positions in the political and administrative system. In general, each provides a brief summary of an individual's history before 1949 followed by a relatively detailed account of his or her career thereafter. In addition to name lists of national, central and provincial leaders as of June 1980, the appendices include historical records of the Communist Party's Central Committee Politburo and provincial first secretaries, the ministers of the People's Republic, the commanders of the military regions and China's ambassadors, all from 1949 to June 1980.

390 **Biographical dictionary of republican China, volume i-v.**
Edited by Howard L. Boorman. New York: Columbia University Press, 1967-71.

The series contains comprehensive, objective life stories of some six hundred leading Chinese during one of the most turbulent periods of Chinese history, from October 1911 to October 1949. Volume five provides complete indexing of all persons mentioned in the original four volume dictionary. Extensively cross-referenced and complete with an up-to-date and thorough bibliography, the index is an invaluable guide to many minor leaders of the Republican period.

391 **Diplomats in crisis: United States-Chinese-Japanese relations, 1919-1941.**
Edited by Richard Dean Burns, Edward M. Bennett.   Santa Barbara, California: ABC-CLIO Press, 1974. 346p.

This is a useful collection of biographical essays on thirteen Pacific-East-Asia diplomats of Japan and the United States during the interwar period.

392 **Dictionary of Ming biography: 1368-1644, two volumes.**
Edited by Carrington L. Goodrich, Zhao Yingfang.   New York: Columbia University Press, 1976. 1,751p.

Based largely upon original Ming documents, the dictionary explores the lives of nearly 650 representative figures, both Chinese and foreign, who influenced the course of almost 300 years of Chinese history. Edited by L. Carrington Goodrich and Chao Ying Fang (Zhao Yingfang) and written by scholars throughout the world, the articles span all classes, professions and fields of endeavour, from emperors, empresses and imperial concubines to soldiers, scholars, writers, artists, philosophers, musicians, missionaries, workers, physicians, architects, pirates, shipbuilders and even a solitary lacquer maker.

393 **Biographical dictionary of Chinese communism 1921-1965.**
Donald W. Klein, Anne B. Clark.   Cambridge, Massachusetts: Harvard University Press, 1971. 2 vols.

In these 433 biographies, the authors include information on 200 major policy makers as well as on individuals from the military, bureaucratic, economic and cultural spheres of mainland Chinese life. Biographies start with a brief identification of the individual: an initial paragraph provides a summary of his career and its significance and a more detailed account of his life follows.

394 **The biographies of eminent Chinese in the Republic of China.**
Li Xin, Sun Sibai.   Peking (Beijing): Chung Hwa Publications (Zhong Hua Publications), 1978. 408p.

This book, compiled by Li Hsin (Li Xin) and Sun Ssu-pai (Sun Sibai), is one of the three projected works prepared by the Institute of Modern History in the Chinese Academy of Social Sciences, as a foundation programme intended for the eventual writing of an official history of the Republic of China. The Institute is planning to write a total of 1,000 biographies for eminent leaders of the first level, together with a biographical dictionary of 4,000 eminent Republicans of the second level.

395 **The Chinese Communists: sketches and autobiographies of the old guards.**
Helen Foster Snow.   Westport, Connecticut: Greenwood, 1972. 398p.

Edgar Snow's ex-wife, (also publishing under the pseudonym Nym Wales), an accomplished journalist, updated her 1937 *Red Dust* interviews with expanded biographical material on the individuals who were to become China's new élite. The new edition also contains about 120 shorter biographical sketches of revolutionary leaders.

396 China directory.
Tokyo: Radio Press, 1981. 648p.

The directory contains 6,000 leading Chinese personalities, listed in Pinyin, Wade-Giles and in Chinese ideographs with title and/or position confirmed or identified at the time of the third session of the fifth National People's Congress. Particularly useful for businessmen is the section on China's foreign trade corporatives with not only the official names of managers, but also their principal lines of business.

397 Who's who in Communist China, volumes i and ii.
Hong Kong: Union Research Institute, 1970. 497+399p.

The two volumes contain a total of 2,837 biographies and include appendices listing the membership of the Ninth Central Committee, provincial revolutionary committees, the military hierarchy and the Central Government organization at present and since 1949. The general cut-off date for information is 1 May 1969.

Religion and Philosophy

Religion

398 The syncretic religion of Lin Ch'ao-en.
Judith A. Berling. New York: Columbia University Press, 1980. 360p.

By richly documenting and analyzing the life and teachings of Lin Ch'ao-en (Lin Chaoen), a leader of the Syncretic Movement in Ming China, the author probes the broad question of the nature of Syncretism and its function in the development and interaction of Chinese religious tradition.

399 Bodhisattva of compassion: the mystical tradition of Kuan Yin.
John Blofeld. Boulder, Colorado: Shambhala, 1978. 158p.

This book is based primarily on personal recollections of events and encounters as long ago as four decades in China. It deals chiefly with subjects in Chinese religion, such as Taoism and Buddhism.

400 Taoism: the road to immortality.
John Blofeld. Boulder, Colorado: Shambhala, 1979. 195p.

The author seeks to explain the fundamental concepts of Taoism, tells stories of his masters and offers reflections on Taoist verse. In addition, he writes about his visit to Taoist hermitages in China and his exchanges with contemporary masters. Taoist yoga is also discussed.

401 China, American Catholicism, and the Missionary.
Thomas A. Breslin. University Park, Pennsylvania: Pennsylvania State University Press, 1980. 167p.

The author presents a valuable summary of the work of American Catholic missionaries in China from about 1920-1950. The overall strategy of the American missionaries, according to the author, contributes to their decline. Entering China after the First World War, they never succeeded in building a church which could accommodate itself to Chinese society. They were fearful of the modernizing tendencies in the cities and attempted to build a peasant church for a peasant society.

402 Religion in communist China.
Richard C. Bush, Jr. New York: Abingdon Press, 1970. 432p.

Inevitably, most space is given to the fate of the Christian churches. The author also covers not only Islam and Buddhism but also the philosophical debate in China about the understanding of Confucius and traces the persistence of the Taoist folk religion of the Chinese masses.

403 The Chinese transformation of Buddhism.
Kenneth K. S. Chen. Princeton, New Jersey: Princeton University Press, 1973. 345p.

The author Kenneth Ch'en (Chen) deals with the adaptation of Buddhism to the circumstances of Chinese culture. The sinification of Buddhism resulted in a new emphasis on filial piety, a special relationship between the state and monastic order and changes throughout the economic, social, educational and literary life of the Buddhist community.

404 Hua-yen Buddhism: the jewel net of India.
Francis H. Cook. University Park, Pennsylvania: Pennsylvania State University Press, 1969. 141p.

The author has undertaken the formidable task of introducing Hua-yen (Huayan) Buddhism, a major Chinese philosophical school, by showing its relevance to some critical problems faced by the contemporary world, providing a glimpse into the historical and ideological background of its evolution in India and China and discussing its basic ideas in a cogent and comprehensive manner.

405 S. J. Rodrigues the interpreter: an early jesuit in Japan and China.
Michael Cooper. New York: Weatherhill, 1974. 416p.

This is a book about the life of Joao Rodrigues, the young Portuguese boy who joined the Jesuits in Japan and spent 21 years there. This was followed by 23 years in Macao, whence he travelled on important missions to China. Several times Rodrigues accompanied Portuguese businessmen to the Canton (Guangzhou) Fair, a biannual event, as it is now, and he discovered how difficult it is for foreigners to do business in China.

406 **James G. Endicott: rebel out of China.**
Stephen Endicott. Toronto: University of Toronto Press, 1980. 432p.

James G. Endicott has been one of the most controversial figures in recent Canadian history. His turbulent career as a united Church missionary working in China, his support of the Chinese Communists, his role as a leader in the World Peace Movement and his charges against the US of using germ warfare during the Korean War, challenged the views of church and nation and sparked off widespread criticism in the press.

407 **The missionary enterprise in China and America.**
Edited by John K. Fairbank. Cambridge, Massachusetts: Harvard University Press, 1974. 373p.

In his introduction, Fairbank argues that it is high time that the interactions between China and the United States be examined more closely and systematically by scholars. For him, missionaries stand close to the centre of the complex exchange he describes. The book is an attempt to map the field, indicate the topography and urge further endeavour.

408 **The religion of the Chinese people.**
Marcel Granet, translated, edited and introduced by Maurice Freedman. New York: Harper, 1976. 200p.

Marcel Granet (1884-1940), one of the fathers of modern Chinese studies, wrote *La religion des Chinois* in 1922 as an introduction to the topic and a summary of his own views. Maurice Freedman has translated this book as a contribution to the history of Western perceptions of Chinese religion. The translation is also intended as a tribute to Granet and to the interpretation of the traditional Chinese culture he represents.

409 **In the footsteps of the Buddha.**
Rene Grousset, translated from French by J. A. Underwood. New York: Grossman, 1971. 337p.

This book presents the history, legends and metaphysics of medieval Buddhism. By means of the account of the Chinese pilgrim in the 7th century AD, the book describes many aspects of medieval Buddhism in India as well as in China. Much material from modern scholarship and archaeological research is brought in as background and thus we learn as much history as religion and art.

410 **Our ordered lives confess: three nineteenth-century American missionaries in East Shantung.**
Irwin T. Hyatt, Jr. Cambridge, Massachusetts: Harvard University Press, 1976. 323p.

In an overly modest introduction, the author says that its 'chief introduction' is simply to recount what seem to be three interesting stories of missionaries in China in the late 19th century. In fact, all the broad themes of missionary histography are there: imperialism, missionary cases, contributions to reform in China, the contrast between different Protestant groups, etc.

411 **Discourse on the natural theology of the Chinese.**
Gottfried Wilhelm Leibnitz, translated with an introduction
and commentaries by Henry Rosemount, Jr., Daniel J.
Cook. Honolulu: University Press of Hawaii, 1977. 168p.

Usually referred to as the 'Letter on Chinese philosophy', this is Leibnitz's
response to two works on Chinese religion sent to him by Catholic missionaries.
His discussion deals with the Chinese conception of God, universal principles,
spiritual substance, souls and the correlations between Leibnitz's binary mathematical notation and *I-Ching* (*Yi Jing*).

412 **Religious policy and practice in communist China: a.
documentary history.**
Edited by Donald E. MacInnis. New York: Macmillan,
1972. 392p.

The book's 117 documents, primarily from Chinese sources, cover three broad
topics: first, official policy toward religion; second, the actual relations between
the government on one hand and Christian churches and Taoist and Buddhist
temples and monasteries on the other; and third, Maoism as a new religion in the
life of the people.

413 **Folk Buddhist religion: dissenting sects in late traditional
China.**
Daniel L. Overmyer. Cambridge, Massachusetts: Harvard
University Press, 1976. 295p.

This is a survey of Chinese folk religious sects from the Han era to the 20th
century, with an emphasis on those of Buddhist orientation. Focusing on the
rituals and beliefs of such groups as the White Lotus, the author describes how
many of these sects, although regarded as illegal, developed their own traditions
of organization, leadership and scripture and maintained active congregational life
for long periods of time as well as politically-oriented life with distinctive ideas
and goals.

414 **Mandarins, Jews and missionaries: the Jewish experience in
the Chinese empire.**
Michael Pollak. New York: Jewish Publication Society of
America, 1980. 436p.

In 1605, Matteo Ricci, a Jesuit priest in China, discovered an isolated, but still
flourishing Jewish community in Kaifeng (K'ai-feng), the ancient capital of
Honan (Henan) province. The author provides a fascinating historical account of
this exotic community, from its earliest and legendary beginnings in the biblical
period, to its tragic and almost complete disappearance by the 20th century.
Beyond the confines of Jewish history, this saga sheds much light on China's past,
especially its treatment of minorities.

415 **The home base of American China missions, 1880-1920.**
Valentin M. Rabe. Cambridge, Massachusetts: Harvard
University Press, 1978. 299p.

The author describes how Protestant mission activists in the home base of American China Mission were, by 1900, constructing something quite different from the

enterprise that had preceded it. Institutionally, financially and in terms of person-nel, a veritable revolution took place.

416 Church and China: toward reconciliation?
Joseph J. Spae. Chicago: Chicago Institute of Technology and Culture, 1980. 167p.

The author, a former European Catholic missionary, asks if reconciliation is possible between the Catholic Church and China. His approach is ecumenical in both a political and religious sense. He raises the troublesome question as to whether the degree of freedom in China is sufficient to ensure a human life.

417 The West in Russia and China: religions and secular thought in modern times. Volume i, Russia, 1472-1917; volume ii, China 1582-1949.
Donald W. Treadgold. Cambridge, Massachusetts: Harvard University Press, 1973. 324+251p.

The author traces the development and impact of Western thought in Russia from the 15th century and in China from the 16th century through the break-down of their respective traditions to the victory of Communism. The second volume on Western intellectual influence in China opens with an extensive treat-ment of the Jesuit mission from 1582-1774 and the highly successful and con-troversial accommodation policy of Matteo Ricci.

418 Buddhism under Mao.
Holmes Welch. Cambridge, Massachusetts: Harvard University Press, 1972. 666p.

The author describes the uneasy and unequal relationship between the Chinese government and the Buddhist clergy. While the government wishes to see Budd-hism die out, the clergy finds limited protection in constitutional freedom of religion, the utility of Buddhism in foreign relations and the continued religious proclivities of at least some of the Chinese masses.

419 Facets of Taoism: essays in Chinese religion.
Edited by Holmes Welch, Anna Seidel. New Haven, Connecticut: Yale University Press, 1979. 302p.

This book contains papers from the 1972 Conference on Taoism at Tateshina in Japan and selections from well-known articles by Japanese scholars hitherto unav-ailable in English translation. The papers deal with the ideology of the popular scripture, the *T'aiping Ching* (*Taiping Jing*); popular religion; the Taoist theoc-racy at the northern Wei court; Taoist monastic life; and the formation of the Taoist canon.

420 Religion and ritual in Chinese society.
Edited by Arthur P. Wolf. Stanford, California: Stanford University Press, 1974. 377p.

These papers use abundant and illuminating data to substantiate worthwhile theoretical points. They attempt to provide information on several aspects of Chinese religions and ritual experience, primarily based on the field research conducted in Taiwan and Hong Kong.

421 Buddhist leader in Ming China: the life and thought of Han-shan Te-ch'ing.

Xu Songbang.   University Park, Pensylvania: Pennsylvania State University Press, 1979. 221p.

Han-shan Te-ch'ing (Hanshan Deqing) (1546-1623) was an active Buddhist monk, scholar, teacher and preacher during the final decades of the Ming dynasty. The book is a thorough study of his life and thought against the intellectual and social background of the period. In the process, the author, Hsu Sungpeng (Xu Songbang) suggests that Ming Buddhism was a living religion, a new type of Buddhism which penetrated more deeply into the fibre of Chinese society and culture.

422 Religion in Chinese society.

C. K. Yang.   Berkeley, California: University of California Press, 1975. 483p.

This is a study of the contemporary function of religion in Chinese society. The author also looks at the historical background.

423 Religion, nationalism and Chinese students: the anti-Christian movement of 1922-1927.

Ka-Che Yip.   Bellingham, Washington: Western Washington University, 1980. 133p.

The author surveys the complex interrelationships between the Chinese anti-Christian movement of the 1920s and a range of other phenomena of that decade: nationalism, anti-imperialism, the Kuomintang (Nationalist Party) and Communist Party, new intellectual currents, and, most importantly, the student movement. He concludes that during the 1920s the Chinese movement veered progressively to the left.

424 The renewal of Buddhism in China: Chu-hung and the late Ming synthesis.

Yu Zhunfang.   New York: Columbia University Press, 1980. 328p.

This study explores the life, work and teaching of Chu-hung (Zhu Hong) (1535-1615), who emerged as a charismatic preacher and successful advocate of monastic reform during the late Ming dynasty. The author, Yu Chun-Fang (Yu Zhunfang), provides both an imaginative intellectual biography of a major Buddhist figure and a vivid cultural portrait of one of the most active and creative eras in Chinese intellectual history.

Philosophy

425 The secret and sublime: Taoist mysteries and magic.
John Blofeld. New York: Verry, 1973. 217p.
A discussion of philosophical Taoism. This book contains stories, anecdotes and descriptions of personal visits to recluses in isolated huts and to large, brilliantly-painted monasteries. The author relates stories of the after life, of exorcisms, of invulnerability and other physical feats and of spirit-oracles delivered by monks possessed by gods/demons.

426 Tao Te Ching.
Chu Dagao. Winchester, Massachusetts: Allen & Unwin, 1982. 128p.
This is the acknowledged masterpiece of Taoist philosophy. Starkly simple in form yet infinitely enigmatic in meaning, it is written in a language of great subtlety, tantalizing and fascinating readers of every kind for more than 2,000 years. This translation, the first by a modern Chinese scholar, powerfully conveys the beauty and vigour of the original.

427 China, India and the ruins of Washington.
Austin Coates. New York: Day, 1971. 370p.
The author examines oriental cultural patterns and the fabric of the oriental mind by juxtaposing the roots of Chinese and Indian thought patterns with Western life-styles. To the suggestion that orientals might learn to understand the West, the author would reply that the habits of 4,000 years cannot be altered and also that orientals do not understand each other, the Indian mind being adrift in the clouds and the Chinese entrenched in the kitchen.

428 What is Taoism?
Herlee G. Creel. Chicago: University of Chicago Press, 1977. 192p.
This volume affords one of the first detailed views of Taoism and its relationship to governmental pattern as then developed in the late Chou (Zhou), Ch'in (Qin) and Han dynasties.

429 The Tao and Chinese culture.
Da Liu. New York: Shocken Books, 1979. 168p.
The author has written this work to communicate to Westerners an authentic Taoist (Daoist) understanding of Tao (Dao) and its significance, based on first-hand experience. The best section of the book describes Taoism (Daoism) in such areas as warfare, magic and medicine.

430 The unfolding of Neo-Confucianism.
Edited by William Theodore De Bary. New York: Columbia University Press, 1975. 593p.
The main contention of this book seems to be that the latest phase in the unfolding of Neo-Confucianism was neither a static philosophy nor a set of fixed

doctrines, but a movement which grew precisely through successive efforts to refine tradition and reformulate orthodoxy.

431 **Principle and practicability: essays in Neo-Confucianism and practical learning.**
Edited by William Theodore De Bary. New York: Columbia University Press, 1979. 544p.

The essays in this book explore from various perspectives the continuities and discontinuities between the Neo-Confucian thought of Ming China and the practical learning of the 17th and 18th centuries. The authors point out the need for a deeper examination of the complex relation between traditional and modern thought and values.

432 **How to consult the I Ching (Yi Jing): the oracle of change.**
Alfred Douglas. New York: Putnam, 1972. 251p.

This book examines the history, wisdom and influence of the Chinese *Oracle of Change*, gives instructions on how to use and understand it and includes a new translation of the basic text. The author is writing for the reader primarily interested in divination. His text is clear and avoids the mystifying symbolism of a more literal translation. His introduction is informative and the instructions for using the *I Ching* (*Yi Jing*) are easy to follow.

433 **The legend of Miao-Shan.**
Glen Duobridge. London: Ithaca Press, 1978. 128p.

The pervasive presence of religious themes in Chinese popular literature since the Sung (Song) dynasty is starting to receive the scholarly attention it deserves. The legend of Miao-shan is a happy choice for such a study. It was through this particular legend that the cult of the compassionate Bodhisattva Kuan-yin (Guanyin) became an essential feature of modern Chinese religion at all levels of society.

434 **Centrality and commonality: an exploratory essay on Chung-Yung.**
Du Weiming. Honolulu: University of Hawaii Press, 1976. 157p.

The author, Tu Wei-ming's (Du Weiming) approach is interpretative, an attempt to gain insight into the underlying themes of the text and to make clear that there is a deep, integral structure in the Confucian classic *Chung-Yung* (*Zhong Yong*).

435 **Neo-Confucian thought in action: Wang Yang-ming's youth (1472-1509).**
Du Weiming. Berkeley, California: University of California Press, 1976. 222p.

This is an intellectual biography of the Chinese philosopher's formative years, which culminated in the formulation of his doctrine of the unity of knowledge and action. Through analysis of the philosopher's poems, essays and other writings, the author, Tu Wei-ming (Du Weiming) tries to penetrate into Wang's inner life with his philosophy. He also examines Wang's intellectual links with

Taoism, Buddhism, and his Neo-Confucian predecessors and uses these links to help explain the development of Wang's thought.

436 The limits of change: essays on conservative alternatives in republican China.
Edited by Charlotte Furth. Cambridge, Massachusetts: Harvard University Press, 1976. 426p.

The thirteen essays discuss the range of responses of conservatives in the Republican period. Individual papers analyze the early Republican National Essence movement, the new Confucian humanism of the 1920s and afterwards, political ideology under Republican military dictatorship and the ideas of modern literary conservatives.

437 Chuang Tzu: the inner chapters.
Translated by A. C. Graham. Winchester, Massachusetts: Allen & Unwin, 1981. 293p.

This book is a classic of Taoism, the Chinese philosophy of mystical spontaneity which is ancestral to Zen Buddhism. The author offers a new translation of the chapters ascribed to Chuang Tzu (Zuan Zi), and of the essays of the 'Primitivist', the 'Yangist Miscellany', the Syncredist writings, as well as a selection of other texts classified by topic.

438 Chuang Tzu (Zuan Zi): textual notes to a partial translation.
A. C. Graham. Winchester, Massachusetts: Allen & Unwin, 1982. 65p.

In these detailed notes, the author discusses textual variations and parallels from other authors. He offers reconstructions of sections whose original order seems to have been altered or where original material must have been lost.

439 Hu Shih and the Chinese renaissance: liberalism in the Chinese revolution, 1917-1937.
Jerome B. Grieder. Cambridge, Massachusetts: Harvard University Press, 1970. 420p.

Guided by the same liberal spirit of reason, science and empirical detachment which animated Hu Shih (Hu Shi), the author has composed a biography to describe Hu's contribution to the Chinese Renaissance and liberalism in the Chinese Revolution.

440 Critiques of Confucius in contemporary China.
Kan Kouwie. New York: St. Martin's Press, 1980. 186p.

In this volume, the author examines the changing attitudes of Chinese intellectuals toward Confucius and Confucianism over the course of this century, particularly since the beginning of the Communist period in 1949. The book is organized chronologically and throughout, the author devotes particular attention to three major themes: the significance of Confucius' class background, his theories of ethics and his ideas on education. An extensive bibliography enhances the work's usefulness for all students of contemporary Chinese culture.

441 **Mencius.**
Translated by D. C. Lau. New York: Penguin Books, 1976. 264p.

For two thousand years *Mencius* was required reading among Chinese scholars, since it was a significant part of Confucian texts. *Mencius* is a deeply felt defense of morality in personal and public life. This translation preserves the vigour of the original.

442 **Tao Magic: the Chinese art of the occult.**
Laszlo Legeza. New York: Random House, 1973. 128p.

This book contains a beautiful, lavishly-illustrated introduction to the world of Taoist calligraphy and Chinese mysticism still scarcely known in the West.

443 **Confucius: Confucian analects, the great learning and the doctrine of the mean.**
James Legge. New York: Dover, 1971. 503p.

This book contains Chinese texts with translation, exegetical notes and a dictionary of all the characters.

444 **I Ching games.**
H. Y. Li, Sibley S. Morrill. New York: Cadleon Press, 1971. 138p.

Trangrams, the ancient Chinese puzzle in seven geometrical shapes, can be used to make an infinite number of silhouettes depicting objects, people and animals. This book includes many of these possible shapes and relates the use of this ancient Chinese puzzle with *I Ching* (*Yi Jing*), the *Book of Changes*, making a game which can be played by one or more players. The puzzle can be addictive and the authors claim, there is a feeling of harmony that comes from solving these *I Ching* (*Yi Jing*) puzzle games. The book comes shrink-wrapped with two die-cut puzzle sets, one of fifteen pieces and one of seven.

445 **The introduction of socialism into China.**
Li Yuming. New York: Columbia University Press, 1971. 138p.

The author, Li Yu-ming (Li Yuming) examines the way in which Western socialism was introduced through Japanese socialist writings and other sources into the cultural mainstream of China at the beginning of the 20th century.

446 **Chinese geomancy.**
Evelyn Lip. Singapore: Times Books International, 1979. 126p.

Chinese geomancy is a system of symbols, instruments and rules of topographical interpretation for siting graves, homes and important buildings, at the same time orienting and adjusting the fates of the social units focused on them. This book falls between being a practical handbook and an investigation of geomantic practice.

447 **Ways to paradise: The Chinese quest for immortality.**
Michael Loewe. Winchester, Massachusetts: Allen &
Unwin, 1979. 270p.

In this book, the author examines some of the spectacular archaeological finds in
recent years and places them in the context of other archaeological evidence as
well as contemporary literature and philosophy. The book also enables the author
to review Han ideas on life, death, human nature and methods of divination and
the recurrence of various motifs in Han art.

448 **Chinese ideas of life and death: faith, myth and reason in the**
Han period (202 BC-AD 220).
Michael Loewe. Winchester, Massachusetts: Allen &
Unwin, 1982. 226p.

Archaeological discoveries of the last decade have radically transformed the
history of the Ch'in (Qin) and Han empires. The discoveries have made this a
subject that arouses lively interest among members of the public and the media.
The book is for those who wish to pursue this interest and would like to learn
more about the religious and intellectual background of the period.

449 **The Confucian vision.**
Edited by William McNaughton. Ann Arbor, Michigan:
University of Michigan Press, 1974. 164p.

Selections from Confucian literature are here presented chronologically within
four chapters, each devoted to a basic idea of Confucian philosophy. The editor
provides his own translations with an introduction to discuss some of the most
important Confucian terms and personalities and the influence of Confucianism
outside China.   227592

450 **Escape from predicament: Neo-Confucianism and China's**
evolving political culture.
Thomas A. Metzger. New York: Columbia University
Press, 1976. 303p.

In this detailed examination of the intellectual roots of modern Chinese society,
the author provides a provocative, original interpretation of major aspects of
Neo-Confucian and 20th-century thought. He dicusses the parallels between Neo-
Confucianism and late imperial bureaucratic culture, then demonstrates how knowl-
edge of traditional Chinese orientation casts new perspectives on Maoism and modern
Chinese liberalism.

451 **The Chinese mind.**
Edited by Charles A. Moore. Honolulu: University Press of
Hawaii, 1977. 6th ed. 258p.

The articles in this book range from simple introductory discussions to the more
profound topics of Chinese metaphysics, ethics and political thought.

Religion and Philosophy. Philosophy

452 **The concept of man in contemporary China.**
Donald J. Munro. Ann Arbor, Michigan: University of
Michigan Press, 1977. 248p.

The author compares present Chinese notions of man not only with those held traditionally but also with those current in the Soviet Union and the liberal West. Among his topics are: government and educational theories and practices. He includes an analysis of the goal of equality and concludes with an assessment of the strengths and weaknesses of the Chinese concept.

453 **Invitation to Chinese philosophy: eight studies.**
Edited by Arne Naess, Alastair Hannay. New York:
Columbia University Press, 1977. 283p.

This is an introduction to Chinese philosophy, suitable for the general reader as well as students of philosophy. The articles in the book focus on the main ideas of Chinese philosophers in the different, though related, traditions of Taoism, Confucianism, Neo-Confucianism and Buddhism.

454 **To acquire wisdom: the way of Wang Yang-ming.**
Julia Qing. New York: Columbia University Press, 1976.
373p.

The author, Julia Ch'ing (Qing) presents a study of the thought of the 16th-century Chinese philosopher-official Wang Yang-ming (Wang Yang-ming). It is organized around Wang's relationship to Confucian orthodoxy. There follows an examination of the major conceptual stages in the evolution of Wang's philosophical quest.

455 **Confucianism and Christianity: a comparative study.**
Julia Qing. Tokyo: Kodansha International, 1977. 234p.

The goal of the study is not to scrutinize historical development or analyze religious doctrines but to initiate a religious dialogue between the two traditions, so that one may learn from the other. The author Julia Ch'ing's (Qing) method is problem-oriented and she has built her study around three central problems -man, God and self-transcendence.

456 **Individual and state in ancient China.**
Vitaly A. Rubin. New York: Columbia University Press,
1976. 149p.

This book contains essays on four Chinese philosophers - Confucius, Mo Tze (Mo Zi), Shang Yang (Shang Yang) and Chuan Tze (Zuan Zi) - written by a leading Soviet sinologist who emigrated to Israel in 1976.

457 **The master who embraces simplicity: a study of the
philosopher Ko Hung AD 282-343.**
Jay Sailey. San Francisco: Chinese Material Center, 1978.
658p.

Ko Hung (Ge Hong) was a very articulate representative of the educated gentry of the Wu area during the traumatic period following the loss of north China to barbarian rule and the establishment of the Eastern China dynasty in Nanking (Nanjing) in the early 4th century. He is the voice of the underpriviledged

100

southern majority, viewing with somewhat testy detachment, the sad estate to which the government, morals, philosophy and literature has fallen in his beloved land. Sailey has translated about half of the fifty chapters making up the 'Outer Chapters' (*Wai-P'ien - Waipiang*) of the *Pao-P'u-tzu* (*Baopuzi*) which deal with these subjects, but each chapter chosen has been translated intact, with generous annotation.

458 Researches on the I Ching.
Iulien Shchutskii, translated by William L. MacDonald, edited by Tsuyoshi Hasegawa, Hellmut Willhelm. Princeton, New Jersey: Princeton University Press, 1979. 359p.

One of the most important books in the world's literature, the *I Ching* (*Yi Jing*), or the *Book of Changes*, is one of the first efforts of the human mind to place itself within the universe. The book makes available a wealth of critical essays on the lore associated with this profound book.

459 Ch'i (Qi): a Neo-Taoist approach to life.
R. G. H. Siu. Cambridge, Massachusetts: MIT Press, 1974. 351p.

This volume completes Siu's Tao (Dao)-time trilogy - *The Tao (Dao) of Science* (1958) and *The man of many qualities* (1969). His subject here is the time-light-life continuum. Following the ancient Chinese style, he begins with a synoptic text consisting of some short expositions, synthesized by extended commentaries keyed to each one. He explains the continuum via a synthesis of philosophical and scientific ideas.

460 Confucius.
Howard D. Smith. New York: Scribner, 1973. 240p.

The author first reconstructs the historical setting from which the sage of ancient China emerged and then presents the essentials of his life and teachings. The book is written in clear and intellectual fashion for both scholars and laymen.

461 The Tao is silent.
Raymond M. Smullyan. New York: Harper, 1977. 225p.

In his introduction to Taoism (Daoism), the author uses dialogues between a Taoist and a moralist to explore such questions as free will and determinism, man's relations to ultimate reality and ethics and the West. Other topics such as egotism, altruism, enlightenment and human nature are also treated.

462 Commentary on the Lao Tze.
Wang Bi, translated by Ariane Rump, Wing-tsin Chan. Honolulu: University Press of Hawaii, 1980. 475p.

Of the several hundred extant commentaries on the *Lao Tze* (*Lao Zi*) in China, Korea and Japan, the one by Wang Pi (Wang Bi) (226-249) is the first and most philosophical. It is not an exaggeration to say that Chinese metaphysics began with Wang's commentary on the *Lao Tze* (*Lao Zi*).

463 The complete works of Chuang Tzu.
Burton Watson. New York: Columbia University Press, 1970. 397p.

The complete works of one of the two great exponents of the Taoist (Daoist) school of thought are made available in their entirety in this new translation by Burton Watson.

464 Basic writings of Mo Tzu, Hsun Tzu, and Han Fei Tzu.
Burton Watson. New York: Columbia University Press, 1971. 450p.

Each of these translations of the writing of Mo Tzu (Mo Zi), Hsun Tzu (Xun Zu) and Han Fei Tzu (Han Fei Zi) is provided with an introduction by the author which places the individual philosophers in the context of Chinese history and thought.

465 Tao: the watercourse way.
Alan Watts. New York: Pantheon Books, 1975. 134p.

This book has a chapter on the Chinese language, followed by an explanation of the meaning of Tao (Dao) (the flow of nature), Wu-wei (not forcing things) and Te (De) (the power which comes from this). When Watts died suddenly in late 1973 he was contemplating the completion of this book by adding a discussion of the political and technological implications of Taoism (Daoism) and its significance for our time. Al Chung-Liang Huang (Al Zhongliang Huang), friends and colleagues completed the text and provided much of the Chinese calligraphy.

466 Heaven, earth and man in the book of changes: seven Eranos lectures.
Hellmut Willhelm. Seattle, Washington: University of Washington Press, 1977. 230p.

The aspects of the *I Ching* (*Yi Jing*) explored here include the concept of time; the creative principle; human events and their meaning; the city as a stage of formation; the interaction of heaven, earth and man; the wandering of the spirit and the interplay of image and concept.

Society and Social Structure

General

467 Land and lineage in China: a study of T'ung-Ch'eng county, Anhwei, in the Ming and Ch'ing dynasties.
Hilary J. Beattie. Cambridge, England: Cambridge University Press, 1979. 208p.
This is a study of social stratification, social mobility and the socio-economic functions of lineages in Ming and Ch'ing (Qing) China in T'ung-ch'eng (Tongcheng) county, a region north of the Yangtze (Yangzi) River and about one hundred miles from Nanking (Nanjing).

468 Essays on Chinese civilization.
Derk Bodde, edited and introduced by Charles Le Blanc, Dorothy Borei. Princeton, New Jersey: Princeton University Press, 1980. 504p.
This book contains 21 articles written by a leading American sinologist, Derk Bodde. The essays are grouped under four main categories: 'The formations of Chinese culture'; 'Man in society'; 'Man in the cosmos' and 'Text studies'.

469 China in old photographs, 1860-1910.
Burton F. Beers. New York: Scribner, 1978. 160p.
This collection of photographs provides a view of life in 19th-century China. The photographs show the peasants of China farming, fishing, spinning, peddling and pulling heavily loaded wheelbarrows or rickshaws. Alongside pictures of a bridge being carried in a sedan chair, lounging opium smokers, and a girl with bound feet, there are photographs of electric light poles along the narrow Shanghai streets, steamboats on the Yangtze (Yangzi) River and soldiers posing next to a

Western-style cannon. All of the photographs come from the collection of the
Museum of the American China Trade in Milton, Massachusetts.

470 A year in Upper Felicity: life in a Chinese village during the Cultural Revolution.
Jack Chen. New York: Macmillan, 1973. 383p.

An urban intellectual, Ch'en (Chen) was sent from Peking (Beijing) in 1969
during the Cultural Revolution to learn from the revolutionary peasants. He
found himself assigned to the old, sick and disabled work team in Upper Felicity,
Honan (Henan) in North China. There he observed the amalgam of rural
customs and new socialism in the lives of his neighbours.

471 The dragon's village.
Chen Yuanzong. New York: Pantheon Books, 1980. 178p.

This novel by Ch'en Yuan-tsung (Chen Yuanzong), describes the efforts, in 1951,
of an enthusiastic troupe of young Shanghai cadres, proudly sporting their new
soldier-style jackets and caps to carry Mao's theory of land reform to a remote
village in a northern province.

472 Popular movements and secret societies in China, 1840-1950.
Edited by Jean Chesneaux. Stanford, California: Stanford
University Press, 1972. 328p.

This volume which was derived from the sessions on modern Chinese secret
societies held at the 1965 Conference of Chinese Studies, contains papers by
scholars of various nationalities. The papers are arranged chronologically to provide characterization and analysis of the societies and discussions of representative
instances of the relations between these primitive rebels and such large movements as the Taiping (T'aiping) Rebellion and the 1911 Revolution. The editor
stressed the secret societies as a means of self-protection which no other social
institution, including lineages, would provide.

473 Han social structure.
Chu Tongzu, edited by John L. Dull. Seattle, Washington:
University of Washington Press, 1973. 570p.

The author first presents scholarly essays on kinship, marriage, the position of
women, social classes and powerful families. The second part of the book is a
translation of texts of incidents drawn from the Han histories which illustrate and
provide evidence for points made in the essays.

474 The politics of marriage in contemporary China.
Elizabeth Croll. Cambridge, England: Cambridge
University Press, 1981. 210p.

This book is a useful overview of the various stages in marriage, from the initial
search for a mate to setting up the household after the wedding. The author had
to painstakingly piece together evidence from press articles, reading between the
lines, to find clues to what kinds of marriage behaviour were typical. Her data
convinced her that very few people in rural or urban China conform fully to the
official ideals, and that in rural areas parents take more of the initiative and have
more control, while in the cities young people have more say in the matter. So,
marriage is an arena in which the younger generation is competing with the older
for control, in an effort to escape from traditional customs.

475 The Chinese welfare system.
John Dixon. New York: Praeger, 1981. 462p.
This is the first comprehensive study of the welfare system of the People's Republic of China. Based on every major source available, including translation services, visitors' reports, the author's own observations on two visits to China, refugee reports and a wide range of secondary sources, the study reports in detail on the development of the Chinese welfare system since 1949, placing each development into the social context which influenced it.

476 Chinese industrial society after Mao.
Rosalie L. Dong. Lexington, Massachusetts: Heath, 1982. 384p.
This is a detailed comprehensive examination of Chinese industry and the various political, social, economic and cultural forces which shaped China's industrial society. Tung's (Dong) incisive analysis of management practices is based on first-hand data and interviews.

477 The Chinese city between two worlds.
Edited by Mark Elvin, William G. Skinner. Stanford, California: Stanford University Press, 1974. 384p.
This volume contains twelve essays spanning a wide range of topics and demonstrating impressive scholarship. Eight papers deal with late 19th- and early 20th-century social history, touching on treaty ports, modern banking, chambers of commerce, peasant insurrections, warlordism, educational reform, philanthropy and city government. The remaining articles deal with urbanization in Taiwan.

478 The revenge of heaven: journal of a young Chinese.
Gen Ling, English text prepared by Mirigan London, Daling Li. New York: Putnam, 1972. 413p.
This is an account by Ken Ling (Gen Ling) of life inside China today. It appears that the Chinese Communist revolution did not produce a 'New Chinese man' and that the population continued to obey parents, revere ancestors, worship gods, propitiate demons, marry by arrangement, gamble for entertainment, etc.

479 Organization behavior in Chinese society.
Edited by Sidney L. Greenblatt, Richard Wilson, Amy Wilson. New York: Praeger, 1981. 288p.
In this volume the individual authors have come up with a variety of strategies for dealing with what has happened in China from Mao's era to Deng's (Teng) ascendency. The authors were plagued by a problem which has been troubling many scholars: when seeking to understand today's China, can one safely forget Mao's China? Organizational behaviour in Chinese society is built around four topics: the application of Western organizational models to the Chinese experience, behaviour within specific organizational settings (e.g. educational institutions, the military, the Communist Party, the courts), management of organizational processes (e.g. personnel practices, incentives, career cycles, tension management, conflict resolution) and organizations in the large environment (e.g. rural and industrial organizations, business practices, articulation of interests).

480 Social interaction in Chinese society.
Edited by Sidney L. Greenblatt, Richard Wilson, Amy
Wilson. New York: Praeger, 1982. 260p.

The volume, produced by the Committee on Scholarly Communication with the
People's Republic of China, provides a framework for the critical assessment of
both theoretical generalizations about interactional behaviour and generalizations
derived from study of interaction in Chinese cultural and social settings. In the
editors' views, theoretical work on interactive behaviour and data from Chinese
and other social systems is essential to an understanding of the impact of revolution, social and cultural change and continuity and discontinuity in Chinese
society.

481 The dynamics of revolution: a cybernetic theory of the dynamics of modern social revolution with a study of ideological change and organizational dynamics in the Chinese revolution.
Thomas G. Hart. Stockholm: Stockholm University Press,
1971. 203p.

Essentially all Hart says about China is that from time to time Mao has reas-
sessed the threats to the Chinese revolution from external enemies and internal
rivalries emphasized one or the other of these dangers and increased or slowed
down the processes of revolutionary change accordingly. In particular, Mao has
tried to balance and reconcile the conflicting requirements of stability and change
by altering ideology, rather than forms of organization and the valued element of
continuity.

482 A memoir of revolutionary China, 1924-1941.
Ruth V. Hemenway, edited and introduced by Fred W.
Drake. Amherst, Massachusetts: University of
Massachusett Press, 1977. 220p.

This memoir is based on diaries of a strong-willed New Englander who worked
for 18 years as a medical missionary in warlord-dominated rural China. She
attempts to convey to Western readers something of the quality of life in China
during the painful decade before the Communist revolution. With the editorial
assistance of historian Fred W. Drake, she has produced a description of both
missionary life and rural southern and western China in the two decades before
the Second World War.

483 Childhood in China.
Edited by William Kessen. New Haven, Connecticut: Yale
University Press, 1975. 241p.

This book was carefully compiled by a group of distinguished American social
scientists who visited China for three weeks late in 1973 as the American Delegation on Early Childhood Development in the People's Republic of China. The
delegation was composed mainly of developmental psychologists, but also included
two sociologists, a pediatrician, a nursery school teacher and a staff member of
the Committee on Scholarly Communication with the People's Republic of China.
The delegation concentrated on observing and reporting, attempting to keep interpretation and explanation to a minimum.

484 **Chinese ways in warfare.**
Frank A. Kierman, Jr., John K. Fairbank. Cambridge,
Massachusetts: Harvard University Press, 1974. 401p.

A Harvard symposium of 1969 provides seven case studies in Chinese military
history and a penetrating introductory summation which stressed the Chinese
insistence on the end, not the means of warfare; the goal is to change an
opponent's mind and violence is not always the best technique.

485 **Class conflict in Chinese socialism.**
Richard Curt Kraus. New York: Columbia University
Press, 1981. 376p.

This book examines the political struggles over the rise of an embryonic bureaucratic class in the wake of revolution. The book also analyzes the changing class
relationships - and definitions of class - that have characterized the post-liberation
period.

486 **Rustication of urban youth in China.**
Edited by Peter J. Seybolt, introduced by Thomas P.
Bernstein. White Plains, New York: Sharpe, 1977. 200p.

This is a useful collection of materials dating from 1973 to 1976 on the rural
transfer programme. The bulk of the book translates a 1975 Peking (Beijing)
compendium of emulation models and guidelines. In addition, it includes several
supplementary documents.

487 **The city in late imperial China.**
Edited by William G. Skinner. Stanford, California:
Stanford University Press, 1977. 820p. maps.

This book contains sixteen papers by special scientists and institutional historians
which examine various aspects of the traditional Chinese city. It is illustrated
with 58 maps showing the cities of China in 1894, classified according to size,
administrative level and economic importance.

488 **The studies of Chinese society: essays by Maurice Freedman.**
Edited by William G. Skinner. Stanford, California:
Stanford University Press, 1979. 515p.

The book contains twenty-four major essays by the late Maurice Freedman, a
brilliant scholar and teacher who profoundly affected the course of anthropological research into Chinese society. The essays cover his chief interests: overseas
Chinese communities, kinship and religion and the disciplinary problems for
anthropologists who study ancient and complex societies.

489 **The pivot of the four quarters: a preliminary inquiry into the
origins and character of the ancient Chinese city.**
Paul Wheatley. New York: Aldine-Atherton, 1971. 602p.

This is a comparative study of the origins of cities with particular reference to
the development of urbanism in ancient China. The basic conclusions reached are
that the cities of early China, in much the same fashion as cities elsewhere in the
world, came into being as religious centres and were laid out in accordance with
the dictates of religious belief.

Society and Social Structure. General

490 Deviance and social control in Chinese society.
Edited by Amy Wilson, Sidney L. Greenblatt, Richard Wilson. New York: Praeger, 1977. 227p.

This collection attempts to apply various disciplinary and interdisciplinary perspectives to defining and examining questions of deviance and social control (reactive and pre-active) in the Chinese political cultural framework. What the editors have managed to do is to study the criminal justice field in the context of social life in China.

491 Value change in Chinese society.
Edited by Richard Wilson, Amy Wilson, Sidney L. Greenblatt. New York: Praeger, 1979. 309p.

This book begins with an introduction in which Wilson reviews the essential properties of values. The designation of certain goals as desirable and the maintenance of self-esteem are, to Wilson, the two critical functions that values serve in helping to organize individual behaviour. Value change occurs when conventional modes of behaviour are seen as inappropriate for a new problem and when people begin to feel distressed about this condition.

492 Moral behavior in Chinese society.
Richard Wilson, Amy Wilson, Sidney L. Greenblatt, foreword by Thomas A. Metzger. New York: Praeger, 1981. 232p.

Exploring the role of morals in Chinese society, this book covers such issues as defining morals within a Chinese social context, the role moral values play in maintaining social cohesion in Chinese society, the role of specific social organizations in maintaining 'moral boundaries', the treatment of individuals who fall outside 'moral boundaries' and the teaching and learning of morals.

493 Studies in Chinese society.
Edited by Arthur P. Wolf. Stanford, California: Stanford University Press, 1978. 391p.

This book is intended to serve the needs of students in courses taught by anthropologists, sociologists and historians. It is also very useful in a general undergraduate course on Chinese society and culture. It proves very useful as a compact and inexpensive source of a variety of ethnographic descriptions of selected aspects of Chinese society, religion and ritual, kinship and marriage.

494 Marriage and adoption in China, 1845-1945.
Arthur P. Wolf, Huang Jieshan. Stanford, California: Stanford University Press, 1980. 359p.

Based on a detailed analysis of Japanese household registers for an area of the T'aipei (Taibei) basin, the authors Wolf and Chieh-shan Hwang (Huang Jieshan) make two general points. One is that the choice between minor, major and uxorious marriages can only be understood in the context of economic options and demographic changes. The other, bringing in data from other parts of Taiwan and from the Chinese mainland, is that Chinese family organization varied sharply from region to region, to the point where forms of marriage that were nearly unknown in one region were actively preferred in another.

495 Sociology and socialism in contemporary China.
Sui-lun Wong. London: Routledge, 1979. 147p.

This book gives a brief, balanced summary of Chinese social investigation work prior to 1979. Despite recent events, this summary will remain useful to scholars entering the field who want a brief bibliography of major studies and an historical context in which to place them.

496 The Chinese heritage: a new and provocative view of the origins of Chinese society.
K. S. Wu. New York: Crown, 1982. 512p.

This is the first systematic study in the English language of the origins of Chinese society. The history begins with the first appearance of the Chinese written language and ends when China's basic political, cultural, and social institutions were well enough established to codify in book form. It spans a period from approximately 2500 BC to AD 1100. The author discusses ancient Chinese customs, ancestor worship and religion, attitudes toward women, political organization, warfare, the origins of Confucianism and the creation of China's centralized state bureaucracy.

497 China and the West: Society and Culture, 1815-1937.
Jerome Zhen. Bloomington, Indiana: Indiana University Press, 1979. 488p.

This book is organized into two parts. The first covers agents of change: Western perceptions of China and Chinese perceptions of the West, missionaries, scholars, foreign communities in China and Chinese immigrants abroad. Part two describes the legal, political, economic, social and cultural transformations during the period.

Family

498 Chinese family and kinship.
Hugh D. R. Baker. New York: Columbia University Press, 1979. 243p.

Using 20th-century field work to illustrate features of the traditional family, the author examines the composition of the family, lineage, the clan, ancestor worship and the relations of family and lineage to state and society in China. He is well aware of the heterogeneity of Chinese kinship structure and so draws heavily upon historic and current sources for his description of family life in China. The interplay of kinship and Chinese social structure in general is particularly well delineated.

499 Chinese family law and social change in historical and comparative perspective.
Edited by David C. Buxbuam.   Seattle, Washington:
University of Washington Press, 1978. 533p.

This book arises out of a conference (1968) on family law. Much of the material in the book has been superceded by subsequent work, particularly with respect to the research on Taiwan.

500 The aristocratic families of early imperial China: a case study of the Po-ling Tsui family.
Patricia Buckley Ebrey.   New York: Cambridge University Press, 1978. 537p.

The author traces the history of the most famous aristocratic families over the course of 800 years (from the 1st through the 9th centuries), showing how the influence of the aristocracy fluctuated and how the basis of its power and influence changed.

501 Family and kinship in Chinese society.
Edited by Maurice Freedman.   Stanford, California:
Stanford University Press, 1970. 375p.

This is a comprehensive picture of the current state of knowledge on family, kinship and marriage in Chinese society during the last 100 years. The papers in the book deal with both traditional patterns and contemporary realities including family structure; socialization; demographic features of farming, family and lineage organizations; kinship and ritual and kinship terminology. The final paper discusses Japanese kinship in comparison with Chinese.

502 The people of Taihang: an anthology of family histories.
Edited by Sidney L. Greenblatt.   White Plains, New York:
International Arts and Sciences Press, 1976. 305p.

The book consists of 17 family histories selected from among 70,000 similar records from the Taihang mountain region of China. They were collected as part of the family history writing phase of the rural socialist education campaign of 1962-64.

503 China man.
Maxine Hong Kingston.   New York: Knopf, 1980. 308p.

The men from China on whom the author focuses are her father, other male ancestors and her brothers. She also describes the lives of men who came from China to work on the railways of the West and on the sugar plantations of Hawaii.

504 Marriage law and policy in the Chinese People's Republic.
M. J. Neijer.   Hong Kong: Hong Kong University, 1972. 369p.

This is the first comprehensive study of Chinese marriage law and policy since 1949. The book represents the first systematic survey of any branch of modern

Chinese legislation, covering the historical, political and social context as well as the construction and application of the law.

505 **Village and family in contemporary China.**
William L. Parish, Martin King Whyte. Chicago: University of Chicago Press, 1978. 419p.

The authors employ interviews with their Hong Kong informants, former residents of a selected sampling of 63 villages in adjacent Kwangtung (Guangdong) Province, to construct a portrait of the South Chinese countryside over the period 1969-1974. They concentrate on which aspects of pre-1949 village and family life have been altered and which have not, what factors promote or oppose change and why change occurs in some villages but not in others.

506 **Old Madam Yin: a memoir of Peking life.**
Ida Pruitt. Stanford, California: Stanford University Press, 1979. 286p.

The book is an affectionate, revealing portrait of an aged, wealthy widow and her family in Peking of the 1920s and early 1930s. Through the memoirs of Lao Tai-tai (Lao Taitai), the reader is given an intimate glimpse of the life of an upper-class urban family: the relationship between husband and wife; between wives and concubines; the interactions among brothers; and the construction of gardens and the courtyards according to precise rules. The reader is shown the enormous importance to the Chinese protocol etiquette and reciprocal obligation. Above all, the memoirs capture the essence of pre-war Chinese cultural and social values.

Women's status

507 **Women's liberation in China.**
Claudie Broyelle, translated from the French by Michele Cohen, Gary Herman, preface by Han Suyin. New York: Humanities Press, 1976. 174p.

This book is based on Broyelle's 1971 trip to China. It contains five parts: the economic, domestic, maternal, familial and sexual aspects of women's oppression in the capitalist world; the failure of Soviet policies; Chinese intentions to cope with these problems; and the progress made by the Chinese toward women's liberation.

508 **Asian women in transition.**
Edited by Sylvia A. Chipp, Justin J. Green. University Park, Pennsylvania: Pennsylvania State University Press, 1980. 262p.

This book is a compilation of papers on women in various East, Southeast and South Asian societies. Their common theme is a discussion of the economic, social, political, ideological and religious factors that already do or potentially affect the process of role and status change among women. An article on China, written by Kay Ann Johnson, summarizes the political and economic reforms which have been designed to redefine women's roles and status in China and examines the reasons why it has been difficult to implement some of these reforms.

509 The women's movement in China: a selection of readings, 1949-1973.

Elizabeth Croll. London: Anglo-Chinese Educational Institute, 1974. 150p.

This book contains five parts: women's separate organization; their role in the family; their role in society; their ideological emancipation; and the continuing revolution. A theme running throughout the book is that for centuries women have felt inferior.

510 Feminism and socialism in China.

Elizabeth Croll. London: Routledge, 1978. 363p.

The author traces the movement for equality for women in China in the past 100 years. She points out interesting motifs: foreign women and missionaries in China had helped start the anti-footbinding movement in the 1890s but once the further freedom of women became part of an organized political effort in the May 4th movement of 1919, foreigners and Christians could no longer lead the way. Nationalism excluded the foreigners and Christianity avoided politics. The new marriage law of 1949 was a milestone and she traces the interplay since then between the women's movement and the social transformation of which it is a part.

511 Woman works: women and the Party in revolutionary China.

Dalia Davin. New York: Oxford University Press, 1976. 244p.

After surveying in an introduction the position of women before 1930, the author describes Communist Party policy towards women in the period of the Jiangxi (Chiang-hsi) Soviet, the anti-Japanese War and the Civil War and the development of the Women's Federation which has directed the women's movement since 1949. Then in separate chapters she analyzes more closely the difficulties of introducing a new style of marriage and family life to the conservative countryside. She discusses the relationship between women, production and the land, showing the effects of land reform and collectivization on women's economic position; she examines the life of women in the towns. The growth and reform of the educational system and progress which has been made in public health and medicine are two themes of these changes.

512 The divine women: dragon ladies and rain maidens in T'ang literature.

Edward H. Schafer. Berkeley, California: University of California Press, 1973. 191p.

This is the cluster of ancient associations linking women with water fertility and receptivity and the realization of these qualities in the figures of water goddesses. This volume takes as its subject the shamanesses and water-goddesses of early religion and legends, glimpsed only in fragments, the transformation and alteration of these legends into literary conventions and the occasional transformation of these conventions by poets of genius.

513 **Portraits of Chinese women in revolution.**
Agnes Smedley, edited and introduced by Jan Mackinnon,
Steve Mackinnon, afterword by Florence Howe. London:
Feminist Press, 1976. 203p.

This collection of portraits brings together in one volume much of Agnes Smedley's writings about Chinese women. The sketches and stories reprinted here are selected from Smedley's newspaper and magazine articles and from her books: *Chinese destinies* (1933), *China's Red Army marches* (1934), and *Battle hymn of China* (1943). The book describes the harsh life of women in China during the revolutionary years of the 1920s and 1930s.

514 **Women in Chinese societies.**
Edited by Margery Wolf, Rozane Witke. Stanford,
California: Stanford University Press, 1975. 315p.

A number of important themes appear in the papers collected in this volume, three of which are especially interesting: conflicting cultural images or stereotypes are shown to contribute to the confusing social context; the complex relationship of feminism and revolution are placed in the Chinese context; the role of women in productive labour is discussed and its relation to their oppression.

515 **Women in China.**
Edited by Marilyn Young. Ann Arbor, Michigan: Center
for Chinese Studies, University of Michigan, 1973. 259p.

The collection provides a history of the struggle for the rights of women in 20th-century China. The lesson of the Chinese experience, as presented in this volume, is clear: with or without revolution, women have to fight their own battles.

Population

516 Population and health policy in the People's Republic of China.
Chen Pizhao.   Washington DC: Smithsonian Institution
Interdisciplinary Communication Program, 1976. 157p.

The author, Ch'en Pi-chao (Chen Pizhao), places his primary emphasis on the
content of population policy. His concern is the medical service and the planned
birth programme evolved in China's rural areas since the Cultural Revolution.
Not only does he analyze the content of this policy but also tries to evaluate it in
a comparative perspective.

517 Rural health and birth planning in China.
Chen Pizhao.   Research Triangle Park, North Carolina:
International Fertility Research Programme, 1981. 115p.

This book begins with a brief summary of population policy developments in
China since 1949 and gives an overview of the political administrative system, to
which the author, Ch'en Pi-chao (Chen Pizhao), attributes much of China's success in health care, perinatal care and family planning. The author describes the
contraceptive programme from its inception and the current campaign to get
Chinese couples to limit themselves to one child. He presents his model estimates
and projections of population and vital rates from 1953 to the end of the century.

518 China's forty millions.
June Teufel Dreyer.   Cambridge, Massachusetts: Harvard
University Press, 1977. 333p.

This is the most comprehensive study yet produced of Chinese Communist policy
toward the strategically-located national minorities. The author shows that unlike
the Kuomintang, the Communists have exhibited flexibility and willingness to
modify general programmes in response to local conditions and sensitivities. This
has brought them some success, but assimilation and modernization efforts continue to produce tensions and resistance in minority areas.

519 **China's population: problems and prospects.**
Liu Zheng, Song Jian (and others). Beijing: Foreign
Language Press, 1981. 180p.

The book contains 13 essays on population growth, policies and problems in
China by some of the country's leading population specialists. The authors cite
many population data not previously available to scholars outside China.
Although all of the essays reflect the current official views on population and the
use of data is more interpretative than analytical, the style of the essays are, for
the most part, objective and straightforward.

520 **Chinese approaches to family planning.**
Leo A. Orleans. New York: Macmillan, 1980. 228p.

In contrast to their earlier efforts to reduce the nation's fertility, the author
concludes that the expanded 'planned birth' campaign in the early 1970s has
shown the world that even an overwhelmingly rural, developing nation can succeed in achieving a significant decrease in the birth rate.

521 **Every fifth child: the population of China.**
Leo A. Orleans. Stanford, California: Stanford University
Press, 1972. 191p.

The author suggests that Chinese agriculture can feed 800 million people; that
population pressure will not be a motive for expansion; and that the ratio of
Chinese to the total world population is not increasing but declining. In this
account of China's population, the author describes such recent phenomena as the
decline in China's death rate as a result of improved public health and medicine
and speculates on the possible effects of density pressure on migration, on China's
ethnic minorities and on foreign policy.

522 **China's population struggle: demographic decisions of the
People's Republic 1949-1969.**
H. Yuan Tian. Columbus, Ohio: Ohio State University,
1973. 479p.

The author, H. Yuan T'ien (H. Yuan Tian) characterizes population problems as
social and economic problems which have to be seen in developmental perspective.
He covers population numbers (rural and urban distribution), relocation and
education and training. In addition, he devotes his introduction to a survey of
Malthusianism and the Chinese negative response to its implications.

523 **Population theory in China.**
Edited and introduced by H. Yuan Tian. White Plains,
New York: Sharpe, 1980. 129p.

This is a translation of *Renkou Lilun* (*Jen-kou Li-Lun*) (*Population theory*)
which appeared in Beijing (Peking) in 1977. Translated in this volume is the first
systematic and comprehensive disclosure from the People's Republic of China
since the 1950s of how China has gone about developing a demographic theory
and methods for the practical application of population controls.

115

524 **Rural health in the People's Republic of China.**
US Department of Health and Human
Services. Washington, DC: US Government Printing
Office, 1980. 207p.

In June 1978, the eleven-member Rural Health Systems Delegation visited China
to study in detail the three-tiered prevention and treatment network for medical
care in the Chinese countryside, the training work of barefoot doctors and the
integration of medical and social systems. The report includes assessments of
medical issues, social and administrative problems, questions related to education
and training and micro- and macro-level glimpses of the rural health and perinatal care.

Overseas Chinese

525 **Silent invasion: the Chinese in Southeast Asia.**
Garth Alexander. London: MacDonald, 1974. 264p.
This is an account of the overseas Chinese in Southeast Asia, emphasizing the links between racism, Communism and political power. Events such as the anti-Chinese excesses in Indonesia, the 1969 riots in Kuala Lumpur, the Yuyitung case in the Philippines are dealt with in detail. The final chapter points to the need to develop an equitable distribution of economic and political power as the underlying goal of the region to unite Southeast Asians and local Chinese.

526 **Columbus was Chinese: discoveries and inventions of the Far East.**
Hans Bruer, translated from German by Salvator Attanasio. London: Herder & Herder, 1980. 281p.
This book contains discussions of examples of Chinese technology such as the seismograph, the compass, firearms, paper, printing and the Great Wall. The author describes the 'Silk Road' trade in detail. The final chapter 'Columbus was Chinese' argues the major thesis of the book: that the Chinese were the first people to reach the shores of North, Central and South America.

527 **The sandalwood mountains: readings and stories of the early Chinese in Hawaii.**
Tin-yuke Char. Honolulu: University Press of Hawaii, 1975. 359p.
This book seeks to cover the historical background of the Chinese in Hawaii from the 9th century to the Second World War. It deals with economic and political aspects of immigration, Chinese organizations and religious faith. In the final chapter, five immigrant families are presented through narrative accounts.

528 **The Chinese of America: from the beginning to the present.**
Jack Chen. New York: Harper, 1980. 288p.
This is an up-to-date history of Chinese-Americans from their own point of view. The author, Jack Ch'en (Chen), tells the full story of their part in building the

West, early anti-Chinese agitation, and the Exclusion Laws, in the context of American social growth.

529 Chinese migration and settlement in Australia.
C. Y. Choi.   Sydney: Sydney University Press, 1975. 129p.

The author divides the history of the Chinese in Australia into three periods coinciding with changes in immigration restrictions, residence patterns, economic activity and migrations (1861-1901, 1901-47, 1947-66). The book provides a useful summary and analysis of the demographical figures on marriage ages for different categories of Chinese, on occupational distribution and mobility.

530 The Chinese in America, 1820-1973, a chronology and fact book.
William L. Dong.   Dobbs Ferry, New York: Oceana, 1974. 150p.

The author William Tung (Dong) has organized his book into three sections: a brief chronology, a collection of the major documents relating to Chinese immigration to the United States and a bibliography.

531 The southern expansion of the Chinese people.
C. P. Fitzgerald.   New York: Praeger, 1973. 217p.

The author traces the southward expansion of Chinese influence, culture and power into Yunnan and Vietnam. He also traces the massive migration of Chinese individuals, which has resulted in large Chinese minorities in many Southeast Asian countries today. The author examines the cultural, economic and political effect of this migration on the countries concerned. He challenges the view, widely held in the West, that the Chinese population in Southeast Asia is a potential fifth column for Mao Tse-tung (Mao Zedong).

532 China and the overseas Chinese: a study of Peking's changing policy, 1949- 1970.
Stephen Fitzgerald.   New York: Columbia University Press, 1972. 268p.

This is an examination of the policy of the People's Republic of China towards the overseas Chinese, mostly in Southeast Asia. These overseas Chinese have often been regarded as a kind of fifth column used by the Chinese Communist Party to stir up revolution in their host countries. The author demonstrates the falseness of this view. He traces the development of overseas Chinese policy by the Chinese Communist Party after its accession to power in 1949, through a decline in interest after 1954, down to a vanishing point during the Cultural Revolution.

533 Southeast Asia's Chinese minorities.
Mary F. Somers Heihues.   New York: Hawthorn, 1974. 125p.

The author begins with a few pages on the realities behind Chinese population figures in the Nanyang, turns to the economic roles and activities of the Chinese in Southeast Asia and then writes chapters on 'Assimilation' and 'The organizational life of Chinese minorities'.

534· From Canton to California: the epic of Chinese immigration.
Corinne K. Heoxter.   New York: Four Winds, 1976. 304p.
This book contains a two-part overview of Chinese immigration to America. The first section gives a general history of the Chinese in the United States from 1850 to the beginning of the 20th century, including Chinese participation in the Gold Rush, railway building, agriculture and city life. The second section is a biography of Ng Poon Chew, founder of the first daily Chinese language newspaper in the United States in 1900.

535 The Mississippi Chinese: between black and white.
James W. Loewen.   Cambridge, Massachusetts: Harvard University Press, 1971. 237p.
This is a study of the 1,200 Chinese descendents who came to the Mississippi delta area in the last 19th century. The author describes how they improved their status gradually, and achieved, in 1940s and early 1950s, status very nearly equal to that of the whites.

536 Chinese Americans.
Stanford M. Lyman.   New York: Random House, 1974. 213p.
This volume discusses the origins, history in the United States and current situation of Chinese Americans. Chapters on the social organization of South China in the 19th and early 20th centuries are followed by analyses of Chinese social organization in the United States, the anti-Chinese movement of the 19th century, the social organization of Chinese Americans, the Chinese American middle class and inner-city Chinatowns.

537 The Chinese in Indonesia: five essays.
Edited by J. A. C. Mackie.   Honolulu: University Press of Hawaii, 1976. 358p.
The essays analyze the changes in the position of the Indonesian Chinese since the 1950s. They describe how the Chinese have tried to fit themselves into the changing circumstances of Indonesian society in the 20th century; how their political attitudes and influence have evolved; the implications of the anti-riot policy of the Indonesian government in the 1950s and 1960s; and the crucial role of the Chinese in Indonesian economic development.

538 An illustrated history of the Chinese in America.
Ruthanne Lum McCunn.   San Francisco: Design Enterprises, 1979. 133p.
The author concentrates on the second half of the 19th century, attempting to explain why many thousands of Chinese men came here without their families, describing the role they played in the development of the West and how rivalry and bigotry caused them to be excluded systematically from one means of livelihood after another and finally from the United States altogether. Readers learn why so many Chinese operate laundries or restaurants, why Chinatowns developed and still exist, why new immigrants continue to be exploited and why most Chinese Americans tend to be non-political.

539 Thousand pieces of gold.
Ruthanne Lum McCunn.   San Francisco: Design
Enterprises, 1981. 308p.

This is a moving true story of the Chinese-American pioneer, Polly Bemis, who
struggled against extraordinary odds to survive and carve out a life for herself in
the United States. Sold to bandits by her starving family in China, she later
worked in saloons in California's Gold Country and finally settled to farm with
her husband. Through many struggles, this remarkable woman captured the
hearts of all who knew her.

540 Longtime California: a documentary study of an American Chinatown.
Victor G. Nee, Brett De Bary.   New York: Pantheon
Books, 1973. 410p.

In their examination of San Francisco's Chinatown, the authors seek to describe
by interviews with residents of the area, three distinct societies - the bachelor
society, the small-business centered family society and an emerging society of
working class families (composed of new immigrants who have entered the community in large numbers since 1965). The authors have produced probably the
most vivid, essential guide for anyone who wants to understand the experience of
Chinese immigrants in America.

541 Fusang: the Chinese who built America.
Stan Steiner.   New York: Harper, 1979. 259p.

The author examines the role of the Chinese in America. The book is divided into
three parts. It deals with the Chinese discovery of America, the Chinese contribution to the building of America and the role of the Chinese in contemporary
America.

542 The Chinese minority in Indonesia: seven papers.
Leo Suryadinata.   Singapore: Chopmen Enterprises, 1978.
175p.

The book is comprised of seven essays, including a well-written political biography
of Liem Koen Hian (Lin Qunxian). The paper traces Liem's (Lin) development
from Chinese to Indonesian nationalist and back again, shedding interesting light
on political events in Indonesia as we pass through them. Other papers deal with
the history of the Chinese press in Indonesia, and a review of the literature on
the Chinese there.

543 Eminent Indonesian Chinese: biographical sketches.
Leo Suryadinata.   Singapore: Institute of Southeast Asian
Studies, 1978. 230p.

The book is a research aid consisting of brief items of personal information
(birth, occupation, religion, major events, etc.) on 310 prominent Indonesian
Chinese. The names are cross-indexed, so that a person can be identified by
Chinese names in their local spelling and in romanized mandarin (usually characters also supplied) as well as by names in Bahasa Indonesian.

544 Peranakan Chinese politics in Java, 1917-42.

Leo Suryadinata. Singapore: Institute of Southeast Asian
Studies, 1976. 184p.

This book is based on a thorough study of primary sources, especially Indonesian-
and Chinese-language newspapers and fills in an important gap in our knowledge
of the subject. The author is himself a Peranakan so that he is emotionally
involved in the topic. Because of this, the book has undoubtedly increased in
value.

545 Political thinking of the Indonesian Chinese, 1900-1977: a source book.

Edited by Leo Suryadinata. Singapore: University of
Singapore, 1979. 251p.

The author has prepared a source book by bringing together a number of statements by prominent or typical Indonesian Chinese spokesmen on the role of the
Chinese in Indonesian politics, ranging from separatist to assimilationists. The
author believes the major political problem for the Indonesian Chinese is one of
identity.

546 Working daughters of Hong Kong: filial piety or power in the family?

Janet W. Salaff. Cambridge, England: Cambridge
University Press, 1981. 317p.

Building on a combination of in-depth interviewing of some 28 young women of
Hong Kong over a period of 6 years and occasional abbreviated 'participant
observations' of their family and social lives, the author offers some important
new perspectives on the impact of industrialization upon family relationships in a
particular highly-urbanized Chinese setting. Although she sees some expansion of
opportunity for unmarried working daughters in terms of marriage choice, the
utilization of personal earnings, peer-group activities, and affections and prestige
within the family, she suggests that largely because of the nature and ideology of
the Chinese family system, the position of men remains superior in virtually all
respects to that of women.

547 Emigration and the Chinese lineage: the man in Hong Kong and London.

James L. Watson. Berkeley, California: University of
California Press, 1975. 240p.

Watson guides us through complex ecological changes leading to the village's loss
of its traditional rice-growing economy based on brackish land reclaimed from the
sea. He shows why emigration was the best solution to its problems and how it
was able to organize a large exodus of people. The emigrants' life in London is
described, as well as their continuing relationship with the home community.
Finally, the total impact of emigration on the life and social organization of the
village is considered.

Overseas Chinese

548 **The overseas Chinese and the 1911 revolution.**
Yan Qinghuang.   New York: Oxford University Press,
1977. 439p.

The author Yen Ching Hwang (Yan Quinghuang) presents a thoroughly
researched and minutely documented study of T'ung-ming Hui (Tongming Hui)
activities in the overseas Chinese communities in Singapore and Malaya.

Education

549 Chang Chih-tung and educational reform in China.
William Ayers.   New York: Oxford University Press, 1971.
182p.
This volume contains descriptions of Chang Chih-tung (Zhang Zhidong), one of
the last great Confucians of Imperial China, who regarded Western-inspired educational reforms as fundamental to preserve the Chinese state.

550 The 1978 college entrance examination in the People's Republic of China.
Edited by Robert D. Barendsen.   Washington, DC: US
Department of Health, Education and Welfare, 1979. 146p.
This is a timely publication that presents English translations of the official
review outline for the 1978 exam and the actual tests in six of eight subjects
comprising the examination. Of special interest are commentaries on the various
subjects by American specialists assessing the level of knowledge reflected in the
Chinese materials and attempting, where possible, to compare it with American
standards and with Chinese educational materials of the 1950s.

551 1978 Chinese English language examination.
Translated by Robert D. Barendsen.   Washington, DC: US
Government Printing Office, 1980.
A review of the examination provides some insight into what level of English-
language ability Chinese education officials had expected of their first group of
exchanges and visiting scholars. In turn, American officials may be better able to
assess a Chinese applicant's language proficiency from a reading of the examination.

Education

552 Lectures in China, 1919-1920.
John Dewey, translated from the Chinese and edited by Robert W. Clopton, Zuichen Ou. Honolulu: University Press of Hawaii, 1973. 144p.

China specialists will welcome the present volume for its contribution to a more precise delineation of Dewey's role in China's intellectual revolution which was in a critical phase at just the time Dewey was in China.

553 The East is red: a simulation game.
James F. Dunnigan, Redmond A. Simonsen. New York: Simulations Publications, 1974.

Games of strategy are often regarded as a rather esoteric hobby, something like that of collecting toy soldiers. 'The East is red' persuasively demonstrates some of the ways in which a game can be a useful paradigm of the interpretation of military, political and historical events.

554 Chinese education and society: a bibliographic guide, the Cultural Revolution and its aftermath.
Stewart E. Fraser, Guangliang Xu. White Plains, New York: International Arts and Sciences Press, 1972. 204p.

The authors provide a bibliography of sources on education in China since 1966, with sources annotated in many cases, divided into topical categories and cross referenced to other categories. English, Chinese, Japanese, French, Italian and German sources are included, with references to English translations of most of the foreign language materials. In an introductory chapter there is a summary of the range of research centres, publications and translation series which deal with Chinese education and related topics.

555 Red and expert: education in the People's Republic of China.
Ruth Gamberg. New York: Shocken, 1977. 299p.

The author visited China in June 1973 and returned for a tour in the summer of 1975. She has written a lively account of educational policy in the People's Republic of China, concentrating on ideological questions rather than institutional changes. Her concept of education is a broad one, ranging from formal institutions of nursery school through university to adult study groups, literary classes and political campaigns.

556 China's intellectuals: a devise and dissent.
Merle Goldman. Cambridge, Massachusetts: Harvard University Press, 1981. 276p.

This volume is a persuasive analysis of the interaction between political factionalism and intellectual dissent in China during the past twenty years.

557 Intellectuals and the state in modern China.
James B. Grieder. New York: Free Press, 1981. 395p.

The tumultuous century before the founding of the People's Republic of China in 1949 witnessed China at a crossroads, confused by the pull of modernity. It was the intellectuals who debated over policy in dealing with the West as China was wrenched from its planned isolation. This period and those who shaped it, are explored in this work.

558 Mao Tse-tung and education: his thoughts and teachings.
John Hawkins. Hamden, Connecticut: Linnet, Shoe String, 1974. 260p.

Drawing from both official and non-official collections of Mao's works covering a period of more than half a century, the volume traces the historical development of Mao's pedagogical philosophy and always the important features in educational policy during the various stages of the Communist Party's development.

559 Education and social change in the People's Republic of China.
John Hawkins. New York: Praeger, 1982. 335p.

The study explores critical educational and social issues in an analytical manner and assesses the positive and negative features of China's educational programme during and after the Cultural Revolution. The current 'Four modernizations' campaign is also examined. The author contends that China's experience in utilizing education as a force for social change provides lessons for both developed and developing nations.

560 Toward a New World outlook: a documentary history of education in the People's Republic of China, 1949-76.
Hu Shiming, Eli Seifman. New York: AMS Press, 1976. 335p.

The authors' stated objectives are to identify a number of distinct periods of educational development, to analyze the distinctive features of each of these educational periods and to offer a selection of materials from Chinese sources which document and illustrate the nature of each of these periods of educational development.

561 From muskets to missiles: politics and professionalism in the Chinese army, 1945-1981.
Harlan W. Jencks, Harvey L. Nelsen. Boulder, Colorado: Westview Press, 1982. 322p.

This book provides a detailed description and evaluation of the military, political, economic, social and educational context within which the People's Liberation Army officers have functioned since the civil war (1945-49). Its aim is to evaluate the personal commitments and professional implications of a military career in the People's Republic of China.

562 The Dewey experiment in China: educational reform and political power in the early republic.
Barry Keenan. Cambridge, Massachusetts: Harvard University Press, 1977. 335p.

John Dewey spent 2 years (1919-21) touring China and lecturing. In this volume, the author examines Dewey's 78 lectures delivered, translated and published in China to discover what made them so attractive to the Chinese who regarded Dewey as a modern-day sage.

Education

563 Chinese educational policy: changes and contradictions 1949-79.
Jan-Ingvar Lofstedt. Atlantic Highlands, New Jersey: Humanities Press, 1980. 284p.

The author portrays the zigzag development of China's educational policies as a product of the political/ideological debates that have dominated the 30 years of the People's Republic of China. He offers a broad ideological interpretation through his discussion of Marxist educational theory and the Chinese approximation of that theory with reference to basic concepts of Marxist thought. He also traces the development of Soviet educational policy in terms of its impact on the evolution of the Chinese system.

564 Fei Hsiao-t'ung: the dilemma of a Chinese intellectual.
Edited by James P. McCough. White Plains, New York: Sharpe, 1979. 160p.

This volume presents the views and positions of one of China's leading social scientists and those of his critics, providing unparalleled documentation on the fate of a Chinese intellectual. It makes an important contribution to our understanding of the social and political background of the present revival of social science activity in the People's Republic of China.

565 China's school in flux: report by the State Education Leaders Delegation, US; US National Committee on US-China relations.
Edited by Ronald Montaperto, Jay Henderson. White Plains, New York: Sharpe, 1980. 200p.

This is one in a series of reports from American educators who visited schools in China in 1977. There are chapters on such items as early childhood education, admission, curricula, decision-making structures, and family and community involvement. It provides a good overview of trends and issues.

566 Education in modern China.
R. F. Price. Boston, Massachusetts: Routledge, 1980. rev. ed. 385p.

The book examines the clash between tradition and the Cultural Revolution in the educational system and focuses on reversals since Mao's death. The book belongs to a series on world education designed for students of comparative education. The author summarizes clearly Mao's thoughts on education, the educational policies since 1949 and the historical, economic and sociological background of educational change in China.

567 Education and popular literacy in Ch'ing China.
Evelyn Sakakida Rawski. Ann Arbor, Michigan: University of Michigan Press, 1979. 294p.

For a long time it was assumed that the vast majority of Chinese in the late imperial period were illiterate. Using a variety of analytical strategies and many different data, the author concludes that elementary education in the Ch'ing (Qing) period was extremely cheap and therefore available to almost any male Chinese (even those from poor rural areas) who wanted it badly enough, that it was possible to acquire functional literacy relatively quickly; that by the late 19th century 30 to 45 per cent of China's men and almost 2 to 10 per cent of its women 'knew how to read and write', making an average of almost one literate person per family; and that the male literacy rate at this time was comparable to those of contemporary Japan and 17th-century England.

568 The making of a model citizen in Communist China.
Charles P. Riley, Paul Godwin, Dennis Doolin. Stanford, California: Hoover Institution, 1971. 402p.

The volume analyzes the political, social and technological values that China is teaching its youth. It helps explain the course and violence of the Red Guards' movement. The analysis is based on school texts used on the mainland and the second half of the book is composed of translations of selections from these texts.

569 Red Guard factionalism and the Cultural Revolution in Guangzhou.
Stanley Rosen. Boulder, Colorado: Westview Press, 1981. 320p.

This study examines the causes of factionalism within China's Red Guard during the Cultural Revolution. Focusing primarily on middle-school students in Guangzhou (Canton), but looking also at university students, the author reaches two primary conclusions: that the class origin of middle-school tended to determine whether they joined forces with the rebel or the conservative factions and that the Cultural Revolution was contested most fiercely at those secondary schools that contained significant numbers of students of cadre and intellectual family origin - the good schools. He examines the interests of each of the factions, their constituencies and sources of support and the issues that divided rebels and conservatives, as viewed in light of post-Mao politics.

570 Revolutionary education in China: documents and commentary.
Edited by Peter J. Seybolt. White Plains, New York: International Arts and Sciences, 1973. 460p.

The volume illustrates and analyzes recent revolutionary changes in the Chinese educational system and provides background and perspective. The material translated from the current period focuses on the radical departure of Chinese education from both traditional and Western goals and methods and helps explain why the Chinese regard the transformation of their educational system as indispensable for the transformation of their society.

571 Educators' source book on China: a selected list of information resources.
Alice H. Songe, Pauline B. Mangin. Munich, GFR: Saur Verlag, 1981. 80p.

The authors have compiled a modest but useful list of education sources on China for elementary and secondary school teachers as well as for the general reader at the post-secondary and college level. The book contains over 1,000 bibliographic entries from 1970 to 1980 that include books, monographs, dissertations, journals, audiovisual materials and teaching packets. Sources are conveniently divided by educational level and subject. Also found are lists of China-related journals (in English), publishers and audiovisual distributors.

572 Mathematics education in China: its growth and development.
Frank Swetz. Cambridge, Massachusetts: MIT Press, 1974. 364p.

This book consists of a description and assessment of the main trends in mathematical education at the primary and middle-school levels in China. He argues that in contrast to previous concepts of education as an 'elitist activity', education was now geared to fulfill the industrial and socio-economic necessities of the country.

573 China's intellectual dilemma: politics and university enrollment, 1949-1978.
Robert Taylor. Vancouver, British Columbia: University of British Columbia Press, 1980. 306p.

In analyzing the conflicting philosophies which have shaped educational systems and events leading up to the national conference of 1978, the author deals with issues that are central to understanding China's modern development and the goals of Chinese society as a whole.

574 Education under Mao: class and competition in Canton schools, 1960-1980.
Jonathan Unger. New York: Columbia University Press, 1982. 293p.

This volume contains a detailed analysis of the educational system of the People's Republic of China, highlighting the debate between Maoists and modernists.

575 Party and professionals: the political role of teachers in contemporary China.
Gordon White. Armonk, New York: Sharpe, 1980. 273p.

The author provides a comprehensive view of teacher recruitment, working conditions, social status and wages and benefits, as well as the complex interactions between the Communist Party and these professionals. He also provides a systematic perspective on the situation of teachers, viewed through the framework of the distribution of social goods. The accompanying appendix of documents is well selected and organized and provides a valuable complement.

576 The Maoist educational revolution.
Theodore Xien Chen. New York: Praeger, 1974. 295p.

The book consists of a description and analysis of Chinese education after the Cultural Revolution, with an appended set of educational documents from the Chinese press, mostly dating from the post-Cultural Revolution period. Throughout the book, the author, Theodore Hsi-en Ch'en (Xien Chen), utilizes the Cultural Revolution notion of two opposing educational lines: the bourgeois revisionist line and the Maoist revolutionary line, which he calls the educational revolution.

577 **Chinese education since 1949: academic and revolutionary models.**
Theodore Xien Chen.   New York: Pergamon Press, 1981.
259p.

The author, Theodore Hsi-en Ch'en (Xien Chen) portrays the zigzag development of China's educational policies as a product of the political/ideological debates that have dominated the 30 years of the People's Republic of China. He examines these shifts in terms of two contending development models of education.

578 **An introduction to education in the People's Republic of China and US-China educational exchange.**
Washington, DC: US-China Education Clearinghouse, 1980.
130p.

This volume contains four sections of material. Part I provides an overview of China's higher education, institutions of higher education and research institutes. Part II summarizes current education exchanges with the People's Republic of China including an overview of the fields of study of Chinese students and scholars in the United States and an outline of numbers in various countries. Current US-China governmental education-related agreements are also summarized. In part III, the US-China educational exchange process and related issues are discussed. The final section has appendices listing Chinese 'key' universities, institutions of the Chinese Academy of Sciences, China's major ministries and agencies with academic concerns, US organizations involved in exchanges with China, key contacts within the US government and bibliographies on education and science and technology in China.

China: a resource and curriculum guide.
See item no. 1368.

Higher education and research in the People's Republic of China: institutional profiles.
See item no. 1420.

Medicine and Health

579 **Health care in the People's Republic of China: bibliography with abstract.**
Shahid Akhtar. Ottawa, Canada: International
Development Research Center, 1975. 182p.
The major emphasis of the literature surveyed is on the Chinese approaches to health care both in rural and urban areas from 1949 through 1974. The majority of entries are published works, including books, articles or chapters in books and articles appearing in professional journals. Unpublished documents and theses were listed if relevant. The bibliography also includes a list of the names and addresses of the authors and researchers, research and university study centres and libraries with special collections in the field of China's public health.

580 **An American transplant: the Rockefeller Foundation and Peking Union Medical College.**
Mary Brown Bullock. Berkeley, California: University of
California Press, 1980. 280p.
The author sees adaptation and assimilation as crucial to cultural transplantation. On this basis she prevents a mixed picture of the Peking (Beijing) Union Medical College's achievements and non-achievements. Among the former were public health works inspired by John B. Grant and midwife's training guided by Marian Yang as well as the curing of endemic diseases like kala-azar.

581 **Proceedings, US-China pharmacology symposium.**
Edited by J. J. Burns, Patricia Jones
Tsuchitani. Washington, DC: National Academy of
Sciences, 1980. 354p.
This report includes selected papers presented by the Chinese Pharmacology Delegation and the American participants at the three-day meeting at the National Academy of Sciences, Washington, DC, 29-31 October 1979. The symposium was the first bilateral scientific symposium between the United States and China to be held in the United States.

130

582 **Essentials of Chinese acupuncture.**
Compiled by Colleges of Traditional Chinese Medicine of
Beijing, Shanghai, and Nanjing, Acupuncture Institute of
the Academy of Traditional Chinese Medicine. Beijing:
Foreign Language Press, 1980. 275p.
This book is a translation and updated English edition of the famous *Zhongguo
Zhenjuxue Gaiyao* (*Chung-Kuo Chen-Chiu-Hsueh Kai-yao*). This edition is
clearly illustrated and presents the basic theories of traditional Chinese medicine
and its benefits in clinical practice.

583 **More than herbs and acupuncture.**
Grey E. Dimond. New York: Norton, 1975. 223p.
The author was a member of the first American medical delegation to the
People's Republic of China in 1971. He gives a first-hand account, based on his
first trip and two subsequent ones, of Chinese medicine and health care. Although
he discusses acupuncture, he devotes most of the book to medical education in
China and the way in which it has been moulded to fit the needs of the great
mass of people.

584 **Chinese herbs and therapy.**
Hengyan Xu, William S. Peacher. New York: Oriental
Healing Arts, 1976. 233p.
In conjunction with the Oriental Healing Arts Institute, the authors, Heng-yen
Hsu (Hengyan Xu) and William Peacher, have compiled a comprehensive study
to introduce the 5,000 year-old Chinese system of medicine to Americans. The
book will do much to introduce traditional Chinese herbal medicines to the
interested Western practitioner.

585 **Cancer in China: the report of the American Cancer
Delegation's visit to the People's Republic of China.**
Edited by Henry S. Kaplan, Patricia Jones
Tsuchitani. New York: Liss, 1976. 240p.
Topics of special interest covered in the report are the impact of migration on
epidemiology; the unusual phenomenon and demographics of nasopharyngeal,
liver, embryonic and oesophageal cancer epidemics; the use of amputation and
reimplantation for treating neoplasms of extremities; and the incorporation of
Chinese traditional medicine into treatment protocol. The report also evaluates
the methods and facilities for diagnosis and treatment of various cancers, examines research findings and assesses the beneficial and problematic results associated with the Chinese approach to cancer prevention.

586 **The politics of medicine in China: the policy process,
1949-77.**
David M. Lampton. Boulder, Colorado: Westview Press,
1977. 301p.
The study has the objective of examining and explaining changes in Chinese
health care policy during the 1949-77 period. The questions which this study
seeks to answer are: why have policies changed, why have they moved in the
directions they have and what does this tell us about the Chinese policy process?.
Several areas of medical policy will be considered: medical education, medical

research, the structure of the health care delivery system, service financing, the conditions of employment for physicians, traditional medicine and the campaign to bring medicine to the masses.

587 **Patients and healers in the context of culture.**
Arthur Leinman.   Berkeley, California: University of California Press, 1980. 153p.

Drawn from field studies, primarily in Taiwan, this book is a contribution to medical anthropology and cross-cultural psychiatry that inquires how clinical categories and processes are organized in society.

588 **Chinese medical modernization: policy continuity across revolutionary periods.**
AnElissa Lucas.   New York: Praeger, 1982. 220p.

The goal of Chinese state medicine has been to build a national network of medical and health care institutions serving the needs of both rural villagers and urban centres. The author examines Chinese efforts to extend medical services to the entire population through this network. She also discusses the basic problem of attracting medical personnel to work in the rural sector.

589 **Health policies and services in China, 1974.**
Leo A. Orleans.   Washington, DC: US Government Printing Office, 1974. 42p.

The author reviews the emphasis placed on preventive health, describes some of the operating characteristics of the health system, evaluates the status of efforts to integrate functionally Chinese and Western medicine and analyzes the changes in China's approach to the recruitment and training of medical, paramedical and auxiliary staff.

590 **The theoretical foundations of Chinese medicine: system of correspondence.**
Manfred Porkert.   Cambridge, Massachusetts: MIT Press, 1978. 286p.

This volume is the first in a projected series aimed at elucidating for Western readers the theoretical and practical aids of diagnosis, pathology, pharmacology, acupuncture and chemotherapy in the classical Chinese medical tradition.

591 **Acupuncture.**
Shanghai College of Traditional Medicine, translated and edited by John O'Connor, Dan Bensky.   Beijing: Eastland Press, 1981. 741p.

First published in 1974 by one of China's most prominent schools of medicine, this book has become recognized throughout the world as the most comprehensive textbook in the field of acupuncture. The present edition marks the first complete translation in a Western language. Included are descriptions of more than a thousand acupuncture points, hundreds of prescriptions, both ancient and modern, for the treatment of numerous diseases and a detailed discussion of a variety of acupuncture techniques and modalities ranging from ear, head, hand and foot acupuncture to moxibustion, ultraviolet and surgical techniques.

592 The health of China.
Ruth Sidel, Victor W. Sidel.   New York: Beacon Press, 1980. 228p.

In 1978, Ruth and Victor Sidel were members of the first US medical delegation to China in more than 20 years. From their first-hand observations on that and subsequent trips, they have written a new and complete overview of the revolutionary changes that took place in Chinese medicine, urban organization, child care and education during the 1970s. The authors examine the ways in which China is assimilating Western influences while maintaining her own distinctive health and human services methods.

593 Serve the people: observations on medicine in the People's Republic of China.
Victor W. Sidel, Ruth Sidel.   New York: May, 1973. 317p.

Stressing the post-Cultural Revolution period, the nine chapters in the book cover the development of health services, health care in the cities, health care in the countryside, the role of the community and the patient in health care, medical education, the integration of traditional and Western medicine, treatment of mental illness, health administration and research and a summary.

594 Acupuncture and moxibustion: a handbook for the barefoot doctors of China.
Translated by Martin Elliot Silverstein, Yilok Zhang, Nathaniel Macon.   New York: Schocken Books, 1975. 118p.

This book is sub-titled 'The official handbook for the barefoot doctors of China' and it is the actual handbook used by the barefoot doctors of Hopei (Hebei) province. The aim is to meet the urgent need of the medical workers who serve the farming community and it is a selection of material culled from past medical publications of interest to farm-community practitioners.

595 Rural health in the People's Republic of China.
US Rural Health System Delegation.   Washington, DC: Department of Health and Human Services, 1980. 207p.

The report includes assessments of medical issues, social and administrative problems, questions related to education and training and micro- and macro-level glimpses of the rural health care system. The report raises some provocative questions regarding the integration of Chinese traditional medicine with Western medical concepts and the transferability of the Chinese experience to America.

596 The complete book of acupuncture.
Stephen Thomas Zhang.   Beijing: Celestial Arts, 1976. 244p.

The author discusses the philosophy and development of acupuncture and stresses that acupuncture, unlike Western medicine, is natural and preventive. Illustrations and charts accompany the discussion of acupuncture points, the method of diagnosis and treatment for common diseases.

597 **Acupuncture anaesthesia in the People's Republic of China, a trip report of the American Acupuncture Anaesthesia Study Group.**

Washington, DC: National Academy of Sciences, 1976. 73p.

The delegation went to 16 hospitals and observed 48 surgical procedures which used acupuncture anaesthesia to control pain. They concluded: in addition to lacking a theoretical basis for explaining acupuncture, there also is no standardization of needle placement or methods of stimulation. While Chinese scientists are making efforts to study this phenomenon, their work is only in its early stages. The report includes an evaluation of each operation observed and discusses the effectiveness of acupuncture in controlling operative pain and factors affecting the success of acupuncture as an anaesthetic. It also discusses the implications of acupuncture for Western surgery and describes Chinese and Western research efforts with acupuncture.

598 **A barefoot doctor's manual: the American translation of the official Chinese paramedical manual.**

New York: Running Press, 1977. 948p.

This volume is a compilation of the techniques that Chinese paramedical workers use in the countryside to improve the health of the people and provide basic medical care. It includes certain techniques of acupuncture, the use of medicinal herbs, basic hygiene and much more.

Law

599 **Dictionary of Chinese law and government.**
Philip R. Bilancia. Stanford, California: Stanford
University Press, 1980. 840p.

Indispensable to anyone studying the institutional life of contemporary China, this new dictionary contains more than 25,000 Chinese terms, at least 15,000 examples of usage and over 30,000 cross-references. The coverage extends from 1930 to 1977, and treats virtually every aspect of every activity dealt with by government in China since 1939; terms of political, historical and sociological interest, as well as terms related strictly to law and administration. The dictionary uses the Wade-Giles system of transliteration, but it also contains a Chinese transliteration conversion table for easy conversion to Pinyin and other systems.

600 **Law in imperial China.**
Derk Bodde, Clarence Morris. Philadelphia, Pennsylvania:
University of Pennsylvania Press, 1978. 386p.

This is the first book to provide a comprehensive picture of the basic concept and function of imperial Chinese law.

601 **Law and justice: the legal system in China, 2400 BC to 1960 AD.**
Philip M. Chen. New York: Dunellen, 1973. 234p.

The author, Philip Ch'en (Chen) tries to explain the typicality of Chinese law and the endurance of traditional Chinese principles which are fundamentally divergent from the principles of law in the state under the rule of law. He assimilates the rules of socialist community life with the rites of Confucian philosophy and calls them 'Communist Li'.

602 Contemporary Chinese law: research problems and perspectives.
Edited by Jerome Alan Cohen. Cambridge, Massachusetts: Harvard University Press, 1970. 380p.

Thirty specialists in various disciplines explore the possibility of interpreting Communist Chinese law. Problems confronted include accessibility of materials, modern Chinese legal terminology and difficulties in translating Japanese, Soviet and Nationalist Chinese studies on the topic.

603 China's practice of international law: some case studies.
Edited by Jerome Alan Cohen. Cambridge, Massachusetts: Harvard University Press, 1972. 417p.

This book deals with aspects of Chinese foreign policy involving international law - notably disputes with Russia, Japan and India, as well as cases dealing with foreign diplomats and foreign organizations. Cohen and his collaborators conclude that China's approach to the law, like that of other countries, is pragmatic, not principled.

604 People's China and international law: a documentary study.
Jerome Alan Cohen, Qiu Hongda. Princeton, New Jersey: Princeton University Press, 1974. 1970. 2 vols.

The authors pieced together 524 items of literature derived from pertinent official acts and statements, editorials of Communist Party and government organs, dispatches of Chinese and foreign news agencies, as well as opinions of individual specialists in the field. The items are arranged in 47 chapters, which in turn are divided into 10 parts. Each part is preceded by a concise introduction to what follows and each chapter or item is generally supplemented by a number of lucid explanatory notes with detailed bibliographic information. At the end of the study, there is a 12-page glossary, an exhaustive 66-page bibliography, a page list of source materials in the Chinese and Japanese languages and an index.

605 Essays on China's legal tradition.
Edited by Jerome A. Cohen, Randle Edwards, Fumei Zhang Chen. Princeton, New Jersey: Princeton University Press, 1980. 420p.

Essays spanning Chinese history from the Zhou (Chou) through Qing (Ch'ing) dynasties, cover law in commercial transactions, code commentaries on judicial process, law and slavery. Their analysis of previously neglected aspects of the traditional legal system illuminates the impact of the past upon specific areas of Chinese life and, in so doing, stimulates a reappraisal of imperial Chinese justice that is long overdue.

606 English-Chinese law dictionary.
William S. H. Hong. Hong Kong: Chinese University, 1972. 179p.

The author practiced and taught law in Shanghai in the 1930s at a time when the new Chinese civil code was being put into effect. This short dictionary is a product both of that experience and of the need, in Hong Kong, of translating accurately into Chinese the complex and sometimes obscure terminology of the English legal system.

607 **The T'ang code: general principles.**
Translated by Wallace Johnson. Princeton, New Jersey:
Princeton University Press, 1979. vol. 1. 364p.

In its aim to maintain a strict hierarchy of privilege and liability for punishment among the members of society and harmony between the human and the natural world, the T'ang (Tang) code reflects the primary purpose of traditional Chinese law. The code, first promulgated in AD 653, has been the single most important collection of laws in the history of East Asia and the volume is the first complete translation into any Western language.

608 **Law in Chinese foreign policy: Communist China and selected problems of international law.**
Shaozhuan Leng, Qiu Hongda. New York: Oceana, 1972. 387p.

Using mainland Chinese sources as their research base, the authors examine the international legal positions taken by China with regard to space, the UN, the status of Taiwan and other problems. Particular attention is given to the theoretical tension between a universal system (China) and the multiplicity of the traditional legal system.

609 **Law and politics in China's foreign trade.**
Edited by Victor H. Li. Seattle, Washington: University of Washington Press, 1977. 467p.

This volume contains thirteen papers originally presented at a conference hosted by the School of Oriental and African Studies, Contemporary China Institute in London in 1971. Most have been updated to cover events through 1973. Seven of the papers examine China's bilateral trade with individual countries, six treat more general topics and an illuminating introduction has been added by the editor.

610 **Law without lawyers: a comparative view of law in the US and China.**
Victor H. Li. Boulder, Colorado: Westview Press, 1978. 110p.

The author offers an invaluable understanding of Chinese society today as well as his own appraisal of the legal system. The book opens with a discussion of historical and ideological reasons for China's rejection of Western-style law, with its codes, fixed procedures and preference for stability and predictability. Such a system, the author argues, would be inappropriate in revolutionary China, where rapidly changing social and economic conditions require an equally rapid change in the law.

611 **Treaties of the People's Republic of China, 1949-1978: an annotated compilation.**
Victor H. Li. Boulder, Colorado: Westview Press, 1978. 110p.

This annotated compilation investigates the Chinese use of treaties to pursue foreign policy aims. The treaties reflect the political, economic and ideological currents that shape the course of international relations that have been established or are about to be established. They are listed in five groups - friendship, boundaries, commerce, consular and dual nationality - each of which begins with a brief essay analyzing the importance of the specific treaties.

612 Agreements of the People's Republic of China: a calendar of events, 1966-80.
Qiu Hongda. New York: Praeger, 1981. 350p.

This book deals with agreements concluded by the People's Republic of China between 1966-80. The main role of this calendar is to emphasize the role of treaties in China's international relations. This volume includes all official and semi-official exchanges of commitments in their widest sense, involving the People's Republic between 1966 and 1980.

613 The People's Republic of China and the law of treaties.
Qiu Hongda. Cambridge, Massachusetts: Harvard University Press, 1972. 178p.

The author argues that China's concept of treaty-law does not differ substantially from that of the West, except in her development out of her own historical experience of the concept of unequal treaties. International law, for China as for other nations, will be respected only as long as it serves political ends.

614 Chinese treaties: the post-revolutionary restoration of international law and order.
Garry L. Scott. New York: Oceana, 1975. 312p.

A quantitative study of Chinese treaty-making leads to the conclusion that the People's Republic of China follows the normal practices of the status quo powers in its international obligations and regards treaty commitments less seriously than do more ideologically conservative nations.

615 Law and policy in China's foreign policy.
James Jie Xiong. New York: Columbia University Press, 1972. 435p.

The author deals with such matters as sovereignty, territorial jurisdiction and the law of treaties. He examines Chinese conduct in various crises which involved its compliance with treaties and its attitude toward force in international relations. The Chinese are shown to be tough and unrelenting negotiators, but once the terms of a treaty have been settled, they are described as diligent in carrying out their commitments.

616 Political imprisonment in the People's Republic of China: an Amnesty International report.
Amnesty International Publications: distributed in the United States by Random House, 1978. 176p.

This report is a compilation from official documents and unofficial refugee reports concerning the status of political and civil freedoms in China.

Politics and Government

History

617 **The bureaucracy of Han times.**
Hans Belenstein.   New York: Cambridge University Press, 1980. 385p.
In this comprehensive and fully-documented study of Chinese bureaucracy during the periods 202 BC-AD 9 and AD 25-189, the author analyzes and describes the central and local administrations, the army, civil service recruitment and power in government. He includes alphabetical lists of all Chinese official titles with their English and Chinese equivalents.

618 **The Chinese Machiavelli: 3,000 years of China statecraft.**
Dennis Bloodworth, Jingbing Bloodworth.   New York: Farrar, Straus, 1976. 346p.
In this book, the veteran correspondent for *The Observer* (London), and his wife study the Chinese power game in the framework of chronological history intending to provide the general reader with an historical perspective on current Chinese attitudes and policies.

619 **Urban change in China: politics and development in Tsinan, Shantung, 1890-1949.**
David D. Buck.   Madison, Wisconsin: University of Wisconsin Press, 1978. 296p.
This book clearly reflects the author's prodigious exploitation of the published and unpublished, primary and secondary sources available outside of China, but the results are also constrained by the limitations of these materials themselves.

620 **Rebels and bureaucrats: China's December.**
John Israel, Donald W. Lein. Berkeley, California: University of California Press, 1976. 305p.

The December 9'ers take their name from the 1935 student demonstrations held in Peking (Beijing) in protest of Japanese encroachments in North China. The account examines the December 9'ers from three perspectives. First, it discusses the concerns which caused the students to protest. Then, it describes from contemporary records the characters of several student leaders. Finally, it traces the careers of these former student rebels from 1936 to 1966. They suffered heavily in the Cultural Revolution. An eminent survivor is Ambassador Huang Hua.

621 **Selected papers no. 3, proceedings of the NEH Modern China Project, 1977-78: political leadership and social change at the local level in China from 1850 to the present.**
Susan Mann Jones. Chicago: Center for Far Eastern Studies, University of Chicago, 1980.

This book includes Ch'en Yung-fa's (Chen Yongfa) 'The wartime bandits and their local rivals'; Susan Mann Jones' 'The organization of trade at the county level'; Philip A. Kuhn's 'Local taxation and finance in Republican China'; David Strand and Richard R. Weiner's 'Social movements and political discourse in 1920's Peking (Beijing)'; Tang Tsou (Dang Zou), March Blecher and Mitch Meiser's 'Organization, growth and equality in Xiynag (Hsi-Yang) county'; and Guy S. Alitto's 'Rural elites in transition'.

622 **Szechwan and the Chinese Republic: provincial militarism and the central power, 1911-1938.**
Robert Rapp. New Haven, Connecticut: Yale University Press, 1974. 198p.

The author looks at the experience of Szechwan (Sichuan) under warlord rule in the 1920s and 1930s, and at its distant but complicated relationship with the Nanking (Nanjing) government during the latter part of that period. Besides its discussion of a region, this book is also a study of a particularly relentless and brutal form of warlordism.

623 **The politics of Chinese Communism: Kiangsi under the Soviets.**
Ilpyong J. Kim. Berkeley, California: University of California Press, 1973. 232p.

This volume focuses on the development of Chinese Communism during the Kiangsi (Jiangxi) Soviet and especially on the political changes initiated by Mao Tse-tung (Mao Zedong). The author emphasizes Mao's theory of mass politics and the techniques used to achieve his goals. Specific topics discussed include Mao's theories on administration, local government, and cadre education, and his development of mass campaigns in the areas of land investigation, cooperatives and economic construction.

Politics and Government. History

624 Region and nation, the Kwangsi clique in Chinese politics 1925-1937.
Diana Lary. Cambridge, England: Cambridge University Press, 1975. 276p.

By focusing on the Kwangsi (Guangxi) clique, the book is able to deal with two important matters at the same time: military activities and political changes in Kwangsi (Guangxi) province and the participation of regional militarists in Kuomingtang politics. The Kwangsi (Guangxi) clique was a loose grouping of military leaders who in 1928 controlled 350,000 troops, four of China's southern provinces and the major cities of Canton (Guangzhou), Wuhan and Peking (Beijing). A year later, the clique's power burst and leaders retired to their base in south-west China, and there they carried out a campaign of local reform.

625 Political institutions in traditional China: major issues.
Edited by James T. C. Liu. New York: Wiley, 1974. 156p.

This is a modest book of 150 pages consisting of reprinted selections of well-known articles and books. It ought to be useful to students of China's traditional policy who want a quick round-up of some of the influential ideas of the 1950s and 1960s.

626 The consolidation of the South China frontier.
George V. H. Mosely. Berkeley, California: University of California Press, 1973. 225p.

Large ethnic minorities along the southern Chinese frontier from the Himalayas to the Pacific pose a special problem for Peking (Beijing). The author's findings, based on first-hand research in the field as well as published sources, attempt to define an historical continuity between China's modern and pre-Revolution minority policy.

627 Peking politics, 1918-1923: factionalism and the failure of constitutionalism.
Andrew J. Nathan. Berkeley, California: University of California Press, 1976. 318p.

Although political discussion in early Republican China centred on the faith that a proper constitution could make China strong, political behaviour, structured by factions, repeatedly brought constitutions to naught. In analyzing both the sources of the Constitutionalist faith and the destructive effects of factionalism, the author studies two important episodes of conflict: struggles involving President Hsu Shi-Ch'ang (Xu Shichang), 1918-20, and those surrounding the restoration of Li Yuan-hung (Li Yuanghong), 1922-23.

628 Documents of the Chinese Communist Party, 1927-1930.
Edited by Hyobom Pak. Hong Kong: Union Research Institute, 1971. 769p.

Many of the documents, mostly from the 1927-29 period, assembled and translated by the editor, reveal numerous details on earlier factional struggles and on other inescapable problems that followed the Nationalist destruction of the first United Front.

629 **Cadres, commanders and commissars: the training of the Chinese Communist leadership, 1920-45.**
Jane L. Price. Boulder, Colorado: Westview Press, 1976. 226p.

The author places the subject in an historical context. Tracing the evolution of the Chinese Communist educational system for higher-level leadership cadres from the May 4th Movement to the end of the Sino-Japanese War, she is able to convey a sense of continuity and development in the Chinese Communist Party's cadre policy.

630 **Warlords politics: conflict and coalition in the modernization of Republican China.**
Lucian W. Pye. New York: Praeger, 1971. 212p.

This study deals primarily with Chinese politics north of the Yangtzu (Yangzi) between 1920 and 1928. In his analysis, the author examines the relationships between the warlords and their shifting coalitions, their relations with the Republic's cabinets and the composition and function of the cabinets. He treats the warlords' problems in building and financing their organizations and their propaganda techniques. His material is historical, but in presenting a series of case studies of alliance formation and dissolution, he also shows the political operation of the warlord system and its impact on China's modernization.

631 **The government and politics of China, 1912-1949.**
Qian Tuansheng. Stanford, California: Stanford University Press, 1970. 257p.

This volume by Ch'ien Tuan-sheng (Qian Tuansheng) casts new light on the collapse of Nationalist China. Appendices give texts of the various constitutions and a bibliography is included.

632 **Warlord politics in China, 1916-1928.**
Qi Xisheng. Stanford, California: Stanford University Press, 1976. 282p.

After a description of the emergence of military factions after the death of Yuan Shih-k'ai (Yuan Shikai), the author, Ch'i Hsi-sheng (Qi Xisheng), analyzes their membership, goals, capabilities and sources of cohesion, offering a convincing explanation in balance-of-power terms for the baffling advances, retreats, clashes and changes in allegiance that have puzzled students of the era.

633 **A madman of Ch'u: the Chinese myth of loyalty and dissent.**
Laurence A. Schneider. Berkeley, California: University of California Press, 1980. 231p.

The author's wide-ranging study traces the evolution of one of China's most enduring and controversial madmen, the legendary southern poet Ch'u Yuan (Chu Yuan), for two thousand years a central figure in art, folklore and political debate.

634 **Provincial militarism and the Chinese Republic: the Yunnan Army, 1905-25.**
Donald S. Sutton.   Ann Arbor, Michigan: University of Michigan Press, 1980. 318p.

The Yunnan Army of 1916 was disciplined, devoted to a cause, supported by the people. Ten years later, the same army was wrecking provincial finances, oppressing its neighbours, dealing in opium and avoiding battle at all costs. From revolutionary militarism to warlordism, the story of the Yunnan Army reflects recurring themes in modern Chinese history.

635 **China: a political history, 1917-1980.**
Richard C. Thornton.   Boulder, Colorado: Westview Press, 1981. 500p.

The author puts the events of the past eight years in China into historical perspective in this updated and expanded version of his textbook on China's political history since 1917 (first published in 1973). With the additional material, the book now stands as the most detailed account available. He deals with every significant issue that has confronted the leaders of revolutionary China and discusses the origins of the political landscape of the People's Republic of China.

636 **Government and politics in Kuomintang China 1927-1937.**
Hongmao Tian.   Stanford, California: Stanford University Press, 1972. 226p.

This volume analyzes the Nationalists' political and administrative institutions in both the capital and the province, covering such topics as leadership, recruitment and finance. The author, Hung-mao T'ien (Hongmao Tian) seeks to identify the country's political élites, to show how they operated and to assess their performances in terms of the régime's goals of national unity and political order. Information is also given on the main Kuomintang factions (the Blue Shirts, the Communist cliques and the Political Study Clique), on the social composition and educational backgrounds of provincial governors and other élites.

637 **The Chinese high command: a history of Communist military politics, 1927-71.**
William W. Whitson, Chenxia Huang.   New York: Praeger, 1973. 638p.

Campaigns and battles are described in meticulous detail, the careers of the main participants are unravelled and illuminated. This huge mine of information is accompanied by numerous elaborate maps and charts, as well as name and subject indices.

638 **Revolutionary leaders of modern China.**
Zhundu Xue.   New York: Oxford University Press, 1970. 368p.

This book contains original articles and reprints concerning important Chinese leaders, not all of them familiar to Westerners, of the three revolutions of modern China: the T'aiping (Taiping) rebellion, the Republican Revolution and the Communist movements.

639 **China's examination hell: the civil service examinations of imperial China.**
Ichisada Yiyazaki, translated from Japanese by Conrad Schirokauer. New York: Weatherhill, 1976. 145p.

This is not a history of the examination system but a study of the way in which it operated in its fully-developed form, with background glances at formative periods in its long history.

Hu Shih and the Chinese renaissance: liberalism in the Chinese revolution 1917-1937.
See item no. 1245.

China's uninterrupted revolution: from 1840 to the present.
See item no. 1254.

Chinese revolutionary memoirs: 1919-1949.
See item no. 1261.

Contemporary

640 **Militarism in Peking's policies.**
G. Aplain, U. Mitayev. Moscow: Progress, 1980. 244p.

The authors discuss post-Mao development in China and conclude that Leftist Maoism has been replaced by pragmatic Maoism designed to secure the 'hegemonistic aspirations of Peking (Beijing)'. According to the authors, the strengthening of the present régime and the expansion of China's economic and military power may lead to greater Chinese bellicosity in the international arena.

641 **Chinese politics and the Cultural Revolution.**
Byung-joon Ahn. Seattle, Washington: University of Washington Press, 1976. 392p.

The heart of this book deals with the dramatic eight year period from the Great Leap Forward in 1958 to the beginning of the Cultural Revolution in 1966. Proceeding chronologically, the author first describes the retreat from the Great Leap Forward between 1958 and 1962, focusing on both the policy adjustments undertaken by the Communist Party and the criticism of the Leap by intellectuals and ranking Party leaders. Then, he analyzes the disputes within the central Party leadership between 1962 and 1965 over such issues as rural organization, industrial management, agricultural mechanization, education, public health, culture and foreign policy. Finally, he outlines the process of making and implementing the Cultural Revolution - a process that occurred, in his analysis, between November 1965 and the 11th Plenum of August 1966.

642 The 11th central committee of the Communist Party of China.
Wolfgang Bartke.   Hamburg, GFR: Institut für
Asienkunde, 1977. 145p.

In this brief booklet, the author has provided an instant summary and analysis of both the newly-elected 11th Central Committee and the changes wrought with comparison to the 10th Central Committee.

643 Prelude to revolution: Mao, the Party, and the peasant questions: 1962-66.
Richard Baum.   New York: Columbia University Press,
1975. 222p.

This book concentrates on the socialist education movement which immediately preceded the Cultural Revolution. It was a clash between two lines represented by Mao Tse-tung (Mao Zedong) and Liu Shao-ch'i (Liu Shaoqi). As a result it was more than a mere power struggle. It was an attempt by Mao to rekindle the flames of revolution by shaking up the Communist Party while reemphasizing the class struggle.

644 Yundong: mass campaigns in Chinese Communist leadership.
Gordon A. Bennett.   Berkeley, California: University of
California Press, 1976. 133p.

This short interpretative essay on mass movements in China will serve as a very useful supplementary text in intermediate and advanced courses on Chinese politics.

645 Micropolitics in contemporary China: a technical unit during and after Cultural Revolution.
Marc Blecher, Gordon White.   White Plains, New York:
Sharpe, 1979. 135p.

This study is based entirely upon detailed interviews conducted in Hong Kong with a 'Mr Ji (Chi)', who worked in a technical post from 1968 until about 1973. The authors use Mr Ji's (Chi) recollections to describe the situation in a technical unit before the Cultural Revolution and the dynamics of that campaign.

646 Heirs apparent: what happens when Mao dies?
Dennis Bloodworth, Jingbing Bloodworth.   New York:
Straus, 1973. 236p.

The object of this study is to examine, through Chinese eyes and in Chinese terms, the Chinese political situation in order to discover who will probably control the country in the coming years. It is a study of the leaders - almost unknown to Westerners - who may rule China, not only in terms of their positions on the political chess-board, but as individuals whose ambitions and loyalties and rivalries can only be understood against the setting of Chinese society. As far as an heir apparent is concerned, it is suggested that Chou En-lai (Zhou Enlai) is the person likely to emerge from the complex political situation as the moderate leader of China after Mao dies.

Politics and Government. Contemporary

647 Revolution at work: mobilization campaigns in China.
Charles P. Cell. New York: Academic Press, 1977. 221p.

The author has systematically studied thirty-six mobilization campaigns in China, dividing them into three categories: ideological, economic and revolutionary. He sets forth fourteen hypotheses, drawn from the observations of other theorists on campaign effectiveness and tests these hypotheses by weighing shortcomings against achievements in each of the categories. He also presents a brief chronology of mobilization campaigns from 1949 to 1975.

648 The execution of Mayor Yin and other stories from the Great Proletarian Cultural Revolution.
Chen Ruoxi. Bloomington, Indiana: Indiana University Press, 1978. 200p.

The author, Ch'en Jo-hsi (Chen Ruoxi), is a Taiwan- and American-educated Chinese who returned to China in 1966 in an idealistic frame of mind and left in 1973 in disillusionment. Her social and psychological observation is sharp, but each reader will have to decide how representative such stories are of Chinese realities. The eight stories in this volume were originally published in Taiwan and Hong Kong.

649 The Chinese Red Army: campaigns and politics since 1949.
Gerard H. Corr. New York: Schocken Books, 1974. 175p.

The author contends that the Chinese army is not aggressively expansionistic, pointing out that the People's Republic of China has engaged in only four conflicts - in Tibet, Korea, India and Russia - each of which was fought under provocation to defend her borders. The author views Chinese military achievements as a single developing story which he sees in close relation to the political and social development of the People's Republic.

650 China's hundred weeds: a study of the anti-rightist campaign in China (1957-59).
Naranarayan Das. Calcutta, India: Bagchi, 1979. 244p.

The author brings clarity and balance to the complex campaign which in paradoxical ways planted the seeds for the Cultural Revolution. At every juncture he lays out sequentially all the authoritative and popular interpretations of the events he is describing and then with sharp critical judgements, he evaluates each and arrives at his conclusions. In the same disciplined fashion he reviews the positions and the statements of the conflicting participants.

651 Yellow earth, green jade: constants in Chinese political mores.
Simon De Beaufort. Cambridge, Massachusetts: Harvard University Press, 1978. 90p. (Harvard Studies in International Affairs, No. 41).

In this essay, the author distils his many years of familiarity with China and concludes that China is both 'Communist' and 'Chinese'. The main reasons behind this view are that the imperial mandarinate survives in the bureaucracy of the People's Republic, that social and political methods of control are remarkably similar to those used by the Ch'ing (Qing) court and that, while Marxism-

Politics and Government. Contemporary

Leninism has replaced Confucianism, it plays the same ideological role for the new cadre-mandarins.

652 **China after the Cultural Revolution: politics between two congresses.**
Jurgen Domes, with a contribution by Marie-Luise Nath, translated from the German by Annette Berg, David Goodman. London: Hurst, 1977. 283p.
This book is a very competent analysis of Chinese politics between 1969 and 1973. The author concludes that China is mak'ng a transition to institutionalized leadership. He believes that China's charismatic leadership phase under Mao Tse-tung (Mao Zedong) ended in the late 1950s and that since 1959 China's political system has been under transitional leadership.

653 **The internal politics of China, 1949-1972.**
Jurgen Domes, translated from the German by Rudiger Machtzki. London: Hurst, 1973. 258p.
This is a lucid and dispassionate short history of Chinese government and politics since the Revolution. The author views the Cultural Revolution as a success for the military only, a drastic defeat for the genuine Maoist Left and an ironic victory for Liuist bureaucratic rationality, moderation and order.

654 **Socialism in the Chinese countryside.**
Jurgen Domes. London: Hurst, 1980. 192p.
This is an account of agricultural policies in the People's Republic of China, from the land reform of 1950-53 to the present in the context of intra-party conflicts since the late 1950s. The author also evaluates the social and economic performance of the various parties.

655 **Socialist planning.**
Michael Ellman. London: Cambridge University Press, 1979. 300p.
In his introduction, the author outlines the evolving rationale of planning in the broad sense of state intervention in both market and socialist situations. In subsequent chapters he deals with agriculture, investment, labour, incomes and foreign trade.

656 **Coming of grace.**
Edward Hammond. New York: Lancaster-Miller, 1980. 196p.
This book documents the life and times of Chou En-lai (Zhou Enlai) with a fascinating and unprecedented collection of photographs gathered from archives in the United States and China. Much of the brief but comprehensive text has been derived from original Chinese sources that have never before been translated into English.

Politics and Government. Contemporary

657 **To embrace the moon.**
Edward Hammond.   New York: Lancaster-Miller, 1980.
192p.
This illustrated biography of Mao reveals the real man and his times. Drawing on an unprecedented collection of photographs, this exceptional book portrays every phase of Mao's long career.

658 **From the other side of the river: a portrait of China today.**
Edited by W. H. Fan, K. T. Fan.   New York: Doubleday,
1975. 429p.
The writings collected here are reproduced from the *Peking* (Beijing) *Review*, *China Reconstructions*, and other publications of the Foreign Language Press in Peking (Beijing) and they deal with broad topics - people, places, social and economic development and the liberation of education and philosophical thought -as well as contemporary politics. Included are pieces on the family and marriage, women's liberation, children and youth, cities and commune, agriculture, industry, commerce, finance, ecology, revolution, reform of intellectuals and the movement to deprecate Confucius and his influence.

659 **China's quest for independence: policy evolution in the 1970s.**
Edited by Thomas Fingar.   Boulder, Colorado: Westview
Press, 1980. 245p. (Westview Special Studies on China and
East Asia).
The book addresses two central questions: how durable were foreign and domestic policies during the 1970s, and what is the relationship between foreign and domestic policy. Studies of five broad policy areas reveal that most policies were very stable during this period and that foreign policy was linked to domestic interests.

660 **The military dimension of the Chinese revolution.**
Edmund Fung.   Vancouver, British Columbia: University of
British Columbia Press, 1980. 250p.
In this work, the author describes the military reforms which led to establishment of China's new army, the army's relationship to the social order, the processes of military subversion and the new army's pivotal role in the Republican Revolution in 1911.

661 **Chinese politics and the succession problems.**
John Gardner.   New York: Macmillan, 1982. 280p.
This is a well-documented analysis of the major political upheavals in China since the death of Mao. This includes the arrest and trial of the Gang of Four and the re-emergence of Deng Xiaoping (Teng Hsiao-ping) in the political arena. There are discussions of the social and economic policies that have emerged as well as the new directions in foreign relations.

662 **A Chinese view of China.**
John Gittings.   New York: Pantheon, 1973. 216p.
This book, which consists of translations from Chinese writers about their own society and history, was prepared to complement a series of radio programmes on

148

China, but stands perfectly well on its own. These excerpts span 2,500 years beginning with the rise and fall of the imperial dynasties and the romantic heroes that dominate Chinese literature and continuing through the wars with Western powers in the 19th century and early Chinese descriptions of Western customs. Moving into the 20th century, it portrays such different aspects of Chinese life as the struggle for land reform in the 1930s, 'Love in a mountain village', Red Guard wall posters and scenes after the Cultural Revolution. This collection contains 34 excerpts from Western and Chinese sources, including some English-language magazines published in the People's Republic.

663 **Beijing street voices: the poetry and politics of China's democracy movement.**
David Goodman. New York: Boyars, 1980. 192p.
This book includes some 40 poems selected from the unofficial publications, appearing in Beijing (Peking) in the winter of 1978-79 during the so-called Democracy Movement for greater political and cultural freedom. The author sketches the origins and development of this movement and gives a sample of its representative poems. His aim is to place both movement and poetry in their social and political contexts.

664 **Chinese Watergate: political and economic conflict in China, 1969-1977.**
Leo Goodstadt. Atlantic Highlands, New Jersey: Humanities Press, 1979. 219p.
The book contains a well-informed recreation, by a longtime Hong-Kong-based observer, of the power struggle in China in the year immediately prior to Mao's death. The author concentrates almost exclusively on the struggle for power without analyzing in sufficient depth the economic, social and foreign policy context in which that struggle took place.

665 **China's intellectuals.**
Merle Goldman. Cambridge, Massachusetts: Harvard University Press, 1981. 256p.
The account is a study of the writers, philosophers, historians, journalists and scientists, who, in the period climaxed by the Cultural Revolution, debated the political issues and steered the course of public policy.

666 **China's new development strategy.**
Edited by Jack Gray, Gordon White. New York: Academic Press, 1982. 342p.
The death of Mao Zedong (Mao Tse-tung) and the arrest of his principal supporters inaugurated a period of massive change in China. As Vice-premier Deng Xiaoping (Teng Hsiao-ping) asserted his authority in place of Mao's favoured successor Hua Guofeng (Hua Kuo-feng), the transformation deepened. The papers in this book describe and evaluate the changes which have occurred and relate them to earlier policies and experience. The problems of development occurring as late as 1980 and early 1981 are taken into account.

667 The Chinese Communist Party in power, 1949-1976.

Jacques Guillermaz, translated from French by Anne
Destenay. Boulder, Colorado: Westview Press, 1976. 614p.

This revised and updated translation of the 1972 French edition is a history of
the Chinese Communist Party from the founding of the People's Republic of
China to the death of Mao Tse-tung (Mao Zedong). The text is thorough and
scholarly with ample citation and some quotation of major primary documents, a
good supply of tables, maps and charts and judicious personal observations drawn
from the author's many years of service in China as a soldier and diplomat.

668 My house has two doors.

Han Suyin. New York: Putnam, 1981. 655p.

This is the fourth and final volume of this world-renowned author's personal
account which describes revolution and change in China, covering the years from
1949 to 1979.

669 Organizing China: the problem of bureaucracy, 1949-1976.

Harry Harding. Stanford, California: Stanford University
Press, 1980. 349p.

This is a history of the development of Chinese organizational policy from 1949
to the death of Mao Tse-tung (Mao Zedong) in 1976. The author argues that
Chinese organizational policy has been controversial because of the complexity of
the administration of power and status, and the philosophical dilemma of whether
the efficiency of modern bureaucracy outweighs its social and political costs.

670 Political China observed: a western perspective.

Peter Harris. New York: St. Martin's Press, 1980. 220p.

The author seeks to set the current leadership of the People's Republic of China
in historical context while considering the meaning of totalitarianism. He explores
the present political situation inside China and examines the Communist Party,
the state and the army. This book attempts to analyze how the new orientation in
Chinese politics will affect international relations, particularly with the Soviet
Union and the United States.

671 Soviet and Chinese personalities.

Wilhelm S. Heiliger. Lanhan, Maryland: University Press
of America, 1980. 221p.

The author has taken up very challenging and historically significant questions
about the differences and similarities of Russian and Chinese characters after
their respective immersions in Communism. His approach is to review objectively
what Western scholars have to say about Soviet and Chinese personalities, then
the ideals of the 'new man' in each society and finally the theories and findings
of Soviet and to a much lesser degree, Chinese psychologists.

672 The People's Republic of China, 1949-1979: a documentary survey.

Edited by Harold C. Hinton. Wilmington, Delaware: Scholarly Resources, 1980. 5 vols. 3,000p.

All major policy-related documents produced over the first thirty years of the People's Republic of China have been assembled in this important new resource collection. Included are hundreds of official statements on ideology, politics, economics and foreign policy in China from the war of liberation to and including the normalization of relations with the United States. All documents are unabridged, as released by the Chinese government, in English translation. The editor provides introductory commentaries for each selection.

673 An introduction to Chinese politics.

Harold C. Hinton. New York: Praeger, 1973. 323p.

In an introductory chapter the author discusses the ways in which the West has viewed China and how the Chinese have viewed themselves. A very short chapter on 'The legacy of the past' is followed by two longer ones on political history from 1949 to 1972. Thereafter, the book treats in somewhat greater depth the conventional range of topics, such as ideology, the Communist Party, the leadership, the armed forces, foreign policy and the Taiwan question.

674 After Mao what? Army, party, and group rivalries in China.

J. P. Jain. New Delhi: Radiant, 1975. 276p.

The book seeks to identify various group rivalries which might play significant roles in determining Chinese leadership. He concludes that the Army is not an independent entity or a clearly distinguishable group struggling for power and/or top leadership positions. He also discounts the likelihood of a de-Maoism. The eventual conclusion of the book is that the moderates and radicals would try to avoid serious conflicts and adopt decisions by consensus and compromise.

675 The politics of the Chinese Cultural Revolution: a case study.

Hong Yung Lee. Berkeley, California: University of California Press, 1978. 382p.

The author argues that those who attacked the status quo during the Cultural Revolution were expressing dissatisfaction with their own social positions, while those who defended the status quo generally belonged to favoured groups. The author gives an account of the student Red Guard and worker-rebel factions whose battles and power seizures shook China from 1966 to 1968. Based on Red Guard newspapers, his analysis seeks to reveal the composition of the mass organization, their ideology and their links to Central Party politicians.

676 Party leadership and revolutionary power in China.

Edited by John Wilson Lewis. New York: Cambridge University Press, 1970. 422p.

Twelve American and British scholars discuss China's political system, the divergent attitudes toward the organization of power, the changing roles of the Communist Party and its élite and the new view of power occasioned by the Cultural Revolution.

Politics and Government. Contemporary

677 Broken image: essays on Chinese culture and politics.
Simon Leys. New York: St. Martin's Press, 1980. 156p.

This book should not be read as an introduction to contemporary China. As part of an advanced course for those who have already studied China, it contains some stunning insights. The book conveys the human side of Chinese life well.

678 China: management of a revolutionary society.
Edited by John M. H. Lindbeck. Seattle, Washington: University of Washington Press, 1971. 391p.

The ten papers in the volume cover the usual academic spectrum from pedestrian fact-catching to tenuous speculation.

679 Red Guard: from schoolboy to 'Little General' in Mao's China.
Ken Ling. London: MacDonald, 1972. 413p.

This book is a highly personalized account of the role of a leading Red Guard in Fukien (Fujian) Province during the Cultural Revolution. Using a racy narrative style, it attempts to go beyond a recital of events to convey the thoughts and feelings of the central character and his associates.

680 Party recruitment in China.
Robert Martin. New York: East Asian Institute, Columbia University, 1981. 116p.

This is a profile of changing approaches to Communist Party recruitment over time. The author details the major recruitment campaign of 1954-56 and shows how a Maoist model of leadership, implemented during the campaign, established the basic characteristics of Party recruitment through 1976. He also discusses problems and prospects for recruitment policy in the post-Mao era.

681 Chinese Communist power and policy in Xinjiang 1945-1977.
Donald H. McMillan. Boulder, Colorado: Westview Press, 1979. 383p.

This is the first in-depth study of Chinese Communist rule in Xinjiang (Sinkiang), a muslim region lying along the Sino-Soviet border in Central Asia. The degree of similarity and difference between the power and policy perspectives of the regional leadership and those of the central authorities in Peking (Beijing) after 1949 is a central concern of the book.

682 Opposition and dissent in contemporary China.
Peter R. Moody, Jr. Stanford, California: Hoover Institution, 1977. 342p.

The author provides an analysis of Chinese attitudes to political opposition, the handling of opposition by the Communist régime, potential sources of opposition to the régime and the ideas and behaviour of opposition movements in China, from 1949 until the riots in Peking (Beijing) in April 1976. The main contribution of the study lies in its relatively comprehensive catalogue of critics of the régime.

Politics and Government. Contemporary

683 The politics of the eighth central committee of the Communist Party of China.
Peter R. Moody, Jr.   Hamden, Connecticut: Shoe String Press, 1973. 346p.

This account of élite-level politics in the decade preceeding the Cultural Revolution attempts to explain China's failure to achieve political stability. Rejecting the simplistic notion of the Communist Party as an institutional entity, the book adopts grouping rather than policy preferences as the motor force of Chinese politics. It contributes a statistical analysis of the groups according to background and organizational and systematic affiliation.

684 The Chinese military system: an organizational study of the Chinese People's Liberation Army.
Harvey L. Nelsen.   Boulder, Colorado: Westview Press, 1977. 266p.

This book offers a picture of the Chinese military system which differs sharply from that of previous studies. Against commonly held assumptions - such as the People's Liberation Army's multifunctional character, its social and political role in Chinese society, and its highly decentralized structure - the author argues that the Chinese Communist-armed forces are presently centralized and strongly committed to a purely military function, similar to the armies of other major powers.

685 A rage for China.
Robert Payne.   New York: Holt, 1977. 276p.

The author's descriptions of recent events, notably the countless denunciations of Mao's widow, Chiang Ch'ing (Jiang Qing) and the Gang of Four on posters and in meetings, stand against a backdrop of delight at the beauty of the Chinese landscape and the artistic heritage. The result is a perceptive report which unlocks part of the puzzle of contemporary China.

686 Fundamentals of the Chinese Communist Party.
Edited by Pierre M. Perrolle.   White Plains, New York: Sharpe, 1978. 252p.

This book is one of the most comprehensive and authoritative treatments of the Communist Party and its development since the Cultural Revolution. It provides a discussion of the theoretical nature of Party rule in China and thereby invites consideration of the changing of that rule.

687 The dynamics of Chinese politics.
Lucian W. Pye.   Cambridge, Massachusetts: Delgeschlager, 1981. 307p.

This book focuses primarily, on how the Chinese élite, behind a conspiracy of consensus, carry out their politics and decision-making. Much of the book examines propositions about factional behaviour: the bases of factions; the relationships between the rules of factional politics and public policies; the ways in which factional politics give both stability and instability to the Chinese system; and above all, the likelihood that the factions will alter the current Chinese consensus about the Four Modernizations in domestic policies and foreign relations with the USSR.

153

688 **The dynamics of factions and consensus in Chinese politics: a model and some propositions.**
Lucian W. Pye. Santa Monica, California: Rand Corporation, 1980. 115p.

The author views China's political factions as dominated more by bureaucratic interests and generated differences than by specific policy or ideological biases - although policy is indeed affected by the outcome of factional tensions.

689 **Teng Hsiao-ping: a political biography.**
Qi Xin. New York: Cosmos, 1978. 271p.

This book is the first work in English about China's most controversial politician and influential contemporary leader, Teng Hsiao-ping (Deng Xiaoping). The Ch'i Hsin (Qi Xin), includes a series of documents from the Chinese press.

690 **Political behavior of adolescents in China: the Cultural Revolution in Kwangchow.**
David M. Raddock. Tucson, Arizona: University of Arizona Press, 1977. 242p.

This book attempts to explain attitudes of male adolescents toward participation in the Cultural Revolution, as a consequence of authority patterns between fathers and sons. The author bases his argument on the assumption that father-son relations in contemporary Chinese families are steadily becoming less vertical-authoritarian and more progressively horizontal and one-to-one.

691 **Our world: the People's Republic of China.**
Margaret Rau. New York: Messner, 1974. 128p.

The first half of the book gives a short survey of Chinese history, emphasizing recent times, the development of Communism and the contributions of Mao Tse-tung (Mao Zedong). The remainder describes China as it is today - education, industry and agriculture -and ends with a few questions about the future.

692 **China: politics and government.**
Tony Saich. New York: Macmillan, 1981. 280p.

This book presents in a single volume a concise yet comprehensive history of the Chinese Communist Party and the major political, economic and social developments in China from 1945-1980. It includes discussions of the latest events, in particular the new policy direction and the trial and sentence of the Gang of Four. It makes extensive reference to all important successes in China and includes new interpretations of past events in the light of recently-disclosed information.

693 **Élites in the People's Republic of China.**
Edited by Robert A. Scalapino. Seattle, Washington: University of Washington Press, 1972. 672p.

Fourteen American specialists present detailed papers on Chinese Communist leadership, considering in particular why some politicians were/are more successful than others in achieving and maintaining power.

694 **Authority, participation and cultural change in China.**
Edited by Stuart R. Schram. New York: Cambridge
University Press, 1973. 350p.

The eight essays in this book present the Cultural Revolution as not merely a
power struggle but as a genuine social and cultural revolution. Factory management, educational life, local politics - all are significantly different, indicating a
move towards a more democratic society.

695 **Through Chinese eyes.**
Edited by Peter J. Seybolt. New York: Praeger, 1974. 2
vols. 294p.

This book does not try to explain China but to show it. It does not offer 'expert'
analysis by outside observers, but rather, attempts to recreate the reality of everyday life as experienced by the Chinese people. Interpretation is left to the reader.
It contains selections from Chinese fiction, poetry, autobiography and political
commentary - all of which are logically organized and coherently presented.

696 **China: the politics of revolutionary reintegration.**
James D. Seymour. New York: Crowell, 1976. 285p.

The book begins with a review of some of the literature in political science on the
subject of political modernization and political development. The author draws
from this review the concept of integration as being a particularly useful way to
understand modern China's political history.

697 **Competitive comrades: career incentives and student strategies
in China.**
Susan L. Shirk. Berkeley, California: University of
California Press, 1982. 256p.

More than 30 years after Mao's rise to power, his crusade to transform social
consciousness has left people more, rather than less, alienated from one another
and from the state. How can we explain his failure to realize the Maoist vision?
The author analyzes this subject by looking at the city high school as a micro-
cosm of Chinese society. She introduces the concept of 'virtuocracy' to describe
revolutionary régimes that attempt to achieve the moral transformation of society
by awarding career opportunities to persons who exemplify the moral virtue of the
régime.

698 **The great road, the life and times of Chu Teh.**
Agnes Smedley. New York: Monthly Review Press, 1972.
460p.

The author travelled with the People's Liberation Army and wrote this biography
from notes and interviews en route. Like Snow's *Red Star over China* (q.v.) this
is a history of the Long March and the Yenan (Yanan) period - as well as a
biography of the commander-in-chief of the Red Army.

699 **Regional government and political integration in southwest China: a case study.**
Dorothy J. Solinger. Berkeley, California: University of California Press, 1977. 300p.

This is the first analysis of the role in the takeover process of the greater administrative regions, which existed from 1949 to 1954. The focus is on the administrative arrangements by which the provinces of south-west China were welded into stronger units and also integrated into the national polity.

700 **Mao's revolution and the Chinese political culture.**
Richard H. Solomon. Berkeley, California: University of California Press, 1971. 583p.

The book demonstrates that Mao's principal task in reshaping the Chinese polity has been to change the way people think and shows that institutions cannot be changed until attitudes have been altered to accept Mao's guiding principles. The author suggests that these principles have been correct - but with paradoxical consequences. The book offers absorbing details that demonstrate the social configurations of both old and new China.

701 **A revolution is not a dinner party: a feast of images of the Maoist transformation of China.**
Richard H. Solomon. New York: Anchor Press, Doubleday, 1976. 208p.

This brief study analyzes the fundamental and continuing transformation of China under Mao with both scholarly perception and journalistic readability. The author's explanation of Chinese language idioms such as 'eating bitterness' and 'paper tiger' strengthen his interpretations. The photographs on nearly every page are exceptionally well chosen and well integrated with the text.

702 **Politics and purges in China: rectification and the decline of party norms 1950-1965.**
Frederic C. Teiwes. White Plains, New York: Sharpe, 1980. 744p.

This volume relates the story of control and discipline within the Chinese Communist Party. Rectification was Mao's distinctive approach to élite discipline. Devised in the early 1940s, rectification underwent continuous modification. The emergence of a distinctive Chinese doctrine of Party rectification before 1949 and its increasingly controversial and problematic implementation in the fifteen years prior to the Cultural Revolution constitute the theme of this study.

703 **Provincial leadership in China: the Cultural Revolution and aftermath.**
Frederic C. Teiwes. Ithaca, New York: Cornell University, 1977. 170p.

This book concentrates on the related themes of the fear of a resurgence of provincial localism and the working out of the difficult party/military relationship in the post Cultural Revolution period. The author concludes, that, despite the arguments to the contrary, political power has not become decentralized in the last seven years.

Politics and Government. Contemporary

704 The future of China: after Mao.
Ross Terrill.   New York: Delacorte Press, 1978. 331p.

The author discusses the leadership crisis in China that occurred in 1976-77 with the passing of Chou En-lai (Zhou Enlai) and Mao Tse-tung (Mao Zedong). The personalities of Hua Kuo-feng (Hua Guofeng) and Teng Hsiao-ping (Deng Xiaoping) are discussed as well as the story of the Gang of Four. He also takes up issues in China's foreign relations, such as relations with the United States and the Soviet Union, Taiwan and China's world role.

705 Political participation in Communist China.
James R. Townsend.   Berkeley, California: University of California Press, 1972. 2nd ed. 233p.

Distinguished by clarity in presentation, lucid, concise analysis, and broad historical perspectives, the author examines ways in which the ordinary worker and peasant, the men and women of contemporary China, participate in the political process.

706 Politics in China.
James R. Townsend.   Boston, Massachusetts: Little, Brown, 1980. 2nd ed. 377p.

One of the intriguing aspects of this book is the avowed effort to use social science concepts. This book is part of a series in comparative politics under the overall editorship of Gabriel A. Almond, James S. Coleman and Lucian Pye. As such, the book has been structured around the analytical categories that were developed in the book, *Comparative politics: a developmental approach*, by Gabriel A. Almond and G. Bingha Powell.

707 Chang Ch'un-ch'iao and Shanghai's January revolution.
Andrew G. Walder.   Ann Arbor, Michigan: University of Michigan, Center for Chinese Studies, 1977. 150p.

This book deals primarily with the Cultural Revolution in Shanghai during 1966-67. It provides a new, revisionist interpretation of Shanghai's January revolution and Chang Ch'un-ch'iao's (Zhang Chunqiao) role in the insurrection.

708 The government and politics of the People's Republic of China.
D. J. Waller.   New York: New York University Press, 1982. 3rd. ed. 1982. 24p.

The first edition of this introductory text was published in 1970. The revised edition (1973) was modestly expanded to include President Nixon's visit to China and the presence of the People's Republic in the United Nations. The latest edition includes all significant events since the death of Mao - the rise and fall of the Gang of Four, the new economic strategies, re-establishment of the legal system, normalization of the relationship with the United States, changing attitudes to education and national minorities.

Politics and Government. Contemporary

709 Shu Ch'ing.
Clae Waltham. New York: Allen & Unwin, 1972. 174p.

The *Shu Ch'ing* (*Shu Qing*) is one of the ancient classics of China. In a great variety of documents it chronicles the 1,700 years from 2357 BC to 631 BC - the dynasties of Hsia (Xia), Shang and Chou (Zhou) - the rise of the clan system and feudalism - and the lives of the great and poor, the powerful and the petty in one of the world's first civilizations.

710 The politics of class and class origin: the case of the Cultural Revolution.
Gordon White. Canberra, Australia: Australian National University, 1976. 97p.

The central problem of the Communist Party's class policy on the eve of the Cultural Revolution was how to treat the class designations which indicated former relationships to the means of production. For young people, born since liberation and without class designations, the question was one of family background. Should the ascribed status of birth take precedence over the achieved status of political activism? The author effectively relates these positions to the social situations of their advocates.

711 Careers in Shanghai: the social guidance of personal energies in a developing city, 1949-1966.
Lynn T. White, III. Berkeley, California: University of California Press, 1978. 272p.

This book is a detailed consideration of ideological versus material incentives in the modernization of a socialist country. Drawing on local newspaper accounts as well as more conventional data, the author shows how Communist Party élites charged with guiding modernization linked the allocation of jobs, school admissions, household registrations, food rations, and other benefits, to the performance of tasks defined as being in the community interest. The origins of the Cultural Revolution, an urban movement, can partially be traced to these economic changes.

712 The military and political power in China in the 1970s.
Edited by William W. Whitson. New York: Praeger, 1972. 390p.

This book provides a comprehensive evaluation of the Chinese military establishment and its role in Chinese politics. The papers focus on trends of the past and prospects for the future, including the military role, selection criteria for generals, the organization of military power and strategies and tactics.

713 Chinese domestic politics and foreign policy in the 1970s.
Allen S. Whiting. Ann Arbor, Michigan: Center for Chinese Studies, University of Michigan, 1977. 85p.

By applying quantitative research formulas and content analysis, the author has been able to reconfirm that the radical group around Madame Mao had not been undermining Peking's (Beijing) policy of detente towards the United States and that its attitudes towards the Taiwan issue was probably more disengaged than that of the Teng (Deng) group after the fall of the Gang of Four. Secondly, he found that the opposition of this group to the prospect of China's growing reliance on foreign countries in her modernization, tends to enjoy much greater support among the Chinese élite than the radical programme could ever gain.

714 **Small groups and political rituals in China.**
Martin K. Whyte. Berkeley, California: University of California Press, 1974. 283p.

This is an analysis of the functioning of small group political study and mutual-criticism rituals in which much of the population of Communist China regularly participates. In the course of more than 700 hours of interviews with former residents of China, the author explored the significance of these groups and rituals in the daily lives of officials, students, workers, peasants and inmates of penal institutions. He presents case studies constructed from these interviews to illustrate the range of successes and failures of small-group rituals in China.

715 **China's higher leadership in the socialist transition.**
Paul Wong. New York: Free Press, 1976. 316p.

The author asks two broad questions to determine the extent of integration: firstly, has there been a concentration of power in China? Secondly, is society as a whole equally represented in the élite? He bases his interpretation on the patterns that emerge from the aggregation and correlation of information on the backgrounds and role attributes of the Chinese élite.

716 **The Chinese Cultural Revolution.**
A. Xia. New York: McGraw Hill, 1972. 254p.

This is a thorough analysis and critique, based on many previously inaccessible or little-known Chinese publications and documents, of the turmoil that existed in China during the mid-1960s. The author, Hsia (Xia), examines current trends in various strata of Chinese society - youth, intellectuals, peasants, workers, as well as the Communist Party and the army - and then focuses on the contradictions and stresses in Chinese society both before and after the Cultural Revolution.

717 **Chen Yi and the Jiangxi-Guangdong base area.**
Yang Shangkui. Beijing: Foreign Language Press, 1981. 256p.

This is an account of some of the major battles fought between the Communist armies and the Kuomingtang forces during the War of Liberation. The book details events in the life of one of the leading Communist generals, Chen Yi (Ch'en Yi).

718 **The People's Liberation army and China's nation-building.**
Yingmao Gau. White Plains, New York: International Arts and Science Press, 1973. 407p.

The author, Ying-mao Kau (Yingmao Gau), contends that despite continual temptations to Right and Left deviation, the Maoist model of military performance will last as long as the older generation retains power and as long as no other institutions are capable of doing the army's present jobs. The 32 documents are chosen to provide clear, pointed policy statement on all major aspects of the army's extra-military role and it is useful to have them brought together and translated.

Politics and Government. Political philosophy

719 **Power to politics in China.**
Parris H. Zhang. University Park, Pennsylvania:
Pennsylvania State University Press, 1978. 2nd ed. 325p.
This is a study by Parris Chang (Zhang) of Chinese politics, emphasizing the leadership's relative moderation, openness and flexibility in decision-making, as compared to other Communist governments.

720 **Factional and coalition politics in China: Cultural Revolution and its aftermath.**
Y. C. Zhang. New York: Praeger, 1976. 144p.
In this study, the author, Y. C. Chang (Zhang) examines the major factions and coalitions that have vied for control of the Chinese Communist Party since the start of the Cultural Revolution. His narrative includes sections on the rise and fall of Lin Piao (Lin Biao), the influence of Chiang Ch'ing (Jiang Qing), and the reorganization of the Chinese Communist Party following Lin Piao's (Lin Biao) death. His goal is to make some sense out of this period by putting together known information on events and personalities and organizing them into a coherent narrative.

Political philosophy

721 **The protracted game: a Wei-Chi interpretation of Maoist revolutionary strategy.**
Scott A. Boorman. New York: Oxford University Press, 1973. 139p.
The author provides a detailed description of Wei-Chi (Weiqi) and then suggests parallels between Wei-Chi's (Weiqi) and Mao Tse-tung's (Mao Zedong) strategies against Chiang Kai-shek (Jiang Jieshi) and the Nationalist armies during the Chinese Civil War.

722 **Documents of dissent: Chinese political thought since Mao.**
Translated by J. Chester Chen. Stanford, California:
Hoover Institute, 1980. 180p.
The author J. Chester Ch'en (Chen) here translates four documents dated between December 1975 and October 1977. Taken together these four documents provide a rare glimpse into the inner dynamics of the formation of official ideology and contribute to an understanding of current ideological factions in China.

723 **The Chinese political thought in the twentieth century.**
Chester C. Dan. New York: Doubleday, 1971. 390p.
This book explores the significance of each of the political and social movements that are considered to have shaped China's destiny: Sun Yat-sen's (Sun Yixian) republican and national revolutions; Ch'en Tu-hsiu's (Chen Duxiu) New Culture Movement of 1916; Hu Shih's (Hu Shi) Human Rights Movement of 1929; Chiang Kai-Shek's (Jiang Jieshi) New Life Movement of 1934; the emergence of the Third Force; and the rise of the Chinese Communist Party.

Politics and Government. Political philosophy

724 **Master of Chinese political thought: from the beginning to the Han dynasty.**
Edited by Sebastian De Grazia. New York: Viking Press, 1973. 430p.

This book contains the works of Mencius and Hsun Tzu's (Zun Zi) the *Art of war*. The editor presents analytical essays to introduce each selection and convey how deeply the thinking of the ancients has touched all aspects of life in China.

725 **Revolutionary ideology and Chinese reality: dissonance under Mao.**
Paul J. Hiniker. Beverly Hills, California: Sage Publications, 1977. 320p.

The author offers us yet another explanation of the Cultural Revolution, an episode that has fascinated Western analysts of Chinese politics for the past decade. Although he presents no new evidence, he does provide a content analysis of previous research which has the merit of interdisciplinary cross-fertilization and rigorous quantitative analysis.

726 **Imperialism and Chinese politics.**
Hu Sheng. Peking (Beijing): Foreign Language Press, 1981. 332p.

This is a penetrating analysis of the three-way conflict between the Chinese people, the imperial-feudal system and the foreign imperialist powers from 1842 to 1924.

727 **Autopsy on the people's war.**
Chalmers Johnson. Berkeley, California: University of California Press, 1973. 118p.

The author analyzes both the evolution of the people's war doctrine as well as the campaigns in the 1960s. The book follows six stages: the historical and ideological origins of the Chinese doctrine of people's war; the high tide of the doctrine during the 1960s; the Vietnam War and its significance for the doctrine; the Soviets' attack on the doctrine, yet their support of people's war; contemporary inconsistencies in the Chinese position; and a spinoff from the doctrine, the myth of the guerrilla.

728 **Ideology and politics in contemporary China.**
Edited by Chalmers Johnson. Seattle, Washington: University of Washington Press, 1973. 390p.

Does ideology grow out of experience? Or is experience guided by ideology? Crucial questions are not only for the leaders of ideological movements but for scholars who study leadership. These ten papers discuss whether political ideology proceeds or follows political activity and whether the two interact and evolve as a movement grows and attains state control.

Politics and Government. Political philosophy

729 **Glossary of Chinese political phrases.**
Lau Yee-Fui, Ho Wan-Yee, Yeung Sai-Cheng. Hong
Kong: Union Research Institute, 1977. 590p.

This glossary contains over 2,000 phrases, some from earlier Communist history,
but mostly from 1949 onwards, arranged in alphabetical order according to the
pinyin transliteration system, giving the Chinese script (unabbreviated) and an
English translation of the phrases. Each entry is followed by an explanation
skilfully culled from the Chinese press which usually not only explains the meaning of the phrase but also indicates the date and political context of its origin.

730 **Political culture and group conflict in Communist China.**
Allan P. L. Liu. Santa Barbara, California: ABC-CLIO
Press, 1976. 205p.

The author hopes for a future 'revolution' in which conflict is regulated by
explicit rules, predictable behaviour and continuity, a hope not likely, he grants,
to be satisfied. This is a study of the Cultural Revolution. The author attempts to
make use of Western theoretical studies of group conflict to analyze the Cultural
Revolution.

731 **States and social revolutions: a comparative analysis of
France, Russia, and China.**
Theda Skocpol. New York: Cambridge University Press,
1979. 407p.

This is a comparative historical analysis of the French, Russian and Chinese
Revolutions. Part I discusses the structural and historical conditions for
emergence of objective revolutionary situations in old-régime France, Russia and
China. The logic of comparison in part I primarily stresses ways in which France,
Russia and China were similar. Part II attempts to demonstrate how the conflicts
unleashed in the revolutionary crises led to social-revolutionary outcomes, with
certain patterns common to all three Revolutions and others distinctive to one or
two of them.

732 **Ideology and culture: an introduction to the dialectic of
contemporary Chinese politics.**
John Bryan Starr. New York: Harper & Row, 1973. 300p.

The author provides the reader with a clear and succinct guide to post-1949
China - on the nature of ideology, the peasantry, urban residents, the Communist
Party, the state, the People's Liberation Army and foreign affairs. This book can
be used in any course on modern China.

733 **The arts of war.**
Sun Zi, translated from the Chinese by Samuel B.
Griffith. New York: Oxford University Press, 1972. 90p.

Sun Tzu's (Sun Zi) essays on the art of war, written more than a thousand years
ago, have never been surpassed and might well be termed the concentrated
essence of wisdom on the conduct of war. Terse and aphoristic, they contain
principles still acted upon by Chinese generals today.

162

734 **Methodological issues in Chinese studies.**
Edited by Amy Wilson, Sidney L. Greenblatt, Richard
Wilson. New York: Praeger, 1982. 208p.

This study draws upon the expertise of scholars in various disciplines, including
philosophy, political science and sociology - to explore concerns of special interest
to China scholars including methodological problems related to field observation
and documentary interview and survey analysis as well as more general issues
related to the adequacy of currently-favoured conceptual political and social
models.

735 **A history of Chinese political thought, volume i: from the beginning to the sixth century AD.**
Xiao Gongzhuan, translated by F. W. Mote. Princeton,
New Jersey: Princeton University Press, 1978. 386p.

The author Hsiao Kung-chuan (Xiao Gongzhuan) systematically treats leading
thinkers, schools and movements, displaying a consummate mastery of traditional
Chinese learning and of Western analytical and comparative methods in this
complete translation. The volume covers the period of creativity which begins with
the birth of Confucius (551 BC) and part of the subsequent period from 227 BC
to 1376 AD, when there was an extended debate among schools of thought
originating in the earlier age.

736 **Ideology and practice: the evolution of Chinese Communism.**
James Jie Xiong. New York: Praeger, 1970. 359p.

The author, James Chieh Hsiung (Jie Xiong) has some interesting ideas about
neo-Confucian and Taoist influences on Chinese Marxism-Leninism. He traces
Mao's evolution as a Marxist and his gradual adaptation of Leninist principles of
political action to the conditions of Chinese society.

737 **Moving a mountain: cultural change in China.**
Edited by Goodwin C. Zhu, Frances Xu. Honolulu:
University Press of Hawaii, 1980. 325p.

While social and political changes in China have received much attention among
scholars, this volume represents the first major attempt to examine changes in
culture through the prism of communication as a fundamental social process. The
authors Goodwin Chu (Zhu) and Frances Hsu (Xu) draw on data from a wide
range of disciplines, including anthropology, economics, history, journalism, political science and sociology, to illustrate the period from the 1950s to the aftermath
of the Gang of Four.

Foreign Relations

History

738 The Chinese and Americans.
Jules Archer. New York: Hawthorne Books, 1976. 227p.

This is a history of US-Chinese relations from their beginnings to the present. The author discusses American business interests and missionaries in China, Chinese immigrants in America, the alliance during the Second World War, the US role in China's Civil War, relations during the Korean and Vietnamese wars and recently increasing communication between the two countries.

739 China and Japan at war, 1937-1945: the politics of collaboration.
John Hunter Boyle. Stanford, California: Stanford University Press, 1972. 430p.

This book describes the attempts at wartime collaboration between the two nations in the late 1930s which was ultimately consolidated into a single national collaborationist régime in Nanking (Nanjing) under Wang Ch'ing-wei (Wang Qingwei). To the Japanese, this government offered a wide range of military, political and economic advantages. The problem was to make it sufficiently attractive to the Chinese people to win them away from their allegiance to Chungking (Zhongqing) or Yenan (Yanan), or simply to overcome their hatred of the Japanese invader. Despite the support of able and well-intentioned Chinese - notably Wang, a patriot and Guomindang (Kuomintang) leader at the time of his decision to collaborate in 1940 - the problem was never solved.

740 America's response to China: an interpretive history of Sino-American relations.
Warren I. Cohen. New York: Wiley, 1971. 242p.

The author has produced as comprehensive textbook which should be of great and continuing use in university courses. This is an examination of the essence of the American failure in China. While the author is concerned primarily with the perceptions and behaviour of American historical figures and politicians, he also

ventures to discuss the Chinese setting - conditions in China, the national interest
of China and Chinese provocation of and response to American policy.

741 **China and Japan: a search for balance since World War I.**
Edited by Alvin D. Coox, Hilary Conroy.   Santa Barbara,
California: ABC-CLIO Press, 1978. 468p.
This is a collection of essays loosely joined together by their common interest in
20th-century Sino-Japanese relations. These articles are of value because of their
diversity and freshness of approach.

742 **Dragon by the tail: American, British, Japanese, and Russian**
encounters with China and one another.
John Paton Davies, Jr.   New York: Norton, 1972. 448p.
Davies, a US diplomat in China in the 1930s and 1940s, stresses his service as
Stilwell's diplomatic aide. He takes the reader through almost 200 pages of
historical review before beginning his personal involvement. As a result, the general reader will gain from the lengthy background but may find the detailed
exposition of personal and bureaucratic infighting over US China policy in
1943-45 a bewildering labyrinth.

743 **China and the foreign powers: the impact of and reaction to**
unequal treaties.
W. L. Dong.   Dobbs Ferry, New York: Oceana, 1971.
326p.
This book deals with China's foreign relations from the middle of the century to
the present time. It attempts to explain the underlying anti-imperialist policies of
Chinese political parties and the basic reasons for the present hostility of China
to the Soviet Union and the United States. His main theme is to prove that
although China's troubles were partly due to her own importance, the Chinese
attitude toward foreign powers in recent decades has had much to do with the
national humilation endured during the past century.

744 **Diplomacy and enterprises: British China policy: 1933-37.**
Stephen Lyon Endicott.   Vancouver, British Columbia:
University of British Columbia Press, 1975. 209p.
The author has worked painstakingly through the recently-opened British official
archives for the 1930s. He manages to recount British official thinking on the Far
East from 1933 in great detail. He is primarily concerned with policy towards
China alone and is clearly fascinated with the decision-making process.

745 **Aspects of Sino-American relations since 1784.**
Edited by Thomas H. Etzold.   New York: New Viewpoints,
1978. 173p.
The six essays offer interesting insights into American foreign policies toward
China and American treatment of Chinese immigrants. Each essay is accompanied by an annotated bibliography drawn from recent literature on American diplomatic history. It carries the basic theme that American intentions in Asia in
general and toward China in particular have been hazy and policies and actions
inconsistent.

746 The World and China, 1922-1972.
John Gittings.   New York: Harper, 1974. 303p.

Gittings, China correspondent of the *Manchester Guardian*, has written an intensely lucid analysis of the long-term continuities in Chinese foreign policy. His principal theses are: when nationalism and socialism conflict, national goals win out; when domestic and foreign constraints conflict, foreign ones predominate; when Mao and other leaders debate, Mao is victorious.

747 The American image of China.
Edited by Benson Lee Grayson.   New York: Ungar, 1979. 332p.

This volume is a collection edited by Grayson of extracts of opinions about China from Samuel Shaw, who led the first commercial mission to China in 1784, to Cyrus Vance and President Carter on the most recent links. There are many quotations from presidents and other officials.

748 The hidden history of the Sino-Indian frontier.
Karmakar Gupta.   Calcutta, India: Minerra Associates, 1974. 176p.

While he covers a great deal of ground, the author devotes particular attention to the fascinating story of the attempt by the old British Indian government to alter the content of their own official publication on the question of the validity of the McMahon Line.

749 Frontier defense and the open door: Manchuria in Chinese-American relations, 1895-1911.
Michael E. Hunt.   New Haven, Connecticut: Yale University Press, 1973. 281p.

Between 1895 and 1911, Manchuria, endangered by Japanese and Russian advances became for the first time a major point of contact between China and the United States. Basing his study on Chinese and American archives, Hunt sheds important new light on the interaction of late Ch'ing (Qing) foreign policy and American expansionism under the Roosevelt and Taft administrations. The Open Door policy called for the equality of commercial opportunity in China. The book analyzes the reasons why for a brief period before the Republican Revolution of 1911, China's frontier defense and American Open Door policy became synonymous.

750 The Chinese and the Japanese: essays in political and cultural interactions.
Edited by Akira Iriye.   Princeton, New Jersey: Princeton University Press, 1979. 393p.

Focusing on the period between 1800 and 1945, the essays approach the modern history of Chinese-Japanese relations. They do so, not in terms of broad categories like imperialism and nationalism, but in terms of the actual points of contact between the two countries' ideas, institutions and individuals.

751 **Scratches on our minds: American views of China and India.**
Harold R. Isaacs.   White Plains, New York: Sharpe, 1978.
452p.

Previously reprinted as *Images of Asia*, this book is a gold mine of information for political scientists, psychologists, economists, philosophers and any thoughtful readers who want to understand the background to American policy in Asia.

752 **Japan and China: from war to peace 1894-1972.**
Maurius B. Jansen.   Chicago: Rand McNally, 1975. 547p.

This volume contains 12 essays which move chronologically from the Sino-Japanese war of 1894-95 to the normalization of relations between Japan and the People's Republic of China in 1972. This is the first effort which concentrates on the ways in which the ideas, the politics and the military actions of one - as well as the mutual perceptions arising from these points of contact - significantly affected the modern history of the other.

753 **The China lobby in American politics.**
Edited by Ross I. Koen.   New York: Harper, 1974. 279p.

Serving a dual purpose, this book not only offers an explanation for America's loss in the late 1940s, but is itself an historical document which helps to explain why no second chance arose in the 1950s and 1960s. The author describes the activities of groups and individuals sympathetic to the Chinese Nationalist government who sought to persuade American opinion and government policy to be favourable toward Chiang Kai-shek (Jiang Jieshi) and the Kuomintang.

754 **Britain and the Sino-Japanese war 1937-39.**
Bradford A. Lee.   Stanford, California: Stanford University Press, 1973. 319p.

The author questions the views of the victorious powers, and those which arose from the proceedings of the international military tribunals for East Asia on the motives and intentions of imperial Japan. He concludes that while in Europe, Britain adhered on the whole to a policy of appeasement during the late 1930s, in East Asia she chose a firmer course.

755 **The Japanese army in north China, 1937-1941: problems of political and economic control.**
Lincoln Li.   Tokyo: Oxford University Press, 1975. 278p.

The author provides a useful account of the successive policies and organizational devices used by the Japanese in attempting to control north China and offers insight into the background of Japanese actions there. His central conclusion is that inadequate manpower prevented the Japanese from doing much more than holding cities and trunk communications lines. At the same time, he argues that the Japanese army in the end refused to turn over any real power to its Chinese collaborators. The focus is on the Japanese: what they did and why.

Foreign Relations. History

756 **The McMahon line and after: a study of the triangular contest on India's north-eastern frontier between Britain, China and Tibet 1904-1947.**
Parshotam Mehra.   New York: South Asia Books, 1975. 497p.

The account begins with the history of 1903 Younghusband expedition to Tibet and then preceeds through World War I when Sir Arthur Henry McMahon, diplomatic plenipotentiary for British India, negotiated the tripartite treaty with China and Tibet, which for all practical purposes laid down the frontier line that has lasted with small changes until our own time. There follows a discussion of British Indian foreign policy concerning this frontier during the 1920s and 30s. An epilogue brings the northeastern frontier story to the Chinese-Indian border clash of 1962.

757 **Tanaka Guichi and Japan's China policy.**
William Fitch Norton.   New York: St. Martin's Press, 1980. 329p.

Tanaka Guichi, Japanese military leader and Prime Minister from 1927 to 1929, had a formative influence on the development of Japanese policy towards China. In this book, the author has drawn widely from primary sources of the period and particularly from Tanaka's private papers, to provide a pioneering study of Tanaka's career and of the factors influencing Japanese relations with China during the first third of this century.

758 **Russia and the roots of the Chinese revolution 1896-1911.**
Don C. Price.   Cambridge, Massachusetts: Harvard University Press, 1974. 303p.

The early contacts and sympathies between the Chinese and Russian Revolutions have retained their significance in spite of the violent feuding between their present-day heirs. Western historians have paid considerable attention to these relations beginning with the second decade of the 20th century. The author looks further back to the years between the Reform movement of 1896-98 and the Revolution of 1911.

759 **Whither China: the view from the Kremlin.**
Morris Rothenberg.   Washington, DC: Advanced International Studies Institute in association with the University of Miami, 1977. 310p.

This is not a book about China but one about what Soviet leaders think about China and what sort of impact their thinking may have on Soviet global policies. The author makes two important points: that the China factor looms much larger in Soviet thinking than is generally realized and that the Soviet view of China is by no means static.

760 **The United States and China in the twentieth century.**
Michael Schaller.   New York: Oxford University Press, 1979. 199p.

The book is as much an interpretation of US policies as it is a history of diplomatic relations with China. The author has delivered a highly readable and refreshingly outspoken survey of America's relations with China up to and including the advent of normalization in early 1979.

761 The US crusade in China, 1938-1945.
Michael Schaller.   New York: Columbia University Press, 1978. 364p.

The author provides many novel insights, particularly in revealing the extent of US involvement in the Chinese Nationalist-Communist power struggle. He also discusses American plans for the contemplated assassination of Chiang Kai-shek (Jiang Jieshi), covert military operations, the training of Kuomintang secret units and other characteristics of US escalating involvement in Vietnam two decades later.

762 The Amerasia papers: some problems in the history of US-China relations.
John S. Service.   Berkeley, California: Center for Chinese Studies, University of California, 1971. 220p.

In this volume, Service, who was discharged from the Foreign Service in 1951, offers a welcome clarification of a record that appears to discredit not only Service himself, but also his government. His analysis of the American papers and the security investigations of the early post-Second World War period is important in that it reveals a way in which the American experience in China was utilized to serve particular ends in American politics.

763 Origins of the war in the east: Britain, China and Japan, 1937-39.
Aron Shai.   London: Croom Helm, 1977. 267p.

This study of the origins of the Second World War is confined to British policy in East Asia. Britain can be said to have pursued a policy of appeasement towards Japan during these years.

764 China and Japan: past and present.
M. I. Sladkovsky, edited and translated by Robert F. Price, Guld Breeze.   New York: Academic International Press, 1975. 286p.

This is a translation from the Russian edition of a book published in Moscow in 1971 by the head of the Far Eastern Institute of the USSR, Academy of Science and editor of its official journal, *Problems of the Far East*. After briefly surveying the earlier history of China and Japan, Sladkovsky devotes most of his attention to the political and economic development of these two nations and their inter-relationships in the 20th century.

765 China's response to the West: a documentary survey, 1839-1923.
Siyu Deng, John K. Fairbank.   Cambridge, Massachusetts: Harvard University Press, 1979. 462p.

This documentary survey by the authors, Ssu-yu Teng (Siyu Deng) and John Fairbank, through an excellent selection of material, makes available in English the most important documents of each period.

766 **The limits of foreign policy: the West, the League and the Far Eastern crisis of 1931-33.**
Christopher Thorne. New York: Putnam, 1973. 442p.

The author challenges the accepted version of the origins of the Second World War and seeks to cast a new light on modern foreign policy. Traditionally, the Far Eastern crisis of 1931-33, when Japan seized Manchuria from China in open defiance of the League of Nations, is said to have prepared the way for the subsequent acts of aggression of the 1930s. Drawing upon papers that have just become available and upon the results of recent Japanese research, the author offers a reconstruction of the actual events as well as an in-depth analysis of the roles of the major powers involved.

767 **Britain and East Asia, 1933-1937.**
Ann Trotter. London: Cambridge University Press, 1975. 277p.

During the period just before the 1937 Marco Polo Bridge Incident, Britain's position in China was being steadily eroded, partly by the growth of nationalist sentiment, but even more by the extension of Japanese influence and control. The author tends to concentrate on the Japanese angle and writes a straight-forward narrative history.

768 **The closing of the door: Sino-American relations 1936-46.**
Paul A. Varg. Ann Arbor, Michigan: University of Michigan Press, 1973. 300p.

This book is very much the diplomatic historian's approach. The author discusses why the door on Sino-American diplomatic relations closed when the government of the People's Republic of China assumed power in 1949. Beginning with the years immediately preceeding Pearl Harbor, the book closes with an examination of the factors that caused the failure of the Marshall Mission in 1949. The focus is on the internal developments in China immediately after the Second World War.

Lost chance in China: the World War II dispatches of John S. Service.
See item no. 234.

American and Chinese Communists: 1927-1945, a persuading encounter.
See item no. 258.

Contemporary

769 **China, Iran, and the Persian Gulf.**
A. H. H. Abidi. Atlantic Highlands, New Jersey: Humanities Press, 1982. 325p.

This is the study of China's relations with Iran. Although there are brief sections on the period since the Iranian Revolution, most of the book deals with relations with the Shah. China has taken a special interest in Iran because of its concern to keep the USSR out of Asia.

770 **The Sino-Soviet territorial dispute.**
An Daisong. Philadelphia: Westminster Press, 1973. 254p.
The author An Tai Sung (An Daisong) in chapter one gives the historical back-ground to Sino-Soviet territorial disputes from the earliest conflicts until the Communist victory in China in 1949. Chapter two describes the brief Russo-Chinese honeymoon in 1949 to the growing discord in the 1960s. Chapter three focuses on the 1969 border clashes on the Ussuri River and subsequent relations and the final chapter considers the possibility of a Sino-Soviet war, concluding that there probably will not be one.

771 **Revolutionary diplomacy: Chinese foreign policy and the United Front doctrine.**
J. D. Armstrong. Berkeley, California: University of California Press, 1977. 369p.
United Front is the strategy of isolating a principal enemy and cooperating against it with a number of other governments whose ideologies are different from one's own and at the same time trying to win those states over to one's own ideology by persuasion and revolution. The author concludes that China's foreign policy is sometimes ideologically based and sometimes not, depending upon whether or not there are important balance-of-power interests at stake.

772 **The political economy of war and peace: the Sino-Soviet-American triangle and the national security problematique.**
Richard K. Ashley. London: Pinter, 1980. 384p.
This book discusses the sources of conflict and violence between the United States, USSR and China. It covers more than 20 years (1950-72) of interaction between the three great powers and in passing makes some interesting points. The notion that the uneven pace of growth of the three states can have lethal consequences suggests that we need to pay attention to more than rational calculation or careful crisis management. The notion that the three bilateral axes of communication in the triangle are all intertwined is equally important.

773 **The committee of one million 'China Lobby' politics, 1953-71.**
Stanley D. Bachrack. New York: Columbia University Press, 1976. 371p.
This is an analysis of the origins and activities of the Committee of One Million against the admission of the People's Republic of China to the United Nations. The author identifies the major personalities involved in the China lobby, describing their methods of operation and evaluating the influence they were able to exert over the formulation of American policy toward China. He also hints that there may have been CIA involvement in the organization of the Committee.

774 **China and America: the search for a new relationship.**
Edited by William J. Barnds. New York: Columbia University Press, 1977. 254p.
The merit of this collection of essays on American policy in China is that it offers a variety of formulae to meet the need for the normalization of Sino-American relations without abandoning Taiwan.

775 China and the major powers in East Asia.
A. Doak Barnett. Washington, DC: Brookings, 1977. 416p.

This is an analysis of relationships of the People's Republic of China with the Soviet Union, Japan and the United States. The author assesses the ideological, political and economic components of those relationships and concludes that the current leadership will continue Mao's policy and emphasizing strategic considerations and balance-of-power policies in its dealings with the other major powers.

776 China policy: old problems and new challenges.
A. Doak Barnett. Washington, DC: Brookings, 1977. 131p.

The author reviews the changes in the Sino-American relationship that have occurred since the start of the 1970s and attempts to analyze the problems that lie ahead. Relations between the two countries are still fragile and unless they are strengthened, he asserts that there is a danger they will retrogress. On the crucial issue, how to normalize relations without abandoning Taiwan, the author advocates ending the defense treaty with Nationalist China and replacing it with a strong unilateral statement. The United States should remove all of its military forces but continue to allow the sale of military equipment to Taiwan.

777 A new US policy toward China.
A. Doak Barnett. Washington, DC: Brookings, 1971. 132p.

This examination of Sino-American political relations is divided into three parts. Chapters 1-4 deal with the historical background and current setting. Chapters 5-7 deal in more depth with three aspects of policy: questions relating to Taiwan; the UN membership problem; and the nuclear issue. In a concluding section, the author outlines action that he thinks should be taken by the United States and looks forward to a reduced but still important American military role in Asia. The ideas presented in this little book, published just before the table-tennis tour, became shortly thereafter the model for US diplomacy in China.

778 The United States and China: the next decade.
A. Doak Barnett, Edwin O. Reischauer. New York: Praeger, 1970. 276p.

Two of America's foremost experts on Asian affairs bring together thought-provoking discussions by such experts as Lincoln P. Bloomfield, Richard M. Pfeffer, George E. Taylor and Harrison E. Salisbury on some of the most urgent topics of the 1960s. What is the significance of the Cultural Revolution? Who will lead China after Mao? What are the prospects of future trade with China? What policies toward China should the United States adopt in the 1970s?

779 China's economic aid.
Wolfgang Bartke. New York: Holmes & Meier, 1975. 215p.

This volume lists all of China's foreign aid projects and briefly analyzes their impact. The most favoured projects include textile mills and medical groups. The most favourable recipients include Pakistan and Tanzania.

780 **Britain and the People's Republic of China 1949-74.**
Robert Boardman. London: Macmillan, 1976. 210p.

This book is a description of Anglo-Chinese relations during 1949-74, stressing the years 1949-55 as the formative period. His account of British relations with China concentrates on particular points: the recognition question of 1949 and British reaction to it, the SEATO treaty and the containment of China, the restrictions on trade, the Quemoy and Matsu crises in 1954 and 1958, the final exchange of ambassadors after the Cultural Revolution and the seeking of Western European allies against the Russians.

781 **Understanding foreign policy decisions: the Chinese case.**
Edited by Davis B. Bobrow, Steve Chan, John A.
Krigen. New York: Free Press, 1979. 242p.

This book seeks to derive the operational codes of the élite of the Chinese Communist Party in formulating foreign policy and to demonstrate that these operational codes will predict changes in behaviour and provide explanations for them across a variety of substantially interesting foreign policy situations.

782 **Uncertain years: Chinese-American relations, 1947-50.**
Edited by Dorothy Borg, Waldo Heinnichs. New York:
Columbia University Press, 1980. 336p.

Nixon's 1972 visit to Peking (Beijing) and the newly-opened Washington archives have led some to replace the old debates on the loss of China with a new one on the 'lost chance'. If the United States had responded to indirect feeders from Mao and Chou (Zhou) in the 1940s, China might have become an Asian Yugoslavia. Papers in this volume debate the stance of Secretary of State, Dean Acheson, of the China lobby, of Chiang Kai-shek (Jiang Jieshi), of Mao and consider the concept of the US defense perimeter in the Pacific.

783 **Soviet-Chinese relations, 1945-1970.**
O. B. Borisov, B. T. Koloskov, edited with an introduction by Vladimir Petrov. Bloomington, Indiana: Indiana University Press, 1975. 384p.

Written by two Soviet experts on the basis of extensive research in the secret Communist Party and government archives, this study is the official Soviet version of the Sino-Soviet conflict. The central theme of this work is that petty bourgeoisie nationalist elements in the Chinese Communist Party, led by Mao, bided their time until China was developed with Soviet aid, then usurped power and set China on an anti-Soviet course.

784 **Israel, the Korean War and China: images, decisions and consequences.**
Michael Brecher. Jerusalem, Israel: Academic Press, 1974. 148p.

Although some details of Israel's exchange with China have been revealed and published elsewhere, this study is indubitably the most thorough, detailed and penetrating to date. It relies heavily on the Israeli Foreign Ministry archives, to which the author was given access and on elaborate interviews and communications with most of those who had taken part in the decision-making. On the basis of the information provided by these sources, the author analyzes six basic decisions.

785 China among the nations of the Pacific.
Edited by Harrison Brown, with a foreword by J. William Fulbright. Boulder, Colorado: Westview Press, 1982. 136p.

The authors address such fundamental issues as China's economy, demography, food and energy supplies and relations with the rest of Asia. Will China become a major exporter of energy? Will it remain a major importer of food? Is China destined to become one of Japan's major suppliers of raw materials? Can China resolve its maritime jurisdiction disputes with neighbouring countries? How will the perceptions of the nations of Southeast Asia concerning China and the Chinese influence the future course of events? The discussion of these and other questions adds a new dimension to the study of China's external relations.

786 US China policy and the problem of Taiwan.
William M. Bueler. Boulder, Colorado: Colorado Associated University Press, 1971. 140p.

In this study, the author traces the development of China policy from the Truman to the Nixon administrations. He argues for an independent Taiwan governed by the Taiwanese and suggests that an independent, disarmed, neutral Taiwan that posed no threat and made no claim to sovereignty in China might just be acceptable to Peking (Beijing) in the long run. He recommends that Taiwan be granted full self-determination in order to extract the United States from its dilemma of wishing to develop friendly relations with two antagonistic Chinese régimes.

787 China: the People's Republic of China and Richard Nixon.
Claude A. Buss. San Francisco: Freeman, 1974. 118p.

The author begins by reviewing modern Chinese history, the development of the Chinese Communist Party and the internal and external policies of the People's Republic of China since its creation. In a final chapter, he evaluates the US response to China in those years. He concludes that the new era in Sino-American relations derived more from historical forces within China and within the United States than from the sagacity or will of their respective leaders. He also appraises the meaning of the Nixon visit.

788 Chinese foreign policy: the Maoist era and its aftermath.
Joseph Camileri. Seattle, Washington: University of Washington Press, 1981. 311p.

The author examines three phases of Chinese foreign policy: a revolutionary period (1949-68), a transitional period (1969-73) and a post-revolutionary period (1977 onward). The author takes China's rapprochement with the United States as evidence of a gradual movement away from the revolutionary path. The author believes China became comfortable with a non-revolutionary policy once certain basic goals had been achieved - especially international recognition of China as a major power.

789 **China and the three worlds.**
Edited by King C. Chen, Michael Y. M. Gau. White
Plains, New York: Sharpe, 1977. 400p.

This is a collection by King Ch'en (Chen) and Michael Kau (Gau) of Chinese internal and public documents written or published by and large between 1972 and 1977. The book contains Chinese policies toward and relations with, the three worlds, including the theory of evolutionary diplomacy. Sino-American rapprochement, anti-super power hegemonism, support for the Third World and relations between foreign affairs and modernization.

790 **Chinese perception of the world.**
G. W. Choudhury. Washington, DC: University Press of
America, 1977. 105p.

A former Pakistani government official who left Pakistan in 1971 but has since returned to China on several occasions for extended stays provides a useful addition to the literature on recent Chinese foreign policy. His focus is on how the Chinese leaders view the outside world.

791 **China in world affairs: the foreign policy of the PRC since
1970.**
G. W. Choudhury. Boulder, Colorado: Westview Press,
1982. 310p.

Drawing on original sources and first-hand experience, the author examines China's global policy, diplomatic options and strategy in the context of the triangular relationship of Washington, Moscow and Beijing (Peking). His discussion covers China's quest for security, the breakthrough in US-Chinese relations, the course of Sino-Soviet rivalry, the role of the People's Republic of China in the United Nations since 1971, how China has championed Third World countries and the new, dynamic elements in post-Mao Chinese foreign policy.

792 **P'yongyang between Peking and Moscow: North Korea's
involvement in the Sino-Soviet dispute, 1958-1975.**
Chung Ching O. University, Alabama: University of
Alabama Press, 1976. 230p.

Relying almost exclusively on official press reports from Korea, China, Soviet Union and elsewhere, the author has produced a fluent and concise analysis of the shift in North Korea's position in the Sino-Soviet dispute from 1958 to 1975.

793 **The United States, China and arms control.**
Ralph N. Clough, A. Doak Barnett, Morton H. Halperin,
Jerome H. Khan. Washington, DC: Brookings, 1975. 153p.

Written primarily for a Washington audience, the Brookings Study systematically and cautiously discusses the role of nuclear weapons in Chinese foreign policy and the impact of those weapons on US defense policies and arms control thinking. The major recommendations of this study are that: China be brought into arms-control discussion; the United States considers a nuclear no-first use pledge toward China; and an agreement be sought renouncing the use of force and establishing a nuclear-free zone in Korea.

Foreign Relations. Contemporary

794 Island China.

Ralph N. Clough. Cambridge, Massachusetts: Harvard
University Press, 1978. 251p.

In this book the author has analyzed political, economic and military trends in
Taiwan and the evolving relationships between Taiwan and mainland China and
between Taiwan and its close neighbour, Japan, in the hope of providing a more
informed basis on which to reach judgements as to future US policy toward the
People's Republic of China and Taiwan.

795 China and Russia: the great game.

O. Edmund Clubb. New York: Columbia University Press,
1971. 578p.

In this book, which covers three and a half centuries of relationships between
China and Russia, the author examines not only the course of those relations but
also the internal developments in Russia, China and Central Asia which have
influenced those relationships. He states that his theme is the growth of the two
empires and the long struggle for dominance between them, which continued even
after they discarded their imperial aspects.

796 Taiwan and American policy: the dilemma in US-China relations.

Jerome Allan Cohen (and others). New York: Praeger,
1971. 187p.

This Taiwan-oriented work, a collection of commentaries originated in Washington in March 1971 at a conference jointly sponsored by the League of Women
Voters and the National Committee on US-China Relations. It focuses on old
imagined obstacles to changes in Taiwan's status.

797 The dynamics of China's foreign relations.

Edited by Jerome Allan Cohen. Cambridge, Massachusetts:
Harvard University Press, 1971. 129p.

These essays examine the specific problems that the People's Republic of China
has encountered in various areas of the world and place these in the broader
context of China's overall relations with each area.

798 China's global role.

John Franklin Copper. Stanford, California: Hoover
Institute, 1980. 181p.

This is a very hard-nosed realistic assessment of China's national power capabilities. Using numerous comparisons and a variety of carefully compiled statistics,
the author demystifies the sleeping dragon theory and concludes that China must
be regarded as a second-rank power.

799 China's foreign aid: an instrument of Peking's foreign policy.

John Franklin Copper. Lexington, Massachusetts:
Lexington Books, 1976. 197p.

This is a survey of China's foreign aid programme which shows relatively big
Chinese investments in Asian Communist neighbours, North Vietnam, North

Korea and Cambodia; a continuing commitment to Pakistan; and a new emphasis since 1970 on aid to non-Communist countries, particularly Africa. The author also shows how aid programmes virtually came to a halt during the Cultural Revolution and have since been revived. He contends that Peking (Beijing) uses aid rather than trade as a means of creating and rewarding friends.

800 American policy toward Communist China: the historical record, 1949-1969.

Foster Rhea Dulles.   New York: Crowell, 1972. 273p.

The book has a foreword by John K. Fairbank. The author seeks to show how a combination of many factors, including domestic partisan politics, McCarthyism and the dread of international communism, the China bloc in Congress and the obduracy of the Chinese Communists, made Sino-American relations over the years so controversial and involved. The author shows how America became a victim of its own anti-Communist obsessions and pursued a policy that led to the isolation of China, confrontation in Korea and the disaster of Vietnam.

801 China and South-east Asia since 1945.

C. P. Fitzgerald.   London: Studies in Contemporary China, 1973. 110p.

The author surveys China's dealings with Vietnam, Cambodia and Laos; with Indonesia; with Burma, Thailand and the Philippines; and with Malaysia and Singapore. The country-by-country survey is followed by a brief treatment of China in relation to the overseas Chinese.

802 China's decision for rapprochement with the United States.

John W. Garver.   Boulder, Colorado: Westview Press, 1982. 174p.

Since China's historic rapprochement with the United States in 1971, most experts have cited the 1969 Sino-Soviet border conflict and subsequent fear of Soviet attack as China's primary motive for seeking better relations with the United States. In the detailed account of the events leading to China's move toward rapprochement, the author argues that the domestic political objectives of the Chinese leaders and their views of the shifting balance of power in Asia might have weighed more heavily in their decision.

803 Technology, defense, and external relations in China, 1975-78.

Harry O. Gelber.   Boulder, Colorado: Westview Press, 1979. 229p.

This is a useful survey of Chinese economic defense and science policy since the death of Mao. The author describes the enormous setbacks to the development of science and technology during the Cultural Revolution and then lists the various steps that have been taken to chart a new course; the new stress on intellectual excellence rather than political enthusiasm; the new priority given to higher education; the revival of major research facilities; the importing of foreign technology and the sending of Chinese students to study in the West.

804 China's nuclear and political strategy.
Edited by S. K. Ghosh. New Delhi: Young Asia
Publications, 1975. 298p.

This book examines China's nuclear and armed forces. The papers survey Chinese involvement in the Indian Ocean, foreign aid, basic ideologies, the border dispute with India and international trade. They conclude that Peking's (Beijing) approach to international relations is not very different from that of other major powers.

805 China: rationalizing the domestic: theoretical approaches to the Chinese Communist world view.
Jan H. Ginsburg. New York: Vantage Press, 1972. 153p.

There are two chapters, the first entitled 'Symbolic structures, insecurity generation and the Chinese press' and the second 'Belief systems, moral Maoism, and the Chinese view of the world'.

806 The Sino-Soviet territorial dispute, 1949-64.
George Ginsburgs, Carl F. Pinkele. New York: Praeger, 1978. 145p.

This book is an analysis of the context as well as the content of all Chinese and Soviet statements, official and unofficial, pertaining to the Sino-Soviet border problem as it evolved down to the fall of Khrushchev. It is a fascinating but frustrating book.

807 China under threat: the politics of strategy and diplomacy.
Melvin Curtov, Huang Broong-Moo. Baltimore, Maryland: Johns Hopkins University Press, 1978. 368p.

This volume contains Chinese foreign policy analyses and examines decision-making during the Korean War, Taiwan Strait Crisis (1958), Sino-Indian Border War (1962), Vietnam War and 1969 Sino-Soviet Border conflicts.

808 China and Southeast Asia: the politics of survival.
Melvin Gurtov. Baltimore, Maryland: Johns Hopkins University Press, 1971. 234p.

This is a study of foreign policy interaction. The author is concerned with Peking's (Beijing) relationships with three countries: Cambodia, Burma and Thailand. He examines each country in detail and then discusses the internal struggles in China and their impact on Chinese policy. He seeks to show that Chinese policy is capable of responses to specific changing needs. He puts into perspective his conclusion that China's ideological and practical needs dictate the formation and implementation of its policy which has resulted in co-existence with neutral governments and support of revolutionary movements.

809 The Peking bomb: the psychochemical war against America.
Gerd Hamburger, translated from the German by Sarah Banks Forman. New York: Luce, 1975. 256p.

The author argues that the Chinese Communists have been attempting - and with success - to use drugs as a weapon in political conflicts, thus conducting a kind of chemical warfare to demoralize troops and people, so that by now the youth of the world have become infected with the desire to use such drugs and the narcotic wave has reached epidemic proportions. The first target was Japan. The next was the US soldiers in Vietnam in a growing and secret narcotic war eventually involving the entire capitalist world.

810 China, oil, and Asia: conflict ahead.
Selig S. Harrison. New York: Carnegie Endowment, 1977. 269p.

This is a comprehensive report on Peking's (Beijing) offshore oil and gas programme. The author shows why a growing Chinese offshore capability could foreshadow significant clashes with neighbouring countries and thus affect the future of Taiwan and South Korea and Sino-Filipino relations. In projecting long-term production capabilities, the author is more optimistic than recent CIA studies, but he continues to stress that Peking (Beijing) is unlikely to have a large surplus for export to other countries with the notable exception of Japan.

811 China and Japan: a new balance of power.
Edited by Donald C. Hellmann. Lexington, Massachusetts: Lexington Books, 1976. 306p.

This book is one of seven geographic studies prepared for the Commission on Critical Choices for Americans. Dealing with the two most important countries in Asia and their relations with the United States, it is a collection of six generally well-written, provocative essays by some of America's leading academic experts on China and Japan.

812 The bear at the gate: Chinese policy-making under Soviet pressure.
Harold C. Hinton. Washington, DC: American Enterprise Institute for Public Research, 1971. 112p.

The book combines the ideological with the operational components of policy. The author reminds readers of the obvious differences between rhetoric and action. In action, Peking (Beijing) has engaged in a long odyssey to escape the constraints represented by Soviet pressure on its policy-making.

813 China's turbulent quest.
Harold C. Hinton. New York: Macmillan, 1970. 340p.

This book is an appraisal of the many imponderables in China's foreign relations since 1945. The analysis includes China's place as a thermonuclear power, the uncertain results of the Cultural Revolution, the unresolved Sino-Indian and Sino-Soviet border disputes.

814 The Sino-Soviet confrontation: implication for the future.
Harold C. Hinton. New York: Crane Russak, 1977. 71p.

The author traces the origins of the Sino-Soviet conflict, assesses its current state and suggests possible directions that these relations might take in the future, i.e. rapprochement, detente or conflict. In his final chapter, he discusses how each might affect American interests and suggests possible responses.

815 China and the Taiwan issue.
Hongda Qiu.   New York: Praeger, 1979. 310p.

Including the US recognition of China, the author, Hungdah Chiu (Hongda Qiu) examines the status of Taiwan from historical, economic, political, legal and diplomatic perspectives. Essays are supported by documents that are central to the legal and historical questions involved. Included is Taiwan's role from Peking's (Beijing) perspective and the role of Taiwan as it relates to Sino-American relations.

816 Worlds apart: China 1953-55, USSR 1962-65.
Trevelyan Humphrey.   London, Macmillan, 1972. 320p.

The book contains the author's records of conversations with Premier Chou En-lai (Zhou Enlai), in particular his conversation of 5 January 1955, at the height of the first Taiwan Crisis. His position as head of the British Mission in Peking (Beijing) and Moscow gave him an unusual chance to see the men behind the policies.

817 China's African revolution.
Alan Hutchinson.   Boulder, Colorado: Westview Press, 1976. 313p.

This study is of special value to students of China's foreign policy not only because it provides data concerning the relationship between China and Africa, but also because it is written from an African point of view. As such, it presents a provocative account of the impact on domestic African situations of Chinese aid and trade policies.

818 China, Pakistan and Bangladesh.
Edited by R. K. Jain.   New Delhi: Radiant, 1974. 270p.

This book examines China's attitudes and actions relating to the emergence of Bangladesh in the context of the 'Han imperialistic aims' in Asia and particularly of Sino-Indo-Pakistan relations from 1952 to the war of 1971. It also chronicles Chinese moves in the United Nations and elsewhere.

819 Taiwan's future?
Jo Yung-Hwan.   Hong Kong: Union Research, 1974. 351p.

This book is the result of an international symposium on Taiwan's future in perspective. Within the limited space of some 350 pages the book may rightly claim to represent a wide spectrum of all political opinions (Nationalists, Communists, Taiwanese, Overseas Chinese, American, Japanese, Russian and British) as well as to exhaust the topic of discussion from all conceivable angles - political, economic, social, legal, technological and international. However, no conclusions are reached.

820 Communist China and Latin America 1959-1967.
Cecil Johnson.   New York: Columbia University Press, 1970. 287p.

The major theory of people's war is systematically analyzed and compared with the strategy articulated by Regis Debray, Che Guevara and Fidel Castro. The author examines the Sino-Cuban ideological and political controversy in the context of the Sino-Soviet conflict and the global struggle with the United States.

Another topic is the Chinese efforts to establish pro-Chinese parties and movements to implement their views. Employing the technique of content analysis of Chinese and Spanish documents, the author frames his study within the dialectical concept of the nature of reality.

821 **The pattern of Sino-American crises: political-military interactions in the 1950s.**
J. H. Kalicki.   New York: Cambridge University Press, 1975. 279p.

This book traces the pattern of Sino-American relations from Korea to the Taiwan Strait Crisis of 1958. He finds first that crisis does not dull perceptions but sharpens them: Chinese and American policy-makers deal with each other better under pressure; second, that nations can learn from crisis: what was a dialogue of the deaf in 1950 became almost accurate communication by the end of that decade.

822 **The Japan-China phenomenon.**
Shuichi Kato, translated from Japanese by David Chibelt.   New York: Kodansha International, 1975. 254p.

These essays compare current life in China and Japan and trends in their past and present thought. The author discusses the reasons for both countries' failure to understand the West and, in particular the alternatives facing them in foreign policy. He throws light not only on recent events, but on the long-term Japanese and Chinese attitudes to life and on differences between them.

823 **China, the United Nations, and world order.**
Samuel S. Kim.   Princeton, New Jersey: Princeton University Press, 1979. 581p.

This book focuses in great detail on Chinese behaviour at the United Nations. It is particularly rich in detail on Chinese attitudes to international law and North-South issues. Focusing on the years 1971-77, the author bases his analysis of China's participation in the United Nations on the World Order Model Project developed at the Princeton Center for International Studies.

824 **A matter of two Chinas: the China-Taiwan issue in US foreign policy.**
William R. Kintner, John F. Copper.   Philadelphia, Pennsylvania: Foreign Policy Research Institute, 1979. 127p.

The authors argue that the US recognition of the People's Republic of China was based on an exaggerated view of Chinese power and that playing the China card could be dangerous to US-Soviet relations. The authors also argue that relations between the United States and the People's Republic should not include the sacrifice of Taiwan.

825 **China and Africa, 1949-1970: the foreign policy of the People's Republic of China.**
Bruce D. Larkin.   Berkeley, California: University of California Press, 1971. 350p.

This is a study of Chinese political and economic activities on the African continent. The author demonstrates that China has exercised characteristic flexibility and prudence in dealing with both the various liberation movements and the African governments which have made overtures to her. He also reviews the successes and failures of the People's Republic over the past 21 years in developing and promoting revolutionary ferment in Africa, as well as respect for China as the foremost spokesman for the Third World.

826 **China's foreign relations since 1949.**
Edited by Alan Lawrence.   Boston, Massachusetts: Routledge, 1975. 261p.

This book is largely comprised of a well-organized collection of official Chinese statements on the Sino-Soviet relationship, policies toward its Asian neighbours and the Third World and stances during and since the Cultural Revolution.

827 **Communist China's policy toward Laos: a case study, 1954-67.**
Chae Jin Lee.   Lawrence, Kansas: Center for East Asian Studies, University of Kansas, 1970. 161p.

This book deals with China's policy towards Laos during the years 1954-67. The author argues that Peking's (Beijing) foreign policy towards Laos has been rational and cautious.

828 **Japan faces China.**
Chae Jin Lee.   Baltimore, Maryland: Johns Hopkins Press, 1976. 242p.

This is a study of the highly unstable, paradoxical relationship between Japan and the People's Republic of China between 1949 and 1972. The author traces the fluctuations in Japanese policy toward China. He gives particular attention to the divergent orientations of the ruling Liberal Democratic Party which, throughout the 20-year period, was tied to US-China policy and the opposition of Japan's Socialist Party, which forcefully advocated a neutralist policy and the normalization of economic and diplomatic relations with China.

829 **Sino-Soviet diplomatic relations, 1917-1926.**
Sow-Theng Leong.   Honolulu: University of Hawaii Press, 1976. 361p.

To anyone interested in the likely future of Sino-Soviet relations, this historical study is indispensable background. Based on Nationalist archives, it vividly demonstrates the continuity between Soviet and imperial Tsarist policy toward China even in the very first decade of Bolshevik rule. The Bolsheviks quickly detached Outer Mongolia from the Chinese Republic and re-established Russian dominance in north Manchuria.

830 De-recognizing Taiwan.
Victor H. Li. New York: Carnegie Endowment, 1977. 41p.

This is a timely investigation of the legal problems that would result from the withdrawal of US recognition of Taiwan and the formal recognition of the People's Republic of China. Li argues that a legal framework can be constructed for continuing to deal with Taiwan as a *de facto* government without *de jure* recognition.

831 The future of Taiwan: a difference of opinion.
Edited by Victor H. Li. White Plains, New York: Sharpe, 1980. 260p.

This volume records the conversations of a political balanced group of prominent Chinese-American scholars who met to try to come to grips with the future of Taiwan. Widely differing views are a reflection of a highly complex situation. Taiwan is not just a piece of real estate. There are 17 million people living there.

832 China as a nuclear power in world politics.
Yueyun Liu. New York: Taplinger, 1972. 125p.

The author takes a cool look at China's thermonuclear intercontinental capacity and sees these consequences: the vigour with which Chinese foreign policy goals are pursued will increase; the United States and the Soviet Union will accelerate their own programmes to defend against two potential opponents rather than one; India, probably, and Japan, possibly, will feel compelled to develop nuclear weapons; alliances will break up as security guarantees become less credible.

833 China and People's war in Thailand, 1964-1969.
Daniel D. Lovelace. Berkeley, California: University of California Press, 1973. 99p.

This is a careful, concise and fairly cogent study of China's policy towards insurgency in Thailand between 1964 and 1969. The author uses Chinese sources to understand Beijing's (Peking) policy towards Bangkok power holders, rebels in the rural Thai hinterland and revolutionary front groups in China.

834 The Sino-Soviet dispute.
Alfred D. Low. Madison, New Jersey: Fairleigh Dickinson University Press, 1978. 364p.

The book is basically a chronological review of the Sino-Soviet polemics. It is one of the few careful analyses of those polemics up to the early 1970s and will be useful to anyone interested in tracing the twists and turns of this crucial relationship.

835 Sino-American relations, 1949-1971.
Roderic MacFarquhar. New York: Praeger, 1972. 267p.

This volume contains a useful compendium of documents on the postwar course of Sino-American relations as well as essays by China scholars which attempt to assess the consequences of this course. The editor writes brief but incisive introductions to each of the seven sections of documents.

836 **Southeast Asia and China: the end of containment.**
Edward Martin. Boulder, Colorado: Westview Press, 1977. 114p.

This is a survey of China's relations with the Southeast Asian nations by a former US Ambassador to Burma. In Martin's view, China's policy in the mid-1970s stressed normal state relations and the independence of the Southeast Asian states; nor is there much likelihood that internal rebellion or Japanese, Soviet, or American interference will destabilize the region.

837 **India's China war.**
Neville Maxwell. Harmondsworth: Penguin, 1971. 475p.

This edition includes a postscript specially written by the author to cover new material on the Sino-Indian dispute including the memoirs of the director of the Intelligence Bureau at the time of the 1962 border war. It is based on interviews with authorities and soldiers, unpublished files and government reports and on-the-spot observations. The author offers some sensible views on how the Sino-Soviet dispute affected Chinese action and how the contemporary crisis over Cuba influenced events.

838 **China policy: new priorities and alternatives.**
Edited by William Meyers, M. Vincent Hayes. New York: Gordon & Breach, 1973. 86p.

This slim volume is the product of a conference held in February 1971 to determine what US policy should be towards China. The conference was attended by prominent Democratic senators including McGovern and Edward Kennedy, as well as a number of academicians and journalists. They came to the conclusion that US policy should change.

839 **The duel of the giants: China and Russia in Asia.**
Drew Middleton. New York: Scribner, 1978. 241p.

Middleton believes that war between Russia and China is probable, that the Chinese will need extensive outside military assistance in order to continue their resistance and that the US will not be in a position to supply it. On the bases of a late visit to China and conversations with Soviet, Chinese and Western military experts, *New York Times* reporter Middleton sketches the military doctrine and weapons capabilities.

840 **Remaking China policy: US-China relations and government-decision-making.**
Richard Moorsteen, Morton Abramowitz. Cambridge, Massachusetts: Harvard University Press, 1971. 130p.

The authors propose an innovative plan for improving US-China relations and analyze deficiencies in the way the US government now develops its China policy. They propose organizational and procedural changes, including new modes of interaction between government China specialists and their policy-making superiors.

841 **Chinese policy toward Indonesia 1949-1967.**
David Mozingo. Ithaca, New York: Cornell University
Press, 1976. 303p.

The author considers that Chinese policy toward Indonesia is intended to encourage Indonesian independence from the major capitalist countries and the Soviet Union, rather than to maximize Chinese or Communist influence for its own sake. He believes that it came near to success but was in the end undermined by the inability of the Chinese to control internal political events, including the behaviour of the PKI (Partai Kommunis Indonesia). The author gives more detail of the earlier years of the period under discussion.

842 **China and Japan: emerging global powers.**
Peter G. Mueller, Douglas A. Ross. New York: Praeger,
1975. 218p.

This Canadian study is thorough, concise and solidly sensible. Its conclusion: Japan and China, both three-quarter powers, need each other more than they need conflicts between them. Limited rapprochement is the likely pattern for the future with the Chinese side wielding somewhat greater influence.

843 **Two Chinese states: US foreign policy and interests.**
Edited by Raymond H. Myers. Stanford, California:
Hoover Institute, 1978. 81p.

The Sino-American decision to establish diplomatic relations with China was taken with great secrecy. This book and subsequent events suggest why President Carter had to move stealthily and swiftly to recognize the People's Republic of China. The purpose of the book is to chart a policy for the United States in its future relationship with the two régimes, the Republic of China and the People's Republic of China, that will be in its own best interest. The essays argue in favour of the equilibrium strategy.

844 **India, Russia, China and Bangladesh.**
J. A. Naik. New Delhi: Chand, 1972. 163p.

The 1971 civil war in Pakistan, which resulted in the creation of Bangladesh, provides an interesting case-study of the factors that determine the foreign policies of the great powers. Naik attempts to explain the policies of Peking (Beijing) and Moscow with only brief reference to Washington's role during the conflict. He foresees a change in Chinese policy in view of the altered situation on the subcontinent.

845 **China's policy on Africa, 1958-71.**
Alaba Ogunsanwo. New York: Cambridge University
Press, 1974. 310p.

The study traces the evolution of Chinese policy in Africa from the halcyon period, when revolutionary ideology coincided with national interest in seeing the overthrow of existing governments as the first priority, to the more complicated present, when zeal preaches revolution but power politics dictates cautious pragmatism and compromise.

846 **Dragon and eagle: United States-China relations, past and future.**
Edited by Michel Oksenberg, Robert O. Oxnam. New York: Basic Books, 1978. 384p.

Instead of searching in vain for some set of policy recommendations, the authors of this volume are concerned that the greatest need is for a new way of thinking about the relationship between the world's most populous society and the world's most affluent society. This group of essays is particularly strong on the historical and cultural background to Chinese-American relations.

847 **The shaping of Chinese foreign policy.**
Greg O'Leary. New York: St. Martin's Press, 1980. 320p.

This book adopts the long discredited tautological view that national interest is whatever the ideology deems it to be and that the ideology in turn is under constant reformation in the light of new developments. The book is a major re-examination of the period when China turned to the West between 1969 and 1973.

848 **Harry Truman's China policy: McCarthyism and the diplomacy of hysteria, 1947-51.**
Lewis McCaroll Purifoy. New York: New Viewpoints, 1977. 316p.

The author is sympathetic towards Truman's policy in the Chinese civil war, noting that to save the Nationalists would have required full-scale intervention - a step which neither he nor American public opinion could accept. Senator McCarthy's attack on Communists in the State Department forced Truman to be excessively aggressive when the North Koreans attacked South Korea. The result, says Purifoy, was that Truman committed American military force much further than the policy of containment dictated and that began a tragic policy of involvement on the Asian mainland.

849 **Soviet and Chinese influence in the Third World.**
Edited by Alvin Z. Rubinstein. New York: Praeger, 1975. 2nd ed. 230p.

This book attempts to find out how and to what degree Peking (Beijing) and Moscow have been able to influence the behaviour and policies of the Third World countries. Thus one may have to study not only the foreign policy but also the domestic politics of the Third World. The message is that the ability of the great powers to influence the behaviour and policies of smaller nations is very limited.

850 **Asia and the road ahead: issues for the major powers.**
Robert A. Scalapino. Berkeley, California: University of California Press, 1975. 337p.

This study provides an overview of the Asian political scene. Its primary concerns are with six nations critical to the future of the Pacific-Asian area: Japan, the People's Republic of China, India, Indonesia, the United States and the Soviet Union. In each case, the author first explores the domestic situation so as to provide a context in which to view foreign policies. He seeks to view problems from the perspectives of the leadership and people involved. At no point does he restrict himself to one approach or single solution although he clarifies the most probable developments and, in connection with the United States, his own preference.

851 **Through Russian eyes: American-Chinese relations.**
S. Sergeichuk, translated from the Russian by Elizabeth Cody-Rutter. Arlington, Virginia: International Library, 1975. 220p.

The Russian author seeks to provide a concise historical outline of American policy with regard to China. The book is based more on newspaper and magazine reports, eyewitness accounts and current documents, than on archival research. The Sino-American rapprochement of the past few years has deeply disturbed Moscow's leaders.

852 **The Middle East in China's foreign policy, 1949-1977.**
Yitzhak Shichor. New York: Cambridge University Press, 1979. 268p.

According to the author, since the mid-1940s the Chinese leadership has viewed the Middle East as part of an intermediate zone in the world which should be free from imperialism. In the immediate post-Second World War years this meant that the People's Republic of China backed efforts to reduce Western influence, especially that of the United States, in the region. In the early 1960s the Chinese broadened their concern with outside influence in the Middle East to include opposition to the Soviet Union.

853 **China's world: the foreign policy of a developing state.**
J. D. Simmons. New York: Columbia University Press, 1971. 260p.

The author sees Chinese policy as dictated mainly by the need for an external enemy to spur domestic effort. The author contends that so long as China remains overwhelmingly agrarian its chief concerns will be food, education and population control and foreign relations will, to a great extent, be dictated by these problems. Danger from external enemies, especially the United States and the Soviet Union, has been exaggerated to motivate the Chinese people to work harder.

854 **Asian security in the 1980s: problems and policies for a time of transition.**
Edited by Richard H. Solomon. Santa Monica, California: Rand Corporation, 1980. 336p.

These articles discuss the problems and policy goals which the United States and other countries must acknowledge in formulating a regional security strategy for Asia in the 1980s. They focus on both Asian and American perspectives of the forces affecting security along the rim of the Western Pacific and offer an unusally diverse and rich exchange of views.

855 **The China factor: Sino-American relations and the global scene.**
Edited by Richard H. Solomon. Englewood Cliffs, New Jersey: Prentice-Hall, 1981. 323p.

This is a collection of essays which analyze the ways in which China's re-emergence on the world scene has affected international affairs. Several authors offer some advice on relations between the United States and the People's Republic of China. As Strobe Talbot puts it: these relations should be gradually extricated from US calculation about the Soviet Union and given a value of their own. The emphasis of such an American policy should be on building human contacts, on opening the doors of US universities to help train Chinese intellectuals and on expanding trade. Michel Oksenberg points out that the US-China relationship needs to be institutionalized so that it will survive the almost inevitable leadership struggles and political changes ahead.

856 **Nations in darkness, China, Russia and America.**
John C. Stoessinger. New York: Random House, 1980. 197p.

The author examines ten empirical case studies in which misconceptions had concrete and specific effects on policy decisions. Five of these deal with Chinese-American relations and the other five concern Russo-American relations. He shows how great nations struggle not only with each other, but also with their perceptions of each other. All too often, he finds, prejudice, single-factor analysis, ego, false analogy or perhaps simply wishful thinking has caused a leader to misperceive reality and as a result adopt the wrong course of action.

857 **China, the Soviet Union and the West: strategic and political dimensions for the 1980s.**
Edited by Douglas T. Stuart, William T. Tow. Boulder, Colorado: Westview Press, 1981. 310p.

This book is based on the decade's first major conference on Sino-Soviet relations, held during May 1980 in Garmisch, West Germany. The articles explore such topics as sources of Sino-Soviet conflict, contrasts and competition between the two powers and Western policy options vis-á-vis the relationship.

858 **The road to confrontation: American policy toward China and Korea, 1947-1950.**
William Whitney Stueck. Chapel Hill, North Carolina: University of North Carolina Press, 1981. 326p.

In this study of post-Second World War US Far Eastern policy, the author contends that the United States confronted China and Korea from the position that the maintenance of the credibility of American foreign policy required a firm and generally inflexible stance against Communism - a policy that had disastrous consequences. The study is well documented and the bibliography is excellent.

859 **The coldest war: Russia's game in China.**
C. L. Sulzberger. New York: Harcourt Brace, 1974. 113p.

The author analyzes the ideological differences and reviews the long history of difficulties between China and Russia. He maintains that, although Russia has developed armed forces along the Sino-Soviet frontier, it does not intend an outright military assault against China; instead by infiltrating agents, disseminating propaganda and subverting important Chinese, it hopes to impose a pro-Russian régime after the death of Mao Tse-tung (Mao Zedong).

860 **Chinese foreign policy after the Cultural Revolution, 1966-1977.**
Robert G. Sutter.   Boulder, Colorado: Westview Press, 1978. 176p.

This volume reviews and analyzes developments in recent Chinese foreign affairs. The first part focuses on major turning points since 1966. The second concentrates on Peking's (Beijing) policies toward specific countries and regions and those issues critical to China's interests, e.g. Sino-Soviet relations, Europe and the Middle East. He also shows how Chinese policy toward the United States began to change in the late 1960s.

861 **China-watch: toward Sino-American reconciliation.**
Robert G. Sutter.   Baltimore, Maryland: Johns Hopkins University Press, 1978. 155p.

Drawing heavily on analyses of Chinese communications during the past 30 years, the author throws fresh light on several aspects of Chinese policy, particularly on the dialogue with Washington in 1955-57 over Taiwan. He suggests that Peking (Beijing) demonstrated much greater flexibility on the Taiwan issue at that time than is generally assumed.

862 **Eighth voyage of the dragon: a history of China's quest for seapower.**
Bruce Swanson.   Annapolis, Maryland: Naval Institute Press, 1982. 352p.

Although China has a vast coastline and more than three million offshore islands, she has always been a continental rather than a maritime power. This book explores the reasons for this orientation and demonstrates that since Mao's death, China has undergone a vast maritime buildup. By early 1981, the commercial fleet of the People's Republic of China was capable of transporting 70 per cent of its contracted cargo, a remarkable achievement considering that it could haul virtually nothing in 1970. Moreover, although still technologically backward, the Navy of the People's Republic of China is now the third largest in the world in terms of the number of major combatants.

863 **China and Pakistan: diplomacy of an entente cordial.**
Anwar Hussain Syed.   Amherst, Massachusetts: University of Massachusetts Press, 1974. 259p.

The author sees the pattern of Sino-Pakistani relations as being not so much that of a formal alliance, or even of a client-patron situation, but rather that of two states, albeit of differing sizes which have discovered that they share certain interests in common. The entente cordial appears strange for two reasons: the rhetoric which claims that God-fearing Islam cannot make common cause with God-less Communism, and the creation and continuance of the association while Pakistan was in alliance with the United States. The author gives close attention to these apparent contradictions and attempts to resolve them in the name of *realpolitik*.

Foreign Relations. Contemporary

864 China and Southeast Asia: Peking's relations with revolutionary movements.
Jay Taylor. New York: Praeger, 1974. 384p.

This is a country-by-country study of China's relations with revolutionary movements in Southeast Asia. The historical analysis, drawn largely from government announcements, newspapers and radio reports, includes two chapters on Vietnam, one on Indonesia, one on Burma and a composite chapter on the allied states, which includes Thailand, Malaysia, Singapore and adjacent areas plus a brief summarizing section.

865 China, the struggle for power, 1917-1972.
Richard C. Thornton. Bloomington, Indiana: Indiana University Press, 1973. 403p.

There are three general topics which the author treats in this book. The first is the struggle between Nationalists and Communists for power. Second is the growth and development of the Chinese Communist Party and the rise to power of Mao Tse-tung (Mao Zedong). Finally comes the establishment and decay of the Sino-Soviet alliance and the history of the post-1949 period extending up to the present day. The work emphasizes the attempts by outside forces to influence the Chinese Communist movement.

866 Revolution and Chinese foreign policy: Peking's support for wars of national liberation.
Peter Van Ness. Berkeley, California: University of California Press, 1970. 266p.

This is a study of how the Maoists have interpreted the Chinese Communist Party's experience in making revolution in China from 1921 to 1949, and how they have applied the results to their attempts to foment the overthrow of governments in Asia, Africa and Latin America.

867 Peking's UN policy: continuity and change.
Byron S. J. Weng. New York: Praeger, 1972. 337p.

In the 22 years between the founding of the People's Republic of China and its seating in the United Nations, Peking's (Beijing) policies toward the world body went through many transformations - from the optimistic appointment of a delegation in early 1950, through the bitter denunciation of the early 1960s, to renewed interest in membership in the post-Cultural Revolution period. The book seeks to trace these policy twists and reveal some underlying themes.

868 The Chinese calculus: India and Indochina.
Allen Whiting. Ann Arbor, Michigan: University of Michigan Press, 1975. 299p.

The author seeks to present a framework for anticipating Chinese political-military behaviour. He reconstructs China's response to the perceived threat from India in 1962 and reveals the pattern of Peking's (Beijing) secret military participation in the Indochina war from 1964-1968. He then compares these conflicts with Chinese behaviour in Korea and on the Sino-Soviet border.

869 **Sino-Soviet crisis politics.**
Richard Wich. Cambridge, Massachusetts: Council on East
Asian Studies, Harvard University 1980. 313p.

Through an analysis of political perception and communication, this book explains
the structural change in the international political landscape that followed the
1968 Soviet intervention in Czechoslovakia. It examines the shifts in China's
global policies and analyzes the complex signaling process through which that
change was accomplished.

870 **China and the Great Powers: relations with the United
States, the Soviet Union, and Japan.**
Edited by Francis O. Wilcox. New York: Praeger, 1974.
103p.

This volume is comprised of four lectures given in the Christian A. Herter Lecture Series at the Johns Hopkins School of Advanced Studies in 1973. In his
introduction, Wilcox observes that the United States has had to pay an 'extremely
heavy diplomatic price' for the China policy it followed for so long. Since it is
still paying for the errors associated with that policy, the several treatments in
this book hold much topical interest.

871 **Issues in Japan's China policy.**
Mendle Wolf. New York: Oxford University Press, 1978.
178p.

The purpose of this book is to analyze the issues in Japan's China policy and to
consider the question of whether, over the past years, there has emerged a distinctive approach to China which not only signals a change from the policies and
perceptions of the previous half-century, but also offers some indication of future
trends. The issues are examined under headings such as trade, Taiwan, security
and China as a factor in domestic politics.

872 **China and the world since 1949: the impact of independence,
modernity and revolution.**
Wang Gung Wu. New York: St. Martin's Press, 1977.
190p.

This book attempts to weave together an analysis of the international relations
and domestic development of the People's Republic of China during the period
from 1949 through Mao's death in September 1976. The author identifies three
themes in this period of Chinese history - independence, modernity and revolution
- and constructs his interpretation on the basis of relationships among these
central Chinese themes.

873 **The strategic ridge, Peking's relations with Thailand,
Malaysia, Singapore and Indonesia.**
Yuanli Wu. Stanford, California: Hoover Institution, 1975.
97p.

The author, Yuan-li Wu (Yuanli Wu), argues that the United States does have
long-term strategic interests in safeguarding the non-Communist future of the
land-ridge (Thailand, Malaysia and Singapore) - while China is anxious to exploit
the weakness of the regions there to export revolution. Furthermore, Russia and
Japan are interested in preventing the closure of the strategic waterways between

the Indian Ocean and the South China Sea, as well as seeing that the strategic materials of the area remain available to all nations. To prove his assertions, the author analyzes the relations of the People's Republic of China with Thailand, Malaysia, Singapore and Indonesia.

874 Sino-American detente and its policy implications.
Edited by Gene T. Xiao. New York: Praeger, 1974. 319p.

The Sino-American detente of 1972 had far reaching implications for the balance of power in the world and for the patterns of international relationships, particularly in the Asia-Pacific region. This book examines these implications, covering such topics as the new balance of power in East Asia; the impact of the detente on Russia, Japan, Korea, Taiwan, Indochina, India and NATO allies; China's record in the United Nations; and prospects for Sino-American trade.

875 Sino-American normalization and its policy implication.
Edited by Gene T. Xiao, William R. Feeney. New York: Praeger, 1982. 300p.

This book begins by analyzing the process that led to the normalization of relations between China and the United States after President Nixon's visit to Peking (Beijing) in 1972. The authors, Hsiao (Xiao) and Feeney, then study the impact of normalization on the strategic situation in East Asia where the security interests of the four major powers, China, the United States, Japan and USSR, interact. They next examine the extent to which Chinese and American national interests are coincidental on the major global issues and the extent to which they differ from each other. Other topics include: political implications or normalization for the rest of the world; the implication of normalization for the development of bilateral trade and economic relations, scientific and technological exchanges, the need of China's modernization programme for American financing, the problems of China's ability to repay, the possibility of establishing joint ventures in China and the prospects of joint development of Chinese resources; problems of technological transfer to China; and the implications of American legal institutions for economic relations with China.

876 China in the global community.
Edited by James C. Xiong, Samuel S. Kim. New York: Praeger, 1980. 288p.

The authors Hsiung (Xiong) and Kim begin with a chapter on the methodology of its study, suggesting a globalistic view which relates every single act to an overall design, or a reactive model, in which China can be seen as reacting to external stimuli and demands. It follows with a discussion of Mao's concept of world order and specifically China's refusal to join the superpower club, choosing instead to cast its fate with that of the Third World.

877 China's role in world affairs.
Michael B. Yahuda. London: Croom Helm, 1978. 293p.

The main operational concepts and the themes of China's foreign policy are traced as they developed in the context of current events; the author sees China as an integral component of the world in the conduct of foreign policy, but as a country that conducts domestic affairs in a totally autonomous manner.

878 **The end of Isolationism - China's foreign policy after Mao.**
Michael B. Yahuda. New York: Macmillan, 1982. 240p.
This book examines in depth the changes that have occurred in China's foreign relations since the death of Mao. The relations between China and the United States, USSR, European Economic Community and Third World countries are viewed from China's economic, political and strategic standpoint. The author argues that these changes have occurred not only because of external factors but because of China's internal struggles for modernization. This book provides a fascinating insight into the role China plays in the balance of world power.

879 **China since Mao.**
Edited by Kwan Ha Yim. New York: Macmillan, 1980. 200p.
This book adopts a developmental approach in analyzing events which have occurred in China since the death of Mao. It provides a narrative account of domestic and foreign events in what is essentially an analytical look at recent changes in policy.

880 **China's African policy: a study of Tanzania.**
George T. Yu. New York: Praeger, 1975. 200p.
This study of a diplomatic relationship of unequals concludes that the Sino-Tanzanian alliance endures in part because it serves not only the international but also the domestic interests of both partners.

881 **The foreign relations of the People's Republic of China.**
Edited by Winberg Zhai. New York: Capricorn Books, 1972. 420p.
This is a book of readings and historical synoposes meant to serve as introductory texts in courses dealing with Chinese foreign policy. The author, Winberg Chai (Zhai), arranges his selections by analytical categories. The documents are grouped under seven headings: the meaning of Maoism, Sino-American relations, Sino-Soviet disputes, Chinese strategies in developing areas, policies on overseas Chinese, boundaries and disputed territories and world order.

882 **Dimensions of China's foreign relations.**
Zhundu Xue. New York: Praeger, 1977. 293p.
The author Chun-tu Hsueh (Zhundu Xue) examines the basic factors that motivate China's foreign policy and attempts to illustrate this foreign policy. Case studies include China's relations with Japan, Nepal, the Soviet Union, the United States, Latin America and the Middle East.

883 **China's foreign relations: new perspectives.**
Zhundu Xue. New York: Praeger, 1982. 224p.
In this volume, edited by Chun-tu Hsueh (Zhundu Xue), the contributors examine China's foreign relations with the superpowers, Japan, Korea, the ASEAN states, France, Western Europe, Eastern Europe and Latin America with particular attention given to questions of security and how perceptions influence policy. Special attention is given to China's grand strategy of the international united front, the theory of the three worlds and the editor's thesis that China's foreign policy is based on a balance with the two superpowers. When Peking's

(Beijing) relations with one or both of them changed, its relations with many other countries invariably changed accordingly.

884 **China: US policy since 1945.**
Washington, DC: US Government Printing Office for the *Congressional Quarterly*, 1980. 387p.

This is a revision and updating of a 1968 *Congressional Quarterly* publication. It contains a 70-page introduction, a chronology of events between 1945 and January 1980, biographical sketches of both Chinese Nationalist and Communist leaders, brief notes on US policy-makers, the text of significant American and Chinese documents and a number of maps, charts, tables and a summary of information. The book has been digested from US and foreign news accounts, journals, government publications and the writing of China specialists.

Economy

885 The political economy of the Chinese revolution.
Eric Axilrod. Hong Kong: Union Research Institute, 1972.
541p.

The author attempts to review and interpret China's agricultural progress since 1949. He provides his own unique assessment of China's economic performance, mainly agricultural and lengthily attempts to formulate the economic laws of a collective economy, largely based on the Chinese experience.

886 The Chinese agricultural economy.
Edited by Randolph Barker, Radha Sinha, Beth
Rose. Boulder, Colorado: Westview Press, 1982. 266p.

In this book, the authors present an array of views analyzing the past successes and failures of China in its efforts to increase agricultural production and improve its people's standard of living. Throughout their discussions the authors emphasize that the economic development of China is dependent on many factors, including social institutions, natural resource potential, technological development and government policy and its implementation. Information on these factors is presented along with a view of Chinese agricultural development in a comparative international context.

887 China's economy in global perspective.
A. Doak Barnett. Washington, DC: Brookings, 1980. 776p.

In this study, the author analyzes the recent changes in China's policies at home and abroad, the new problems that the Chinese face, the likely prospects for future growth in their domestic economy and foreign trade and the policy issues that China's growing participation in the international economy pose for other nations, particularly concerning technology imports, financial prospects and policy issues in US-Chinese economic relations.

Economy

888 **China's four modernizations: the new technological revolution.**
Edited by Richard Baum. Boulder, Colorado: Westview
Press, 1980. 307p.

This is a collection of articles on one of the core issues in China's modernization
drive: China's ability to acquire, use and disseminate modern technology. The
authors offer different responses to one crucial question. How effective can a
highly bureaucratized political system be in encouraging innovation and disseminating technology in the absence of a market mechanism?

889 **A Chinese/English dictionary of China's rural economy.**
Kieran Broadbent. Slough, England: Commonwealth
Agricultural Bureau, 1978. 406p.

This dictionary thoroughly covers terminology common in materials on the rural
areas (emphasizing the People's Republic of China), including agrotechnical, economic, political and administrative terms and phrases.

890 **The Chinese economy.**
Jay Deleyore, translated from French by Robert
Leriche. London: Deutsch, 1973. 207p.

This is the English version of M. Deleyore's study of post-1949 economic developments, first published in French in 1971. There are chapters on China's economic
heritage, economic management and organization; population and employment;
agriculture, industry and transport; technical and scientific developments; foreign
trade; and the economy during and after the Cultural Revolution.

891 **China's development experience in comparative perspective.**
Edited by Robert F. Dernberger. Cambridge,
Massachusetts: Harvard University Press, 1980. 360p.

This volume contains essays on the Chinese economy concentrating on income
distribution, industrial technology and public health. It also includes speculation
on the transferability of China's experience to other Third World countries.

892 **China's economic development: the interplay of scarcity and
ideology.**
Alexander Eckstein. Ann Arbor, Michigan: University of
Michigan Press, 1975. 389p.

This volume contains 12 essays written over a couple of decades by the acknowledged 'American Dean' of the scholars of Chinese economics. Two of the essays
investigate some aspects of general development theory, two are on the pre-
Communist economy of China and the remaining eight follow the convolutions of
the People's Republic of China over the quarter-century of its growth. All of the
essays are distinguished by their lucidity and many by their instructive comparisons of China's experiences with those of Eastern European countries, especially
the USSR.

893 China's economic revolution.
Alexander Eckstein.   New York: Cambridge University
Press, 1977. 340p.
This is a study of China's efforts in the last twenty-five years to achieve rapid
modernization of its economy within a socialist framework. The author concludes
that, barring a repetition of the Great Leap Forward, the Cultural Revolution, or
a similar upheaval, China should be able to sustain a six per cent rate of growth
to the end of this century. This would quadruple the gross domestic product and
make China one of the five largest economies in the world.

894 Quantitative measures of China's economic output.
Edited by Alexander Eckstein.   Ann Arbor, Michigan:
University of Michigan Press, 1979. 386p.
Eckstein organized and coordinated the papers which comprise this volume so as
to clarify the issues surrounding China's major macro-economic indicators, such
as agriculture and industrial production, capital formation and gross national
product. After Eckstein's death in 1976, Robert Dernberger took over the editorship to prepare the volume for publication. The result is a rich legacy of Alexander Eckstein's scholarship and public service.

895 Socialist planning.
Michael Ellman.   New York: Cambridge University Press,
1979. 300p.
In his introduction, the author outlines the evolving rationale of planning in the
broad sense of state intervention in both market and socialist situations. In subsequent chapters he deals with agriculture, investment, labour, incomes and foreign
trade. Readers of this book will find China treated at some length.

896 The pattern of the Chinese past: a social and economic interpretation.
Mark Elvin.   Stanford, California: Stanford University
Press, 1973. 346p.
This book examines the evolution of Chinese society from the 2nd to the 19th
century in terms of changing patterns in the economics of technology. The author
deals in turn with three major questions. Firstly, by what virtue did the Chinese
empire remain united when the Roman Empire and all other historic empires
ultimately collapsed? Secondly, what caused the technical revolution that made
12th-century China the most advanced nation in the world? Finally, why did
Sung China's flair for technology disappear and fail to produce the equivalent of
the Industrial Revolution in the West? Particular attention is paid to the manner
in which economic and military technology both affected and were affected by
social and political institutions. China was caught in what the author terms a
'high-level equilibrium trap'. The book closes with some of the implications of this
theory for Chinese development in this century.

897 **The foreign establishment in China in the early twentieth century.**
Albert Feuerwerker. Ann Arbor, Michigan: Center for China Studies, University of Michigan, 1976. 120p.

This book offers the reader a precise but static description of the foreign interests in China between 1910 and 1920, which marked the apogee of their impact on China. As the author remarks, foreign imperialism in China is often discussed but is as yet uncharted. In his essay, he has begun to fill this gap.

898 **Economic trends of China, 1912-1949.**
Albert Feuerwerker. Ann Arbor, Michigan: Center for Chinese Studies, University of Michigan, 1979. 123p.

The book is intended as a discussion of the wider aspects of rebellion in 19th-century China. After giving a brief factual account of various rebellions, the author goes on to consider their economic and social origins, rebel ideologies and rebel social groups, with equal importance being given to religious and ethnic minorities, to lineage organizations, to peasant militias, to sects, bandits and secret societies.

899 **The development of cotton textile production in China.**
Gang Zhao. Cambridge, Massachusetts: Harvard University Press, 1977. 402p.

The author, Kang Chao (Gang Zhao) presents significant information about the history of cotton textiles in China. He deals with several aspects of handicraft textiles that are fundamental to an understanding of the role of that sector in Chinese economic history.

900 **China's changing role in the world economy.**
Edited by Bryant G. Garth. New York: Praeger, 1975. 222p.

The book consists of nine articles and a short introduction devoted to the understanding of the complete interplay of international politics and economics in China's present strategy of development. It examines Chinese attitudes toward self-reliance in the context of the changing international political scene.

901 **China's economy and the Maoist strategy.**
John G. Gurley. New York: Monthly Review Press, 1976. 325p.

The first three of the collected essays focus on aspects of economic development and strategy in China; the fourth is entitled 'Mao and the building of socialism'. The fifth essay concerns rural development. The sixth and seventh deal with the financial system, prices and profits. In his concluding essay, the author considers whether Chinese economic systems can be used profitably by other underdeveloped countries.

902 **Crisis and prosperity in Sung China.**
Edited by John W. Haeger. Tucson, Arizona: University of
Arizona Press, 1975. 264p.

This volume contains eight separate essays - covering Sung economic, political
and intellectual history and in the introduction, the editor ties them loosely
together.

903 **Shanghai: revolution and development in an Asian metropolis.**
Edited by Christopher Howe. Cambridge, England:
Cambridge University Press, 1980. 456p.

This volume contains a collection of essays showing how Shanghai was transformed politically, economically and culturally by the Chinese Communist Party
between 1949 and late 1970s. It also contains tables and maps.

904 **China's economy: a basic guide.**
Christopher Howe. London: Elek, 1978. 248p.

The author sets the stage with a brief introduction which identifies the turning
points in recent Chinese economic history and the directions of that change. Six
subsequent chapters review within this framework: the development of population
and human resources, including their education and employment; the organization
and planning of economic activities, with emphasis on state controlled industry
and collective agriculture; the relatively slow development of agricultural production and its gradual modernization; the relatively rapid development of industrial
production, especially in selected industries and the evolution of small-scale industries; the role of trade with the rest of the world, its changing value, structure
and organization; and the implications of all these developments for the structure
of income and rural and urban standards of living. The author's aim is to provide
for a nonspecialist audience a basic factual account of China's recent economic
development.

905 **The development of underdevelopment in China: a symposium.**
Edited by Philip C. C. Huang. White Plains, New York:
Sharpe, 1979. 146p.

This volume critically examines various theories of underdevelopment and
responses to these controversial theories by Mark Elvin, Albert Feuerwerker,
André Gunder, Frank Keith Griffin and Carl Riskin.

906 **Chinese economic planning: characteristics, objectives and
methods - an introduction.**
Gerhard Hulcrants, Hakan Lindhoff, Jan
Valdelin. Stockholm: Economic Research Institute,
Stockholm School of Economics, 1977. 274p.

The authors deal with the origins of economic planning in China, the general
pre-requisites of planning, information systems, planning institutions as they
evolved over time, administrative decentralization and the Great Leap Forward,
procedures of financing planning and control, the Cultural Revolution's effect on
planning and the content and application of economic plans from 1949 to 1975.
The last chapter gives a summary of China's economic achievements under various functional headings.

Economy

907 China as a model of development.
Al Imfeld.   Mary Knoll, New York: Orbis Books, 1976.
159p.

The author sees China as a challenge to most theories of development currently
held in both the developed and developing nations. It is his contention that
China's experience offers to the Third World a more valuable lesson than they
can learn from the industrialized nations which they have so often tried to imi-
tate.

908 A concise economic history of modern China, 1840-1961.
Frank H. H. King.   New York: Praeger, 1970. 243p.

The author struggles with inadequate statistical evidence to probe the important
aspects of the Ch'ing (Qing) economic system and the effects of Western intervention in China and Taiwan. He deals with some major aspects of modern
Chinese economic history in the last 150 years, including traditional economy and
the Western impact, China's attempt at modernization and the economic relations
between India and China in the 19th century, with specific reference to Anglo-
Indian banking in coastal China.

909 Chinese economic planning: translation from Chi-hua Ching-chi.
Edited by Nicholas R. Lardy, translated by K. K.
Fung.   White Plains, New York: Sharpe, 1978. 280p.

This volume contains two series of articles on economic planning which appeared
in *Chi-hua Ching-chi* (*Jihua Jingji*) (*Economic Planning*) during the 1950s. The
first series of 17 articles, entitled 'Lectures on national economic planning',
appeared in 1955 and the second series of 14 articles, entitled 'Lectures on basic
knowledge of national economic plan', appeared in 1957 and 1958. It becomes
increasingly relevant as China's post-Mao leadership stresses anew economic
growth and modernization and a return to more regularized, formalized economic
planning.

910 Economic growth and distribution in China.
Nicholas R. Lardy.   New York: Cambridge University
Press, 1978. 244p.

This is a study of resource allocation and income distribution in China. The
author concludes that China has achieved both a rapid rate of growth and a
relatively equitable distribution of income. Mao's pro-peasant policies were highly
divisive and brought sharp declines in industrial output, strikes and work stop-
pages, some of which required army intervention to put down. This widespread
worker unrest, combined with lagging technological progress, may help explain
the switch to a new development strategy by new leadership.

911 Ch'en Yun's strategy for China's development: a non-Maoist alternative.
Edited with an introduction by Nicholas R. Lardy, Kenneth
Lieberthal.   Armonk, New York: Sharpe, 1982. 357p.

Ch'en Yun (Chen Yun), vice-chairman of the Chinese Communist Party and a
vice-premier of the People's Republic of China is the chief architect of China's
post-Mao economic reforms and a leading critic of Maoist approaches to eco-

nomic development. The texts translated in this volume were published by the Communist Party for internal distribution and widely disseminated in 1981 with the support of a coalition of leaders who favour a less bureaucratic and more market orientated system of resource allocation. The texts provide unusual insights into the economic thinking of Ch'en Yun, the central figure of the reformist group.

912 The dragon's wings: the China National Aviation Corporation and the development of commercial aviation in China.
William M. Lardy, Jr. Athens, Georgia: University of Georgia Press, 1976. 226p.

The first flight of an airplane in China in 1909 ended in disaster. It crashed before a crowd of astonished spectators at the Shanghai race course. This early failure was prophetic of the troubled development of civil aviation in China. The author captures the excitement and drama of aviation in a book packed with action and human interest.

913 The city in Communist China.
Edited by John W. Lewis. Stanford, California: Stanford University Press, 1971. 449p.

This book contains eleven long essays. Each paper reflects the concerns of its author and gives readers only a tangential view of major urban social, political or economic problems.

914 Land reform and economic development in China: a study of institutional change and development finance.
Victor Lippit. White Plains, New York: International Arts and Sciences Press, 1974. 183p.

Economic development always depends on diversifying funds from consumption to investment. This work argues that land reform in China in the early 1950s offered a useful tool to accomplish such saving, by shifting the agricultural surplus away from rent payments to landlords who consumed and into tax payments to a state which invested. The statistical data are carefully selected and the mathematics is ingenious.

915 China: development and challenge: proceedings of the fifth Leverhulme conference.
Lee Ngok, Leung Chi-Keung. Hong Kong: Center of Asian Studies, University of Hong Kong, 1979. 2 vols.

The Leverhulme Conference was designed to promote multi-disciplinary inquiry into the 'Chinese way' and 'to contribute to a re-examination and re-interpretation of the implications and challenge of Chinese development'. Volume I contains two sections: aspects of Chinese historical experience since the mid-19th century and Marxist and Maoist ideology pre- and post-1949, along with a few papers on specific political issues in the People's Republic of China. Volume II also contains two sections: one on theoretical and practical issues of contemporary Chinese political economy and one on geographical studies of spatial and ecological variables in both rural and urban contexts.

Economy

916 **Ten great years: statistics of the economic and cultural achievements of the People's Republic of China.**
Introduction by Fenghua Ma, compiled by Beijing State Statistical Bureau. Bellingham, Washington: Western Washington State College Press, 1974. 154p.

Ten Great Years remains the only official statistical handbook ever published by the People's Republic of China. It is of great importance to students of the Chinese economy as a benchmark against which other data may be judged. It was first published in Chinese in 1959.

917 **The fading of the Maoist vision: city and country in China's development.**
Rhoads Murphey. London: Methuen, 1980. 192p.

This book gives a picture of Chinese society through study of the key role which the city plays in social planning. It is especially valuable in setting China's achievements in the larger context of Third World ideas about problems of national development, particularly those of India.

918 **The outsiders: the Western experience in India and China.**
Rhoads Murphey. Ann Arbor, Michigan: University of Michigan Press, 1977. 299p.

The author attempts to compare the effects of imperialism on India and China, with occasional references to Japan and Southeast Asia. Why did India embrace the Western model while China rejected it? The author finds the answer in the economic, cultural and political vitality of China's traditional order as compared to the weakness and demoralization of India's at the moment of Western impact.

919 **China's developmental experience.**
Edited by Michel Oksenberg. New York: Praeger, 1973. 227p.

This collection of essays suggests that Maoism most notably teaches a belief in the possibility of radical change and a commitment to the humanization of bureaucracy.

920 **China's modern economy in historical perspective.**
Edited by Dwight H. Perkins. Stanford, California: Stanford University Press, 1975. 344p.

The papers discuss the positive and negative effects of foreign imperialism on Chinese economic development, the adequacy of China's financial resources for major economic initiatives, the changing structure of the national product and the distribution of income.

921 **The Chinese economy: problems and policies.**
Jan S. Prybya. Columbia, South Carolina: University of South Carolina, 1978. 258p.

Despite some recent assertions that the Cultural Revolution 'lost' China a decade of growth, Chinese economic development has progressed over the past thirty years. Technical and social reforms have transformed a poor, backward, peasant economy into a socialist state which is able regularly to provide essential food, clothing and housing. A comprehensive overview of this transformation, this volume presents sectoral studies of China's demography, agriculture, industry, banking, transport, trade, health and education.

922 Economic management in China.

Joan Robinson. London: Anglo-Chinese Educational Institute, 1975. 2nd ed. 50p.

This pamphlet by Professor Joan Robinson, the eminent Cambridge economist, stems from a six-week trip to China in May and June 1972. There is no shortage of fresh material: the brief section on finance for instance, provides more detail on recent developments in revenue-sharing than can be found in any Chinese publication or broadcast.

923 The modernization of China.

Edited by Gilberg Rozman. New York: Free Press, 1981. 551p.

This volume packs in a vast amount of data and analysis under some four dozen topics like 'income distribution', 'line of authority', or 'base-level organization'. Its comparisons with Japan and Russia focus on the haunting question of why China, once so relatively advanced in the world, fell behind and had such trouble catching up. To approach the problem by way of the comparative indicators used in modernization studies gives readers a useful perspective.

924 Guerrilla economy: the development of the Shensi-Kansu-Ninghsia border region, 1937-1945.

Peter Schran. Albany, New York: State University of New York Press, 1976. 323p.

This book is mainly about the economic development of the Shen-Kan-Ning (Shen-Gan-Ning) border region by the Chinese Communists during 1937-45. The author examines the economics of an industrially backward, agriculturally poor area of China occupied by the Chinese Communists during the Chinese-Japanese War. He discusses various aspects of development including: labour organization, motivation and incentives, external relations regarding balance of trade, financial aid from the Nationalist Government, budget, deficit, inflation, taxes and the struggle for self-sufficiency.

925 The transition to socialism in China.

Mark Selden, Victor Lippit. Armonk, New York: Sharpe, 1982. 359p.

Ten leading scholars of the Chinese revolution examine the impact of post-Mao economic and developmental policies on the transition and their implications for the future of socialism in China.

926 China's energy: achievements, problems, prospects.

Vaclav Smil. New York: Praeger, 1976. 246p.

Few subjects are of greater or wider importance than China's energy situation. The book attempts to look at the energy sector as a whole and it is a welcome contribution to our knowledge.

Economy

927 Economic growth in China and India, 1952-1970: a comparative appraisal.

Subramanian Swamy. Chicago: University Chicago Press, 1973. 84p.

The author has calculated from the limited data available, the 'value added' for agriculture and industry and has estimated the role of the available service sectors, thereby arriving at overall economic growth rates for India and China.

928 Foreign intervention and China's economic development, 1870-1911.

Stephen C. Thomas. Boulder, Colorado: Westview Press, 1983. 200p.

The author takes the view that foreign intervention had more influence than purely domestic concerns on the nation's industrialization efforts. He points to the year 1897 as a turning point in China's development. Prior to that date, costly levels of foreign intervention hampered, but did not prevent, the successful development of modern enterprises in transportation, mining and manufacturing. Afterward, however, greatly increased levels of intervention destroyed the chances of success of many new ones.

929 China's nationalization of foreign firms: the politics of hostage capitalism, 1949-57.

Thomas N. Thompson. Baltimore, Maryland: School of Law, University of Maryland, 1979. 72p.

This volume focuses on the difficulties that British firms encountered in trying to extricate themselves from their direct investments in Shanghai after 1949. Many of these firms wanted to continue in the China trade, but the new Chinese government adopted laws and practices that made these ventures totally unprofitable.

930 Fundamentals of political economy.

Edited by George C. Wang. White Plains, New York: Sharpe, 1977. 507p.

This volume contains a translation of an introductory treatise on political economy in China in 1974. The book is a clear exposition of Maoist views on economics.

931 Economic reform in the PRC.

Translated and edited by George C. Wang. Boulder, Colorado: Westview Press, 1982. 156p.

In the volume, China's economists offer candid analyses of the strengths and weaknesses of the present economic system. Their lucid and penetrating comments lend insight to our comprehension of China's economic problems and the country's prospects for the future. Each article is based on first-hand information and data, much of which is made available here for the first time.

932 **Mao Zedong and the political economy of the border region: a translation of Mao's economic and financial problems.**
Edited and translated by Andrew Watson. New York: Cambridge University Press, 1980. 397p.

This volume gives important insights into the origins of Mao's thinking on questions of economic development and political economy. It also contains detailed information on the economy of the border region and the innovations introduced by the Communist Party between 1936 and 1942.

933 **The Chinese road to socialism: economics of the Cultural Revolution.**
E. L. Wheelwright, Bruce McFarlane. New York: Monthly Review Press, 1970. 256p.

This is a general survey of the Chinese political economy since 1949. The first section outlines economic developments up to the Cultural Revolution in 1966. The second section examines the significance of the Cultural Revolution. The authors suggest that the major impact lay in increasing moral incentives toward production and planning. The final section briefly assesses the relevance of recent Maoist political-economic strategies to other socialist and nonsocialist developing nations.

934 **Equality and development in the People's Republic of China.**
Gordon White, Peter Nolan. New York: Macmillan, 1982. 232p.

This book is the first comprehensive analysis of the distinctive development strategy of the People's Republic of China which aims at both quantitative economic growth and technological development on the one hand and radical qualitative changes in social and political structure, social relationships and distribution on the other. In analyzing the success and/or failure of this strategy, the authors use comparative data from other societies and address themselves to most of the central questions with which scholars in the field of development are concerned.

935 **China's future: foreign policy and economic development in the post-Mao era.**
Allen S. Whiting, Robert F. Dernberger. New York: McGraw-Hill, 1977. 202p.

In this volume, the authors suggest that the imperatives of China's economic development and the position China occupies in the international economic system will be more important elements in determining China's policies than the particular leaders in power. Dernberger's essay projects a significant but diminished rate of economic growth with little prospect for an agricultural breakthrough. Whiting foresees a growing Chinese relationship with the industrialized nations as the most likely future course for China if those nations are able to respond imaginatively to China's needs.

936 **Economic organization in Chinese society.**
Edited by W. E. Willmott. Stanford, California: Stanford University Press, 1972. 461p.

The contributors deal topically with matters such as agriculture, crafts, industries, marketing and credit and the organization of government relations to commerce, as in the case of the salt monopoly. Several of the articles deal with the 18th and 19th centuries.

937 The international energy relations of China.
Kim Woodard. New York: Columbia University Press, 1980. 487p.

This comprehensive political and statistical analysis treats all aspects of China's energy development and foreign energy policy. Part I describes, analyzes and projects the course of China's international energy relations from 1949 through the year 2000. Part II presents a detailed, coordinated set of statistics on energy balance and nearly 100 statistical tables that give data for the resource, production, consumption and trade stages of each energy industry, with projected statistics to the year 2000.

938 Almanac of China's economy 1981: with economic statistics 1949-1981.
Xue Muqiao. New York: Harper, 1982. 1,128p.

This definitive report from the People's Republic of China offers the only account of the development of China's socialist economy over the past 30 years, making available all statistics and developments since 1949. *Almanac of China's Economy* will be updated annually, providing the only official report by the Chinese themselves of their economic, political and business trends.

939 Current economic problems in China.
Xue Muqiao, edited and translated with an introduction by K. K. Fung. Boulder, Colorado: Westview Press, 1982. 159p.

This book brings together papers and speeches by Xue Muqiao (Hsueh Much'iao), one of China's most prominent economists and one of its key spokesmen for liberal economic reform. Xue (Hsueh) addresses such issues as commune and brigade enterprises, employment, wages and price adjustments; proportional imbalances among industries, within industries, and between capital accumulation and consumption; problems associated with current economic reforms; and proposals for future reforms. The introduction by K. K. Fung traces the development of Xue's (Hsueh) views since the publication of his earlier work (q.v.) and evaluates the implications of China's liberal economic policies for Third World countries.

940 China's economic development: growth and structural change.
Zhuyuan Zheng. Boulder, Colorado: Westview Press, 1982. 535p.

How has the government of the People's Republic of China transformed traditional economic institutions into a socialist, central-planning system? What has been the impact of this transformation on China's economic growth? What is the essence of the Chinese development model and how successfully has it functioned during the past three decades? What are the prospects for the future? In this comprehensive and up-to-date analysis of the Chinese economy from 1949 to the present, the author, Chu-yuan Cheng (Zhuyuan Zheng), answers these key questions as he discusses China's economic development and the operation of its economic system.

941 **China under the four modernizations, part i.**
Washington, DC: US Government Printing Office, 1982.
610p.

This volume is composed of selected papers submitted to the Joint Committee of
the US Congress. According to the specialists who contributed to this volume,
China's overall performance is characterized by strong but erratic growth and
China is one of the few developing nations to have avoided massive foreign debt.
On the other hand, agricultural production is barely keeping up with population;
oil production peaked in 1979 and is declining; and energy shortfalls will be a
brake on growth for the next few years. Finally, inflation, unemployment and
industrial bottlenecks have been increasing and they raise the possibility that the
current emphasis on raising living standards may be only temporary. Thus, there
may be continuing shifts in Chinese economic policy rather than the widely
predicted stability.

942 **Present-day China: socio-economic problems (collected
papers).**
Moscow: Progress Publications, 1975. 248p.

Russian, East German, Bulgarian and Mongolian commentators offer some views
on modern China. Their perspectives range from antagonism to outrage.

943 **Rural small-scale industry in the People's Republic of China.**
American Rural Small-Scale Industry
Delegation. Berkeley, California: University of California
Press, 1977. 266p.

The eleven chapters cover social administrative systems, worker incentives, the
economics of rural small-scale industry, agricultural mechanization and production, small-scale chemical fertilizer and cement technologies, the connection of
small-scale industry with agriculture, the impact of small-scale industry on
Chinese society and expanding knowledge and transforming attitudes in China.

Chinese Watergate: political and economic conflict in China, 1969-1977.
See item no. 664.

Finance and Banking

944 China's finance and trade: a policy reader.
Edited by Gordon A. Bennett. White Plains, New York: Sharpe, 1979. 256p.

This is a survey designed as a text for a course in contemporary Chinese economics and politics. Drawing on current pre-Cultural Revolution primary sources, the book covers the general economic line, planning and markets and banking and investment.

945 China's financial system: the changing role of banks.
William Byrd. Boulder, Colorado: Westview Press, 1982. 150p.

The book provides a detailed account of the institutional structure of China's financial and banking systems; a review of policy and performance in 1949-1976, the key features of post-Mao China's economic reform package and developments in 1976-1982; an evaluation of the success of the main financial and banking reforms, especially in the area of investment financing; and an assessment of the prospects for the future.

946 Bankers and diplomats in China, 1917-1925: the Anglo-American relationship.
Roberta Albert Dayer. London: Cass, 1981. 295p.

The author analyzes official and private pronouncements by British and American diplomats and provides insights into the relations between the diplomats and bankers who led the Second Consortium, the mechanism through which these powers sought to implement their China policy.

947 Capital formation in mainland China, 1952-1965.
Gang Zhao. Berkeley, California: University of California Press, 1974. 196p.

The author, Kang Chao (Gang Zhao), attempts to provide a comprehensive measurement of fixed capital investment in China. He has compiled information both from diverse Chinese publications and from sources in countries that have exported capital goods to China and analyzes facets of the investment drive as well as the relationship between capital accumulation and the major aspects of Chinese economic development. He discusses many details previously unknown to the West.

948 **Money and monetary policy in communist China.**
Katherine Huang Xiao. New York: Columbia University Press, 1971. 298p.

This book shows that an understanding of the Chinese monetary system is a prerequiste to understanding the overall functioning of the economy. The author describes the control of the money supply in detail and has particularly interesting accounts of the 'booms' of 1953, 1956 and 1958 and of the role of the banking system in bringing these under control.

949 **Taxation and government finance in 16th century Ming China.**
R. Huang. New York: Cambridge University Press, 1980. 396p.

This pioneering work should be placed high on the list of books which are essential reading for the history of the Ming-Ch'ing (Ming-Qing) period.

950 **Shanghai old-style banks (Ch'ien-chuan - Qian Zhuan) 1800-1935.**
Andrea Lee McElderry. Ann Arbor, Michigan: Center for Chinese Studies, University of Michigan, 1976. 230p.

The author shows how, after 1935, the enhanced capacity of the central government to control fiscal affairs, including the adoption of a state-controlled currency system and the nationalization of leading private banks, finally tipped the balance of power permanently away from the old-style banks.

951 **China's international banking and financial system.**
Paul D. Reynolds. New York: Praeger, 1982. 128p.

Intended for bankers, corporate planners, lawyers and academics in economics and finance, this book summarizes the banking and financial systems of China and the policies that evolved from 1978 through 1981. The author shows how these years have been filled with startling reversals of traditional practices and marked by intense interest from outside China and an extraordinary openness from within. The book explains the role that China's banks play in both domestic and international economic policy. The Bank of China's unique role in regulating the economy and providing funds for expansion is explained.

952 **Land taxation in imperial China, 1750-1911.**
Yeqian Wang. Cambridge, Massachusetts: Harvard University Press, 1974. 216p.

The author, Yeh-ch'ien Wang (Yeqian Wang), provides a reliable estimate and an in-depth analysis of imperial China's principal source of public revenue, the land tax, in the Ch'ing (Qing) period. The approach used by the author is both institutional and quantitative as he studies how the land-tax system worked and how much revenue was produced from this source.

Finance and Banking

953 **The pawnshop in China.**
J. S. Whelan.   Ann Arbor, Michigan: Center for Chinese
Studies, University of Michigan, 1979. 81p.

In this short book, the author offers readers in the English language a useful
introduction to the oldest credit institution in China - pawnshops. It begins with a
brief sketch of the origins, development and demise of pawnshops in China. The
main body of the book, however, is devoted to a description of the internal
organization and business management of the first-class pawnshops known as *tien*
(*dian*) in the late 19th and early 20th centuries. It also touches on interest rates
charged and government regulation of the industry.

954 **China's nation-building effort, 1927-1937: the financial and
economic record.**
Arthur H. Young.   Stanford, California: Hoover Institution,
1971. 553p.

The first part of the book deals with the fiscal and monetary policy of the
Nationalist government. The latter part of the book deals with aspects of modernization under the Nationalist government, such as developments in agriculture,
transport, foreign trade and foreign aid.

955 **China's allocation of fixed capital investment 1952-1957.**
Zheng Zhuyuan.   Ann Arbor, Michigan: Center for Chinese
Studies, University of Michigan, 1974. 115p.

The author, Cheng Chu-yuan (Zheng Zhuyuan), focuses on the structure of
investment in the People's Republic of China. The study is divided into four
parts. The first part describes the official statistics on capital investment. The
second part presents the broad sectoral allocation of fixed capital investment,
compares the allocation with that of other countries and examines the sectoral
capital-output ratios. The third and fourth sections deal in greater detail with
allocation of investment within the non-agricultural and agricultural sections
respectively.

Trade

956 China and the world food system.
A. Doak Barnett. Washington, DC: Overseas Development Council, 1979. 115p.

After a brief general description of the world food problems, the author devotes his analysis to China's food and agricultural situation. The book presents in clear and precise terms China's place in the 'World food system', thereby allowing the reader to put into perspective the importance of Chinese agriculture and to measure the multiple consequences of a good or bad grain harvest in that country.

957 Trade with China: assessment by leading businessmen and scholars.
Edited by Patrick M. Boarman. New York: Praeger, 1974. 192p.

This is a collection of speeches made at two conferences held in 1972. Some of the talks retain their timeliness to inform businessmen who would like to know about China. These include general and highly realistic assessments by David Wilson, Marshal Green and A. Doak Barnett.

958 Doing business with the People's Republic of China.
O. Bohdan, Maria R. Szuprowics. New York: Wiley, 1978. 449p.

This is a useful industry-by-industry assessment of the economy, geared to Western businessmen interested in the China market.

959 The China trade and US tariffs.
Harry A. Cahill. New York: Praeger, 1973. 170p.

This volume includes a summary of the history and recent changes in US control of trade with China and the changes in the level and structure of China's economy and foreign trade since 1949. The author evaluates various estimates which have been made for the potential trade between China and the US and argues that the reasons why the Chinese export trade to the US did not grow more rapidly was mainly due to poor merchandising practices on the part of US businessmen and the existence of the non-most-favoured-nation tariff.

960 Merchants, mandarins and modern enterprises in late Ch'ing (Qing) China.
Wellington K. K. Chan.   Cambridge, Massachusetts: Harvard University Press, 1977. 323p.

The author traces the development of modern enterprise in late Ch'ing (Qing) China from its traditional roots to the rise of the official entrepreneur. He sees in this development a growing bureaucratization of provincial government involvement, which eventually stifled merchant participation of the earlier forms of business operation. Case histories of individual merchants, firms and bureaucrats reveal a bewildering variety of arrangements, some of which resulted in considerable economic advance, while others foundered. The author concludes that despite a growing inter-relationship between mercantile and official personnel, late Ch'ing (Qing) efforts to modernize China's economy lacked the scale and coherence needed to make a decisive break with the past.

961 US-Chinese trade negotiations.
John W. De Pauw.   New York: Praeger, 1981. 252p.

Although much has been written about the history and activity surrounding US-China trade, little has been published about the process of negotiating with trade officials of the People's Republic. This book determines what impediments are faced by US firms undertaking commercial negotiations with the Chinese government and how these hindrances may be overcome. The author's findings are based on results from questionnaires sent to US companies accounting for a large percentage of all annual US-Chinese trade, personal interviews with US business executives, lawyers and government officials and finally, basic source documents from US companies concerning their negotiations for various commercial contracts.

962 China business manual, 1981.
Compiled by Christopher M. Clark, Katherine L. Dewenter.   Washington, DC: National Council for US China Trade, 1981. 318p.

This is a guidebook for anyone seriously planning to conduct business with the People's Republic of China. It provides a clearly-organized listing of 88 commissions, ministries and state agencies, all top Communist Party and government officials, more than 200 factories and over 100 banks and branches. Included are telephone numbers, indexed by product and organization.

963 China trade prospects and US policy.
Edited by Jerome Alan Cohen, Robert F. Dernberger, John R. Carson, with an introduction by Alexander Eckstein, preface by Robert A. Scalapino.   New York: Praeger, 1971. 329p.

This study focuses on the US controls on trade with China which originated in 1949. The five contributors seek to put into new perspective some of the crucial problems related to the lifting of the US embargo against China and China's easing of legal restraints on foreign trade and offer a projection on aid and trade between the two nations.

964 **The China trade: export paintings, furniture, silver and other objects.**
Carl L. Crossman, with a foreward by Ernest S.
Dodge. New York: Pyne Press, 1975. 275p.

This volume covers art objects and house furnishings imported from China to America from 1784 to 1876. Forty good colour plates and 177 monochromes show sea captains, clipper ships and Chinese ports painted by known Chinese artists, all listed by name. The format is attractive and the writing is direct and factual, yet readable. The notes contain much material for specialists. The book is also an excellent source on Sino-American history, art and trade.

965 **Chinese and exotic rugs.**
Murray L. Eiland. New York: Graphic Society, 1979.
246p.

The author discusses the rugs of China, Tibet, Mongolia, Eastern Turkestan, India, North Africa and the Balkans. For each he gives a brief historical description of the land and its peoples, followed by a lengthier survey of rugs and rug-making, in most cases carried on into the 20th century.

966 **Mid-Ch'ing rice markets and trade: an essay on price history.**
Hansheng Zhuan, Richard A. Kraus. Cambridge,
Massachusetts: Harvard University Press, 1975. 238p.

This book consists of four brief chapters, supplemented by four lengthy methodological and statistical appendices. After a preliminary discussion of the nature and validity of imperial price reports, the authors employ them in two interrelated case studies: a narrowly focused analysis of seasonal rice-price variation in Southern Kansu and a wide-ranging account of price fluctuations and rice trading in several key provinces.

967 **Post-Mao: China and US-China trade.**
Edited by Shaozhuan Leng. Charlottesville, Virginia:
University Press of Virginia, 1978. 156p.

This is a collection of essays edited by Shao-chuan Leng (Shaozhuan Leng) on Chinese-US trade prospects. Robert Dernberger is pessimistic about the likelihood of a significant increase in Chinese exports to the United States even considering the possibility of Chinese oil being exported to the US or China's being granted most favoured-nation status.

968 **China's silk trade: traditional industry in the modern world, 1842-1937.**
Lillian M. Li. Cambridge, Massachusetts: Council on East
Asian Studies, Harvard University, 1981. 288p.

The author describes the volume as an analysis of 'the relationship between the traditional silk industry and the new export market' of the late 19th and 20th centuries. She discusses the development of silk trade from the opening of treaty ports to the 1930s and China's encounter with the modern world market.

Trade

969 **Law and politics in Chinese foreign trade.**
Edited by Victor H. Li. Seattle, Washington: University of
Washington Press, 1977. 488p.

This book consists of papers presented at a conference in 1971, some of which
have been updated to 1972 or 1973. But, as the editor notes, some very important
changes took place in China's foreign trade patterns between 1973 and 1976.

970 **China's foreign trade statistics, 1864-1949.**
Xiaoliang Lin. Cambridge, Massachusetts: Harvard
University Press, 1974. 297p.

This volume contains the data in the original Chinese Maritime Customs report,
about the trade in gold and silver, customs revenues, the distribution of exports
and imports by countries and by ports, foreign exchange rates and shipping statistics according to the flag of the carrier.

971 **The foreign trade of mainland China.**
Fenghua Ma. Chicago: Aldine-Atherton, 1971. 270p.

The author analyzes China's foreign trade system, price problems in foreign
trade, international settlement with trading partners, degree of foreign trade
dependence, trends in trade value, direction, commodity structure and a new
estimate of China's balance of international payment. The book also provides
students of China with a wide array of useful statistical data and generalizations
and analyses about the economic relations of the People's Republic of China with
the rest of the world, communist and non-communist, up to 1969.

972 **The future of the China market: prospect for Sino-American
trade.**
Edward Neilan, Charles R. Smith. Washington, DC;
Stanford, California: AEI-Hoover Policy Studies, 1974. 94p.

The authors contend that China provides American businessmen with important
opportunities for trade and finance. The study, published jointly by American
Enterprise Institute and the Hoover Institution, includes the findings of the authors' poll of leading American government, banking and academic specialists on
the China trade. They discuss political, social and defense considerations, as well
as the short and long-term prospects for Sino-American trade.

973 **Understanding business contracts in China, 1949-1963.**
Richard M. Pfeffer. Cambridge, Massachusetts: Harvard
University Press, 1973. 146p.

This book is indicative of the best of the nascent scholarship on Chinese business
law. The author's diverse background not only permits him to look realistically at
aspects of Chinese law, but also permits him, with his knowledge of Chinese law,
to reflect more objectively on American law.

974 **China's trade with the West: a political and economic analysis.**
Edited by Arthur A. Stahnke.   New York: Praeger, 1972. 234p.

This volume suggests three main things about China's foreign trade: it is shaped more by economic than by political considerations; it is not highly important to the economy; and it can be manipulated to advantage only by the Chinese government.

975 **Doing business with China: American trade opportunities in the 1970s.**
Edited by William W. Whitson.   New York: Praeger, 1974. 593p.

This volume contains a market survey of prospects for the sales of American products in over 25 industries and trade categories to the People's Republic of China. It outlines practical steps whereby management can approach trading with China at the least cost in money and executive time.

976 **The foreign trade of China: policy, law, and practice.**
Gene T. Xiao.   Berkeley, California: University of California Press, 1977. 312p.

The volume is particularly useful on the organization of the Ministry of Foreign Trade in China and on Sino-Japanese trade relations.

977 **Doing business with the People's Republic of China.**
Geneva: Business International, 1973. 122p.

This book seems to incorporate most of the information that has been published in the last few years, including the experiences of firms who have been trading with China and taken part in the national exhibition there.

978 **How to approach the China market.**
Japan External Trade Organization.   New York: Wiley, 1972. 227p.

This is the translation of a Japanese book (*Japan-China Trade Handbook*) prepared by the Japan External Trade Organization for the purpose of assisting Japanese businessmen dealing with China. There are useful details on the organization of China's foreign trade, its composition, quantity and future potential.

Industry

979 China's industrial revolution: politics, planning and management, 1949 to the present.
Stephen Andors. New York: Pantheon, 1977. 344p.

The focus of this book is to determine whether the organization and management of industrial work can be made compatible with democratic and social values. The author maintains that China has discovered a new path to modernization without relying on a technocratic or bureaucratic élite.

980 Oil in the People's Republic of China: industry structure production exports.
Wolfgang Barke. London: Hurst, 1977. 125p.

This book is a good analysis of the Chinese oil industry. The author uses all the information available in the West, especially that officially released by Chinese broadcasts or newspapers. On oil output, the author does not accept the widely-used figures for production in 1973 of 50 million tons.

981 Cultural Revolution and industrial organization in China: changes in management and the division of labour.
Charles Bettelhelm. New York: Monthly Review Press, 1974. 128p.

The report highlights the results of Chinese efforts to fundamentally change the organization of industrial work, its location and management patterns. The extent and originality of these changes, not only in factories but throughout the planning system, is analyzed in terms of the implication for China's future development and for other societies. There is a good analysis in the postscript of the difference between ultra-leftism and Maoist orthodoxy.

216

982 **Democracy and organization in the Chinese industrial enterprise, 1948-1953.**
William Brugger.   New York: Cambridge University Press, 1976. 374p.

The book examines how a new system of factory management was implemented in China after the liberation of 1948-49. At that time the Chinese Communist Party attempted to integrate a commitment to broad participation in management by industrial workers with a rigid system of control derived from the Soviet Union. The integration was not accomplished successfully and the events of the period 1948-53 set the stage for the rejection of the Soviet model in the mid-1950s. The book offers insights into comparative patterns of modernization, industrial democratization and the effect of cultural differences on social forms.

983 **The Tach'ing oilfield: a Maoist model for economic development.**
Leslie W. Chan.   Canberra, Australia: Australian National University Press, 1974. 281p.

The author examines the situation at Tach'ing (Daging) and ponders its future. One of the lessons of Tach'ing, the author points out, is that as critical modern industries develop, large state investments are necessary and self-reliance is less and less relevant. So while the Chinese are urged to emulate Tach'ing, many of the features which make it special are unrepeatable elsewhere.

984 **The development of China's steel industry and soviet technical aid.**
M. Gardner Clark.   Ithaca, New York: New York School of Industrial and Labour Relations, 1973. 160p.

This book is based on two principal types of materials - translations into English from the Chinese press and Russian-language writings on the subject. The author discusses in detail Soviet aid given to the Chinese steel industry from 1950 to 1957 and then describes the contrasting technological pattern adopted by the Chinese when they struck out on an independent path after 1958.

985 **China's oil future: a case of modest expectations.**
Randall W. Hardy.   Boulder, Colorado: Westview Press, 1978. 144p.

This book analyzes soberly the many constraints on China's oil development and comes to the conclusion that China is not the potential oil giant that some writers have contended it is. In fact, he concludes, China in the 1980s could well find itself more in need of development capital from Japan and the United States than they are in need of Chinese oil.

986 **The arms of Kiangnan: modernization in the Chinese ordnance industry.**
Thomas L. Kennedy.   Boulder, Colorado: Westview Press, 1978. 250p.

In the late 19th century, Chinese leaders made efforts to transform the defense industry in China along lines suggested by European and US counterparts; this was the first such instance of a large-scale concerted effort to change a critically important area of government operations. Despite tradition and the semicolonial influence of foreign governments, the major industries were modernized with remarkable speed and success and with some benefit to the Chinese society and economy.

987 The petroleum industry of the People's Republic of China.
H. C. Lin. Stanford, California: Hoover Institute, 1975. 264p.

This study finds the outlook promising for China as an exporter of petroleum. Principal constraints are transportation (pipelines to the north and northwest) and technology (offshore drilling rigs). Both are likely to be overcome with some form of international arrangement.

988 Nationalist China during the Sino-Japanese war 1937-1945.
Edited by Paul K. T. Shi. New York: Exposition-University Press, 1978. 374p.

This book contains a series of papers and commentaries on various phases of the Nationalist administration of wartime China, including industry, education, food production and distribution, transportation, public finance and political, military and diplomatic affairs. The papers were presented at a 1976 Conference under the sponsorship of St. John's University and the University of Illinois.

989 China's transition to industrialism: producer goods and economic development in the twentieth century.
Thomas G. Rawski. Ann Arbor, Michigan: University of Michigan Press, 1980. 211p.

The author provides a comprehensive study of the history and development of a group of industries which have played key roles in China's recent economic gains. The author focuses on engineering, chemicals and allied production industries, showing how the growth of these sectors of the economy sparked a dynamic process of development which has spread to encompass the entire Chinese economy.

990 Rural industrialization in China.
Jon Sigurdson. Cambridge, Massachusetts: Harvard University Press, 1977. 281p.

Two aspects of Sigurdson's work are especially valuable. Firstly, in order to highlight China's emphasis on rural small-scale industry, he explains the importance of China's industrial policy. Secondly, he outlines how China's institutional framework promotes the processes of innovation and technology-transfer at all levels of administration in China.

991 Mineral resources and basic industries in the People's Republic of China.
K. P. Wang. Boulder, Colorado: Westview Press, 1977. 211p.

This handbook is the result of careful assessment of multi-lingual, wide-ranging if necessarily fragmentary data culled from technical journals, international publications, Japanese sources and the press and scientific literature of the People's

Republic of China. The author's overall conclusion is that 'China is one of the world's rich mineral areas fully capable of supporting a modern first-rank industrial economy'.

992 China's petroleum industry: output growth and export potential.
Zheng Zhuyuan.   New York: Praeger, 1976. 244p.

The author, Cheng Chu-yuan (Zheng Zhuyuan), pieces together various first-hand sources in an effort to give the most up-to-date information on the Chinese petroleum industry. He traces the industry's output growth from the early 1950s to the present. The study finds that: the growth of the Chinese petroleum industry has been phenomenal; total reserves are over 30 billion tons; offshore drilling, transport and refining equipment are in short supply and will probably be imported from the United States; and Chinese crude oil available for export (mostly to Japan) may be about 125 million tons per year by 1985.

993 The machine-building industry in Communist China.
Zheng Zhuyuan.   Chicago, New York: Aldine-Atherton, 1971. 339p.

The study examines the composition of the machine-building industry in the People's Republic of China. The author, Cheng Chu-yuan (Zheng Zhuyuan), discusses the qualitative changes and the technical development of the industry and their impact on other sectors of the economy. He also analyzes the factors affecting the growth of machine building and, finally, specifies the contributions of this industry to the national goals. Finally, he evaluates the performance of the machine- building industry and provides comparisons with other countries.

Agriculture and
Rural Development

994 **Rural development: learning from China.**
Sartai Aziz.   London: Macmillan, 1978. 201p.

The author claims that developing countries have much to learn from China's experience of rural development since 1949. His account of rural development in China must be understood in the context of the policies adopted by the Chinese and the events that have followed from them.

995 **Agricultural development in China and India: a comparative study.**
Kalyani Bandyopadhyaya.   New Delhi: Wiley Eastern, 1976. 204p.

The author takes a broad approach to compare the land-labour ratio, land ownership and land reforms and institutional changes in China and India. She underlines the totally different political circumstances under which land reforms took place in both countries and points out the shortcomings of both systems.

996 **Huadong: the story of a Chinese people's commune.**
Gordon A. Bennett.   Boulder, Colorado: Westview Press, 1978. 197p.

The author presents an analysis of Huadong (Hua-tung), a commune about 30 miles north of Guangzhou (Canton). The author presents a unique view of the commune system as a whole through a concise study of one commune, including the concept of commune, commune government, politics, society and culture. He calls attention to important changes over the past few years and points to likely developments in the future.

997 Up to the mountains and down to the villages.
Thomas Bernstein. New Haven, Connecticut: Yale
University Press, 1977. 432p.

The book presents a carefully documented analysis of China's efforts to resettle urban youth in rural agricultural communities. Using published materials, radio broadcasts and interviews with former participants, the author investigates the objectives of the programme, the realities of its recruiting and resettlement operations and the degree to which urban youth become acclimatized to rural life. He anticipates a continued retreat from the ideal of lifetime commitment to rural work by the migrants. He also doubts that other developing countries with problems of urban overpopulation will be able to implement this type of programme.

998 Agricultural mechanization in China: the administrative impact.
Steven Butler. New York: East Asian Institute, 1978. 58p.

This volume describes relationships among the four administrative levels in the Chinese countryside - county, commune, brigade and team. The author shows how agricultural mechanization has heightened the importance of the brigade and county. The author also highlights the ways in which these administrative organs mobilize rural resources to fuel the development process.

999 New earth.
Jack Chen. Carbondale, Illinois: Southern Illinois
University Press, 1972. 258p.

The author, Jack Ch'en (Chen), describes the gradual development of cooperation and collectivization in Hsinteng (Xingdeng), which was a key county in Chekiang (Zhejiang) province. The book gives a vivid description of the different development stages - seasonal and permanent mutual aid teams, cooperative farms and collective farms.

1000 Mass movement in a Chinese village: ten mile inn.
David Crook, Isabel Crook. London: Routledge, 1979.
291p.

The volume is the third and final volume of a trilogy about Ten Mile Inn and the effects of the Chinese Revolution and the arrival of the Communists in the village. The authors detail the final stage of land reform in a North China village where they spent seven weeks in early 1948 with a Communist Party work team.

1001 Socialism in the Chinese countryside.
Jurgen Domes. London: Hurst, 1980. 192p.

This is an account of agricultural policies in the People's Republic of China from the land reform of 1950-53 to the present in the context of intra-party conflicts since the late 1950s and an evaluation of their social and economic performances.

1002 Peasant life in China: a field study of country life in the Yangtze valley.
Fei Xiaotong. London: Routledge, 1980. 300p.

This book was first published in 1939. It was based on materials which the author, Fei Hsiao-tung (Fei Xiaodong), collected during a short period of field-

Agriculture and Rural Development

work in a Yangtse (Yangze) valley in 1936. As a pioneering study of modern Chinese rural communities, this work has been rightly acclaimed for its description and system analysis, which covers property, kinship, agriculture, finance, etc.

1003 Agricultural production in Communist China, 1949-1965.
Gang Zhao. Madison: University of Wisconsin Press, 1971. 278p.

The author, Kang Chao (Gang Zhao), analyzes Chinese agriculture in the 1949-65 period in a three-part study of institutional and technical changes and of farm growth. The book is clearly written and brings a wealth of new material to the subject.

1004 Agriculture in the People's Republic of China: structural changes and technical transformation.
Leslie T. C. Gou. New York: Praeger, 1976. 288p.

Following a brief summary of the socialist transformation of agriculture since 1949, the author examines the national programme for agricultural development, drawn up in 1956 and the extent to which its provisions have been implemented in improving yields, water and soil conservation, fertilization, plant breeding and protection, farm equipment and field management.

1005 Fanshen: a documentary of revolution in a Chinese village.
William Hinton. New York: Random House, 1970. 637p.

This is a grass-roots account of what happened in the village of Long Bow in Shansi province during the period when Communist power was established. The book describes in social and economic terms how the villagers resolved the central question of who should own the land and rule the countryside.

1006 Iron oxen: a documentary of revolution in Chinese farming.
William Hinton. New York: Random House, 1971. 225p.

This is an account of the effects of modern machinery on the farming methods of the Chinese peasantry in the years after the Second World War. This documentary also presents a view of the new breed of farm labourers in the People's Republic of China.

1007 The broken wave: the Chinese communist peasant movement 1922-1928.
Roy Hofbreing, Jr. Cambridge, Massachusetts: Harvard University Press, 1977. 255p.

This is an account of the origins in the 1920s of Mao's strategy of rural revolution. The author gives a hard-hitting attack on those theories of revolution with emphasis on social structure, economics and demography at the expense of politics.

1008 Walking on two legs: rural development in South China.
Elizabeth Johnson, Graham Johnson. Ottawa, Canada: International Development Research Center, 1976. 72p.

This book explains how China's model of rural development works. Much of the concrete information included is the result of a trip the authors made in 1973 to four communes outside Canton (Guangzhou) in Kwangtung (Guangdong) province. The book is aimed at policy-makers and development workers in the Third World and most China specialists will find the descriptions of commune organization fairly accurate and comprehensive.

1009 China's fertilizer economy.
Liu Rongzhao. Edinburgh: Edinburgh University Press, 1971. 173p.

After a short introduction the author, Liu Jung-chao (Liu Rongzhao), examines the development of the domestic fertilizer industry and its efficiency of production. He shows that, in the Chinese context, the fertilizer industry has been highly profitable. However, compared with production costs in other countries, China emerges none too favourably.

1010 The urban origins of rural revolution, elites and the masses in Hunan province, 1911-27.
Angus W. McDonald. Berkeley, California: University of California Press, 1979. 253p.

This is a masterful blending of political, economic, social and intellectual history. It contains a wealth of fascinating data and historical insights on revolutionary politics and social change in China during the 1920s. In a way, the book is meant to describe the failure of the Chinese Communist Party in Hunan.

1011 The Chinese peasant economy: agricultural development in Hopei and Shantung, 1890-1949.
Raymond H. Myers. Cambridge, Massachusetts: Harvard University Press, 1970. 413p.

The author contends that the fundamental problem in agriculture had nothing to do with the rural socio-economic relationship. The real problems were the inadequacy of technology, the failure of the government to promote agricultural improvement and the impact of war, especially after 1937.

1012 Commune: life in rural China.
Peggy Printz, Paul Steinle. New York: Dodd, Mead, 1977. 192p.

This work will be familiar to readers who have viewed the authors' group documentary about Kuang-li (Guangli) People's Commune filmed during their three-week stay there in May 1973. The book, like the film before it, is an informal, honest portrait of life in present-day rural China. Their report is extremely good on commune achievements, yet at the same time they are skeptical of many details supplied by their hosts.

1013 The development of Chinese agriculture, 1950-59.
Peter Schran. Chicago: University of Illinois, 1970. 238p.

The author analyzes the Chinese farm experience of the 1950s in the context of institutional change. In his thesis, land reform, collectivization and communization progressively removed income differentials due to unequal land ownership and moved to unequal labour power distribution in the farm households. Initially, these changes enabled the state to maintain rural stability while expropriating the former landlords' share of farm income to underwrite urbanization and industrialization.

1014 Peasant China in transition: the dynamics of development toward socialism, 1949-1956.

Vivienne Shue. Berkeley, California: University of California Press, 1980. 500p.

The book describes how the Chinese Communist Party's economic policy gradually eliminated the petty-capitalistic options open to peasants while offering them material incentives for joining in cooperative ventures. With documentation and detail the author shows how the Party moulded its policies so as to ease the peasants into increasingly socialist forms of organization and to create a rural constituency in support of each of its steps toward state socialism.

1015 Making green revolution: the policies of agriculture development in China.

Benedict Stavis. Ithaca, New York: Cornell University Press, 1974. 274p.

The author has presented an illuminating picture of the changes that were undertaken in Chinese agriculture in the 1960s. A number of conflicting interpretations of agricultural development in the People's Republic of China have been offered over the years. The author has clarified a number of the issues.

1016 The politics of agricultural mechanization in China.

Benedict Stavis. Ithaca, New York: Cornell University Press, 1978. 288p.

The author contends that China has learned from its mistakes and overcome its proclivities to mandate inappropriate technology for political reasons. He argues that China has so far avoided many negative consequences of mechanization common in developing nations, such as unemployment and internal migration to the cities, although his data do not directly support this point.

1017 The cultural ecology of Chinese civilization: peasants and elites in the last of the agrarian states.

Leon E. Stover. New York: New American Library, 1974. 305p.

This book is about two cultures of traditional Chinese society: the small, politically active élite; and the great economic, political, kinship, class, religious and world view of China's folk culture. Seven chapters discuss the same spheres of life of the élite.

1018 Chinese rural institutions and the question of transferability.

Edited by Jonathan Unger. Oxford, England: Pergamon Press, 1980. 772p.

This volume grew out of a conference held at the Institute of Development Studies, Sussex, in 1977 at which nine China specialists and four other scholars of rural development presented papers. Topics covered include how China has met the basic needs of the people, incentives in rural China, welfare and health care and agricultural research.

1019 Water conservancy and irrigation in China: social, economic and agro-technical aspects.

E. B. Vermeer. The Hague: Martinus Mijhoff, 1977. 350p.

The author covers widely divergent issues, namely, the scales and methods of labour mobilization (including manpower training) and capital allocation, the extent of national calamities and relief programmes, construction standards for anti-flood projects, irrigation and salinization. National, provincial and local data is used where available.

1020 Land reform in the People's Republic of China: institutional transformation in agriculture.

John Wong. New York: Praeger, 1973. 319p.

After brief consideration of land reform policy before 1949, the discussion of development in the People's Republic of China begins with an analysis of the 1950 Agricultural Law and a description of the machinery set up for its implementation.

1021 Food for one billion: China's agriculture since 1949.

Robert C. Xu. Boulder, Colorado: Westview Press, 1982. 156p.

This book examines the agricultural policies and programmes adopted by the Chinese leadership since 1949 and analyzes the role of agriculture in China's changing development strategies. The author gives particular attention to the measures intended to improve agricultural technology and to the sources of funds for agriculture investment. He concludes that, while the collective system has been effective in mobilizing China's rural resources for agricultural development and in promoting progress in labour-intensive agricultural technology, periodic extreme leftist policies and interference by rural Communist Party cadres have caused various kinds of inefficiency, offsetting the advantages gained from collective farming.

1022 Animal agriculture in China.

US Animal Science Delegation. Washington, DC: National Academy Press, 1980. 197p.

The report surveys both species and disciplinary interest, reviewing Chinese animal production practices, animal science research and education programmes and the breeding, management, utilization and processing of swine and poultry, dairy and beef cattle, sheep and goats, horse and mules, water buffalo and rabbits. The report also includes a paper on the characterization and distribution of domestic animals in China prepared by a member of the Chinese Academy of Agricultural Sciences.

1023 Insect control in the People's Republic of China.

US Insect Control Delegation. Washington, DC: National Academy of Sciences, 1977. 217p.

The report focuses on four areas of interest: general aspects: an assessment of teaching programmes, the status of agriculture, integrated pest control, entomological research organizations, literature and library facilities; insect problems and control on different commodities - rice, cotton, grain, soybeans and peanuts, deciduous fruits, vegetables, stored grain and insect pests of man and animal; insect control strategies - insecticide use, biological control, host resistance, insect phero-

Agriculture and Rural Development

mones, hormones and trapping; and lists of institutes visited and people met, identification of common pest insects and mites found in China and books on agriculture and entomology.

1024 Rice Improvement in China and other Asian countries.
Manila, Philippines: International Rice Research Institute and Chinese Academy of Agricultural Sciences, 1980. 308p.

The International Rice Research Institute's report contains the proceedings of the first international workshop on rice research ever held in the People's Republic of China. The report reveals a high degree of consistency in the assessment of the state of the People's Republic of China's scientific development.

Wheat in the People's Republic of China.
See item no. 128.

Vegetable marketing systems in the People's Republic of China.
See item no. 130.

Plant studies in the People's Republic of China: a trip report of the American Plant Studies Delegation.
See item no. 131.

Rice research and production in China: an IRRI team's view.
See item no. 132.

Labour and Employment

1025 **Workers and workplaces in revolutionary China.**
Edited by Stephen Andors.   White Plains, New York:
Sharpe, 1977. 402p.

Ranging from historical materials about the Shanghai docks and a Chinese-owned tobacco company in the 1920s and 1930s to discussions of socialist modes of enterprise administration in the 1970s, this book places recent Chinese work organization experiences into historical perspective. The materials from the 1970s (predating the purge of the 'Gang of Four') stress worker participation in management more than work discipline.

1026 **Popular management and pay in China.**
Roberto M. Bernardo.   Honolulu: University Press of
Hawaii, 1977. 249p.

This book raises questions of major importance about the interrelationships of wages, moral incentives and productivity.

1027 **Historiography of the Chinese labor movement.**
Ming Chan.   Stanford, California: Hoover Institute, 1981.
350p.

This book provides a critical survey of over 700 titles of major Chinese works that are useful for serious study of the Chinese labour movement. It draws attention to and offers solid documentary sources for scholarly research of this subject.

Labour and Employment

1028 Workers and commissars: trade union policy in the People's Republic of China.
Merton Don Fletcher. Bellingham, Washington: Western Washington State College, 1974. 147p.

The author has written an account of changes in the functions, organization and control of trade unions in the People's Republic of China from 1949 to 1973. Most of these changes were in response to major shifts in the general line of the Chinese Communist Party. The range of the changes has been enormous from the founding of trade unions in 1949 as the non-party, semi-autonomous, vanguard of the working class to their abolition at the end of 1966 and their subsequent re-establishment in 1973. Such a variety of change offers many perspectives from which trade union development can be assessed.

1029 The Chinese worker.
Charles Hoffman. Albany, New York: State University of New York Press, 1974. 252p.

The author focuses on the industrial work force in urban areas and consistently places his discussion in the context that includes political goals and human relationships as well as the economic and social problems of the much larger rural-agricultural sector of the Chinese countryside. After a chapter dealing with the economics of development and the general Maoist approach, the main topics covered include: the structure of employment; worker mobility and labour allocation; the Chinese approach to worker motivation; trade unions; and the change in the standard of living of workers.

1030 Work incentive practices and policies in the People's Republic of China, 1953-1965.
Charles Hoffman. Albany, New York: State University of New York, 1970. 148p.

The author is concerned with the details of the incentive system proposed by the Chinese Communist Party, the economic and ideological limits and principles that define the system, to what extent adversity has affected these limits and principles and what incentive techniques have been used under varying economic circumstances and raises an issue on whether the Chinese labourer works better for material or non-material incentives.

1031 Employment and economic growth in urban China 1949-1957.
Christopher Howe. New York: Cambridge University Press, 1973. 185p.

This is a study of China's urban employment problems in the context of the growth and fluctuation of the urban economy between 1949 and 1957. It is the first study in labour problems to use statistical and other information available in the local newspapers published in Chinese cities and materials in the journals of the Chinese Ministry of Labour.

1032 **Wage patterns and the wage policy in modern China 1919-1972.**
Christopher Howe.   New York: Cambridge University Press, 1974. 150p.

This book provides an analysis of changes in the level and structure of wages in China from the 1920s to 1972. He evaluates the degree to which wage policy objectives have been achieved, particularly since 1949. He also explains both fluctuations in policy and discrepancies between plans and reality and examines the mechanism of wage determination. He goes on to argue that the wage system can only be understood within a common analysis of the whole framework of incentives and controls affecting the work force.

1033 **Economic growth and employment in China.**
Thomas G. Rawski.   New York: Oxford University Press, 1979. 269p.

This study investigates the relations between growth and employment in China. It shows that over the past two decades the world's largest developing country has made significant progress towards the full employment of her nearly half a billion people, unlike other developing countries, where industrialization often fails to provide adequate employment.

1034 **Man and the workers: the Hunan labor movement, 1920-1923.**
Lynda Shaffer.   Armonk, New York: Sharpe, 1982. 247p.

Focusing on four major strikes in Hunan in the early 1920s, the author examines the importance of more traditional forms of organization, such as crafts guilds, in the early labour movement and how the failure of those organizations to satisfy modern workers meshed with the goals and methods of the early Communist organizers led by Mao, Liu Shaoqi (Liu Shao-ch'i) and Li Lisan (Li Li-san) in ways that often defy easy Marxist categories.

1035 **Land and labor in China.**
R. H. Tawney.   White Plains, New York: Sharpe, 1978. 216p.

From this book, it is possible to learn why a peasant revolution might give the Communists their opportunity, but it does not explain why the peasant revolution occurred.

1036 **Rural employment and manpower problems in China.**
Curtis Ullerich.   White Plains, New York: Sharpe, 1977. 136p.

This concise study traces the Chinese model of social and economic development through three premises: that China has attained remarkable socio-economic development while achieving a unique synthesis of historical and modern elements of national life and production; that China has encountered and largely overcome problems that are common to most Third World countries today and that China has achieved prototypical production and qualitative improvements in the nation's material and social well-being.

Science and Technology

1037 Chemistry and chemical engineering in the People's Republic of China.
Edited by John D. Baldeschwieler. Washington, DC: American Chemical Society, 1979. 266p.

This is a report of the US Pure and Applied Chemistry Delegation that visited China in May-June 1979. It examines the roots of chemical research and development in China, the institutional structure of chemical research and development, chemistry and chemical engineering in the context of national science policy and chemistry and chemical engineering as components of science education in China. It also includes the issues of basic research in sub-disciplines of the field and assesses the status of research in key areas of technology. There are also sections on the organization of chemical research and development in broad national mission areas and on such elements of infrastructure as scientific communications, scientific manpower, innovation and resource allocation.

1038 American Science and modern China, 1876-1936.
Peter Buck. New York: Cambridge University Press, 1980. 376p.

The author focuses on the transmission of scientific ideas from the US to China showing what modifications were induced by the change in environment and what the modifications imply about the interdependence of scientific knowledge and social life.

1039 Science and technology in the development of modern China: an annotated bibliography.
Genevieve C. Dean. London: Mansell, 1974. 265p.

This reference guide lists secondary materials mainly relating to the period since 1949 and details English, European and Japanese works that have appeared up to 1972. Several unpublished papers of particular relevance are included. There are two appendices listing items on traditional Chinese science and technology and on the introduction of modern science and technology to China prior to the establishment of the People's Republic.

1040 Solid state physics in the People's Republic of China.
Edited by Anne Fitzgerald, Charles P. Slicher. Washington, DC: National Academy of Sciences, 1976. 203p.

The US Solid State Physics Delegation visited China in September-October 1975 and observed Chinese research in semiconductors, lasers, low temperatures, crystal growth and other areas. The book traces the historical development of science in China, focusing on the impact of the Cultural Revolution and describes science education in China, university-factory relations, selection of students and student placement.

1041 Technology, defense and external relations in China, 1975-78.
Harry G. Gelber. Boulder, Colorado: Westview Press, 1979. 229p.

This is a useful survey of Chinese economic, defense and science policy since the death of Mao. The author describes the economical setbacks to the development of science and technology during the Cultural Revolution and then lists the various steps that have been taken to chart a new course: the new stress on intellectual excellence rather than political enthusiasm, the new priority given to higher education, the revival of major research facilities, the importing of foreign technology and the sending of the Chinese students to study in the West.

1042 Astronomy in China: a trip report of the American Astronomy Delegation.
Edited by Leo Goldberg, Lois Edwards. Washington, DC: National Academy of Sciences, 1979. 109p.

The report contains a brief history of Chinese astronomy, its organization, administration and institutions, topics of special interest (including solar physics, satellite observations and orbital determinations, stellar astrophysics, radio astronomy and extragalactic astronomy). The report also describes and evaluates facilities including those under construction as well as education and research at universities.

1043 Aeronautics in China.
Edited by Jerry Grey. New York: American Institute of Aeronautics and Astronautics, 1981. 198p.

This volume is based on the September 1980 visit to China of a 23-person delegation from the American Institute of Aeronautics and Astronautics. Among the 14 chapters are those devoted to aircraft and engine production, materials and structures, flight testing, guidance and control, computers and university education. Especially noteworthy were observations made concerning aerodynamics research and development and testing and propulsion research. In both instances, the American specialists found that China's strengths lay in theoretical research and in basic facilities and weaknesses in instrumentation and computer capacity.

Science and Technology

1044 Earthquake engineering and hazards reduction in China.
Edited by Paul C. Jennings. Washington, DC: National Academy of Sciences, 1980. 189p.

The report is a significant new reference work containing the results of a visit by 12 American earthquake engineers and geoscientists to China in July-August 1978 to learn about Chinese earthquake engineering research and practice, earthquake-prediction capabilities and other efforts of the Chinese to mitigate earthquake hazards, as well as to explore what is known about the disastrous Tangshan (T'ang-Shan) earthquake of July 1976.

1045 Selling technology to China.
Edited by Nicholas H. Ludlow. Washington, DC: National Council for US-China Trade, 1979. 354p.

This volume includes an overview of China's past experience in importing technology and sections on the organization of China's technology acquisition process, licensing, design engineering, bartering, joint ventures and the new areas of counter-trade. The book discusses selling technology to China in fields including ferrous and non-ferrous metallurgy, mining and the petroleum, construction, aircraft and chemical industries.

1046 The grand titration: science and society in East and West.
Joseph Needham. Toronto: University of Toronto Press, 1970. 350p.

This is a collection of previously published essays, lectures and broadcasts. The author discusses East-West scientific and technological relations, why the West moved ahead with its own scientific methodology, the contributions to science by mediaeval Chinese and their effect upon Europe. Included also are chapters on the Chinese scientific tradition, science and social change, science and society in ancient China, social relations of science and technology in China, time and Eastern man and the human law of nature.

1047 Science and civilization in China, volume 5: chemistry and chemical technology, part 4: spagynical discovery and invention: apparatus, theories and gifts.
Joseph Needham. New York: Cambridge University Press, 1980. 746p.

This is the latest installment of the work of ecumenical scholarship which, for more than twenty years, has been revealing facet after facet of the history of science and proto-science in China - always in comparison with parallel developments in the other major civilizations of Eurasia.

1048 Science in contemporary China.
Edited by Leo A. Orleans. Stanford, California: Stanford University Press, 1980. 599p.

The US National Academy of Sciences Committee for Scholarly Communication with the People's Republic of China was established in 1964. It has played a pioneering role, first in stimulating interest on the part of American scientists in Chinese scientific development and then, since 1972, in helping to arrange scientific exchanges between the United States and China. The exchanges have now resulted in dozens of trip reports prepared by visiting American delegations and

Science in Contemporary China grew out of an attempt to distill these reports to make an assessment of the current status of science in China.

1049 Manpower for science and engineering in China.

Leo A. Orleans. Washington, DC: US House of Representatives Committee on Science and Technology, 1980. 137p.

The report provides an updated overview of China's educational policies and trends, offers the latest statistics on higher education in the People's Republic of China, examines the quality of professional manpower in China and delves into several questions of policy in a 'speculative discussion' of the issues.

1050 China space report.

Edited by Wilbur Pritchard, James J. Harford. New York: American Institute of Aeronautics and Astronautics, 1980. 208p.

This report is the outcome of the first American space scientists' visit to the People's Republic of China in November 1979. Among the technological assessments made was the conclusion that in several areas, such as in the development of microwave solid state devices and techniques, research is highly advanced. In the case of communications satellites, theoretical and experimental work is well advanced yet building an operational satellite will require a huge pool of highly-trained people, a manpower problem that can only be solved with time. The report concludes that prospects for cooperation in applications satellites and data utilization are bright.

1051 Technology and science in the People's Republic of China.

Jon Sigurdson. Elmsford, New York: Pergamon Press, 1981. 364p.

The author assesses and reviews the present situation, describes China's objectives and defines the policies that have governed scientific and technological development. He provides clear descriptions of what is meant by 'open door scientific and technological research', 'walking on two legs' and 'self reliance'. Chapters on basic and applied science, mass science, environmental protection and natural resources and electronics round out the study and link the theoretical context of technology policy with Chinese work now underway in specific areas.

1052 Science, technology and China's drive for modernization.

Richard P. Suttmeier. Stanford, California: Hoover Institute, 1980. 133p.

China's bid for modern technology came at a time when its leaders had embraced a new foreign policy. How should the United States respond to Chinese demands for the most advanced science and technology within the context of this new foreign policy? How can the United States properly supervise the export to the People's Republic of China of its most advanced scientific knowledge? Or should it? These and other relevant questions are discussed in depth by this study.

Science and Technology

1053 Research and revolution: science policy and societal change in China.
Richard P. Suttmeier. Lexington, Massachusetts: Lexington Books, 1974. 188p.

This book is an attempt at an interpretive summary of twenty years of Chinese science and technology policies and programmes. After an introductory perspective on research, innovation and developmental science policy, the author concentrates on policy and principles for Chinese scientific development, science organization from 1949-1957, models of science organization and administration in several periods from 1949 to 1971, technological mobilization and concludes with his idea of the 'Chinese model' for scientific development. A bibliography of primary and secondary sources is included.

1054 Environmental protection in the People's Republic of China.
Susan Swannack-Nunn. Washington, DC: National Council for US-China Trade, 1979. 293p.

The report covers China's general policy and philosophy towards environmental protection, the organization of this work and specific, detailed descriptions of environmental problems in China concerning air and water quality, solid waste management, control of toxic substances, preservation of natural areas and environmental health among others. The appendices are valuable in themselves since they contain much of the essential scholarly documents on the subject and lists of commercial activities in the field.

1055 Technology, politics, and society in China.
Rudi Volti. Boulder, Colorado: Westview Press, 1982. 255p.

The author looks at technological change in China as part of a broader process of economic, political, cultural and organizational change, focusing primarily on four key areas - agriculture, energy, land transport and medicine and public health. He emphasizes how technological change has been shaped by political and ideological structures, notes how China's unique cultural heritage has affected adoption of technologies developed outside China and assesses China's success in developing technologies appropriate to its specific needs as an economically and politically developing nation.

1056 Mineral resources and basic industries in the People's Republic of China.
K. P. Wang. Boulder, Colorado: Westview Press, 1977. 211p.

The book examines the world significance of Chinese minerals, the historical growth of China's mineral industry, policy considerations and regional technical factors affecting mineral development and China's mineral trade and its effort to obtain equipment, supplies and new technology. The major mineral sectors of coal and power, oil and gas, iron and steel, nonferrous metals, industrial metals and fertilizers and chemicals, are all discussed in detail. The foreign trade outlook is summarized in the concluding chapter.

1057 **The organization and support of scientific research and development in mainland China.**
Y. L. Wu, Robert B. Sheeks. New York: Praeger, 1970. 618p.

The authors present an extensive history of pre-1949 science and scientific organizations and attempt to define China's science and technology priorities and policies within the context of economic and political goals.

1058 **Science and socialist construction in China.**
Xu Liangying, Fan Dainian, edited with an introduction by Pierre M. Perrolle. Armonk, New York: Sharpe, 1982. 225p.

Originally written in 1956, this treatise on Chinese science policy was reintroduced in 1980 by the Chinese authors Xu Liangying (Hsu Liang-ying) and Fan Dainian (Fan Tai-nien) and an English version published in 1982 under the supervision of Pierre Perrolle. Twenty-five years later the ideas raised in the essay remain relevant. One question debated is how much China should rely on foreign assistance in the development of her scientific enterprises. Other questions discussed are those concerning manpower and the proper relationship between research and education.

1059 **Directory of selected scientific institutions in mainland China.**
Prepared by the Surveys & Research Corporation, produced with the support of the National Science Foundation. Stanford, California: Hoover Institution, 1971. 469p.

The Directory lists 490 selected research institutes, their structure, selected research projects and achievements, publications, chief executives and other related data.

1060 **Oceanography in China.**
Washington, DC: National Academy of Sciences, 1980. 106p.

This is a report of the US Oceanography Delegation that visited China in October 1978. The report describes visits to Chinese laboratories, cities and schools, including several cities not previously seen by American visitors. The report provides not only the delegation's general impressions of China's efforts in oceanography but also valuable insights into the present state of oceanography and marine sciences in China in specific areas.

Language

Beginners' textbooks

1061 Index volume, beginning, intermediate, and advanced texts in spoken and written Chinese.
John De Francis. New Haven, Connecticut: Yale University Press, 1970. 422p.
This volume is an index to nine texts in the series written by De Francis. These are the beginning, intermediate and advanced sections of the transcription and character versions of the conversation series and of the reading series. There are five different indices, the main one being in pinyin, with others giving variants on the theme of strokes and radicals.

1062 Flash cards for beginning Chinese reader.
John De Francis. New Haven, Connecticut: Yale University Press, 1977.
These are four hundred boxed cards, for the basic characters introduced in *Beginning Chinese Reader* (q.v.).

1063 Spoken standard Chinese. Volume i, volume ii.
Parker Bofei Huang, Hugh M. Stimson. New Haven, Connecticut: Yale University Press, 1978. 2 vols.
These two volumes are texts for elementary Chinese in pinyin romanization.

1064 Elementary Chinese comparison.
John C. Jamieson, Lilin Shi. New Haven, Connecticut: Yale University Press, 1975. 418p.
This is a comparable volume to *Elementary Chinese* (q.v.), the elementary text for Chinese published in Peking (Beijing). The comparison offers structural explanations and drills to supplement the intentionally slim, concise Peking (Beijing) volume.

1065 Essential grammar for modern Chinese.
Helen T. Lin. Taibei, China: Zheng & Zui, 1981. 305p.

The author provides a thorough discussion of Chinese grammar and gives examples in simplified characters and pinyin romanization to illustrate the grammatical points and intricacies of the Chinese language.

1066 Reading and writing Chinese.
William McNaughton. New York: Tuttle, 1979. 376p.

This book is an excellent tool for the beginner and intermediate student. It systematically introduces more than 2,000 basic characters and lists stroke order for each character, nonsimplified forms, English definition and important compounds. It has an index by nonsimplified character and useful appendices.

1067 Practice sheets for beginning Chinese reader.
Simon Zhang. New Haven, Connecticut: Yale University Press, 1978.

This is an explanation by Simon Chang (Zhang) of the principles involved in the writing of Chinese characters. Practice sheets include the 400 characters introduced in *Beginning Chinese Reader* by John De Francis (New Haven, Connecticut: Yale University Press, 1977. 2nd ed. 2 pts. 126+134p.).

1068 Chinese for beginners.
Beijing: Foreign Language Press, 1976. 201p.

This volume contains 24 lessons from the 'Language corner' of *China Reconstructs*. It is a compact text designed for self-study. It includes a concise introduction to pronunciation and writing, word-by-word pinyin transliteration, an English translation of each lesson and a Chinese-English vocabulary.

1069 Chinese reader.
Beijing: Foreign Language Press, 1972. pt. 1-4. 1,092p.

This is a four-volume series of *Elementary Chinese* (q.v.). Parts one and two continue the instruction in simple conversation and enable the student, with the help of a dictionary, to read newspapers and popular literature. Parts three and four include current stories and essays with English explanations of vocabulary and grammar.

1070 Elementary Chinese.
Beijing: Foreign Language Press, 1972. pt. 1-2. 641p.

This book is a comprehensive two-volume course for beginners learning Chinese as a foreign language. It includes extensive pronunciation drills, fundamental grammar points and model sentence structure. Part two includes a Chinese-English vocabulary given as an appendix.

1071 Elementary Chinese readers.
Beijing: Foreign Language Press, 1980. pt. 1-4. 1,166p.

These volumes contain a comprehensive course for beginners who want to learn Chinese as a foreign language. Edited by the Beijing Language Institute, each lesson contains exercises aimed at helping students reinforce what they have learned. The material furnishes concise explanations of Chinese grammar and expressions, supplemented by drills in speech and writing. To further aid the students, all simplified characters are accompanied by their original forms. After completing these four volumes, students will have mastered the basic sentence patterns and about 1,600 common expressions in modern Chinese. Cassette tapes, Chinese character exercise books and 1,000 flash cards are available to accompany the course. Each flash card has one simplified Chinese character with pinyin pronunciation on the reverse side.

1072 **Modern Chinese readers.**
Beijing: Foreign Language Press, 1977. pt. 1-2. 679p.

These books are updated texts for beginners with emphasis on practical conversation, substitution drills and a complete introduction on pronunciation, tones and the writing of Chinese characters. Part two includes a Chinese-English glossary.

Intermediate textbooks

1073 **Annotated quotations from Chairman Mao.**
J. De Francis. New Haven, Connecticut: Yale University Press, 1975. 147p.

This is an addition to the De Francis Chinese language textbook series. The volume presents the original Chinese text of Mao's 'little Red Book' with a pinyin transcription. The annotation includes vocabulary, notes to difficult passages, stroke index of various forms and pinyin romanization.

1074 **Supplementary readers for intermediate Chinese reader, 5 volumes.**
Edited by John De Frances. New Haven, Connecticut: Yale University Press, 1975. 5 vols.

The five volumes are additions to the De Francis Chinese language series. They are: *The white-haired girl* (by Ho Chih-yu - He Zhiyou); *Red detachment of women* (by Ho Chih-yu - He Zhiyou); *Episodes from dream of the red chamber* (by Louis H. Li); *Sun Yat-sen* (*Sun Yixian*) (by Yung Teng Chia-yee - Yong Deng Jia-Yee); *Wo Soong* (*Wu Song*) *kills a tiger* (by Yung Teng Chia-Yee - Yong Deng Jia-Yee).

1075 **Acoustical studies of mandarin vowels and tones.**
John Marshal Howie. New York: Cambridge University Press, 1976. 164p.

This is one of the first books in any language to apply the techniques of acoustic phonetics to Mandarin Chinese. The book describes the acoustic cues for the perception of nine vowels and four tones.

1076 Modern mandarin conversation.
Shirley C. Leong. San Francisco: China Books & Periodicals, 1981. 161p.

This conversation book is primarily for tourists and businessmen planning to visit China, who need a quick reference on day-to-day conversation and business expressions. It contains 32 chapters on topics which are frequently used in daily life in China. Vocabularies are selected on the basis of being essential and practical. The important aspect of this book is the introduction of the new system of pinyin presently used in China, as well as up-to-date expressions and phrases. It is packaged with cassette tape.

1077 Intermediate reader for modern Chinese.
Isabella Bingyi Mao. New Haven, Connecticut: Yale University Press, 1978. 315p.

The book presents ten contemporary and traditional selections with annotations.

1078 Readings in the Chinese Communist Cultural Revolution.
Qi Wenxun. Berkeley, California: University of California Press, 1971. 384p.

Those who wish to learn written Chinese as it is used in China today will find here materials published during the Cultural Revolution. The author, Chi Wenhsun (Qi Wenxun), includes official documents and articles that highlight the ideological conflict between Mao Tse-tung (Mao Zedong) and his opponents. He also includes explanatory sections in English, glossaries and vocabularies.

1079 Introduction to Chinese cursive script.
Wang Fangyou. New York: Far Eastern, 1972. 240p.

The book is an introduction to the deciphering of cursive Chinese. It breaks down cursive shorthand into components and explains each one and includes handwritten texts.

1080 Chinese romanization self-study guide.
Dennis Yee. Honolulu: University Press of Hawaii, 1975. 55p.

The book has detailed comparisons of Yale/pinyin and pinyin/Wade-Giles romanization systems. It points out pitfalls and includes practice exercises.

1081 Readings from the People's Daily.
Vivian Ling Xu. New Haven, Connecticut: Yale University Press, 1976. 184p.

The author presents fifteen selections from the *People's Daily*, fully annotated with grammar notes for beginners and intermediate students of the Chinese language.

Chinese-English dictionaries

1082 A dictionary of the Chinese particles.
W. A. C. H. Dobson. Toronto, Canada: University of Toronto Press, 1974. 907p.

This dictionary treats close to 700 particles, that is, words that are neither substantives nor verbs. Entries are arranged in alphabetical order by the pinyin system. The book is a very useful reference work for beginners in classical Chinese who cannot read Chinese easily.

1083 A Chinese-English dictionary of Communist Chinese terminology.
Dennis Doolin, Charles P. Ridley. Stanford, California: Hoover Institution, 1973. 569p.

This dictionary contains 17,000 entries of primary words and phrases, either coined or given new currency by the People's Republic of China during the period between the 1920s and the present.

1084 Five thousand dictionary: Chinese-English.
C. H. Fenn. Cambridge, Massachusetts: Harvard University Press, 1973.

In this basic tool for the study of the Chinese language, words are arranged in the alphabetical order of their romanized form. It contains the phonetic and the usual translations. It includes indications as to whether the character is colloquial or literary and whether it is used as a classifier, numerator, or surname. Other readings of the same character and indications as to its frequency are also included.

1085 Comprehensive glossary of Chinese Communist terminology.
Warren Guo (and others). Taibei, China: Institute of International Relations, 1978. 907p.

This dictionary contains a glossary of roughly 2,300 terms of the political languages used prominently in the media of the People's Republic of China. It is organized with alphabetical entries in Wade-Giles romanization (plus tones) and additional Chinese characters in their unabridged forms.

1086 Lin Yutang's Chinese-English dictionary of modern usage.
Lin Yutang. Hong Kong: Chinese University of Hong Kong, 1973. 1,720p.

Supporting the dictionary proper are an 182-page English index and several useful tables, including a list of simplified characters. This work seeks to present idiomatic English equivalents for all the words in the Chinese national language that the modern reader is likely to encounter. It treats the words linguistically, indicating parts of speech and meanings derived from context.

1087 A dictionary of military terms, Chinese-English and English-Chinese.

Joseph D. Lowe. Boulder, Colorado: Westview Press, 1977. 579p.

This dictionary contains some 2,500 entries of military terms and political terms which often appear in military documents and appendices of essential Chinese military, geographical and political administrative information. A conversion table giving frequently used simplified characters and their complex forms is also provided.

1088 Mathews' Chinese-English dictionary.

R. H. Mathews. Cambridge, Massachusetts: Harvard University Press, 1975. 1,226p.

The encyclopaedic dictionary of traditional Chinese lists over 100,000 compounds. The book is excellent for early 20th-century literature and classical Chinese. It is arranged alphabetically by Wade-Giles romanization with nonsimplified characters. It has a radical index.

1089 A compilation of Chinese dictionaries.

J. Mathias, Sandra Hixson. New Haven, Connecticut: Yale University Press, 1976. 120p.

This is a comprehensive first history of all Chinese dictionaries on all subjects and in all languages.

1090 Chinese-English dictionary of contemporary usage.

Qi Wenxun. Berkeley, California: University of California Press, 1977. 484p.

The compiler, Chi Wen-hsun (Qi Wenxun), has added a great amount of new material gleaned from other dictionaries and contemporary publications, especially the *People's Daily* and the theoretical journal *Red Flag*. In addition to technical and political terms, the dictionary also contains a larger amount of general vocabulary which the compiler thinks will be useful to the reader of recent mainland prose.

1091 Pinyin Chinese-English dictionary.

Compiled by the Beijing Foreign Language Institute, under the editorial direction of Wu Jingrong. New York: Wiley, 1979. 977p.

Representing the work of more than fifty contributors over eight years, the dictionary is the most up-to-date, authoritative reference of its kind anywhere. It is the only dictionary that reflects both the recent simplification of Chinese characters and the adoption of the pinyin system for the English spelling of Chinese personal and place-names.

1092 A Chinese-English dictionary.
Edited by Wu Jingrong (and others). Beijing: Commercial Press, 1978. 1,318p.

This is the most useful middle-sized Chinese-English dictionary to have been published in recent years. A better quality, more expensive identical volume is also available under the title *A pinyin Chinese-English dictionary* (Pitman). This dictionary is the most significant general purpose lexical tool currently available to all those from professional translators to beginners who have need of a clearly-printed, easy-to-use aid that will meet the needs of most situations.

1093 The Sino Chinese-English dictionary.
New York: Sino-Publishing, 1980. 592p.

This Sino Chinese-English dictionary is an abridged version, published by the Beijing (Peking) Foreign Language Institute in 1979. This dictionary incorporates all of the special features and approach of the original edition (which contains over 5,000 single-character entries and over 80,000 compound-character entries). Only rarely used words, unfamiliar allusions and strongly-localized illustrative examples have been deleted.

English-Chinese dictionaries

1094 China beginner's/traveller's dictionary.
New York: Eurasia Press, 1980. 176p.

It is a useful dictionary for visitors to China and language students. It has over 1,500 words and phrases translated from pinyin to English and from English to pinyin.

1095 Concise English-Chinese dictionary.
Beijing: Commercial Publishing, 1972. 1,208p.

This dictionary has 26,000 entries, simplified characters, but no romanization. It translates idiomatic English into Chinese.

1096 English-Chinese dictionary of idioms.
Beijing: Commercial Publishing, 1981. 1,898p.

This dictionary is excellent for those wishing to know the Chinese equivalents of English idioms. Thousands of American and British idioms, both modern and archaic, are given. Excerpts from English literature are included to show how the idiom is used in its native context, along with the Chinese equivalent for each entry. Each literary example also has a Chinese translation.

1097 An English-Chinese dictionary of technology.
Qinghua University Group. Beijing: Defense Industry Publications, 1978. 2,437p.

This dictionary is a new encyclopaedia of scientific and technical terms. It translates words in context, has simplified characters, but has no romanization.

1098 **A junior English-Chinese dictionary.**
Beijing: Foreign Language Press, 1977. 1,022p.
This is a new and expanded version of the popular *Pocket English-Chinese Dictionary*. It has translations of English phrases and simplified characters, but no romanization.

Chinese-Chinese dictionaries

1099 **Ci Hai.** (T'zu Hai.)
Beijing: Zhong Hua, 1979. 4,301p.
This new edition (1979) is the most comprehensive reference work for Chinese characters, phrases and terminology. It has 107,000 entries including idioms, famous personalities, scientific terms and historical events. It is indexed by radical, stroke count and pinyin. Ten appendices include translations of Western names, a chronological table and a gazetteer.

1100 **Hanyu Chengyu Cidian.** (Han Yü Tz'u Tien.)
Gansu Normal University. Shanghai, China: Shanghai Education Press, 1978. 889p.
It is a new and expanded dictionary of the most popular four-character phrases. It has pinyin romanization and a stroke-count index.

1101 **Xiandai Hanyu Cidian.** (Hsien Tai Han Yü Tz'u Tien.)
Beijing: Commercial Publishing, 1977. 1,400p.
It is the most comprehensive medium-sized modern Chinese-Chinese dictionary, listing thousands of compounds. It is arranged by pinyin romanization, with radical and four-corner indices. It has simplified characters.

1102 **Xinhua Zidian.** (Hsin Hwa Tz'u Tien.)
Beijing: Foreign Language Press, 1975. 618p.
It has pinyin romanization, simplified and nonsimplified characters, extensive appendices and a radical index.

Linguistic studies

1103 **Selected works of Peter A. Boodberg.**
Edited by Alvin P. Cohen. Berkeley, California: University of California Press, 1978. 400p.
The late Peter A. Boodberg was a philologist of outstanding creativity. He was a scholar of the history and nature of the Chinese language and script and the history of the period of the Northern and Southern Dynasties, of the Chinese

frontier and of Inner-China. This volume includes his most important essays together with selections from his rare privately-published serials and an unpublished lecture.

1104 Aspects of Chinese sociolinguistics, essays by Yue Ren Chao.
Selected and introduced by Anwar S. Dil. Stanford, California: Stanford University Press, 1976. 415p.

This book presents 24 essays by one of the most distinguished Chinese linguists of our time, Yue Ren Chao (Yueh Jen Ch'ao). They cover a half-century of the author's pioneering researches on various aspects of the Chinese language, including his field studies of Chinese dialects and his work on the unification and standardization of Chinese.

1105 Language and linguistics in the People's Republic of China.
Edited by Winfred P. Lehmann. Austin, Texas: University of Texas Press, 1975. 168p.

This is an expanded account of a brief visit (from 16 October-13 November 1974) to the People's Republic of China by a delegation of American linguists, Chinese and general. It describes the delegation's experience and gives sporadic glimpses of what its members were able to observe directly.

1106 Character indexes of modern Chinese.
N. H. Leon. London: Curzon Press, 1981. 508p.

The book arranged all the characters listed in the standard monolingual dictionary *Xinhua Zidian* (*Hsin Hua Tz'u Tien*) according to the four systems most widely used in China today: alphabetically on the basis of pinyin, by the new 189 radicals introduced as a consequence to the simplification of characters, by the so-called Four-Corner system and by the recently introduced Rapid Stroke-Order system. Each arrangement is preceeded by a description of the given system and an account of its history. There are two appendices, one of which presents the characters proposed for further simplification in 1977 (the proposal was later rejected) and the other gives lists of Chinese characters used in modern Japanese.

1107 About Chinese.
Richard Newhan. Harmondsworth, Middlesex: Penguin, 1971. 188p.

The author explains, in simple terms, the nature of the Chinese language, both written and spoken, giving a brief introduction to grammar as well as a description of romanization systems and an account of language reform. The book also lists a number of introductory textbooks and dictionaries.

1108 A handbook on Chinese language structure.
Henry Henne Ole Bjorn Gongen, Lars Jul Hansen. Oslo: Universitets Forlaget, Scandinavian University Book, 1977. 293p.

The authors' aim in this handbook is to provide an introduction to Chinese language structure for students of Chinese and a reference grammar for general readers interested in the composition of Chinese.

1109 Language reform in China: documents and commentary.
Edited by Peter J. Seybolt, Gregory Guige Jiang.   White
Plains, New York: Sharpe, 1977. 400p.

The book, edited by Seybolt and Kuei-ke Chiang (Guige Jiang), contains translations of the pertinent documents that record the prolonged debates engendered
by the bold attempt to modernize both written and spoken Chinese. The introduction analyzes the reasons for language reform, its political and cultural implications, steps to be taken to implement it and the numerous problems - technical,
historical and psychological - encountered by promoters of reforms.

1110 Chinese writing: an introduction.
Diane Wolff.   New York: Holt, 1975. 46p.

This book introduces material about the different styles of calligraphy, the way in
which it reflects the heart and mind of the scribe and the materials used. The
book also includes instructions for practicing the art of Chinese writing.

1111 Speaking of Chinese.
Raymond Zhang, Margaret Zhang.   New York: Norton,
1978. 197p.

The authors, Raymond and Margaret Chang (Zhang), state at the outset that
their book is for anyone who wants to know more about Chinese without learning
to speak or write it. The complexities of written and spoken Chinese are examined and an account of the language from mythical times to the present is
provided, touching on political and literary history as well and Chinese names,
proverbs and cooking are treated from the perspective of language.

Literature

Texts

1112 Revolutionary literature in China: an anthology.
Edited and introduced by John Berninghasen, Ted Huter. White Plains, New York: Arts & Sciences Press, 1977. 103p.

The extensive introduction furnishes an overarching historical and theoretical framework for viewing something of the process by which the revolutionary literature of contemporary China developed. The volume contains complete translations of seven essays, eight short stories and a *Yang Ko* (*Yangge*) spanning the years 1914 to 1966. Presenting these in chronological order, with brief introductions, it succeeds in giving the reader a clear sense of the developmental aspect of the new literature.

1113 Anthology of Chinese literature: from the fourteenth century to the present day.
Edited by Cyril Birch. New York: Grove Press, 1972. 375p.

This book includes Yuan San Chu (Yuan San Zhu), ghost stories from the Ming and Ch'ing (Qing) periods, poems from Kao Chih (Gao Zhi) and Yuan Mei, Ch'ing Tz'u (Qing Ci) and his autobiography; and the last two-fifths of the book are given over multifariously to modern literature.

1114 Studies in Chinese literary genres.
Edited by Cyril Birch. Berkeley, California: University of California Press, 1974. 416p.

The contributors seek to define and describe major genres. Six essays deal with classical poetry from the Book of Songs to the lyrics (tz'u - Ci) of the Sung (Song) period. There are two essays on drama (Yuan and Ming), two on the vernacular short story and one on the novel of the military romance category whose exemplars bring the readers to the 19th century.

1115 The Chinese novel at the turn of the century.
Edited by Milena Dolezelova-Velingerova. Toronto:
University of Toronto Press, 1980. 376p.

This collection of nine essays analyzes the Chinese novel of the late Qing (Ch'ing) period (1897-1910) in its transitional role between traditional and modern Chinese fiction. The introductory essay explains literary and cultural changes in a political and social context. An appendix provides biographical data for authors.

1116 Chinese literature for the 1980s: the fourth congress of writers and artists.
Edited with an introduction by Howard
Goldblatt. Armonk, New York: Sharpe, 1982. 175p.

The Fourth National Congress of Writers and Artists held in Beijing (Peking) in the autumn of 1979 was a momentous event in the Chinese literary world. It was the first such congress since Mao's death and thus provided the first official occasion to assess the state of the literary ranks and of literature since the purges of the Cultural Revolution. The editor has selected pieces to represent the standpoints of a broad range of Chinese literary professionals at the Congress, from older Communist Party officials, to formerly jailed 'rightists' and to younger popular novelists.

1117 Modern Chinese literature in the May Fourth era.
Edited by Merle Goldman. Cambridge, Massachusetts:
Harvard University Press, 1977. 464p.

Goldman has skillfully edited this collection of essays dealing with the literature of the 1920s and 1930s. The work concentrates on three themes: foreign and domestic influences on May 4th literature, key figures in the literary movement and the lasting impact of the new genres.

1118 Unwelcome muse, Chinese literature in Shanghai and Peking, 1937-1945.
Edward Gunn. New York: Columbia University Press,
1980. 320p.

The period of Japanese occupation in Shanghai and Peking (Beijing), 1937-1945, was a surprisingly productive time for Chinese literature. Making much of this literature available in English for the first time, the volume shows how Chinese writers found new literary directions despite the hardship of occupation.

1119 Twentieth-century Chinese drama: an anthology.
Edited by Edward Gunn. Bloomington, Indiana: Indiana
University Press, 1983. 560p.

Many themes, genres and styles are represented and the plays included cover the Republican period, the Japanese occupation, Mao's ascendancy, the Cultural Revolution and after. This anthology is valuable for its insights into the social and historical development of 20th-century China as well as for its presentation of first-rate dramatists for the most part unknown in the West.

1120 The Chinese short story: studies in dating, authorship, and composition.
Patrick Hanan.   Cambridge, Massachusetts: Harvard University Press, 1974. 279p.

The author examines 149 accessible vernacular short stories from the mid-13th to mid-17th centuries. Using a variety of techniques, but principally that of linguistic-stylistic analysis, he is able to place nearly every story in one of three time periods, early (ca. 1250-1450), middle (ca. 1400-1575) and late (ca. 1550-1627).

1121 Heroes and villains in Communist China: the contemporary Chinese novel as a reflection of life.
Joe C. Huang.   London: Hurst, 1973. 345p.

The volume contains an examination of some twenty works which the author believes to be representative. All were written in the last quarter-century and depict various aspects of the socialist revolution and construction. The central strength of this book lies in its sweeping impassioned survey of the Chinese novel as a portrayal of the contemporary life in China.

1122 Chinese vernacular fiction: the formative period, volume iii.
W. L. Idema.   Leiden, Netherlands: Brill, 1974. 146p.

This is a survey of the early history of Chinese vernacular fiction. The author has cast doubt on earlier theories about the development of Chinese vernacular fiction and presented many new and often provocative ideas. Some of these ideas, however, tend to be impressionistic and speculative and should be accepted only as hypotheses or, at most, tentative conclusions.

1123 Modern Chinese stories and novellas, 1919-1949.
Edited by Joseph S. Lao, C. T. Xia, Leo Oufan Li.   New York: Columbia University Press, 1981. 608p.

This book provides students of modern Chinese literature with one convenient volume containing some of the most historically significant stories and novellas written since the 1919 Literature Revolution. Accompanied by biographies of the authors, an annotated bibliography and an introduction by C. T. Hsia (Xia), the 44 stories collected here, written by 20 different authors, have been selected on the basis of both their intrinsic literary merit and their historical importance, regardless of the writer's political persuasion. All of the selections are representative of the May 4th spirit.

1124 The romantic generation of modern Chinese writers.
Leo Oufan Li.   Cambridge, Massachusetts: Harvard University Press, 1973. 365p.

This volume makes a very unique contribution to the study of the modern literature movement. The author, Leo Ou-fan Lee's (Leo Oufan Li) account is sympathetic, sensitive and well written and it makes extensive use of an array of long-neglected autobiographical materials. This study will be of great interest to social, intellectual and literary historians of the 1920s and 1930s.

1125 Modern Chinese poetry: an introduction.
Julia C. Lin. Seattle, Washington: University of Washington Press, 1972. 204p.

The author attempts to trace the development of modern Chinese poetry from its pre-20th-century origins to the contemporary phase. His presentation is chronological, with three major sections (before 1917, 1917-1937, 1937-1949 and after) divided into seven chapters (tradition, transition, the pioneers, the formalists, the symbolists, the war period and the rise of proletarian poetry and poetry after 1949). He is familiar with the great Western poets and modern critical methods and sensitive to the form, content and history of Chinese verse. The volume is documented by translations of more than 150 poems and extracts.

1126 Stubborn weeds: Chinese literature after the Cultural Revolution.
Edited by Perry Link. Bloomington, Indiana: Indiana University Press, 1983. 320p.

The literature of the People's Republic of China became livelier and more varied during the 'thaw' of 1979-80 than at any other time since the revolution. The editor, who lived in China during that period, has assembled the most representative examples of 'stubborn weeds' - the writing that would not die in spite of the pressures of the Cultural Revolution. This volume includes fiction, drama and poetry, as well as comedian's dialogues and clappertales. The writers range from the prize-winning Jiang Zilong (Chiang Tzu-Lung), to the controversial Bai Hua (Pai Hua), to university students who wrote under pseudonyms in unofficial publications.

1127 Shih-shuo Hsin-yu: a new account of tales of the world.
Liu Yijing, with commentary by Liu Zhun, translated and annotated by Richard B. Mather. Minneapolis, Minnesota: University of Minnesota Press, 1976. 726p.

Professor Mather has spent over twenty years working on this collection of anecdotes, *bons mots* and literary, scholarly and political remarks from the period of the Six Dynasties. He presents a complete translation of the main text of the *Shih-shuo Hsin-yu* (Shishuo Xinyu), traditionally attributed to the Liu-Sung (Liusong) Prince, Liu I-ching (Liu Yijing 403-444) and most of the commentary by Liu Chun (Liu Zhun) (462-521). He further provides ample annotations, along with a detailed glossary of special terms and a short biographical notice for each of the 626 persons mentioned in the text.

1128 Chinese theories of literature.
James J. Y. Liu. Chicago: University of Chicago Press, 1975. 197p.

This book is a clear and worthwhile contribution to both Chinese literary studies and literary theory in general. It has two purposes - to contribute to an eventual universal theory of literature, to make available material which can be used for a synthesis of Chinese and Western views of literature.

1129 An introduction to Chinese literature.

Liu Wuji. Bloomington, Indiana: Indiana University Press, 1978. 246p.

The author, Liu Wu-ch'i (Liu Wuqi) deals with all the principal writers and genres and contains, besides, some interesting insights into Chinese and Western culture. The book includes a comprehensive history of Chinese literature illustrated by passages of prose and poetry from the most important figures.

1130 Chinese literature: an anthology from the earliest times to the present day.

Edited by William McNaughton. New York: Tuttle, 1974. 836p.

This volume offers selections from the literature produced by Chinese authors over nearly 3,000 years. It contains philosophical writings, poetry, legends, short stories and excerpts from novels and drama from traditional China, as well as examples of modern short stories and verse.

1131 Traditional Chinese stories: themes and variations.

Edited by Y. W. Ma, Joseph S. Lao. New York: Columbia University Press, 1973. 603p.

This sizeable volume of sixty-one stories is a major contribution to the body of excellent translations of fiction in readily available anthologies. The editors, Ma and Lau (Lao), drew from what they define to be the full span of Chinese fiction from pre-T'ang (Tang) China to the 20th century. Reflecting the scholarship of the past decade, the editors place the greatest emphasis on the *hua-pen* (*huaben*).

1132 Studies in Chinese poetry and poetics, volume I.

San Francisco; Chinese Materials Center, 1978. 375p.

This book is a collection of ten articles dealing with various aspects of traditional Chinese poetry and poetics with essays to describe the nature and principles of Chinese poetry.

1133 Literature of the hundred flowers.

Edited by Hualing Nieh. New York: Columbia University Press, 1981. 2 vols. 337p.+618p.

From May 1956 until early June 1957, the Communist Party supported independent thinking, debate and creative freedom. The result was the publication of an extraordinary set of literary works and critical essays which openly explored political and artistic issues confronting the modern Chinese writer. The author, Hualing Nieh (Hua-ling Nieh), has tackled a formidable translation project and succeeded in providing both a broad and detailed view of the issues of freedom, dissent and national development which daily affect the lives of millions of Chinese.

1134 **A Chinese look at literature: the literary value of Chou Tso-jen in relation to the tradition.**
David E. Pollard. Berkeley, California: University of California Press, 1973. 183p.

As a literary critic, Chou Tso-jen (Zhou Zouren) divided literature into two classes according to the traditional dichotomy of *Shih Yen Chih* (*Shiyanzhi*) (extempore self-expression) and *Wen i tsai tao* (*Weyi Zaidao*) (didactic literature written in the service of an ideology). To Chou (Zhou), literature in the first category was true literature and that in the second was not literature at all. Chou (Zhou) stressed individualism and individuality and associated Ch'eng (Cheng) (sincerity), Chu-wei (Zhuwei) (taste, sensibility), P'ing-tan (Pingdan) (simplicity) and Tzu-jan (Ziran) (naturalness) with good literature.

1135 **Chinese approaches to literature from Confucius to Liang Ch'i-chao.**
Edited by Adele Austin Rickett. Princeton, New Jersey: Princeton University Press, 1978. 325p.

This is the first comprehensive volume to bring together serious studies of the major text of Chinese literary theory. In addition to its analyses and interpretations, it provides a wealth of factual material regarding writers, texts and editions. Its elucidation of critical terminology will make it particularly useful.

1136 **China and the West: comparative literature studies.**
Edited by William Tay, Yingxiong Zhou, Henxiang Yuan. Hong Kong: Chinese University Press, 1980. 322p.

The editors apply the methods of Western literary criticism to Chinese works, including the problems of theory, methodology, comparison and translation. The volume includes 20 essays as core material to analyze classical Chinese poetry, premodern fiction and drama.

1137 **Lao She and the Chinese revolution.**
Ranbir Vohra. Cambridge, Massachusetts: Harvard University Press, 1974. 199p.

The book is the first large attempt to discover, through Lao She's novels, short stories and plays, the complex truth of Chinese society during the 1920s and 1930s. As the author says in the introduction, 'Political history needs the flesh of social and intellectual history to cover its bone'.

1138 **Early Chinese literature.**
Burton Watson. New York: Columbia University Press, 1972. 311p.

This volume contains answers to some of the questions general readers might have concerning early Chinese literature. It has an excellent introduction.

1139 A history of modern Chinese fiction.
C. T. Xia. New Haven, Connecticut: Yale University Press, 1971. 2nd ed. 701p.

Adequate summaries of the plots of important novels and stories, penetrating analyses of the major characters involved, along with translations of large excerpts, makes this book interesting even to lay readers. The volume, by C. T. Hsia (Xia), is divided into three sections: the early period (1917-27), a decade of growth (1928-37) and the war period and after (1937-57).

1140 The classic Chinese novel: a critical introduction.
C. T. Xia. Bloomington, Indiana: Indiana University Press, 1980. 283p.

The Classic Chinese Novel, by C. T. Hsia (Xia), for its painstaking research, its impeccable scholarship and its fund of invaluable insight is a classic in itself.

1141 Twentieth-century Chinese stories.
Edited by C. T. Xia, Joseph S. Lao. New York: Columbia University Press, 1971. 239p.

The editors, C. T. Hsia (Xia) and Joseph Lau (Lao), have selected works by some writers who are unfamiliar even to specialists of modern Chinese literature. Selection is based on their intrinsic literary merits rather than on extrinsic political or social implications.

1142 Literature of the People's Republic of China.
Xu Kaiyu, Ding Wang, with the special assistance of Howard Goldblatt. Bloomington, Indiana: Indiana University Press, 1980. 976p.

The editors, Hsu Kai Yu (Xu Kaiyu) and Ting Wang (Ding Wang), have assembled a work in six chapters (chronologically) with each part sub-divided into prose (short stories, selections from novels, plays) and verse. The parts follow political watersheds in the People's Republic of China: Yenan (Yanan) to 1955 (Korean War and early land reform); 1956-58 (Hundred Flowers and anti-Rightists campaign); 1959-1961 (Great Leap Forward); 1962-1964 (Socialist education campaign and Mao's partial eclipse); 1964-1970 (Cultural Revolution) and a section from 1971 onwards, entitled 'The fall of the Gang of Four - returns and reversals'. This anthology provides an excellent overview of the type of creative writing produced in the People's Republic of China. Most of these works have been especially translated for this volume.

1143 The Chinese literary scene: a writer's visit to the People's Republic of China.
Xu Kaiyu. New York: Vintage Books, 1975. 349p.

Hsu Kai Yu's (Xu Kaiyu) report is the result of a six-month visit to China in 1973, during which he made tireless attempts to meet with Chinese writers, both active ones and those on the sidelines. He records what he learned, rather than drawing conclusions. About half the book consists of reports on his interviews, the other half on translations of poems, fiction and criticism.

1144 The new realism: writing from China 1979-1980.
Edited by Lee Yee. New York: Sino-Publishing, 1981. 280p.

Before 1978 writings about China by Chinese were nothing more than assembly line propaganda. The material earned international derision and automatic dismissal. Since then the government has encouraged diversity. The result was an outpouring of vivid and realistic profiles of a Chinese society in flux. The new wave of social critics has been called 'The second hundred flowers'. This book represents one of those 'Flowers'.

1145 Chinese literature: popular fiction and drama.
Edited by H. C. Zhang. Chicago: Aldine, 1973. 466p.

This anthology by H. C. Chang (Zhang) features twelve selections illustrative of Chinese colloquial fiction and drama from the 13th to the 18th century. The editor's introductions and footnotes present the historical context for each piece as well as literary and bibliographic details.

1146 Chinese literature ii: nature poetry.
Translated and edited by H. C. Zhang. New York: Columbia University Press, 1977. 124p.

This is an incomparable anthology of traditional Chinese vernacular literature. It is also a fine study of the subject, distilling the best Chinese scholarship on items in the volume. The editor focuses on five poets: T'ao Ch'ien (Tau Qian), Hsieh Ling-yun (Xie Lingyun), Wang Wei, Meng Hao-jen (Meng Haoren) and Lin Tsung-yuan (Lin Zongyuan). The book will provide the general reader with a charming introduction to Chinese nature poetry.

1147 Chinese poetic writing.
François Zheng, translated from French by Donald A. Riggs, Jerome P. Seaton. Bloomington, Indiana: Indiana University Press, 1983. 288p.

The author, François Cheng (Zheng) argues convincingly that Chinese poetry and calligraphy are mutually enhancing in a way in which Western literatures and writing systems are not. A disciple of Roland Barthes, Roman Jakobson and the structuralist school, he offers a fresh approach to the study of Chinese poetry, which is seen as 'an organic ensemble of a semiotic system': phonic, lexical and syntactic as well as mythic. Further helping to illuminate the author's thesis are the 135 poems from the T'ang (Tang) dynasty that constitute the second half of the book. Included are such well-known masters as Wang Wei, Li Po (Li Bo), Tu Fu (Du Fu), Li Shang-yin (Li Shangyin) and Li Ho (Li He).

Lu Xun

1148 The social thought of Lu Hsun, 1881-1936.
Paul Xia Chen. New York: Vantage Press, 1977. 150p.

Detecting a genuine system inherent within the brief and seemingly disconnected sayings of Lu Hsun (Lu Xun), Ch'en (Chen) brings to light this most honoured of modern Chinese writers' unique method of creating a people's literature.

1149 Lu Xun: three stories.
Edited by Paul Kratochril. Cambridge, England: Cambridge University Press, 1970. 217p.

This annotated reader for advanced students gives three short stories of Lu Hsun (Lu Xun), an important Chinese political and literary figure. The stories are reproduced photographically from the Chinese originals. In the introduction, the editor discusses the main issues of post-1919 Chinese literature.

1150 Old tales retold.
Lu Xun, translated by Yang Xianyi, Gladys Yang. Beijing: Foreign Language Press, 1972.

This book by Lu Hsun (Lu Xun) contains eight tales based on fables and legends of ancient China, satirizing Lao Ze (Lao Tsu), Mo Ze (Mo Tsu) and Zhuang Ze (Chuang Tse).

1151 Dawn blossoms plucked at dusk.
Lu Xun, translated by Yang Xianyi, Gladys Yang. Beijing: Foreign Language Press, 1976.

This book by Lu Hsun (Lu Xun) contains ten reminiscences and satirical essays criticizing Confucian morality, feudal customs, scholar-bureaucrats and the cruelty of the old society.

1152 A brief history of Chinese fiction.
Lu Xun, translated by Yang Xianyi, Gladys Yang. Beijing: Foreign Language Press, 1976. 3rd ed. 437p.

This book by Lu Hsun (Lu Xun) traces Chinese literature from its origins in myth and legend through the Qing (Ch'ing) dynasty. It includes detailed analyses of *Dream of Red Mansions*, *Water Margin*, and other classics.

1153 Wandering.
Lu Xun, translated by Yang Xianyi, Gladys Yang. Beijing: Foreign Language Press, 1981. 142p.

In these eleven stories, written in 1924 and 1925, Lu Xun's (Lu Hsun) criticism of feudal society is scathing as he portrays its violation of the human spirit. Often told from a woman's point of view, these stories are masterpieces both in their artistic form and in the significance of their content.

1154 Call to arms.

Lu Xun, translated by Yang Xianyi, Gladys Yang. Beijing: Foreign Language Press, 1981. 149p.

This volume is the first collection of short stories by Lu Xun (Lu Hsun). Written between 1918 and 1922, each of the fourteen stories portrays a certain aspect of pre-liberation Chinese society: the attitude of the intellectual to the peasant (*A small incident*), the conflict of generations (*Storm in a teacup*) and in *The true story of Ah Q*, Lu Xun (Lu Hsun) reveals the most brutal aspects of feudal society. Because of the author's skill in uncovering and presenting people's inner thoughts and emotions, the reader is left with a vivid impression of the author's profound artistic conception.

1155 Lu Hsun's vision of reality.

W. Lyell. Berkeley, California: University of California Press, 1976. 368p.

Lu Hsun (Lu Xun) (1881-1936) is the literary giant of modern China. Though a writer of fiction, he wished to use literature for the betterment of society. A rebel rather than a reformer, he sought the destruction of the Confucian ideology which governed the relationship of man to man in traditional China. The author has written the book with the general reader in mind. The result is a fascinating and perceptive account of Lu Hsun (Lu Xun) the man as well as the artist.

1156 Silent China: selected writings of Lu Xun.

Translated by Gladys Yang. London: Oxford University Press, 1973. 196p.

This book is a collection of stories, reminiscences, poems, prose poems and essays selected, introduced and translated by Gladys Yang. Lu Xun (Lu Hsun 1881-1936) is a great writer of modern China. His striking stories and polemical articles, many of them written in the vernacular, helped to bring about a revolution in language as well as to prepare the way for social and political changes.

1157 Lu Xun: selected works.

translated by Yang Xianyi, Gladys Yang. Beijing: Foreign Language Press, 1980. 4 vols. 1,547p.

Volume one contains selections from Lu Hsun's (Lu Xun) stories, prose, poems and reminiscences. Volumes two to four encompass the most important of his essays written between 1918 and 1936.

1158 The complete stories of Lu Xun.

Translated by Yang Xianyi, Gladys Yang. Bloomington, Indiana: Indiana University Press, 1982. 312p.

The year 1981 marked the centennial of the birth of Lu Xun (Lu Hsun), the most influential writer of this century. His short stories are satiric, vivid, pungently realistic, as satisfying in structure as they are in tone and content. This collection of Lu Xun's (Lu Hsun) short stories is the most complete, accurate and authoritative yet to appear. It includes the preface to his first book, *Call to arms*, in which Lu Xun (Lu Hsun) explains how he came to be a writer.

1159 **A pictorial biography of Lu Xun, 1881-1936.**
    Beijing: Foreign Language Press, 1981. 174p. photos.

This book deals chronologically and comprehensively with Lu Xun's (Lu Hsun) involvement in the drama of developing literary, historical, revolutionary and social movements. It includes several black-and-white photographs as well as essays by various authors who discuss his career as the pioneer of modern Chinese philosophy.

Poetry

1160 **On poetry.**
    Ai Qing, translated by Lou Kinqi. New York: Sino-Publishing, 1981. 196p.

The 1930s, a period of intense suffering and bloodshed in China, saw a blossoming in its literary world. Young poets came forth to sing concern for their tormented country. Of the new breed Ai Qing (Ai Ch'ing) was one of the greatest and most popular poets. His writings during 1938-39 provide extraordinary documentation of the thinking of the Chinese intelligentsia, formulated during that era of great change.

1161 **Kao Shih.**
    Marie Chan. Boston, Massachusetts: Hall, 1978. 176p.

In her preface to the book, *Kao Shih* (*Gao Shi*), the author writes, 'Our taste runs to the sophisticated ambiguity and cynicism of late T'ang (Tang) poetry or its antithesis, the primitivistic spontaneity of nature poetry. Both bodies of poetry offer refuge from proportional certainty'.

1162 **Heaven my blanket, earth my pillow: poems from the Sung dynasty.**
    Jonathan Chaves. New York: Weatherhill, 1975. 118p.

It is a short biographical introduction to Yang (1127-1206), a brief introduction to Sung Shih (Song Shi) poetry, a critique of Yang's own verse and a note 'On the relationship of poetry and painting in China', precede the bulk of the book, which consists of translations of 122 Shih (Shi) and 3 tz'u (ci) (lyrics).

1163 **Mei Yao-ch'en and the development of early Sung (Song) poetry.**
    Jonathan Chaves. New York: Columbia University Press, 1976. 254p.

A study of Mei Yao-ch'en (Mei Yaochen), an 11th century Chinese poet, is divided into five sections: an investigation into the poet's life; a summary of the three major trends in Sung (Song) poetry prior to his time; an examination of Mei's poetry both as a product of these traditions and as an influence upon them; a study of Mei's poetic theory, concentrating on his ideal of *ping-tan* (*bing-dan*) (even and bland) and finally a survey of Mei's most important poems, with commentary and notes.

1164 Selected poems of Ai Qing.
Edited with an introduction and notes by Eugene Chen
Eoyang. Bloomington, Indiana: Indiana University Press,
1983. 476p.

This collection of over fifty poems by one of China's greatest living poets spans
some 45 years, from Ai Qing's first volume, published in 1936, to a group of
poems written in 1981. Ai Qing (Ai Ch'ing) writes about time-honoured themes:
a beggar woman by the side of the road, the selfless love and devotion of a hired
wet nurse, the sense of desolation that accompanies a heavy snowfall. His affinity
to Walt Whitman is immediately apparent, as the editor observes in his introduction, but where the American poet 'spoke as the embodiment of the people, the
poet as the people', Ai Qing (Ai Ch'ing) has assumed a more modest stance: he
has been content to be, from time to time, a poet of the people.

1165 The flowing plum and the palace lady: interpretations of Chinese poetry.
Hans H. Frankel. New Haven, Connecticut: Yale
University Press, 1976. 276p.

The author has selected 106 poems that have special appeal for him and has
organized them into chapters according to their main theme to demonstrate
important aesthetic values in Chinese poetry - fu (rhyme-prose), lu-shih (lushi)
(regulated verse), tz'u (ci) (lyrics), yuey-fu (yuefu) (ballads) and others.

1166 Poetry and politics: the life and works of Juan Chi (AD 210-263).
Donald Holzman. Cambridge, England: Cambridge
University Press, 1976. 316p.

This book is a study of Juan Ch'i (Ruan Ji), one of the 'Seven sages of the
bamboo grove'. It is not only a masterly contribution to the study of Chinese
poetry, but also an original and intriguing inquiry into the intellectual history of
the 3rd century.

1167 Li Qingzhao: complete poems.
Li Qingzhao, translated and edited by Kenneth Rexroth,
Ling Zhun. New York: New Direction, 1972. 118p.

The editors, Kenneth Rexroth and Ling Chung (Zhun), have collaborated to
produce the complete collection of poems (67) of a (female) poet of the Sung
(Song) period. They are in the form of lyric verse popular at that time. Li
Ch'ing-chao (Li Qingzhao) was certainly China's most skillful and fascinating
woman poet. Her eventful life, from happy, congenial marriage to exile, lonely
widowhood and old age during the troubled years of the Sung (Song) empire, is
vividly depicted in these tender lyrics, some poignantly touching and artistically
composed.

1168 **The transformation of the Chinese lyrical tradition: Chiang K'uei and Southern Sung tz'u poetry.**
Lin Shuen-fu. Princeton, New Jersey: Princeton University Press, 1978. 263p.

This volume is a pioneer work of the tz'u (ci) poetry of the Southern Sung (Song). It provides brilliant insights into both Chinese cultural history and literary theory. The book is a landmark publication in every sense.

1169 **The interlingual critic: interpreting Chinese poetry.**
James J. Y. Liu. Bloomington, Indiana: Indiana University Press, 1982. 160p.

As a critical interpretation and evaluation of Chinese poetry, this book is a sophisticated exploration of the poetic experience and the nature of translation and criticism. The book is a valuable contribution to the fields of interlingual criticism and comparative literature.

1170 **Major lyricists of the Northern Sung, 960-1126.**
James J. Y. Liu. Princeton, New Jersey: Princeton University Press, 1974. 275p.

The author introduces us to the writings of six outstanding and representative tz'u (ci) poets and through a critical examination of 28 tz'u (ci) he highlights the similarities and differences between the lyricists.

1171 **Sunflower splendor, three thousand years of Chinese poetry.**
Wuji Liu, Irvin Yucheng Lo. Bloomington, Indiana: Indiana University Press, 1978. 630p.

The book is the largest and, on the whole, best anthology of translated Chinese poems to have appeared in a Western language. It contains about 1,000 poems in classical styles, newly translated by scholars fluent in both Chinese and English. It includes verse by Wang Wei, Li Po (Li Bo), Tu Fu (Du Fu), the five-and-seven word shih, the music bureau ballad, the quatrain, the regulated verse form and popular songs. The original Chinese title for the novel is *Kuei Yeh Chi* (Kui Yeji).

1172 **Paths in dreams: selected prose and poetry of Ho Ch'i-fang.**
Edited and translated by Bonnie S. McDougall. St Lucia: University of Queensland Press, 1976. 244p.

The editor provides valuable information and critical insight that enable the reader to understand better Ho's (He) life and works during those tempestuous years (1931-44). In her translation, she achieves a nearly perfect balance between felicity of expression and faithfulness to the original.

1173 **The poetry of Meng Ch'iao and Han Yu.**
Stephen Owen. New Haven, Connecticut: Yale University Press, 1975. 344p.

The wisdom of attempting a simultaneous exercise in literary history and literary criticism is no longer as obvious as it once was. This volume exemplifies both the advantages and the pitfalls of such a venture, plausible as it appears to interweave the lives and poems of Meng Ch'iao (Meng Qiao) and Han Yu. It is the poems that supply most of the information about both lives and personalities, which, in turn, somehow explain the poems.

1174 The poetry of the early T'ang.
Stephen Owen. New Haven, Connecticut: Yale University Press, 1976. 455p.

The information the author provides is sound; the translations of the poems are accurate for the most part, the discussions are lucid and the opinions expressed on individual poets generally acceptable, if not original.

1175 The orchard boat, women poets of China.
Edited and translated by Kenneth Rexroth, Zhong Ling. New York: McGraw-Hill, 1973. 150p.

This is a brief collection of translated poems by Chinese women from antiquity to the present. The collection ranges from the court poetry of courtesans, palace women and Tao (Dao) priestesses to works by contemporary Chinese women living in the East and West. The collection includes poems by the best-known women poets of China, Li Ch'ing-chao (Li Qingzhao) and Chu Shu-chen (Zhu Shuzhen), as well as selections by writers hitherto unknown to the West.

1176 Fifty-five T'ang poems.
Hugh M. Stimson. New Haven, Connecticut: Yale University Press, 1976. 247p.

This is an instructional text for reading T'ang poetry. The book is organized according to the widely accepted pedagogical principle that one should focus upon one aspect of the language at a time, first sound, then grammar and finally, vocabulary and script.

1177 Chinese poems.
Translated by Arthur D. Waley. Winchester, Massachusetts: Allen & Unwin, 1982. 192p.

The poems represented in this collection were chosen because they lend themselves to literal as well as literary translation. Poems of a highly allusive nature are excluded and annotation, therefore, is kept to a minimum.

1178 The bell and the drum: a study of Shih Ching as formulaic poetry.
C. H. Wang. Berkeley, California: University of California Press, 1974. 176p.

The author analyzes this Chinese classic in light of the modern Parry-Lord theories of oral-formulaic composition, which have developed from the study of Homeric and Old English literature. The author finds this new methodology serviceable and explores the similarity between Chinese and Western literary classics.

1179 **The old man who does as he pleases: selections from the poetry and prose of Lu Yu.**
Translated by Burton Watson. New York: Columbia University Press, 1972. 126p.

The volume includes translations of 60 poems and excerpts from Lu Yu's famous *Diary of a trip to Shu* (1170). This is a delightful book, extremely rich and rewarding reading.

1180 **Su Tung-po: selections from a Sung dynasty poet.**
Translated by Burton Watson. New York: Columbia University Press, 1973. 149p.

These translations provide a revealing selection from the large output of a major Chinese poet of the 11th century, who up to now has been inadequately represented in translation.

1181 **Cold mountain: 100 poems by the T'ang poet Han Shan.**
Translated by Burton Watson. New York: Columbia University Press, 1975. 118p.

This is one of the most important works of Chinese Buddhist poetry. Not only does its language come very close to the original in its simplicity and forcefulness, but its attempt to convey the original feelings and moods is also phenomenally successful.

1182 **Chinese rhyme-prose: poems in the fu form from the Han and Six Dynasties period.**
Burton Watson. New York: Columbia University Press, 1971. 128p.

After an introduction in which he discusses the development and characteristics of fu poetry, the author provides translations, with biographical and critical materials, from the work of 12 poets. The fu, or rhyme-prose, also called prose-poetry, is a type of poetic composition that enjoyed great popularity in China between the 2nd century BC and the 6th century AD.

1183 **The four seasons of T'ang poetry.**
John C. H. Wu. New York: Tuttle, 1972. 225p.

The author's four seasons are a philosophical interpretation of the spirit characteristic of the four traditional chronological divisions. His spring includes the earliest T'ang poets plus Wang Wei and Li Po (Li Bo), summer encompasses Tu Fu (Du Fu) and some poets who wrote about war; autumn is embodied in Po Chu-i (Bo Zhuyi), Han Yu and their respective circulars; Li Shang-yin (Li Shangyin), Tu Mu (Du Mu), Wen Ting-yun (Wen Tingyun) and several other minor poets are included in the season of winter.

1184 **Chinese poetry: major modes and genres.**
Edited and translated by Wai-lim Yip. Berkeley, California: University of California Press, 1976. 496p.

This anthology contains over 150 poems drawn from various periods and representative forms of Chinese verse, the earliest being the Shih Ch'ing (Shi Jing), the latest the Yuan period and nearly half from the T'ang (Tang). Each of the six sections is prefaced with a few pages of introductory remarks concerning the particular period and style. The poems themselves are presented first in Chinese, then, in word-for-character literal English and finally in a more polished rendering.

1185 The poetry of Wang Wei, new translation and commentary.
Pauline Yu. Bloomington, Indiana: Indiana University Press, 1980. 423p.

This volume contains 150 poems by one of the major poets of the T'ang (Tang) dynasty. An extensive introduction relates the work of Wang Wei to Chinese and Western literary traditions. Chinese texts are provided for all translations.

1186 The evolution of Chinese Tz'u poetry: from late T'ang (Tang) to Northern Sung (Song).
Zhang Gangyi Sun. Princeton, New Jersey: Princeton University Press, 1979. 304p.

Chinese tz'u (ci) poetry was the most prominent poetic genre of the Sung (Song) dynasty (960-1279). By concentrating on five major poets whose works represent milestones in the development of the tz'u (ci) from the 9th through the 11th centuries, the author, Chang Kang-I Sun (Zhang Gangyi Sun), demonstrates the importance of the evolution of poetic genres for the study of literary history. She combines an analysis of the form, structure and function of the tz'u (ci) with an examination of its conventional poetic requirements to show how the genre's development is intimately related to the individual talents of the leading poets and to the changing aesthetic and cultural values of the time.

The translation of art: essays on Chinese painting and poetry.
See item no. 1276.

Guide to Chinese poetry and drama.
See item no. 1409.

Fiction

1187 Autumn in Spring and other stories.
Ba Jin. New York: Panda Books, 1981. 147p.

This book contains four stories, an essay and an interview by one of China's most celebrated novelists. The characters are Westernized intellectuals who fall victim to the feudal social system of the 1930s.

1188 Family.
Ba Jin, translated by Sidney Shapiro, Lu Guanghuan, introduced by Olga Lang. New York: Doubleday, 1972. 286p.

Family, as the first part of Pa Chin's (Ba Jin) famous trilogy, has long been well known in Chinese and used to be readily available in an English translation published by the Foreign Language Press in Peking (Beijing) in 1958. This new edition reproduces Sidney Shapiro's Peking (Beijing) translation and adds to it a translation (by Lu Kuan-huan - Lu Guanhuan) of certain passages which were deleted from the 1958 edition as well as a useful introduction to Pa Chin (Ba Jin) and his life by Olga Lang, which includes a description of the dreadful treatment he received during the Cultural Revolution.

1189 The story of the stone: the dream of the red chamber.
Cao Xueqin, vols 1-3 translated by David Hawkes, vol 4 translated by John Minford. Bloomington, Indiana: Indiana University Press, 1979. 1981. 1983.

At his death in 1763, Cao Xueqin (Tsao Hsueh-ch'in) left his masterpiece unfinished. Working from manuscript fragments, the craftsman and artist Gao E (Kao E) finished Gao's (Tsao) book and proved to be a literate, intelligent and conscientious editor. David Hawkes and John Minford complete the landmark translation to capture the nuances of style and tone that distinguish the original novel. No other single book tells us as much about Chinese civilization. The publication of the first four volumes of a projected five-volume set, under the title of *The Story of the Stone*, is on the way to a complete translation into English of the 18th-century Chinese novel, the *Hung-lung Meng (Hong-long Meng)*. The subtitles of each volume are: Volume I, *The Golden Days* (1979); Volume II, *The Crab-Flower Club* (1979); Volume III, *The Warning Voice* (1981); and Volume IV, *The Debt of Tears* (1983).

1190 A dream of red mansions.
Cao Xueqin, Gao E, translated by Yang Xianyi, Gladys Yang. Beijing: Foreign Language Press, 1978. 3 vols.

This is one of the most popular and best-known novels in all Chinese literature. It is the abundantly peopled chronicle of a noble family in the 18th century - rich, powerful, singled out for generations by imperial favour. The splendour of enchanting gardens, pleasure pavilions and a daily life of the most sophisticated refinements hides the symptoms of decline and self-destruction. These volumes mark the first time that the complete novel has been translated into English.

1191 Master Tung's western chamber romance, a Chinese chantefable.
Translated by Lili Chen. New York: Cambridge University Press, 1976. 238p.

Master Tung's (Dong) *Western chamber romance* is a masterpiece of Chinese storytelling literature written in the 12th century in the form of a chantefable known as *Chu-kung-tiao (Zhukongdiao)*. It narrates the charming love story of the beauty Ying-ying (Yingying) and the student Chang (Zhang) - a tale that acquired in China a name comparable to that of Romeo and Juliet in Europe. Ch'en's (Chen) translation is superb. Her notes provide an excellent explanation of the allusions and historical names.

1192 The dragon's village.
Yuanzong Chen. New York: Pantheon Books, 1980. 128p.

This novel describes the efforts, in 1951, of an enthusiastic troupe of young Shanghai cadres, proudly sporting their new soldier-style jackets and caps, to carry Mao's theory of land reform to a remote village in a northern province.

1193 The Hsi yu Chi.
G. Dubbridge. London: Cambridge University Press, 1970.
478p.

This is a study of the early versions of the classic Chinese novel known to English readers as 'Monkey'. The author examines a long tradition of earlier versions in narrative and dramatic form. The study uses Chinese characters both on text pages and in the extensive bibliography.

1194 Lu You.
Michael Duke. New York: Twayne, 1977. 180p.

The author portrays Lu You (Lu Yu) as a microcosmic abstract, a symbol of the classic Chinese tension between the Confucian call to sober social duty and the Taoist invitation to free-flying sensual individualism.

1195 Chinese folk tales.
Louise Guo, Yuanxi Guo. Beijing: Celestial Arts, 1976.
175p.

This book by Louise and Yuan Hsi Kuo (Yuanxi Guo) contains thirty-five tales of Han and minority cultures, each sparkling in wit and plot. The folk-tales, with the notes and illustrations, serve as a valuable introduction to China's diverse cultures.

1196 Chu Yuan.
Guo Moruo. Beijing: Foreign Language Press, 1978. 3rd
ed. 100p.

This book contains a five-act tragedy on the struggle of the famous 3rd-century BC poet-statesman, Chu Yuan (Zhu Yuan) against the tyrants of his day.

1197 Till morning comes.
Han Suyin. New York: Bantam, 1982. 468p.

This new novel is a love story involving an American woman journalist and an officer in Mao's army. It is staged against the entire period from the Second World War to the Cultural Revolution. As always, the author, Han Su-yin (Suyin), portrays with vividness and compassion the effect of major historical changes on individuals.

1198 The golden road.
Hao Ran. Beijing: Foreign Language Press, 1981. 390p.

The novel was an instant success when it first appeared in China in 1972 during the Cultural Revolution. The reader witnesses the painful and exhilarating struggle between these ordinary people who achieve in the humblest setting one of the most daring social reorganizations in human history.

Literature. Fiction

1199 The drawing of an old cat and other stories.
Huang Zhunming, translated by Howard
Goldblatt. Bloomington, Indiana: Indiana University Press,
1980. 288p.

The author, Hwang Chun-ming's (Huang Zhunming) refreshingly simple style, his skillful use of dialect, his humour and above all, his deep concern for people whose lives are complicated by changes beyond their control all come through in Goldblatt's translation.

1200 Straw sandles: Chinese short stories, 1918-1933.
Harold Isaacs, foreword by Lu Xun. Cambridge,
Massachusetts: MIT Press, 1974. 444p.

This is a collection of 23 short stories, one abridged play by Kuo Mo-jo (Guo Moruo), one poem by Yin Fu and notes by Mao Tun (Mao Dun), all of which were written between the years 1918 and 1933. These words were translated by various hands in the early 1930s and were assembled from background information that is important to the understanding of the political meaning of these literary works. The stories in this volume represent the voices of protest, anger and frustration of young Chinese intellectuals in the decade and a half between 1918 and 1933. These stories have a historical and political significance beyond their literary merits.

1201 Modern Chinese stories.
Edited by W. F. Jenner, translated by Gladys Yang. New
York: Oxford University Press, 1974. 2nd ed. 271p.

The twenty stories in this collection cover a period of a half-century up to 1963. The stories describes changes in Chinese life and thought.

1202 Fortress besieged.
Jian Zhongshu, translated by Jeanne Kelly, Nithan K.
Mao. Bloomington, Indiana: Indiana University Press,
1980. 377p.

This is a translation of a novel first published in China in 1947. The volume will delight with its Chinese wit and humour as well as the depth and breadth of the author's erudition. Its translators are to be commended for accomplishing an extremely difficult but rewarding task.

1203 The dream of the red chamber: a critical study.
Jeanne Knoerle, foreword by Liu Wuji. Bloomington,
Indiana: Indiana University Press, 1972. 160p.

This book is the first to analyze the novel in its entirety. The author surveys the historical background and discusses the novel's narrative style, characters, time and space structure and moral view of life.

1204 Rickshaw: the novel Lo-T'o Hsiang Tzu.
Lao She, translated by Jean M. James.   Honolulu:
University Press of Hawaii, 1980. 260p.
The decline and fall of a typical representative of the impoverished masses of early Republican Peking (Beijing) is depicted with fine psychological insight. The hero is a sturdy young rickshaw boy from the country, whose one ambition is to earn enough to buy his own rickshaw. This is one of the most accessible and evocative works of Chinese fiction.

1205 Cat country: a satirical novel of China in the 1930s.
Lao She, translated with an introduction by William A.
Lyell, Jr.   Columbus, Ohio: Ohio State University Press,
1973. 227p.
This is the first unabridged translation into English of the scathing and hilarious satire by one of China's modern writers, who attacks alternately the collectivist philosophy of his troubled homeland and its declining social institutions.

1206 Camel Xiangzi.
Lao She, translated by Shi Xiaoqing, preface by Hu
Jieqing.   Bloomington, Indiana: Indiana University Press,
1981. 240p.
This new, accurate and readable translation of Lao She's unforgettable novel features an afterword by the author as well as a preface by Hu Jieqing (Hu Chieh-ch'ing), Lao She's widow. Honest and industrious Xiangzi (Hsiang-tzu) wants nothing more than to own his own rickshaw. But his fate takes a tragic turn when his wife dies and he is forced to sell the rickshaw to pay off debts. A poignant depiction of a human soul disintegrating in the face of personal misery and social corruption. The novel, with its revolutionary overtones, is a classic of modern China.

1207 Teahouse.
Lao She.   Beijing: Foreign Language Press, 1980. 86p.
The novel follows the life of the owner of a typical, old Beijing (Peking) teahouse and his customers through three stages in modern Chinese history.

1208 Twelve towers.
Li Yu, retold by Nathan K. Mao.   Seattle, Washington:
University of Washington Press, 1979. 154p.
The literary talent of Li Yu, already known to Western readers through the exotic novel, *The prayer mat of flesh*, is superbly displayed in this collection of twelve short stories written around 1658.

1209 In the eye of the typhoon.
Ruth Earnshaw Lo, Katharine S. Kinderman, introduced by
John K. Fairbank.   New York: Harcourt Brace, 1980. 289p.
Midnight raids, loss of work and friends, forced re-education programmes and sharing of one's home were some of the burdens to be borne by middle-class victims of the Cultural Revolution. The author, an American woman and her

Literature. Fiction

Chinese husband, a professor lived through the revolution. The book focuses on the years from 1966, when the Cultural Revolution began, to 1978, when she and her husband and her family were allowed to return to the United States. The book describes her family life at Chung Shang (Zhong Shang) University, near Canton (Guangzhou).

1210 Spring moon.
Bette Lord. New York: Harper & Row, 1981. 400p.

A novel of rare beauty and skill *Spring Moon*, delicately captures the rich fabric of traditional life in China and the cataclysm of her long revolution. The story begins in the region of the Emperor Kuang Hsu (Guang Xu), 1892, in the House of Chang (Zhang) in Soochow (Suzhou), as the slave girl Spring Moon achieves a terrible revenge against the clan. It ends in the early 1970s when five generations of clansmen gather at the site of the family graves to perform the ceremonies that for thousands of years have linked China's past with her present and both with the future.

1211 Three kingdoms: China's epic drama.
Luo Guanzhuan, translated and edited by Moss Roberts. New York: Random House, 1973. 352p.

This book is a beautifully illustrated translation of China's famous historical epic. It tells of the decline of the longest and mightiest of China's dynasties and its breaking in the 3rd century AD into three warring kingdoms. The summation of over a millennium of Chinese reflection on a momentous event in their history is considered by the Chinese to be among the five or six masterpieces in their literary tradition.

1212 Traditional Chinese stories, themes and variations.
Edited by Y. W. Ma, Joseph S. Lao. New York: Columbia University Press, 1978. 603p.

The book is a new anthology of 61 stories from the earliest times to the Republican era. It is arranged thematically: selfless friend, heartless loves, dream adventure, etc. It also includes annotations and bibliographies.

1213 Midnight.
Mao Dun. Beijing: Foreign Language Press, 1979. 2nd ed. 632p.

The central figure in the story is a Shanghai industrialist of the 1930s. He is ruthlessly successful at business until he loses all his money gambling on the Stock Exchange.

1214 Cold night: a novel by Pa Chin.
Translated by Nathan K. Mao, Liu Cunyang. Seattle, Washington: University of Washington Press, 1979. 202p.

Available for the first time in English translation, *Cold Night* (Han Yeh - Han Ye) ranks alongside Pa Chin's (Ba Jin) earlier novel *Family* (Chia - Jia) in importance, both as a masterpiece of Chinese fiction and as a social commentary.

1215 Masks of fiction in the dream of the red chamber.
Lucien Miller.   Tucson, Arizona: University of Arizona
Press, 1975. 345p.
The author proposes to assess the artistry of the author Ts'ao Hsueh-ch'in (Cao
Xueqin) and he invites the readers to embark on a study he regards as mildly
revisionist.

1216 Archetype and allegory in the 'Dream of the Red Chamber'.
Andrew H. Plaks.   Princeton, New Jersey: Princeton
University Press, 1976. 269p.
This book should be of interest to all serious students of Chinese literature,
philosophy or intellectual history. The author's bold hypothesis and the wide-
ranging implications involved call for further careful examination. Also his
masterful contrast of Chinese and Western allegory should make this book important for students of comparative studies.

1217 Hsin-lun and other writings by Huan T'an (43 BC-28 BC).
Translated by Tomotlus Pokora.   Ann Arbor, Michigan:
University of Michigan, Center for Chinese Studies, 1975.
414p.
Pokora has been studying Huan T'an (Huan Tan) and the *Hsin-lun* (*Xinlun*) for
almost twenty years. In this publication he offers a complete translation of all the
known *Hsin-lun* (*Xinlun*) fragments, as well as other writings by Huan, including
a fu, two letters and several memorials.

1218 Selected tales of Liaozhai.
Pu Songling.   New York: Panda Books, 1981. 151p.
These seventeen short tales exemplify the adroit, compressed mingling of dreams,
folk-tales and original plots by a noted 17th-century Chinese writer. Rooted in
magic, Taoism (Daoism), ancient folk-tales and edged with an instinctive awareness of social injustice, these tales are guaranteed to bring a chuckle to the throat
and a prickle to the scalp. Dancing crickets, dreaming wolves, human foxes, a
dictionary of pigeons and miniature armies of men doing battle with bedbugs are
just a few of the delights that enliven this collection.

1219 Water margin.
Shi Naian, translated by J. H. Jackson.   Beijing:
Commercial Press, 1973, 3rd ed. 2 vols. 478p+434p.
It is also known as *All men are brothers*. This is a famous adventure novel of the
13th century, a tale of outlaws and revolt against unjust rulers.

1220 Outlaws of the marsh.
Shi Naian, Luo Guanzhong, translated by Sidney
Shapiro.   Bloomington, Indiana: Indiana University Press,
1981. 2 vols. 1,638p.
Pearl Buck's *All men are brothers* brought part of *The outlaws* to the West. But
Shapiro's effort represents a three-fold improvement: his knowledge of Chinese
makes this version more accurate, his straightforward English proves more grace-

ful and his reliance on earlier editions of the original produces a more comprehensive text.

1221 The death of woman Wang.
Jonathan D. Spence.   New York: Viking Press, 1976. 169p.

The author depicts rural life in an obscure part of Shantung (Shandong) at the beginning of the Ch'ing (Qing) dynasty. The story is a case history of a woman, Wang's brief escape into an adulterous affair, her return to her husband and her death at his hand. The novel provides a detailed social history of the area and time.

1222 Mudan Ting. (The peony pavilion.)
Tang Xianzu, translated by Cyril Birch.   Bloomington, Indiana: Indiana University Press, 1980. 360p.

This sensitive rendering by Cyril Birch captures all the elegance, lyrical beauty and subtle humour of this drama, whose author is perhaps the finest of the Ming dramatists. It is one of the most important translations from Chinese in several years.

1223 The Chinese gold murders, the Chinese lake murders.
Robert Van Gulik.   Chicago: University of Chicago Press, 1979. 214p.

This is an entertaining, instructive and oddly impassive novel. A rich new vein of detective fiction is explored by the author as he describes the world of crime, mystery, violence, lust and corruption in China.

1224 Hai Jui dismissal from office.
Wu Han, translated by C. C. Huang.   Honolulu: University Press of Hawaii, 1972. 150p.

A criticism of the play became a prelude to the Cultural Revolution. The play was accused of criticizing the Great Leap Forward, the People's Communes, rectification campaigns, Communist Party purges and dogmatic class analysis.

1225 The scholars.
Wu Qingzi, translated by Yang Xianyi, Gladys Yang.   Beijing: Foreign Language Press, 1973. 3rd ed. 607p.

This novel is a famous 18th-century satire depicting the old literati and the Confucian examination system.

1226 The field of life and death (1953) - tales of Hulan river (1942).
Xiao Hong, translated by Howard Goldblatt, Ellen Yeung.   Bloomington, Indiana: Indiana University Press, 1979. 291p.

This publication of the two novels in one volume is a major event in a much neglected field called modern Chinese literature. They became a part of China's literary heritage long before they gained the attention of Western students. In both novels, the author portrays the lives of little people - peasants, carpenters, woodmakers, etc. - in typical Chinese villages.

1227 Born of the same roots: stories of modern women.
Edited by Vivian Ling Xu. Bloomington, Indiana: Indiana University Press, 1981. 320p.

This collection of modern Chinese short stories is concerned with Chinese women and the problems and challenges they faced from 1919 through the 1960s. The pieces depict a cross-section of Chinese women, on the mainland, in Taiwan and in the United States.

1228 Excerpts from the classical Chinese novels.
Translated by Yang Xianyi, Gladys Yang. New York: Panda Books, 1981. 295p.

This book contains three selected, translated and annotated tales: *The three kingdoms, Pilgrimage to the West* and *Flowers in the mirror.*

1229 The courtesan's jewel box.
Yang Xianyi, Gladys Yang. Beijing: Foreign Language Press, 1981. 519p. illus.

This is a selection of 20 popular stories from the 10th-17th centuries transcribed from sessions with ordinary street storytellers. The book is illustrated with drawings and paintings from earlier editions.

1230 The journey to the West.
Translated and edited by Anthony C. Yu. Chicago: University of Chicago Press, 1978. 438p.

This is a complete English version of the *Hsi-yu Chi* (*Xiyu Ji*), one of the classics of Chinese narrative. It is a joyful addition to the new rapidly growing body of competent translations of Chinese literature.

1231 Daughters and sons.
Yuan Qing, translated by Sidney Shapiro. Beijing: Foreign Language Press, 1979. 2nd ed. 282p.

It is a novel of the united-front struggle in the countryside against the Guomindang (Kuomintang) and Japanese in the late 1930s and early 1940s.

1232 Sunrise.
Zao Yu, translated by A. C. Barnes. Beijing: Foreign Language Press, 2nd ed. 1978. 839p.

The play was written in 1935 by the author to depict decaying city life under the rule of the Guomindang (Kuomintang) in the early 1930s.

Literature. Fiction

1233 Thunderstorm.
Zao Yu, translated by Wang Zuoliang, A. C. Barnes. Beijing: Foreign Language Press, 1978. 3rd ed. 151p.

The novel was written in 1933 to reflect the conflict between parents and their traditional values and their children. It became his best-known work, a 20th-century classic.

1234 Morning in Shanghai.
Zhou Erfu. Beijing: Foreign Language Press, 1981. 651p.

This is a panoramic look at life in the big city after liberation. In contrast to the avaricious attempts of businessmen to transfer their assets out of Shanghai, a portrayal of the everyday life and struggle of the Chinese workers in the city is contained in this novel.

1235 The hurricane.
Zhou Libo. Beijing: Foreign Language Press, 1981. 450p.

This is a human novel of the dramatic events in a village in northeast China during and after land reform. This best-seller in China won an international prize in 1951 and was made into a popular Chinese film under the same title.

1236 Journey to the sun: folk tales from China.
Beijing: Foreign Language Press, 1981. 140p.

This volume includes nine magical tales which bring to life the diverse and rich cultural heritage of China. Twists of plot and startling new images make these stories a pleasant surprise from start to finish.

1237 The peacock maiden: folk tales from China.
Beijing: Foreign Language Press, 1981. 141p.

This volume includes eleven delightful tales from various nationalities. Many show how cleverly a poor man can make a fool of the rich.

Classical Chinese fiction: a guide to its study and appreciation, essays and bibliographies.
See item no. 1454.

Modern Chinese fiction: a guide to its study and appreciation, essays and bibliographies.
See item no. 1455.

Contemporary Chinese novels and short stories, 1949-1974: an annotated bibliography.
See item no. 1456.

Non-fiction

1238 The Chinese Opium Wars.
Jack Beeching. New York: Harcourt, 1975. 352p.
This is a literary account of how the West opened up China in the mid-19th century by means of the opium trade. The author describes the Western action that reaches its climax when, in 1860, Anglo-French forces loot Peking (Beijing) and the British burn the Summer Palace.

1239 Chinese socialism to 1907.
Martin Bernal. Ithaca, New York: Cornell University Press, 1976. 259p.
This is the first of a projected three-volume literary work devoted to tracing Chinese socialism prior to the May 4th Movement (1919). In this volume, the author explores the role played by British and American missionaries during the 1890s in introducing socialist ideas to Chinese intellectuals. He discusses the impact of the early Japanese social movement upon Chinese radicals and he concludes with a detailed analysis of the shift from socialist democracy to anarchy in China in 1907.

1240 China: a country study.
Edited by Frederica M. Bunge, Rinn-Sup Shinn. Washington, DC: American University, Foreign Area Studies, 1981. 590p.
This is one of a series of country studies published under the 'Area Handbook Program' of the American University. It includes 14 essays by reputable China specialists on topics ranging from the social system to national defense, from education and culture to the political process. The scope of coverage provides an excellent overview of contemporary China.

1241 China called me: my life inside the Chinese revolution.
Percy Chen. Boston, Massachusetts: Little, Brown, 1979. 423p.
Born in 1901 to a wealthy Chinese family in Trinidad and educated in the law in England, Ch'en (Chen) went to China in 1927 to join his father who was then Foreign Minister for the Chinese Republic. In this book, he relates his involvement with China from his arrival through the years before 1949. This informal, episodic autobiography is fascinating for its glimpses of the makers of modern China in *déshabillé*.

1242 China yesterday and today.
Edited by Molly Joel Coye, Jon Livingston. New York: Bantam Books, 1975. 458p.
The editors attempt to combine chronological presentation with a focus on problem-solving over the years of China's history. The book is divided into four sections: physical aspects, Imperial China, China and the West and New China.

271

Literature. Non-fiction

1243 The state of American history and literature studies in the People's Republic of China.

John J. Deeney. Washington, DC: US International Communication Agency, 1982. 172p.

The purpose of this report (dated 15 January 1982) is to assess the present state of the Chinese infrastructure for introducing the United States to China through the study of American history and literature. Data contained in this exceedingly informative report are based on a two-month field-trip to China from May to July 1981, including interviews with 87 Chinese educators and 40 foreign teachers, published and unpublished material accumulated during his trip and earlier reports on American studies in China.

1244 America's cultural experiment in China, 1942-49.

Wilma Fairbank. Washington, DC: Bureau of Education and Cultural Affairs, US Department of State, 1976. 223p.

The author's concise picture of wartime Chungking (Zhongqing) is true and evocative and her brief account of the military and political developments of those years is a fair historical summary of the Kuomintang (Guomindang)-Communist struggle.

1245 Hu Shih and the Chinese renaissance: liberalism in the Chinese revolution 1917-1937.

Jerome B. Grieder. Cambridge, Massachusetts: Harvard University Press, 1970. 420p.

Hu Shih (Hu Shi) spent a lifetime artfully dodging politics. Nevertheless, ardent friends and enemies have almost always cast his reputation in highly politicized terms. Guided by the same liberal spirit of reason, science and empirical detachment which animated Hu Shih (Hu Shi), the author has composed an impressive biography which is refreshingly non-political in its approach.

1246 Memories of Loyang: Yang Hsuan-chih and the lost capital (493-534).

W. J. F. Jenner. New York: Oxford University Press, 1980. 257p.

In its forty-one years as the capital of North China, from 493 to 534, the city of Loyang (Luoyang) was created by imperial command on a deserted site, grew until it contained 1,367 Buddhist monasteries and nunneries and 500,000 inhabitants and was compulsorily abandoned at three days' notice. The book is a study of the origins, history, functions and nature of this remarkable city.

1247 The peach blossom fan.

Kong Shangren, Chen Shixiang, Harold Acton, with collaboration of Cyril Birch. Berkeley, California: University of California Press, 1976. 312p.

This is an elegant English version of a Chinese play originally published in 1699, before the K'ung Shan (Kong Shan) style of the southern drama yielded its primacy to any of the competing regional operatic styles in China. The drama was the finest fruition of the early promises in the ancient medieval traditions of Chinese theatre.

1248 **The unknown war: North China 1937-1945.**
Michael Lindsay.   London: Bergstrom & Boyle, 1975. 112p.
photos.

The author went originally to teach at Yenching (Yanjing) University. Then
following the outbreak of Pacific War in December 1941, he joined the Communists fighting the Japanese, first with General Nieh Jung-chen's (Nie Rongzhen)
forces in North China and from the spring of 1949 with the Chinese Communist
Party Headquarters in Yenan (Yanan). The book is a mixture of personal reminiscences and the history of the Chinese Communist Party's fight against the
Japanese, compiled with photographs which illustrate these two themes.

1249 **Chinese classical prose: the eight masters of the T'ang-Sung
(Tang-Song) period.**
Liu Shishun.   Seattle, Washington: University of
Washington Press, 1979. 406p.

The classical prose of the T'ang-Sung (Tang-Song) period, extending from the
8th to the 11th century AD, emulated the ancient classics in its forceful, unad-
orned literary style and its stress on Confucian teachings. These essays, covering a
wide range of subjects, are presented here by Liu Shih-shun (Liu Shishun) in
parallel Chinese and English texts.

1250 **China scapegoat: the diplomatic ordeal of John Carter
Vincent.**
Gary May.   Washington, DC: New Republic Books, 1979.
370p.

This is a literary account of the diplomatic career of John Carter Vincent, who
joined the US Foreign Service in 1924 and served mostly in China. In 1945, he
became Assistant Secretary for East Asia and the Pacific. In the early fifties, he
was investigated and in 1953, he was offered the option of resigning for poor
judgement as an alternative to being fired as a security risk. The author, while
confirming Vincent's honour and good sense at every turn, has little to say about
the broader implications of China policy or the role of US foreign service officers.

1251 **Mao Zedong 'Talks at the Yanan Conference on Literature
and Art': a translation of the 1943 test with commentary.**
Bonnie S. McDougall.   Ann Arbor, Michigan: Center for
Chinese Studies, University of Michigan, 1980. 112p.

Relatively little comment has been made on the significance of these 'Talks' for
Marxist literary theory in particular and literary theory in general. In the commentary that accompanies the translation, the author seeks to redress this imbal-
ance by redrawing 'attention to those of Mao's comments whose significance is
primarily literary, as distinguished from political or historical'.

1252 **Marco Polo.**
Keith Miles, David Butler.   New York: Dell, 1982. 427p.

This is a novel based on the screenplay for the NBC TV mini-series. It describes
a great adventure focusing on Marco's 17-year stay in China during the Yuan
dynasty with emphasis on historical accuracy. It is written in a popular, readable
style.

Literature. Non-fiction

1253 **Tigers over Asia.**
Bernard C. Nalty.   New York: Elsevier-Dutton, 1978. 182p.

The author gives an account of the American volunteer group, the Flying Tigers and of Claire L. Chennault, who trained and led these men. The success of the Flying Tigers enabled him to gain approval for an aerial campaign in China by a full-fledged air force under his command.

1254 **China's uninterrupted revolution: from 1840 to the present.**
Edited by Victor Nee, James Peck.   New York: Pantheon, 1976. 480p.

The contributors, enthusiastically Maoist, see national economic and political development as linked to permanent revolution and unabating struggle. They defend this perception vigorously against both American modernization theory and Soviet revisionism.

1255 **Chinese narrative: critical and theoretical essays.**
Edited by Andrew H. Plaks, with foreword by Cyril Birch.   Princeton, New Jersey: Princeton University Press, 1977. 365p.

The 13 historical and critical essays examine the narrative tradition in Chinese fiction from the early Tso-chuan (Zuozhuan) period to the 19th century. The principal concerns of the essayists are to break out of Western critical moulds in looking at Chinese fictional techniques, to provide explication for the several levels on which Chinese fiction can be enjoyed and to place Chinese narrative within a universal theory of literature.

1256 **Chinese history and literature: collections of studies.**
Jaroslav Prusek.   New York: Humanities Press, 1971. 587p.

This collection contains twenty articles of the author's studies in sinology. It is divided into two sections, the first dealing with Old Chinese literature and the second with the productions of medieval storytellers. Five of the studies are in French.

1257 **A memoir of China in revolution: from the Boxer Rebellion to the People's Republic.**
Chester Ronning.   New York: Pantheon, 1974. 306p.

This volume contains vivid recollections, based on letters, notes and diaries, by a Canadian diplomat who lived in China for a quarter-century. Some new light emerges on the diplomatic infighting of 1954 over Korea and Indochina, that of 1961 over Laos and of 1966 over Vietnam.

1258 **Selections from records of the historian.**
Sima Jian, translated by Yang Xianyi, Gladys Yang.   Beijing: Foreign Language Press, 1979. 461p.

This volume adds further testimony to the intrinsic value and interest of Ssu-ma Chien's (Sima Jian) literary history. Although translations of the 31 chapters that it covers can almost all be found in other versions, the book is to be welcomed.

1259 The Gang and 900 million: a China diary.
Nihal Singh.   New Delhi: Oxford University Press, 1979.
118p.

This is a very straightforward, unpretentious account by an Indian journalist of a two-week visit to China in April 1979. The volume records some interesting conversations the author had on the Chinese-Vietnam conflict and on the future of Chinese-Indian relations.

1260 The adventure of Mao on the Long March.
Frederic Tuter.   New York: Citadel, 1971. 121p.

This is an account of Mao's famous Long March in the 1930s, when the Communist forces in China managed to avoid being destroyed by the armies of Chiang Kai-shek (Jiang Jieshi).

1261 Chinese revolutionary memoirs: 1919-1949.
Wang Fanxi.   New York: Oxford University Press, 1979.
349p.

The author, born in 1907, joined the Chinese Communist Party whilst a student in Peking (Beijing) during the 1920s and after doing Party work in Canton (Guangzhou) and Wuhan, was sent to Moscow for training. There he came under the influence of the Trotskyist opposition. Expelled from the Party for his Trotskyist views, he spent most of the years from 1931 to 1937 in Kuomintang (Guomindang) prisons, being released from solitary confinement just as the Japanese invaded China. His career as an activist continued until the Trotskyists were purged after Mao's victory in 1949. The author escaped to Macao where he wrote these memoirs, the only published account from a revolutionary's viewpoint of a still largely obscure period in Chinese history.

1262 China: A Handbook.
Edited by Yuanhi Wu.   New York: Praeger, 1973. 915p.

This is a large volume packed with small print and tables which is intended to meet a wide need for information on China by assembling authoritative analyses of various aspects of Chinese affairs by distinguished scholars, both Western and Chinese. The articles are written in a factual, encyclopaedic style suitable to a reference book, with footnotes and annotations offering guidance to further reading.

1263 The people's comic book: red women's detachment and other Chinese comics.
Translated by Endymion Wilkinson.   New York:
Doubleday, 1973. 156p.

Comics are a cornerstone of contemporary Chinese popular culture, widely read by people of all ages and carrying a definite message to the people. This book contains seven complete stories and is a publishing 'first' in the United States.

1264 China image.
Manshih Yonfan.   Beijing: Yonfan Studio, 1981. 186p.

This literary and pictorial interpretation of China reveals a generosity and scope that can only come from an artist's deep identification and love for the country of his birth. It also includes sparkling calligraphy by Huang Yung-yu (Huang Yon-gyu).

1265 **The first revolution in China: a theory.**
Ronald Yelin Zheng. New York: Vantage Press, 1973. 258p.

At the beginning of the 19th century, according to the author, the Chinese government was able to maintain itself and the Manchu monarchy in a state of equilibrium through its outputs and social controls. The result of the contradictions imposed upon China from the West was to overwhelm the capacity of the government to respond, leading naturally to the 1911 revolution.

1266 **Injustice to Tou O (Tou O Yuan - Dou O Yuan): a study and translation.**
Zhungwen Shi. London: Cambridge University Press, 1973. 147p.

Tou O Yuan (Don O Yuan) by Kuan Han-ch'ing (Guan Hanqing), the leading dramatist of the Yuan period (1280-1368), has remained a popular favourite and is still performed in the Peking (Beijing) opera theatres. The author discusses the literary and historical background to the play and the language and conventions of Yuan drama. Each line of Chinese has beneath it a transliteration and a literal translation in English, on the facing page there is a free translation with notes and commentary.

1267 **The travels of Marco Polo.**
Marco Polo, translated by Ronald Latham. New York: Penguin, 1967. 1981. 380p.

This is one of the world's remarkable books. It is a record of Marco Polo's 13th-century journey to China where he met and served the Mongol Emperor, Kubilai Khan. The modern reader will still find it fascinating and rewarding.

The Arts

History

1268 Philosophy of painting by Shih T'ao: a translation and exposition of his Hua-pu.
Earl J. Coleman. The Hague; Paris; New York: Mouton, 1978. 147p.

Living in the late 17th century, when traditionalism was growing increasingly doctrinaire and originality increasingly rare, the Chinese painter Shi T'ao (Shi Tau) was an ingeniously original master. Not so prominent in his own time, his popularity since the late 19th century has kept pace with the growth of modern individualism in China and abroad.

1269 A history of Chinese drama.
William Dobby. London: Elek, 1976. 327p.

This book traces the history of Chinese drama from its origins to its contemporary accomplishments and limitations. Following the chronological division of China's history into dynasties, the first part in six chapters surveys the Chinese drama of the pre-modern period from T'ang (Tang), Sung (Song), Yuan, through Ming; the second part in another six chapters relates in some detail the Ch'ing (Qing) and Republican periods up to the time of the Cultural Revolution in the mid-1960s.

1270 The Dynasties and treasures of China.
Bamber Gascoigne. New York: Viking Press, 1973. 256p.

The author describes some of the art and artifacts associated with the eight major dynasties of China, beginning with ca. 1,000 BC Shang Bronzes, through T'ang (Tang) pottery figures, Ming porcelains, through recent Ch'ing (Qing) achievements. The author has put together elements of the Chinese heritage in an appealing manner for the general reader.

1271 **Artists and traditions: uses of the past in Chinese culture.**
Edited by Christian F. Murk. Princeton, New Jersey: Princeton University Press, 1976. 230p.

This is a collection of fourteen essays based on papers presented at a colloquium held at Princeton University in May 1969. The colloquium was planned in conjunction with an exhibition of Chinese paintings from the collection of Mr and Mrs Earl Mose.

1272 **China: a history in art.**
Bradley Smith, Wan-go Wang. New York: Harper, 1973. 296p. illus.

All the plates are in colour and almost all are drawn from American collections, public and private, or from the old Imperial collection removed by the Kuomintang (Guomindang) to T'aiwan (Taiwan). The book reflects the attitude of an age now closed, in which Western museums rivalled one another in acquiring the most spectacular and ambitious examples of Chinese art which have come onto the market in 50 years.

1273 **A short story of Chinese art.**
Michael Sullivan. Berkeley, California: University of California Press, 1971. 514p.

This volume should prove to be not only the most complete and convenient introduction to Chinese art for students and collectors, but also a most useful textbook, to fulfill a long-felt need.

1274 **The arts of China.**
Michael Sullivan. Berkeley, California: University of California Press, 1977. rev. ed. 287p.

This book is a fascinating and balanced picture from the Stone Age to the present. For this edition the author has made further revisions, based on recent discoveries and research and on the results of his own visits to China in 1973 and 1975.

1275 **Style in the arts of China.**
William Watson. Baltimore, Maryland: Penguin, 1974. 119p.

This book on Chinese art belongs to the type of survey that scans the whole range of figural and decorative arts from the Neolithic to the 18th century, with the sole limitation that it approaches its vast theme from the aspect of artistic style. The author believes that Chinese art should yield to the same criteria applied to other art.

1276 **The translation of art: essays on Chinese painting and poetry.**
Edited by James C. Y. Watt. Hong Kong: Chinese University of Hong Kong, 1977. 216p.

This is a hardcover reissue of a special number, devoted to art, of the journal *Renditions* (no. 6, spring, 1976). The volume offers several translations of modern writings on Chinese art, making them accessible to readers of English.

1277 **Americans and Chinese: purpose and fulfillment in great civilizations.**
Francis L. K. Xu. New York: National History Press, 1970. 493p.

The first edition of this book by Francis Hsu (Xu) appeared under the title *American and Chinese: two ways of life* (1953). The text contrasts the individual-centred American and the situation-centred Chinese way of life. A demonstration comparative analysis of the American movie *Valley of decision*, in which the rebellious son was a hero to American audiences but a villain to the Chinese, sets the tone for other comparisons in the areas of art, literature, sexual attitudes and aberrant behaviour. The author demonstrates the racial dissimilarities between Americans and Chinese and the advantages and disadvantages of each.

1278 **Traditional and contemporary painting in China.**
Washington, DC: US Committee on Scholarly Communication with the People's Republic of China, 1980. 164p.

This report is a scholarly account of the delegation's trip, including notes on many of the paintings seen by the group, their itinerary, chapters on art and the archaeological finds on display in Chinese museums and museum administration and related aspects. The focus is on several areas in Chinese painting including religious paintings, Yuan and Ming paintings, contemporary painting and calligraphy.

Painting and calligraphy

1279 **The Chinese literati on painting: Su Shih (1037-1107) to Tung Chi-ch'ang (1556-1636).**
Susan Bush. Cambridge, Massachusetts: Harvard University Press, 1972. 227p.

This book deals with the literati themselves as artists and calligraphers. This is quite the best book that has appeared in the West on the subject of Chinese art theory. What makes this new treatise so original is the author's readiness to take historical views where others are content to accept authority.

The Arts. Painting and calligraphy

1280 Hills beyond a river: Chinese painting of the Yuan dynasty, 1327-1368.
James Cahill.   New York: Weatherhill, 1976. 198p.

This is a major book, on a major subject, by a major authority. It starts by examining four main aspects of early Yuan painting, continuing in late Sung (Song) styles and carrying through the Ch'ing (Qing) period. The centre of the book is the revolution in Yuan painting with the three great masters of the mid-14th century.

1281 Parting at the shore: Chinese painting of the early and middle Ming dynasty, 1368-1568.
James Cahill.   New York: Weatherhill, 1978. 281p.

This volume is devoted to about two-thirds of the Ming dynasty, a period of both academic revival under restored Chinese rule and the continued pursuit of individualism established under the preceeding Yuan dynasty.

1282 Paintings of Beijing opera characters.
Dong Chengsheng.   Beijing: Zhaohua, 1981. 64p.

This pictorial album was specially compiled by Tung Ch'eng-sheng (Dong Chengsheng) to enable foreign audiences to understand further this unique form of stage opera. The first part provides a basic knowledge of Beijing (Peking) opera with pictures and drawings, including a concise history of its development, types of roles, actors and actresses, musical instruments, dance, make-up, costumes, setting and props. The second part gives a brief introduction to forty items of the Beijing (Peking) opera repertoire.

1283 The field of stones: a study of the art of Shen Chou 1427-1509.
Richard Edwards.   Washington, DC: Smithsonian Institution Press, 1973. 131p.

This is a scholarly work dedicated to a love of nature and filled with a love of family. Shen Chou's (Shen Zhou) scrolls reflect these qualities. The author takes a careful and illuminating look at this famous 14th-century Chinese landscape scroll painter.

1284 Studies in connoisseurship: Chinese paintings from the Arthur M. Sacker collection in New York and Princeton.
Marilyn Fu, Shen Fu.   Princeton, New Jersey: Princeton University Art Museum, 1976. 375p.

This is a study of 41 paintings by 24 artists who lived between the mid-14th and 20th centuries. The authors discuss the painters in their historical context, the approach to connoisseurship and its underlying assumptions, questions of authentication and, in particular, the work of Tao-chi (Daiji). In the catalogue that follows, each entry takes the form of a brief monograph situating the work in the history of Chinese art and answering some of the key questions it raises.

1285 **Traces the brush: studies in Chinese calligraphy.**
Shen Fu, Marilyn Fu, Mary C. Neil, Mary Jane
Clark. New Haven, Connecticut: Yale University Press,
1980. 258p.

Calligraphy in China has been traditionally considered the epitome of artistic accomplishment, superior even to painting. Drawing upon ninety major examples from Western collections this beautifully illustrated book broadens the historical and aesthetic context in which calligraphy has been viewed outside China and captures the elegance and beauty of this exquisite art form.

1286 **Chinese watercolors.**
Text by Josef Hojzlar, photographs by B. Forman. New
York: Mayflower, 1978. 70p.

This book has 20th-century Chinese paintings reproduced in colour, including an extensive selection from Qi Baishi (Ch'i Pai-shih), Li Keran (Li Ko-jan), Lin Feng-mian and Xu Beihong (Hsu Pei-hung) - the 'Shanghai school'. It contains biographical information on the painters and the date of each painting.

1287 **Chinese calligraphy: an introduction to its aesthetic and technique.**
Jiang Yi. Cambridge, Massachusetts: Harvard University
Press, 1973. 3rd ed. 157p.

The *London Times* lauded the second edition (1955) of this masterly work as a splendid book in which the plates alone would be a valuable collection. For the third edition of this art classics series, the author has added two new chapters, 'Calligraphy and painting' and 'Aesthetic principles'. Sixteen new plates further enhance a volume already richly illustrated.

1288 **Ch'i Pai Shih.**
T. C. Lai. Seattle, Washington: University of Washington
Press, 1973. 209p.

This book gives a chronicle of the events of Ch'i Pai-shih's (Qi Baishi) life, largely in his own words, from his birth in 1863 until his 90s. The author supplies translations of the inscriptions on Ch'i Pai-shih's (Qi Baishi) paintings, and in a separate section at the back he also translates many seals sprinkled throughout the text.

1289 **Chinese calligraphy.**
T. C. Lai, introduced by J. L. Zhang. Seattle, Washington:
University of Washington Press, 1973. 252p.

To the Chinese, calligraphy is one of the highest forms of art. For readers unfamiliar with the language and the significance of the characters, this is an excellent visual introduction to the rhythmic vitality of the art.

1290 **Mi Fu and the classical tradition of Chinese calligraphy.**
Luthar Ledderose. Princeton, New Jersey: Princeton University Press, 1979. 364p.

One of the greatest calligrapher-scholars of the Sung (Song) dynasty, Mi Fu (1052-1107) played a pivotal role in the transmission of the classical tradition of the Chin (Jin) masters' art. In his investigation of the origins of the classical tradition and Mi Fu's influence on those who followed him, the author gives us an unprecedented grasp of the evolutionary patterns in the history of Chinese calligraphy.

1291 **Chinese landscape painting.**
Sherman L. Lee. Bloomington, Indiana: Indiana University Press, 1976. rev. ed. 168p.

Beautifully-designed with excellent reproductions carefully coordinated with the text, the author succinctly describes the main stylistic traits of important painters and schools of painting from the Sung (Song) dynasty to the 19th century, including perceptive comparisons with Western landscape painting.

1292 **The art of painting on porcelain.**
Georges Miserez-Schira, translated by Camilla Sykes. New York: Chilton, 1974. 132p.

The author starts with a brief history of painted porcelains illustrated with examples of the ceramicist's art. Then explains how to set up a workroom, what materials and tools to get and how to use them. There is also a section on painting on faience.

1293 **The nine sacred mountains of China.**
Mary A. Mullikin, Anne M. Hotchkis. Hong Kong: Vetch & Lee, 1973. 156p.

This is a delightful account, illustrated with sketches and paintings, of journeys to China's five Taoist (Daoist) and four Buddhist sacred mountains, made by two lady artists during 1935-36.

1294 **Chinese landscape painting in the Sui and T'ang dynasties.**
Michael Sullivan. Berkeley, California: University of California Press, 1979. 288p.

The author continues his detailed study that began with the *Birth of landscape painting in China* (1962) and deals with the 7th-10th centuries. The present volume includes the first study in depth of the artist in T'ang (Tang) society and almost all the material on the life and work of the Sui and T'ang (Tang) landscape painters.

1295 **Chinese landscape painting, volume 2, the Sui and T'ang dynasties.**
Michael Sullivan. Berkeley, California: University of California Press, 1980. 318p.

Volume two is a more cohesive pageant based upon a richer corpus of materials including more recent archaeological discoveries and a more germane literary complement. This allows extended discussions of individual painters and larger issues as well as detailed consideration of particulars.

1296 Symbols of eternity: the art of landscape painting in China.
Michael Sullivan. Stanford, California: Stanford University Press, 1978. 120 plates.

Designed for the general reader approaching Chinese landscape painting as a new experience, this beautifully illustrated volume is an introduction to underlying philosophical ideas, the aims and achievements of the painters and the main stages in the development of the art over nearly 2,000 years. The author takes as his theme the responsibility of the artist to both society and to his own version of nature. Treating this theme historically, he also relates landscape painting to its political and social setting and to the philosophical climate in which the painters worked.

1297 Chinese folk art: in American collections, from early 15th century to early 20th century.
Zeng Yuhe Ecke. Honolulu: University Press of Hawaii, 1977. 176p.

This catalogue compiled by Tseng Yu-ho Ecke (Zeng Yuhe Ecke) is a delight to the eye as well as a highly informative text.

1298 Painting in the People's Republic of China: the politics of style.
Arnold Zhang. Boulder, Colorado: Westview Press, 1980. 130p.

The interaction between policymakers and artists in contemporary China reflects basic conflicts that exist within Chinese society as a whole. The author, Arnold Chang (Zhang), explores this interaction through an in-depth examination of the development of Chinese painting since 1949.

1299 Sung and Yuan paintings.
Metropolitan Museum of Art, introduction by Wen Fong, with catalogue by Marilyn Fu. New York: Metropolitan Museum of Art, 1978. 162p.

This is an introduction to and catalogue of the 25 Chinese paintings of major importance from the Sung (Song) and Yuan dynasties (dated between c 1050 and 1380 AD) acquired by the Museum from the collection of C. C. Wang. Wen Fong (Princeton) has written a series of brief essays specifically directed to issues and qualities found within the paintings.

Pottery, sculpture and crafts

1300 Princes of Jade.
Edmund Capon, William Macquitty. London: Sphere
Books, 1973. 192p.

This is a companion book to the exhibition of Chinese archaeological treasures in
London in autumn 1973. It contains superb photographs plus a background text
on history and art.

1301 Chinese commissionship: the Ko Ku Yao Lun: the essential criteria of antiquities.
Cao Zhao, translated and edited by Sir Percival
David. New York: Praeger, 1971. 267p.

Written by Ts'ao Chao (Cao Zhao), revised successively by Shu Min and Wang
Tao (Wang Dao) (1462), the *Ko Ku Yao Lun* (*Ge Ku Yao Lun*) was a pioneer
work of epochal importance and the earliest comprehensive and systematic
treatise on Chinese art and archaeology. It covers wares in jade, bronze, textiles
and porcelain, as well as painting, calligraphy, ancient zithers and authenticity
and moral criteria.

1302 The Tao of architecture.
Diao Zhang. Princeton, New Jersey: Princeton University
Press, 1980. 88p.

By expanding Frank Lloyd Wright's thoughts on the relationship between modern
architecture and Lao-tzu's (Laozi) philosophy, the author reveals the vitality of
intangible, or negative, elements and shows how these qualities make architectonic
forms 'come alive'.

1303 Chinese lacquer.
Sir Harry Garner. New York: Faber & Faber, 1979. 285p.

The greater part of this book deals with the lacquerwares that were made from
the Yuan Dynasty (1260-1368) onwards. The techniques used involved carving
and inlaying mother-of-pearl, and incised decoration with gold. Pieces dating from
the Han, T'ang (Tang) and Sung (Song) dynasties are also illustrated and discussed and the first products from as far back as the Shang dynasty are identified. After surveys of the nature and preparation of lacquers and the early lacquerwares, the general arrangement is by techniques. In addition to chapters on
the techniques already mentioned there are ones on marbled lacquer, surface
gold-decorated lacquer, painted lacquer and coromandel lacquer.

1304 The Freer Chinese bronzes, volume II, technical studies.
John Gettens. Washington, DC: Smithsonian Institution,
1978. 227p.

The author presents the results of laboratory research on materials and methods
of ancient Asian craftsmen as represented by the collection of ceremonial bronzes
at the Freer Gallery of Art (Volume I, q.v.). Essays on chemical composition,
fabrication, metal structure and corrosion are included. Special emphasis is placed
on X-ray examinations which reveal new information on structures, assembly and
ancient and modern repairs.

1305 **China for the West: Chinese porcelain & other decorative arts for export.**
David Howard, John Ayers, foreword by Nelson A. Rockefeller. New York: Sotheby Parke Bernet, 1978. 2 vols. 689p.

This two-volume catalogue, illustrated from the Mottahedeh Collection, is divided into three parts, the first two of which deal with the principal porcelain styles and Western subject of decoration on porcelain. Each part is subdivided into topical sections, preceeded by brief introductions and followed by check lists of porcelain specimens, not illustrated but of related design, with appropriate bibliographical references. Part III surveys late 18th and 19th century enamels, fans, ivories, silver and reverse paintings on glass. These beautiful volumes represent one of the first attempts to provide a comprehensive history of Chinese export ceramics. There are 700 black-and-white and 103 colour illustrations, each with an extensive and informative descriptive and bibliographical annotation.

1306 **Yan'an (Yenan) papercuts.**
Jiang Feng. Beijing: People's Fine-Arts, 1981. 240p.

This volume, including 190 reproductions of Yan'an (Yenan) papercuts and biographies of the artists, was designed to accompany a major exhibition of papercut art.

1307 **The Chinese garden: history, art & architecture.**
Maggie Keswick. New York: Rizzoll International, 1978. 216p.

The author writes about the long history of the Chinese garden, including its impact on Western civilization and its relationship to Chinese society. Of particular merit is the account of Chinese landscape painting. The book concludes with a sensitive portrait of the philosophy of the Chinese garden.

1308 **Chinese seals.**
T. C. Lai, introduced by J. L. Zhang. Seattle, Washington: University of Washington Press, 1976. 200p.

Seals have been used in China since 1400 BC for purposes of identification and ornamentation. The author introduces his subject through ancient Chinese stories which focus on seals. He then discusses accomplished seal engravers and carvers, the aesthetics of seal engraving and the scripts used on seals, including pictorial script.

1309 **Ancient Chinese Jades from the Greenville L. Winthrop Collection in the Fogg Arts Museum, Harvard University.**
Max Loehr, Louisa G. Fitzgerald Huber. Cambridge, Massachusetts: Fogg Art Museum, Harvard University, 1975. 439p.

Early in 1975, the Fogg Art Museum of Harvard University, held a special exhibition of the already celebrated Chinese jades from the Greenville L. Winthrop Bequest of 1943. The exhibition lasted scarcely two months, but the magnificently produced catalogue, published coincidentaly with the exhibition, will last much longer and remain as an appropriate tribute to the impeccable taste of the man who assembled the collection.

The Arts. Pottery, sculpture and crafts

1310 The Chinese potter: a practical history of Chinese ceramics.
Margaret Medley.   New York: Scribner, 1976. 288p.

This book is concerned with the techniques employed by Chinese potters from the 4th century BC to 1912. While style and ornamentation necessarily are touched upon, the primary factor in this book is the development of techniques, raw materials, glazes and the refinement of the construction of kilns and firing techniques. Line drawings of kilns are included. Potter marks for articles of the Ming and Ch'ing (Qing) dynasties are reproduced in the back of the book.

1311 Chinese ceramics.
W. B. R. Neare-Hill, foreword by Harry Garner.   New York: St. Martin's Press, 1973. 176p.

In his summary of the stylistic and technical development of Chinese ceramics ranging from 2,000 BC through the 19th century, the author sets the artistic development of each dynasty within its own historical context.

1312 The Freer Chinese bronzes, volume I.
John A. Pope, Rutherfold J. Gettens, James Cahill, Noel Barnard.   Washington, DC: Smithsonian Institution, 1978. 688p.

The catalogue contains the famous collection of Chinese ceremonial bronzes at the Freer Gallery of Art. It provides a selective example of the Chinese caster's art from the Anyang period of the Shang dynasty down to Han times and includes a history of the collection in the West.

1313 Ancient Chinese ceramic sculpture from Han through T'ang.
Ezekiel Schloss.   Stanford, Connecticut: Castle, 1977. 2 vols.

Numerous exhibitions have included items borrowed from the extraordinary Schloss Collection of Ming-chi (Mingji) or tomb figurines. More than half of the 250 pieces illustrated here have neither been exhibited nor previously published. The text is well written and informative, including a comprehensive survey of previous scholarship.

1314 Modern Chinese woodcuts.
Shirley Sun.   New York: Chinese Culture Foundation, 1979. 95p.

This book describes the history of the development of wood engravings in China and their influence on modern Chinese art. It includes 77 examples of noted works shown at the 1979 exhibition in San Francisco.

1315 A handbook of Chinese ceramic.
Suzanne G. Valenstein.   New York: Metropolitan Museum of Art, 1975. 251p.

This book is illustrated with black-and-white photographs of 201 objects from the museum's own collection of some 4,500 items. Exhibits from other collections are also included to fill the gaps in the Museum's collection and trace the history of Chinese ceramics from the Neolithic to the early 20th century.

1316 **Chinese porcelain of the 19th and 20th centuries.**
H. A. Van Dort. Locehm, Netherlands:
Uitzeversmaatschapij De Tijdstroom, 1977. 198p.

The author has made a careful inventory of known Hung-hsian (Hong Xian)
pieces in both public and private collections. He divides them into seven categories based on quality, intended use and type of base mark. Although his classifications are based on only 130 known pieces, surely a very small number, their
detailed grouping and study are more timely.

1317 **Imperial China: photography 1850-1912.**
Historical texts by Clark Worswick, Jonathan D. Spence,
with a foreword by Harrison E. Salisbury. New York:
Penwick, 1978. 357p.

This is a collection of photographs gathered for an exhibition under the auspices
of the Asian Home Gallery of the Asian Society and the American Federation of
Arts. It has historical information on the photographers and their works.

Chinese and exotic rugs.
See item no. 965.

Music and dance

1318 **Ballad of the hidden dragon: Lu-Chih-Yuan Chu-Kung Tiao.**
Translated by M. Dolezelova-Velingerova, assisted by J. I.
Drump. New York: Oxford University Press, 1971. 289p.

This is one of the only two complete examples of a form of the medieval Chinese
ballad-singer's art called 'Chu-kung-tiao' (Zhukongdiao). In these ballads, often
of epic length, prose narrative alternated with verse and different musical modes
(Kung-tiao - Kongdiao), were used in the groups or suites of tunes to which the
verse parts were sung.

1319 **The Han rhapsody: a study of the fu of Yang Hsiung (Yang
Xiong) 153 BC-AD 18.**
David R. Knechtges. Cambridge, England: Cambridge
University Press, 1976. 160p.

This is a useful summary of work already written (up to spring 1976) on the *Fu*
in general and on the Han *Fu* and Yang Hsiung (Yang Xiong) in particular.

1320 **Music and tradition: essays on Asian and other musics
presented to Laurence Picken.**
Edited by D. R. Widdess, R. F. Wolpert. Cambridge,
England: Cambridge University Press, 1981. 244p.

A Festschrift for Laurence Picken, this volume includes three articles on the
interpretation and reconstruction of ancient musical scores, three articles on ico-
nographic documents and three on present-day performance practices. The geo-

graphical areas covered include Japan, Korea, China, Burma, northern India, Central Asia, West Africa and England. The variety of topics and localities aptly reflect the broad interests of Laurence Picken himself.

Chinese music: an annotated bibliography (Garland Reference Library of the Humanities, vol. 75).
See item no. 1432.

Theatre and film

1321 **Eight Chinese plays - from the 13 century to the present.**
Translated by William Dolby. New York: Columbia University Press, 1978. 164p.
The author has produced a useful volume on the history of Chinese drama. He has selected eight plays designed to offer a wide sampling of genres and periods.

1322 **Five Chinese Communist Plays.**
Edited by Martin Ebob. New York: Crowell, 1975. 328p.
This collection serves to introduce the layman to the effects of the Cultural Revolution on traditional opera. The author's brief introduction highlights the political struggles that brought to the stage contemporary revolutionary themes, soldiers and workers in street dress, realistic scenary and lighting and Western music. The five plays are: *The white-haired girl*, *The red detachment of women*, *Taking the bandits' strong-hold* (*Taking tiger mountain by strategy*), *The red lantern* and *Azalea mountain*.

1323 **Crime and punishment in medieval Chinese drama: three judge Pao plays.**
George A. Hayden. Cambridge, Massachusetts: Harvard University Press, 1978. 238p.
The author presents preliminary essays on courtroom dramas and the legend of Judge Pao (Bao). The three translations employ a copiously annotated style of translation faithful to the text.

1324 **Contemporary Chinese theater.**
Roger Howard. London: Heinemann, 1978. 138p.
This book is in two parts. The first part gives an extremely brief historical background to Chinese drama to 1949 and then discusses the various forms of theatre, such as Beijing (Peking) Opera, local opera, the spoken play (Hua-Chu - Huaju), acrobatics and balladry. The second part outlines the development of some classifications of drama since 1949. It discusses the period before the Cultural Revolution, the Cultural Revolution itself, 'new workers' and peasants' amateur theatre' and professional productions.

1325 **Dianying (Tien-Ying): electric shadow, an account of films and the film audience in China.**
Jay Leyda. Cambridge, Massachusetts: MIT Press, 1972. 515p.

As an American citizen accompanying his Chinese wife, who had been invited to China as a ballet choreographer, Leyda spent 1959-64 in the China Film Archives in Peking (Beijing) studying old Chinese films and reviewing new ones. This project particularly appealed to him, according to the foreword of this book, because of the fascinating and unresearched avenue which film provides to the study of culture and social history in modern China.

1326 **The Chinese theatre in modern times: from 1840-the present day.**
Colin P. Mackerras. London: Thames & Hudson, 1975. 256p.

A general account of the development of Chinese drama over the past 150 years. Part one deals with the Peking (Beijing) opera up to 1949 and is in large part a restatement of the author's earlier work on the genre. Part two deals with the theatre outside Peking (Beijing) up to 1949 and there are several short chapters on regional opera from south and central China. Part three concerns theatre in China since 1949.

1327 **The rise of the Peking opera 1770-1870: social aspects of the theatre in Manchu China.**
Colin P. Mackerras. New York: Oxford University Press, 1973. 132p.

This book seeks the origins of Chinese drama and in particular the Peking (Beijing) Opera, in Manchu society. The author analyzes the social status of the performers and their general importance in Peking (Beijing) life and describes the theatres of Peking (Beijing) and the restrictions imposed by the government on theatrical performance.

1328 **Modern drama from Communist China.**
Edited by Walter J. Meserve, Ruth J. Meserve. Berkeley, California: University of California Press, 1972. 238p.

The selections provide insight into the political climate of the People's Republic by using Communist Chinese translation. This anthology is arranged chronologically from a dynastic play revised and accepted by Communist Party leaders to the current opera.

1329 **The lute: Kao Ming's Pi-Pachi.**
Jean Mulligan. New York: Columbia University Press, 1980. 335p.

This is the first full translation of the *Lute* (the 14th-century play) into English. The translation flows smoothly and is supplemented by detailed footnotes and an excellent introduction.

1330 **Reminiscences.**

Xin Fengxia. Beijing: Panda Books, 1981. 160p.

This is the life story of a famous Chinese opera actress, Hsin Feng-Hsia (Xin Fengxia). Born in a slum in north China before liberation, the author presents unforgettable vignettes of her family, friends and colleagues, rich men and scoundrels. This book describes the tremendous changes in the status of actors since liberation.

1331 **The golden age of Chinese drama: Yuan Tsa-chu.**

Zhongwen Shi. Princeton, New Jersey: Princeton University Press, 1976. 321p.

In this study of the plays of the Yuan period (1279-1368), the author, Chung-wen Shih (Zhongwen Shi), describes conventional features of dramatic construction, methods of characterization and recurring themes. The central focus is on the use of language, prose passages and lyrics. Attention is also given to the use of musical and physical aspects of staging.

Three kingdoms: China's epic drama.
See item no. 1211.

The peach blossom fan.
See item no. 1247.

Injustice to Tou O (Tou O Yuan - Dou O Yuan): a study and translation.
See item no. 1266.

Guide to Chinese poetry and drama.
See item no. 1409.

Cooking

1332 **Chinese technique: an illustrated guide to the fundamental techniques of Chinese cooking.**

Kem Hom, Harvey Steiman. New York: Simon & Schuster, 1981. 345p. illus.

This is a comprehensive guide for the serious beginner and a reference source for the experienced cook. It contains explicit step-by-step instructions for 100 basic techniques along with more than 1,000 photographs, 100 recipes and 44 colour photographs.

1333 **The Chinese menu cookbook.**

Joanne Hush. New York: Holt, 1976. 274p.

This is an excellent beginners' cookbook. It has a useful and simple introduction to ingredients, equipment and techniques. Another virtue is an excellent three-page discussion of the differences in cooking in the regions of China. Each recipe is denoted by region of origin. The book is well organized and proceeds from simple menus for a dinner for two to a superb dinner of Peking (Beijing) duck.

1334 **The key to Chinese cooking.**
Irene Guo. New York: Knopf, 1977. 532p.

Irene Kuo (Guo) begins with an introduction to general cooking techniques, including 'stir-frying', 'white-cutting' and 'velvetting'. The final section consists of recipes.

1335 **The mandarin way.**
Cecilia Sunyun Jiang. Boston, Massachusetts: Little, Brown, 1974. 274p.

The owner of the Mandarin restaurant in San Francisco, Cecilia Sun Yun Chiang (Sunyun Jiang), reminisces about life in pre-Communist China and presents recipes of mandarin delicacies. She describes the banquets, festivals and customs associated with the changing seasons of the year and also touches on the political climate, literature, opera, etc.

1336 **Chinese cooking for the American kitchen.**
Karen Li. New York: Atheneum, 1976. 303p.

Karen Lee (Li) examines various aspects of Chinese cooking before proceeding with 75 or so recipes. The book ends with 12 dinner party plans with work schedules beginning at least a week in advance.

1337 **Florence Lin's Chinese regional cookbook.**
Florence Lin. New York: Hawthorn, 1975. 342p.

This is a guide to the origins, ingredients and cooking methods of over 200 regional specialities and national favourites. It contains special sections on Chinese eating and cooking utensils, planning and preparation of menus, Chinese tea, wines and spirits. The book is foreworded by Lin Yu-tang (Lin Yudang).

1338 **Chinese cooking on next to nothing.**
Kenneth H. C. Luo. New York: Pantheon Books, 1976. 167p.

This is not a gourmet's cookbook. Kenneth Lo (Luo) has written a practical day-to-day recipe guide for attractive, tasty and inexpensive dishes. As much care is taken with the taste of food as with its balance and nutritional value.

1339 **Chinese vegetarian cooking.**
Kenneth H. C. Luo. New York: Pantheon Books, 1974. 185p.

Kenneth Lo (Luo) gives instructions in the early chapters on stir-frying, steaming, hot marinading, clear simmering, hot assembly and sauces. Later chapters tell how to employ these methods to make a number of items ranging from vegetable broth and plain stir-fried spinach to hot and sour soup.

1340 **The encyclopedia of Chinese cooking.**
Kenneth H. C. Luo. New York: Pantheon Books, 1979. 369p.

Beginning with a comprehensive summary of various preparatory and cooking techniques, Kenneth Lo (Luo) gives over 600 recipes covering all types of dishes from the famous Peking (Beijing) duck to steamed pears in honey. Best for a somewhat experienced cook, the step-by-step instructions can be nonetheless worthwhile for a motivated beginner.

1341 The thousand recipe Chinese cookbook.
Gloria Bley Miller. New York: Grossett & Dunlap, 1970. 926p. illus.

Along with the recipes, the author provides clear, concise directions that make Chinese cooking both easy and enjoyable. It is fully illustrated.

1342 Excel in Chinese cooking.
Lonnie Mock. New York: Alpha Gamma, 1982. 208p.

The book contains homely recipes from soups and main dishes to banquet-style roast duck and delicious teahouse snacks. There are 181 tempting recipes to try, not only for beginners but also for the experienced cook. The author adds helpful suggestions regarding the use of Chinese ingredients.

1343 The People's Republic of China cookbook.
Nobuko Sakamoto. New York: Random House, 1977. 288p.

The author has translated and revised recipes for house kitchens from the *Treatise on famous Chinese dishes* from the Peking (Beijing) Hotel Restaurant, the *Masses cookbook* and the *Cookbook of famous dishes*. She also includes a selection from her own recipes. Recipes from China's four major culinary areas are represented and their characteristics are briefly discussed.

1344 The golden peaches of Samarkand: a study of T'ang exotics.
Edward H. Schafer. Berkeley, California: University of California Press, 1980. 376p.

The author seems to have read all cookbooks that have survived from the T'ang (Tang) period and from them he has concocted a twenty-course meal that is pure delight.

1345 Chinese cooking the easy way, with food processors.
Dee Wang. New York: Elsevier, Nelson Books, 1979. 208p.

The author suggests that the use of a food processor may simplify Chinese cooking. She recommends its use for making dough, mincing and slicing vegetables and meat.

1346 Chinese cookery.
Rose Zheng, Michelle Morris. New York: Harper, 1981. 192p. illus.

Rose Cheng's (Zheng) cookbook is for the experienced cook. It starts with a brief introduction to the basics of Chinese cooking, from ingredients and utensils to the different regional cuisines and contains the most popular recipes. It is beautifully illustrated with colour photographs.

Sport and recreation

1347 Tai Chi handbook.
Herman Kauz.   New York: Doubleday, 1974. 174p. illus.
This volume is a clearly articulated introduction to the philosophy and discipline
of Tai Chi (Taiji), covering exercise, meditation and self-defense. It is illustrated
with photographs.

1348 Sports, politics and ideology in China.
Jonathan Kolatch.   Middle Village, New York: David,
1972. 254p.
This book opens with a brief sketch of sports in traditional China. The remainder
of the book, about 60 per cent, is devoted to the ideology, organization and daily
practices of physical education, paramilitary training and athletic competition in
the People's Republic of China. It also contains a chapter on China's efforts to
participate in international events.

**1349 Acrobats & ping-pong: young China's games, sports &
amusements.**
Isabel Wilcox.   New York: Dodd, Mead, 1981. 144p. illus.
The author describes the wide range of Chinese recreations, commenting on characteristics they share with American leisure activities and stressing their dual
functions of entertaining and teaching. Numerous photographs show young
Chinese enthusiastically skipping rope, playing tug-of-war, sightseeing, dancing
and learning the favourite national sport, ping-pong (ping-pang).

1350 Combined Tai-chi Chuan.
Bow Sim Mark.   Beijing: Chinese Wushu Research
Institute, 1978. 336p.
Created by the Chinese National Athletic Committee, this form of Taiji (Tai-
Chi) represents the collective effort of many great masters of the various styles
and was completed around 1958.

Sport and recreation

1351 Chinese Kung-Fu.
William D. Scott.   New York: Tuttle, 1976. 196p.
This is a manual about one of the oldest, most dynamic defense arts, a derivative of Gongfu developed in southern China over a thousand years ago.

1352 China's sports.
Beijing: Guoji Shudian. 1978- . monthly.
This is an illustrated monthly, with articles on traditional sports, training of Chinese athletes and tournaments at home and abroad.

Libraries, Museums and Archives

1353 Chinese Communist materials at the Bureau of Investigation archives, Taiwan.
Peter Donovan, Carl E. Dorris, Lawrence R. Sullivan. Ann Arbor, Michigan: Center for Chinese Studies, University of Michigan, 1975. 105p.

This survey takes the form of a series of short essays followed by footnotes. The essays cover topics ranging from the Soviet period of 1927-34 to the People's Republic of China and deals with Communist Party affairs, mass movement, cultural and educational affairs, military affairs, the Resistance Base Areas and biographies. Appendices include information on two other government libraries in Taiwan, the Research Library of the Bureau of Intelligence, Ministry of Defense and the Institute of International Relations of the Republic of China.

1354 Oriental Art.
Jan Fontein, Pratapaditya Pal. Boston, Massachusetts: Museum of Fine Arts, 1969. 195p. 40 illus. 95 plates.

The collection in Boston Museum of Fine Arts, which covers a wide range of the nations of Asia, is particularly distinguished for its outstanding works in Chinese, Japanese, Indian and Islamic arts. Of renown is the collection of Chinese paintings from the Han dynasty to the present. This is supplemented by a distinguished assemblage of Chinese bronzes and sculptures.

1355 The development of the Chinese collection in the Library of Congress.
Hu Shuzhao. Boulder, Colorado: Westview Press, 1978. 260p.

This volume by Hu Shu-chao (Hu Shuzhao), is the first comprehensive and in-depth study of the Chinese collection in the Library of Congress, the largest collection of its kind in the Western world. Started in 1869 with some 950 books received in the first exchange of publications between the United States and China, the collection has grown so steadily that in 1978 it numbered more than 430,000 volumes, including 2,000 rare Chinese items, some of which were printed as early as AD 975.

1356 **Directory and guides to the galleries of the Asian Art Museum.**
Edited by Rene-Yvon Lefebvre d'Argence. San Francisco: Asian Art Museum. Reprinted regularly. 3p.

The Avery Brundage Collection of the Asian Art Museum, Golden Gate Park, San Francisco comprises a major part of the museum's collection of Asian art and embraces the major cultures of Asia. It is particularly distinguished in its ancient Chinese bronzes, ceramics and jades. Japanese art is broadly represented in all its historical periods by sculpture, lacquerware, prints, swords and netsukes, with emphasis on ceramics and paintings. Also in the collection are sculptures from China, India and Indonesia dating from ancient times to the modern period. Other publications on this important collection include: Rene-Yvon Lefebvre d'Argence's *Ancient Bronzes in the Avery Brundage Collection*; *Chinese ceramics in the Avery Brundage Collection* (1967. 166p.); *Chinese Jades in the Avery Brundage Collection* and his volume with Diana Turner, *Chinese Korean and Japanese sculpture in the Avery Brundage Collection* (1974. 459p.).

1357 **Guide to the Hoover Institution archives.**
Charles G. Palm, Dale Reed. Stanford, California: Stanford University Press, 1980. 418p.

As the title indicates, this is a guide to the Institution's archival and manuscript holdings which total some 3,569 accessions and occupy approximately 18,000 linear feet of shelving. Entries may be found for North America, Eastern Europe and Russia, Western Europe, East and Southeast Asia, Latin America, Africa and the Middle East and date from the late 19th century for most areas. These items cover political, economic, social and military history and include a wide variety of documentation such as records of organizations, papers of individuals, special collections, audiovisual materials, microfilms, paintings and posters.

1358 **Chinese bronze vessels in the Honolulu Academy of Arts.**
Honolulu: Honolulu Academy of Arts, [n.d.] [unpaginated].

The Chinese collection in the Honolulu Academy of Arts consists of an extensive representation of the major phases of Chinese, Japanese and Korean painting, sculpture, bronzes, ceramics, textiles, lacquer, furniture, folk art and the graphic arts exhibited in a ten-gallery Asian art wing. Other useful volumes include: Gustav Ecke's *Chinese Painting in Hawaii* (1965, 2 vols.); *The Barbara Hutton Collection of Chinese Porcelain* (1965, 36p.) and Gustav Ecke's *Hui Hsien ware in Honolulu* (1954, 41p.).

1359 **Cleveland Museum of Art - handbook.**
Cleveland, Ohio: Cleveland Museum of Art, 1969. 305p.

The Chinese collection is most comprehensive in scope and variety and includes prehistoric pottery, archaic bronzes and jades, Han tiles and mirrors, tomb figurines and gilt bronzes of the Six Dynasties period, ceramics and paintings.

1360 **Freer Gallery of Art, I China.**
Washington, DC: Smithsonian Institution, 1971. 184p. 131 illus.

Oriental art objects of the finest quality have been added from time to time since the gallery was opened in 1905 and the collection now has between 11,000 and 12,000 objects. Most of the countries of Asia are represented, but the special strength of the collection relates to Japan, China, India and Iran and includes Chinese bronzes and Chinese paintings. Other volumes on this topic include John A. Pope, et al, *The Freer Chinese Bronzes* (vol. 1, 1967, 638p. vol. 2, 1969, 227p.); and *Masterpieces of Chinese and Japanese art - Freer Gallery Handbook.*

1361 **Guide to the Metropolitan Museum of Art.**
New York: Metropolitan Museum of Art, 1972. 320p. 431 illus.

The new installation of the museum's Asian art section provides two splendid large halls of Chinese sculpture, perhaps the most important such collection under one roof. The museum's collection contains Chinese pottery and porcelain: especially of note are the Altman and Rockefeller porcelains. There are outstanding examples of archaic bronzes, Chinese and Japanese paintings, especially Japanese painted folding screens and Japanese sculpture. Among the decorative arts of China and Japan, mention should be made of the Bishop Jade Collection. The select Chinese textile collection may be seen by appointment only.

1362 **The Stanford Museum, volume II, volume III, volume IV.**
Stanford, California: Stanford University Press, 1973-76. 3 vols.

Of special note in the collection of Chinese art from the prehistoric period through the 18th century are fifty-three bronze mirrors dating from late Eastern Zhou (Chou) to the Song (Sung) dynasty and a group of small Buddhist sculptures of gilt bronze. Asian countries represented are: Afghanistan, China, India, Japan, Korea, Nepal, Thailand, Tibet. Also useful with respect to this collection are John D. La Plante's *Arts of the Chou Dynasty - introduction and catalogue* (1958, 64p.) and his *The Magnificent Manchus* (1954, 32p.).

1363 **The William Hayes Fogg Art Museum.**
Cambridge, Massachusetts: Harvard University Press, 1973. 3p.

The art of China forms the largest and most important part of the Asian collections and is particularly strong in archaic bronze vessels and metal-work, early and late carved jade and Buddhist sculpture in bronze and stone. Ceramics of all periods are shown but the T'ang (Tang), Sung (Song) and Ming periods are most completely represented. The Chun and Temmoku wares are of particular interest. Another useful publication is Max Loehr's *Ancient Chinese Jades from the Grenville L. Winthrop Collection* (q.v.).

1364 **William Rockhill Nelson Gallery of Art: Handbook of the Collections - volume 1 - Oriental.**
Kansas, Missouri: Nelson Gallery, 1973. [unpaginated].

The extensive Chinese art collection presents varied aspects in the long tradition of an original culture. It includes masterpieces in the fields of scroll painting. Buddhist sculpture and archaic jades, as well as an important group of pottery

Libraries, Museums and Archives

and porcelain dating from the second millenium BC to the Ch'ing (Qing) dynasty. There are also ancient lacquer and silver vessels, furniture of the 17th and 18th centuries and one of the largest collections of textiles.

Scholars' guide to Washington, DC, East Asian studies.
See item no. 1430.

Understanding China: an assessment of American scholarly resources.
See item no. 1434.

Mass Media

1365 Chinese elites: world view and perceptions of the US.
Ralph N. Clough. Washington, DC: US International Communication Agency, 1982. 58p.

This report (US International Communication Agency, Report R-15-82, 6 August 1982) was based on the author's fieldwork in the United States, the People's Republic of China and Hong Kong from September to December 1981 to assess educated urban Chinese perceptions of US-China relations and American society based on interviews with American professionals in close contact with their Chinese counterparts in the People's Republic. The American respondents, 84 per cent of whom are Chinese speakers and most of whom have lived in Beijing (Peking) since 1978, are composed of diplomats, teachers and graduate students, scientists, business people and journalists. The Chinese whose views are represented in this study are urban senior- and mid-level officials, university administrators and faculty members, scholars in leading research institutes and university students.

1366 Government control of the press in modern China, 1900-1949.
Lixia Xu Ding. Cambridge, Massachusetts: East Asian Research Center, Harvard University Press, 1974. 218p.

The author, Lee-Hsia Hsu Ting (Lixia Xu Ding), describes government censorship of the press in modern China, 1900-49.

1367 Communications and national integration in Communist China.
Alan P. L. Liu. Berkeley, California: University of California Press, 1975. 243p.

China has no common language, no adequate roads or railways to connect far off regions and comparatively few literate people capable of communicating over great distances. This book is an account of the role of the mass media in achieving national integration in China today.

Mass Media

1368 China: a resource and curriculum guide.
Edited by Arlene Posner, Arne J. de Keijzer. Chicago: University of Chicago Press, 1975. 317p.

This book is designed as a partial solution to the need for a central channel through which available mass media educational materials on China can be called to the attention of secondary school teachers. The volume contains a list of books, films, filmstrips, packets, slides and tape recordings suitable for secondary school use.

1369 Communication and imperial control in China: evolution of the palace memorial system.
Silas H. L. Wu. Cambridge, Massachusetts: Harvard University Press, 1971. 253p.

The author provides an account of the institutional growth of Ch'ing (Qing) autocracy in the late 17th and early 18th centuries and examines the methods by which the emperors kept abreast of what was happening in their empire.

1370 Moving a mountain: cultural changes in China.
Edited by Godwin C. Zhu, Francis L. K. Xu. Honolulu: University Press of Hawaii, 1979. 264p.

This volume, edited by Godwin Chu (Zhu) and Francis Hsu (Xu) contains a selection of papers from a January 1978 Conference on Communications and Cultural Change in China, which attempt an assessment of the kinds and extent of change achieved through Maoist China's distinctive communications machinery. Topics include the communication system itself, aspects of Chinese political culture, value change and a summary of assessments of the Party's success in inducing change. The articles draw on data from the 1950s to the aftermath of the Gang of Four, and the authors come from a wide range of disciplines, including anthropology, economics, history, journalism, political science and sociology.

1371 Popular media in China: shaping new cultural patterns.
Edited by Godwin C. Zhu. Honolulu: University Press of Hawaii, 1978. 263p.

The essays contained in this volume, edited by Godwin Chu (Zhu) discuss children's folk-songs, serial pictures, revolutionary operas, short stories and big character posters. The study attempts to generalize about the role of the popular media in China on the basis of an examination of the unique 1970-79 period.

1372 Radical change through communication in Mao's China.
Godwin C. Zhu. Honolulu: University Press of Hawaii, 1977. 340p.

The author, Godwin Chu (Zhu), attempts to demonstrate that Chinese development has been unique because the drastic and swift social change has been brought about not by a revolution of technology, nor by the brutal application of force in Stalinist fashion, but rather, primarily by the skilfull use of communication.

Periodicals and Newspapers

Periodicals

1373 Asian Survey.
Berkeley, California: University of California Press, 1960- .
monthly.
This journal carries frequent articles on the People's Republic of China by China scholars.

1374 China Business Review.
Washington, DC: National Council for US-China Trade,
1974- . bimonthly.
This journal is the prime source for current information and analysis on trade and economics in the People's Republic of China. It also serves as a guide to related activities in the United States, including the extensive research and publication programme of the Council.

1375 China Council Report.
New York: China Council, 1978- . quarterly.
The China Council offers a national programme for adult education on China and Sino-American relations. This newsletter covers activities and publications in this area of concern.

Periodicals and Newspapers. Periodicals

1376 China Exchange Newsletter.
Washington, DC: National Academy of Sciences, Committee on Scholarly Communication with the PRC, 1973- . bimonthly.

This newsletter focuses on scientific matters, but also contains leads to information in socio-economic areas.

1377 China's Foreign Trade.
Beijing: Guoji Shudian, 1981- . bimonthly.

A review of China's export trade to foreign countries, with articles on China's economic and scientific development. It is published by the Ministry of Foreign Trade and includes authoritative statements on official trade policy and advertisements of Chinese products.

1378 China Pictorial.
Beijing: Guoji Shudian 1951- . monthly.

A large-format journal with beautiful colour photography and short articles covering China's achievements in many fields.

1379 China Philately.
Beijing: Guoji Shudian, 1982- . quarterly.

Provides news of Chinese stamps, philatelic discoveries, trends at home and abroad and reports on the latest market value of stamps.

1380 China Quarterly.
London: Contemporary China Institute, School of Oriental and African Studies, 1960- . quarterly.

A scholarly publication in China studies. It includes articles on all aspects of contemporary China, book reviews and a bibliography.

1381 China Reconstructs.
Beijing: Guoji Shudian, 1952- . monthly.

A review of China from a Chinese viewpoint, with photographs and feature articles on every aspect of life in the new China.

1382 China Science Abstracts.
Beijing: Guoji Shudian, 1981- . monthly.

This is a new journal from Science Press in Beijing (Peking). It has two editions, one covering mathematics, mechanics, physics and technological sciences; the other, chemistry, life sciences and earth sciences. The journal will aid foreign scholars and scientists to keep abreast of the enormous number of scientific and technical articles now published in China's several hundred technical journals.

1383 China's Screen.
Beijing: Guoji Shudian, 1981- . quarterly.

Covers news and developments in the Chinese film industry and reports on the exchange of films with other countries.

1384 **Chinese Economic Studies.**
White Plains, New York: Sharpe, 1967- . quarterly.
One of the quarterly journals in Sharpe's 'China book project', a series of translated periodicals and books. Other quarterly translated journals include: *Chinese Education, Chinese Law and Government, Chinese Sociology and Anthropology, Chinese Studies in History, Chinese Studies in Philosophy* and *Chinese Science and Technology.*

1385 **Chinese Literature.**
Beijing: Guoji Shudian, 1979- . monthly.
A selection of short stories, novels, essays, poems, plays, operas, and illustrations of art works, both ancient and modern. It sometimes includes the scripts of dramas and articles on literary policy in the People's Republic of China.

1386 **Current Background.**
Hong Kong: US Consulate General, 1956- . monthly.
Each issue focuses on a single topic and includes translations from newspapers, periodicals and books, as well as compilations of information.

1387 **Da Zi Ran.** (Great Nature.)
Beijing: Association of Chinese Museums of Natural Sciences, Beijing Museum of Natural History, 1980- . monthly.
This periodical devoted to popularizing natural sciences, promoting museum work and exchanging results in scientific research began publication in September 1980. It covers biology, palaeontology, anthropology, astronomy, geology, history of science and technology and museum work.

1388 **Far Eastern Economic Review.**
Hong Kong: Far Eastern Economic Review Ltd., 1946- . weekly.
Covers both politics and economics. The journal staff also publishes the *Far Eastern Economic Review Yearbook*, which has useful surveys on countries in the area, including the People's Republic of China.

1389 **Hongqi.** (Red Flag.)
Beijing: Guoji Shudian, 1958- . monthly.
Red Flag (*Hung ch'i*) is the theoretical journal of the Chinese Communist Party under the direct supervision of the Central Committee. It has articles on major policies and reflects the new thinking among the inner circle of Party leaders.

1390 **Instruments and future.**
Beijing: China Instruments and Meters Society, 1980- . monthly.
The first issue of this magazine was published in October 1980. It is a popular science magazine on instruments, meters and automation technology.

Periodicals and Newspapers. Periodicals

1391 The JETRO China Newsletter.
Tokyo: Japan External Trade Organization, 1976- .
bimonthly.
This newsletter supplies readers with the basic knowledge needed for a rational evaluation of the China market. Covering economy, trade and government policies, it is one of the main sources of business information available on the People's Republic of China.

1392 Journal of Asian Studies.
Ann Arbor, Michigan: Association of Asian Studies, 1928- .
quarterly.
Carries frequent articles on China by China scholars and publishes an annual bibliography of Asian Studies, which is the most complete listing available of books, articles, dissertations and other materials on China and Asia.

1393 Modern China.
Beverley Hills, California: Sage, 1975- . quarterly.
A journal intended to liberate US scholarship on China from the 'enemy-watching' syndrome. It is strong in the social sciences.

1394 New China.
New York: US-China People's Friendship Association, 1975-
. quarterly.
Publishes many articles by tourists on contemporary China - living conditions, policy changes and national development.

1395 Pacific Affairs.
Vancouver, Canada: University of British Columbia, 1928- .
quarterly.
A scholarly journal with frequent articles on China.

1396 Peking Review.
Beijing: Pai Wan Chuang, 1958- . weekly.
A weekly journal of political affairs expressing the views of the Chinese government on important domestic and foreign issues. Some of the materials are reprints or condensations from the Chinese official press and media reports.

1397 People's Republic of China Official Activities and Monthly Bibliography.
Hamburg, GFR: Institute of Asian Affairs, 1977- . monthly.
An English-language supplement to the Institute's monthly journal *China Aktuell*. Contents include: the People's Republic of China's agreements with foreign countries; delegations to and from China; activities of the Chinese Communist Party's Politburo members; Chinese articles on the USSR; economic aid to the People's Republic; biographical sketches of several current leaders (with photographs); and a monthly bibliography of articles from and about the People's Republic (in Chinese, English, German and French).

1398 Science and Technology Review.
Beijing: 1980- .

This is a Chinese-language publication with a table of contents in both Chinese and English. Since its inauguration in 1980 this publication has tried to 'promote the exchanges of science and technology' and 'to explore the courses and means of modernization'.

1399 Selections from PRC Magazines.
Hong Kong: US Consulate General, 1956- . weekly.

Formerly *Selections from China Mainland Magazine*, this service now translates all articles from the *Red Flag* and several other Chinese magazines. It also contains translations from scarce periodicals and occasionally from Chinese books and pamphlets.

1400 Social Sciences in China.
Beijing: Guoji Shudian, 1981- . quarterly.

Published by the Chinese Academy of Social Science to deal with Marxism, Leninism and Mao Zedong's (Mao Tse-tung) thought and other questions in philosophy and social science.

1401 Solar Energy Journal.
Beijing: China Solar Energy Society 1981- . quarterly.

This quarterly journal carries articles on China's solar energy science and notes several domestic, agricultural and industrial purposes for which solar power has been used.

1402 Women of China.
Beijing: Guoji Shudian, 1982- . monthly.

This is an illustrated monthly with first-hand views on courtship and marriage, economic and political rights and reports on women's roles in China's culture.

1403 Xinhua Yuebao. (New China Monthly.)
Beijing: Guoji Shudian, 1949- . monthly.

Reproduces texts or condensations of articles from national and local newspapers and periodicals, many of which are not available abroad. Another important feature is its extensive bibliography of articles in Chinese newspapers and periodicals. Lastly, the journal includes a chronology - the only continuously-published chronology available from the People's Republic of China.

China's sports.
See item no. 1352.

Newspapers

1404 Renmin Ribao. (People's Daily.)
Beijing: Central Committee of the Chinese Communist
Party. 1949- . daily.

The *People's Daily* (*Jen-ming Jih-pao*) is the official newspaper of the Communist Party and the biggest most important daily newspaper in China. It publishes
policy statements and foreign press reports on China and international news,
particularly events on Asia and developing nations.

**1405 Summary of world broadcasts, part 3, weekly economic
report.**
London: British Broadcasting Corporation, 1962- . weekly.

The British Broadcasting Corporation provides what is perhaps the best publication for concise factual information on the People's Republic of China on eco-
nomic-related topics, including telecommunications.

1406 Survey of the PRC press.
Hong Kong: US Consulate General, 1956- . weekly.

Formerly *Survey of the China Mainland Press*, this journal includes reprints of
English-language news releases and original translations from the *People's Daily*,
and occasionally other newspapers.

1407 US Foreign Broadcast Information Service Reports.
Washington, DC: US State Department, 1950- . 5 per week.

These contain several brief political analyses on China.

1408 Xinhua News Agency Bulletin. (New China News Agency.)
Beijing: New China News Agency, 1950- . daily.

The New China News Agency, headquartered in Beijing (Peking), has 31
bureaux in China's provinces and maintains 23 foreign branches. In addition to
daily news bulletins in Chinese, English and Russian, the NCNA also issues a set
of captioned glossy photographs every Tuesday, Thursday and Saturday.

Bibliographies and Directories

1409 Guide to Chinese poetry and drama.
Roger B. Bailey.   Boston, Massachusetts: Hall, 1973. 251p.

The annotations in the poetry section cover Chinese poetry from the *Book of Songs*, the oldest collection, to modern vernacular poems, including general anthologies and collections, individual poets and biographical and critical works. The drama section traces the development of drama in China from the Shamanistic rites to the highly literary classical Yuan plays, the Peking (Beijing) opera of the mid-19th century, and the experimental Western-style plays of the early 20th century.

1410 Education in the People's Republic of China: a selective annotated bibliography of materials published in the English language.
Compiled by Robert D. Barendsen.   Washington, DC: US Government Printing Office, 1980. 112p.

This bibliography lists over 198 titles arranged alphabetically under two headings - materials in books, pamphlets and separately published reports and materials appearing in periodicals in the United States and a dozen foreign countries. The index contains 92 categories arranged alphabetically by subject and is extensively cross-referenced.

1411 Development in the People's Republic of China: a selected bibliography.
Patricia Blair.   Washington, DC: Overseas Development Council, 1977. 58p.

It is an up-to-date selection of books and articles on development strategy, economic and social performance and political and social conditions in the People's Republic of China.

Bibliographies and Directories

1412 Professional societies in the People's Republic of China.
Robert O. Boorstin. Washington, DC: National Council for US-China Trade, 1979. 501p.

The bulk of the volume is a listing of the professional societies with details of their activities, leaders, members and publications. Short biographies of members are given where possible. This comprehensive listing is prefaced by an essay on the origin and development of the societies.

1413 An index to Chinese archaeological works published in the People's Republic of China, 1949-1965.
C. M. Chen, Richard B. Stamp. Ann Arbor, Michigan: Michigan Asian Studies Center, University of Michigan, 1972. 75p.

This is a listing, classified by area and period, of articles in Chinese journals about archaeology. The articles are given only in translation.

1414 An annotated bibliography of selected Chinese reference works.
Edited by Deng Siyu, Knight Beggerstaff. Cambridge, Massachusetts: Harvard University Press, 1973. 3rd ed. 250p.

This volume covers pre-20th-century Chinese studies. As compared to the second edition (1950) there are the following changes: 500 titles instead of 400; a new section on the statecraft of the Ming and Ch'ing (Qing) dynasties; more indices to newspapers and periodicals; and the inclusion of more biographical dictionaries that focus on the modern period.

1415 A type of index of Chinese folktales.
Naidong Ding. Helsinki: Finnish Academy of Science and Letters, 1978. 294p.

This volume is arranged by the compiler Nai-tung Ting (Naidong Ding), according to the internationally accepted AT indexing system for folk-tale motifs. The material analyzed by the author comes mainly from the large number of folk narratives recorded and published in the People's Republic of China between 1949 and 1966. Materials from Taiwan and Hong Kong, from earlier collections by European and Chinese folklorists and from Chinese classical literature are also included.

1416 Chinese folk narratives: a bibliographical guide.
Naidong Ding, Lixia Xu Ding. San Francisco: Chinese Materials and Research Aids Service Centre, 1975. 68p.

This guide by Nai-tung Ting (Naidong Ding) and Lee-hsia Hsu Ting (Lixia Xu Ding), consists of three parts: bibliographies; classical literary folk-tales; and modern oral folk-tales. For each part and/or section, there is a brief introduction. Entries of works and collections are annotated.

1417 **Bibliography of Chinese government serials, 1880-1949.**
Julia Dong.   Stanford, California: Hoover Institution, 1980.
136p.

This bibliography contains 527 titles, including items that appeared under the late Ch'ing (Qing) monarchy. During the Sino-Japanese War (1937-1945), the government moved from Nanking (Nanjing) to Chungking (Zhongqing) in Szechwan (Sichuan). Because there was no central government printing office, many government departments contracted with private companies, such as the Commercial Press, to print and distribute their serial publications. Therefore, some of the serials listed bear a non-government publication source.

1418 **The provinces of the People's Republic of China: a political and economic bibliography.**
John Philip Emerson, Robert Michael Field, Michel
Oksenberg, Florence L. Yuan.   Washington, DC: US
Government Printing Office, 1976. 734p.

This book is a bibliographical source book of political and economic developments at the provincial level in the People's Republic of China. It is useful not only for scholars engaged in Chinese provincial political and economic research, but also for China specialists doing research on central-regional conflicts in China and cross-national comparisons using sub-national units of analysis.

1419 **Far Eastern politics: China, Japan, Korea, 1950-1975.**
Compiled by Anthony Ferguson.   Paris: International
Political Science, 1977. 235p.

This bibliography lists those articles about the Far East that have been abstracted in *International Political Science Abstracts* since 1950. The articles originally appeared in selected American and European journals. The information (1,585 entries on China, 771 on Japan and 235 on Korea) is arranged according to country and subject.

1420 **Higher education and research in the People's Republic of China: institutional profiles.**
Compiled by Thomas Fingar.   Washington, DC: the
US-China Education Clearinghouse, 1981. 87p.

This is a valuable addition to the growing body of informational literature related to research or teaching in China.

1421 **Chinese education and society: a bibliographic guide, the Cultural Revolution and its aftermath.**
Steward S. Fraser, Guangliang Xu.   White Plains, New
York: International Arts and Sciences Press, 1972. 204p.

The authors, Steward Fraser and Kuang-liang Hsu (Guanliang Xu), provide a bibliography of sources on education in China since 1966, with sources annotated in many cases, divided into topical categories, with cross-references. English, Chinese, Japanese, French, Italian and German sources are included, with references to English translations of most of the foreign-language materials. In an introductory chapter, there is a summary of the range of research centers, publications and translation series which deal with Chinese education and related topics.

1422 Guide to Chinese philosophy.
Charles Weixun Fu, Wing-tsit Chan. Boston, Massachusetts: Hall, 1978. 262p.

This bibliography is one in a series of guides designed to advance humanistic learning by presenting available resources for the study of Asian philosophies and religions. The materials in this volume are organized both chronologically and topically, with, in most cases, adequate cross-referencing.

1423 The process of industrialization of China: primary elements of an analytical bibliography.
Nicole Ganiere. Paris: Organization for Economic Co-operation and Development, 1974. 137p.

This is an extensive, detailed bibliography dealing with the originality and evolution of and results achieved by industrialization in China. Altogether 500 works of European, American, Japanese and varied translated Chinese source materials are reviewed and classified under appropriate headings.

1424 Subject and author index to Chinese literature monthly (1951-1976).
Donald A. Gibbs. New Haven, Connecticut: Yale University Press, 1978. 173p.

This book provides classified and composite alphabetical indices for the first 25 years of the magazine, ending with the fall of the Gang of Four in 1976. He gives everything in one composite alphabetical index with classified sections and cross-references contained within the composite listings.

1425 A bibliography of studies and translations of modern Chinese literature, 1918-1942.
Donald A. Gibbs, Yunzhen Li. Cambridge, Massachusetts: Harvard University Press, 1975. 239p.

The authors take literature in its broad sense. In addition to fiction, drama and poetry, they also cover expositions, published diaries, reports, literary biographies and autobiographies. The bibliography is divided into three sections: a list of sources, general studies of modern Chinese literature and an alphabetical list of Chinese literature and an alphabetical list of writers and the known English translations of their works.

1426 Chinese local newspapers at SOAS.
David S. G. Goodman, Tony Saich. London: Contemporary China Institute, 1979. 83p.

This guide provides an accurate record of the collection of some 50, mainly provincial, newspapers held in the Library of the School of Oriental and African Studies in London. A useful research tool for students of contemporary China.

1427 A bibliographical guide to Japanese research on the Chinese economy 1958-1970.
W. P. J. Hall.   Cambridge, Massachusetts: Harvard University Press, 1972. 213p.

This bibliography gives chapter headings and ranks works in order of importance. It will obviously be valuable to economists who read Japanese. In addition, scholars who read Chinese will be able to locate tables that may be of value to them and at least help them to be aware of the sort of work in Japan in their own special fields.

1428 A Sung bibliography. (Bibliographie de Sung - initiated by Etienne Balaz.)
Edited by Yves Hervouet.   New York: Columbia University Press, 1976. 598p.

This volume contains bibliographical information and resumés of the most important Sung (Song) works of criticism, philosophy, history, biography, science and literature. It includes 600 biographical notices, along with indices to titles, names and subjects and a listing of journals and reference works used in the notices. Some entries are in French.

1429 Japanese studies of modern China since 1953.
Noriko Kamachi, John K. Fairbank, Chuzo Ichiko.   Cambridge, Massachusetts: Harvard University Press, 1975. 603p.

This volume lists the important monographs and journal articles on modern China, published in Japanese between 1953 and 1969. It begins with general historical studies, continues with domestic and foreign political affairs, ranges over intellectual and cultural history, economy and society and concludes with a list of key reference materials.

1430 Scholars' guide to Washington, DC, East Asian studies.
Hong N. Kim.   Washington, DC: Smithsonian Institution, 1979. 413p.

A guide for specialists and the interested laymen, to the resources on China, Japan, Korea and Mongolia available in Washington, DC.

1431 Essays on the sources for Chinese history.
Edited by Donald D. Leslie, Colin P. Mackerras, Wang Gungwu.   Columbia, South Carolina: University of South Carolina Press, 1975. 364p.

A bibliography on sources for Chinese history, the volume ranges over the whole chronological span of Chinese studies, from prehistoric archaeology to the new terminology of the revolution of the present day. The contributing scholars range from some who are eminent in their fields to others who are not yet widely known and their essays range from definitive summaries to limited introductions.

Bibliographies and Directories

1432 **Chinese music: an annotated bibliography (Garland Reference Library of the Humanities, vol. 75).**
Frederic Lieberman. New York: Garland Press, 1979. 2nd ed. 257p.

The revised and enlarged second edition of Lieberman's works is a compilation of bibliographies, books, articles, masters and doctoral theses, exhibition catalogues and unpublished research papers and reports on Chinese music, dance and drama. The bibliography with 2,441 entries is intended to provide exhaustive coverage of publications in Western languages. The majority of the entries are English-language sources. The bibliography is divided into two lists, 'bibliography and discography' and 'Books and articles'. Each list is arranged alphabetically by author. There is an 'Index to serials' and 'Index to names'.

1433 **A research guide to central party and government meetings in China, 1949-1975.**
Kenneth Lieberthal. White Plains, New York: International Arts and Sciences Press, 1976. 352p.

The author presents data on Central Party and Government meetings, which will be of enormous help in the study of official policies. He also provides a basis for a new analysis of the policy-making process in China.

1434 **Understanding China: an assessment of American scholarly resources.**
John M. H. Lindbeck. New York: Praeger, 1971. 156p.

Concerned about the future of Chinese studies, the Ford Foundation commissioned Lindbeck of Columbia University to survey scholarly resources on China. The report contains his searching analysis, insight, data and recommendations for the future development of the field.

1435 **Notable books on Chinese studies: a selected, annotated and subject-divided bibliography guide.**
C. H. Lowe. Taipei, Taiwan: China Printing, 1978. 228p.

This book is primarily for the layman and the uninitiated in the field of Chinese studies. Its listing of over 1,500 titles, mostly in English, with some in Chinese, presents primarily books published since 1958. The entries are arranged under 18 subject categories, with full bibliographic information given for each, including Chinese characters for names and authors' dates, when known.

1436 **Bibliography on cities and city planning in China.**
Laurence J. C. Ma. Washington, DC: US Government Printing Office, 1980. 158p.

Items included in the bibliography are limited to publications in the English language that are generally available in American libraries. Most of the entries are of publications that have come out in the last two decades, although some older material has been included. Each entry is accompanied by a descriptive annotation indicating the topics and themes covered in the work. The bibliography consists of 194 listings of over 11 categories including basic works on contemporary urban China, city planning, urban housing, urban land use and spatial structure, urban population, urban economy and society, urban politics and administration, urbanization and national development, rustication and urban-rural relations, studies on individual cities and historical and general works.

1437 China and America: a bibliography of interactions: foreign and domestic.

Compiled by James M. McCutcheon. Honolulu: University Press of Hawaii, 1973. 75p.

This volume lists secondary sources in English relevant to the study of Chinese-American relations. Consisting of some 900 selected monographs and theses completed through the spring of 1971, the compilation attempts to give some idea of the scope and nature of Chinese-American contacts and the areas in which these contacts affect Chinese as well as American life.

1438 Source materials in Chinese history.

Edited by Charles Meyer, Ian Allen. London: Warne, 1970. 190p.

With a selection of extracts from documents and commentaries, this book attempts to cover the whole range of Chinese history up to the Cultural Revolution. About half of the content is devoted to the post-1911 period.

1439 Modern China, 1840-1972: an introduction to sources and resource aids.

Andrew J. Nathan. Ann Arbor, Michigan: University of Michigan Press, 1973. 95p.

This book is intended not only as a guide to research aids in all languages but also as an introduction to the primary sources for historical and social science research on modern China. The bibliography is rather thin in certain areas including economics, literature, ethnography, Hong Kong's history and Overseas Chinese history and the history of science and technology.

1440 Bibliography.

Michel Oksenberg, Nancy Baterman, James B. Anderson. New York: East Asian Institute, Columbia University, 1972. 127p.

This bibliography is prefaced with an introduction by the authors which analyzes seven different approaches to contemporary Chinese politics and suggests topics which are deserving of further research.

1441 A bibliography of secondary English language literature on contemporary Chinese politics.

Michel Oksenberg. New York: East Asian Institute, Columbia University, 1970. 112p.

About 1,350 entries dated 1950-70 are classified by a conceptual scheme devised by the author, who prefaces the bibliography with an illuminating essay on social science approaches to the study of China. It includes an author index.

Bibliographies and Directories

1442 Guide to Chinese prose.
Jordan D. Paper. Boston, Massachusetts: Hall, 1976. 116p.
This volume covers 142 items of Chinese prose. It is divided into an introduction to the subject and an annotated bibliography. The material selected is arranged topically and chronologically. Entries in Chinese classics, history, philosophy and general studies occupy one-half of the volume. Other topics included are *belles-lettres*, short stories, novels and modern literature.

1443 China: an index to European visual and aural materials.
Edited by K. L Pratt, D. W. S. Gray. London: Crosby Lockwood Staples, 1973. 129p.
This index sets out to list audio-visual materials on China which are available throughout Europe. The book is divided into a titled 'Commercial' section, listing materials readily available for sale, hire or loan and a research section, listing materials only available by special arrangement with the owners.

1444 Sino-Soviet schism: a bibliography, 1956-1964.
Compiled by Vimla Saran. London: Asian Publishing House, 1971. 162p.
It contains over 2,000 items published between 1956 and the fall of Khrushchev in 1964, of which the great majority are original Chinese and Soviet materials. It has an excellent index. The documents surveyed consist of speeches, statements, resolutions, communiqués, letters, editorials and reports of the Communist and Workers' parties of the world. Non-Communist literature is also covered. In addition to books on the subject, the compiler drew from a most impressive list of periodicals in many languages, Eastern and Western.

1445 Doctoral dissertations on China, 1971-75: a bibliography of studies in western languages.
Compiled and edited by Frank Shulman. Seattle, Washington: University of Washington Press, 1978. 348p.
The author continues his bibliographic work with this supplement to *Doctoral dissertations on China: a bibliography of studies in western languages, 1945-1970*, which he compiled with Leonard H. D. Gordon. The earlier work listed some 2,200 dissertations. The new volume adds nearly 1,600 titles completed in the following five years (as well as 228 pre-1971 theses overlooked in the first compilation). Coverage is broad: dissertations completed in North America, Europe and Australia and dealing in whole or in part with China, Hong Kong, Mongolia, Tibet or the Overseas Chinese, either pre- or post-1949. Listings are by subject and include references to available microfilm copies or published versions.

1446 Modern Chinese society: analytical bibliography. Volume I, publications in western languages, 1644-1972; volume II, publications in Chinese, 1644-1969; volume III, publications in Japanese, 1944-1971.
William G. Skinner. Stanford, California: Stanford University Press, 1973. 802p.+801p.+531p.
This is the first bibliography in the Chinese field to have exploited the potentials of computer type-setting and cross-tabulating for accommodating the last-minute entries, thus making it possible to have an up-to-date, complex and composite

work. The 31,000 items in these three volumes give a representative selection of worthwhile secondary literature in Chinese, Japanese and Western languages on modern Chinese society. The sophisticated annotations and framework of multiple cross-indexing have put a new and powerful weapon in the scholar's hands.

1447 China: an annotated bibliography.
Tsuen-Hsuin Tsien, James K. M. Zheng. Boston, Massachusetts: Hall, 1978. 604p.

This is the most up-to-date and comprehensive compilation on every aspect of Chinese studies through 1977 in English, Chinese and Japanese as well as some titles in French, German and Russian. This book will no doubt remain one of the most important reference tools in Chinese studies for years to come.

1448 The T. L. Yuan bibliography of western writings on Chinese art and archaeology.
Edited by Marrie A. Vanderstappen. Salem, New Hampshire: Mansell Merrimack Book Service, 1975. 654p.

This volume contains over 15,000 items pertaining to Chinese art published between 1920 and 1965 in the Western languages including English, German, Dutch, the Scandinavian, the Slavic and the Romance languages. The bibliography lists books and reviews, catalogues of exhibitions, journal articles and notes - not only on topics specifically Chinese, but also on China-related material from the neighbouring areas including Japan and Korea, Mongolia, Central Asia and Tibet. It is the standard reference guide for students of Chinese art and archaeology.

1449 The Cultural Revolution in China: an annotated bibliography.
James C. F. Wang. New York: Garland, 1976. 246p.

The author presents paragraph-length annotations to 364 English-language books and articles published up to 1975 (with the bulk of the materials published from 1967-71). Arranged by topic, the bibliography includes such subjects as the origins of the Cultural Revolution, its effects on Chinese political leadership, the army, the economy, education and foreign policy. There is an author index and a detailed subject index.

1450 CLIBOC: Chinese linguistics bibliography on computer.
Compiled by William S. Y. Wang. Cambridge, Massachusetts: Harvard University Press, 1970. 513p.

This bibliography includes such areas as diachronic and synchronic dialect studies, Sino-Tibetan linguistics, minority languages within China and the Chinese-language works on linguistic theory. In principle, this first edition of CLIBOC covers those works published before the end of 1967. After the editors' introductory chapter, there is an integrated alphabetical author index and a list of 3,000 books, articles and reviews in Chinese, Japanese and Western languages including Russian. Successive chapters provide topic cross-references to the file of abstracts for several hundreds of items, keys to periodical citations and comparative Romanization tables. Supplementary maps indicate the distribution of the Sino-Tibetan languages and the Chinese dialect groups. The most comprehensive bibliography available on linguistic aspects of the Chinese-language group and related linguistic topics, the book is printed by a lithographic process from the original computer print-out.

Bibliographies and Directories

1451 The history of imperial China, a research guide.
Endymion Wilkinson. Cambridge, Massachusetts: East
Asian Research Center, Harvard University, 1974. 213p.

This book is mainly concerned with the socio-economic history of the Han to the
Ch'ing (Qing) dynasties. The book is divided into two parts, the first entitled
'Research hints' and the second 'Traditional Chinese historical writing and main
categories of primary sources'.

1452 China historiography on the revolution of 1911: a critical survey and a selective bibliography.
Winston Xie. Stanford, California: Hoover Institution,
1974. 100p.

The author, Winston Hsieh (Xie), examines the 20th-century output of Chinese
historians - both Republican and Communist - on the 1911 Revolution and shows
that the interpretation of historical events has usually been coloured by political
ideology or political myth.

1453 Chinese linguistics: a selected and classified bibliography.
Paul Fumian Yang. Hong Kong: Chinese University of
Hong Kong, 1974. 292p.

This book, by Paul Fu-mien Yang (Fumian Yang), in addition to the main body
of the work, contains a list of Chinese, Japanese and Korean publishers; a romanized index of authors' names; and an index to Chinese characters. It contains
3,257 separate entries and is divided into 12 major sections, each dealing with a
well-defined area of Chinese linguistics.

1454 Classical Chinese fiction: a guide to its study and appreciation, essays and bibliographies.
Winston L. Y. Yang, Peter Li, Nathan Mao. Boston,
Massachusetts: Hall, 1978. 302p.

This book is divided into two sections. The first consists of nine chapters of
historical and critical essays on the development of Chinese fiction. The second
section consists entirely of annotated bibliographical entries of approximately 850
English, French and German-language translations and studies. A glossary of
Chinese authors and titles and an author and translator index are included.

1455 Modern Chinese fiction: a guide to its study and appreciation, essays and bibliographies.
Edited by Winston L. Y. Yang, Nathan Mao. Boston,
Massachusetts: Hall, 1980. 356p.

A comparison volume to *Classical Chinese Fiction*, this book is designed for
students, teachers, scholars and general readers in the West. The first section of
the book consists of four essays on modern Chinese fiction from 1917 to 1949,
Taiwan fiction since 1949 and Chinese fiction since 1949. The second part is an
annotated guide to approximately 450 English-language translations and studies,
including books, dissertations and journal articles.

1456 Contemporary Chinese novels and short stories, 1949-1974: an annotated bibliography.
Edited by Meishi Zai. Cambridge, Massachusetts: Harvard University Press, 1979. 408p.

This volume by Meishi Tsai (Meishi Zai), is much more than a bibliography. What the author has done is to read through virtually the entire corpus of China's twenty-five year output of fiction and give succinct summaries and vital bibliographic details, including references to translations. He also furnishes what amounts to a *Who's Who* of the current literary scene.

1457 Bibliography of Asian Studies.
Ann Arbor, Michigan: Association of Asian Studies, 1953- . annual.

This bibliography is published annually by the Association of Asian Studies. It contains a comprehensive list of articles and books written in Western languages about Asia, including the People's Republic of China.

1458 Twentieth century Chinese writers and their pen names.
Baoliang Zhu. Boston, Massachusetts: Hall, 1977. 366p.

This volume includes 7,429 pen names for 2,524 20th-century writers - including both authors of literary works and other cultural figures such as philosophers and publicists. Thus it will be of great value, not only for students of modern Chinese literature but also for political scientists.

1459 A bibliography of Chinese newspapers and periodicals in European Libraries.
Contemporary China Institute. New York: Cambridge University Press, 1975. 1,025p.

This volume is a union list of over 6,000 Chinese serials - journals, newspapers (including Red Guard publications), annuals, yearbooks and series - with a cut-off date of 1970, which are available in 102 libraries from 12 European countries: Austria, Czechoslovakia, Denmark, Germany (East and West), Italy, the Netherlands, the Soviet Union, Sweden, Switzerland and the United Kingdom.

1460 Chinese cooperative catalog.
Washington, DC: US Library of Congress, 1976. annual. 839p.

This catalogue of additions to US libraries began publication in 1975 and the 893 entries in the January issue had grown to 3,283 by November 1975. The annual cumulations, covering three volumes, will supersede the preceding 12 monthly issues. This is a major new bibliographical aid for the cataloguer of new Chinese publications and will serve as a current awareness service to scholars by noting new additions to the most important Chinese-language collections in North America.

Science and technology in the development of modern China: an annotated bibliography.
See item no. 1039.

Directory of selected scientific institutions in mainland China.
See item no. 1059.

Index

The index is a single alphabetical sequence of authors (personal and corporate), titles of publications and subjects. Transliteration has been done according to the *Pinyin* transliteration system. Index entries refer both to the main items and to other works mentioned in the notes to each item. Title entries are in italics. Numeration refers to the items as numbered.

A

Abidi, A. H. H. 769
Abortion 301
Abortive revolution: China under nationalist rule, 1927-37 233
About Chinese 1107
Abramowitz, M. 840
Academia Sinica
  Anyang excavations 138
Acheson, Dean 782
Acoustic phonetics
  Mandarin Chinese 1075
Acoustical studies of mandarin vowels and tones 1075
Acrobats & ping-pong: young China's games, sports & amusements 1349
Acton, H. 1247
Actresses 1330
Acupuncture 591
Acupuncture 301, 582—583, 590—591, 594, 596, 598
  anaesthesia 37, 597

Acupuncture anaesthesia in the People's Republic of China, a trip report of the American Acupuncture Anaesthesia Study Group 597
Acupuncture and moxibustion: a handbook for the barefoot doctors of China 594
Acupuncture Institute of the Academy of Traditional Chinese Medicine 582
Adkinson, D. 367
Administration 83
  decentralization 906
  maps 67
  Shang 138
Adoption 494
Adventure of Mao on the Long March 1260
Aerodynamics research and development 1043
Aeronautics 1043
  imported technology 1045
Aeronautics in China 1043
Africa
  Chinese aid 799, 817
  Communist fifth-columnists 866
  relations with China 817, 825, 845

After Mao what? Army, party, and group rivalries in China 674
Aged, The 107, 113
Ageless Chinese: a history 183
Agreement of the People's Republic of China: a calendar of events, 1966-80 612
Agricultural development in China and India: a comparative study 995
Agricultural Law of 1950 1020
Agricultural mechanization in China: the administrative impact 998
Agricultural production in Communist China, 1949-1965 1003
Agriculture 15, 24, 42, 55, 84, 90−91, 96, 120, 130−131, 303, 658, 691, 890, 894−895, 921, 927, 936, 954, 1002−1003, 1011, 1013, 1015, 1024, 1055
  ancient 148
  animal husbandry 1022
  Chinese immigrants to US 534
  collective 904
  collectivization 999
  communes 996
  comparison with India 995
  economy 885−886
  fertilizers 1009
  field management 1004
  government policy 994, 1001, 1004, 1021
  grain harvests 956
  mechanization 943, 998, 1004, 1006, 1016
  pest control 1023
  research 1018
  resettlement programme 997
  rural development 1008
  socialist planning 655
  yield improvement 1004
Agriculture in the People's Republic of China: structural changes and technical transformation 1004
Ahn, Byung-joon 641
Ai Qing 1160, 1164
Aid, Foreign 42
Air Force, US
  Flying Tigers 1253
Aircraft production 1043
Akhtar, S. 579
Alexander, G. 525
Alitto, G. S. 351, 621
All men are brothers 1219−1220
Allen, I. 1438
Alley, Rewi 72

Almanac of China's economy 1981: with economic statistics 1949-1981 938
Almond, G. A. 706
Along alien roads: the memoirs of a soviet military advisor in China, 1938-1939 243
Alsop, J. 43
Amerasia papers: some problems in the history of US-China relations 762
American and Chinese Communists: 1927-1945, a persuading encounter 258
American and Chinese: two ways of life 1277
American Astronomy Delegation report 1042
American Cancer Delegation Report 585
American China Mission 415
American Committee on Scholarly Communication with the People's Republic of China 483
American Delegation on Early Childhood report 483
American image of China 747
American in China 112
American Institute of Aeronautics and Astronautics Delegation report 1043
American Plant Studies Delegation report 131
American policy toward Communist China: the historical record, 1949-1969 800
American Rural Health Systems Delegation report 524
American Rural Small-Scale Industry Delegation 943
American Science and modern China, 1876-1936 1038
American transplant: the Rockefeller Foundation and Peking Union Medical College 580
Americans and Chinese: purpose and fulfillment in great civilizations 1277
America's cultural experiment in China, 1942-49 1244
Americas, discovery of 526
America's response to China: an interpretive history of Sino-American relations 740
Amherst Mission 171

320

Amnesty International 616
An Daisong 770
Anaesthesia
 acupuncture 37, 301, 597
Ancestor worship 496, 498
Ancient China 135
*Ancient China: the discoveries of
 post-liberation archaeology* 145
*Ancient China: studies in early
 civilization* 142
*Ancient Chinese ceramic sculpture
 from Han through T'ang* 1313
*Ancient Chinese Jades from the
 Greenville L. Winthrop Collection
 in the Fogg Arts Museum,
 Harvard University* 1309
Ancient technology 526
*And Mao makes 5: Mao Tse-tung's
 last great battle* 326
Anderson, J. B. 1440
Andors, S. 24, 979, 1025
Anglo-Indian banking 908
Anglo-Japanese Alliance 221
Animal agriculture in China 1022
Animal husbandry 1022
*Annotated bibliography of selected
 Chinese reference works* 1414
*Annotated quotations from Chairman
 Mao* 1073
Anshan 61
Anthologies
 Chinese revolutionary literature 1112
 drama 1119
 literature 1130, 1142
 Lu Xun 1156—1157
 writings of Mao 336, 348
*Anthology of Chinese literature: from
 the fourteenth century to the
 present day* 1113
Anthropology 31, 47, 134, 143, 488
Anti-Chinese campaigns 525, 528, 536
Anti-Christian Movement 423
Anti-Confucianism 347, 658, 1151
Anti-flood projects 1019
Anti-footbinding Movement 510
Anti-imperialism 360, 423
Anti-Japanese boycott 223
Anti-Japanese War 219, 243—244,
 313, 988
Anti-Manchurianism 152
Anti-Rightist Movement 650
Anti-traditionalism 245
Anyang
 excavations 138

Aplain, G. 640
Archaeology 31, 133, 135, 141—142,
 144—148, 150, 409, 447—448
 bibliographies 1413, 1448
 Great Wall 53
 jade princes 1300
 Manch'eng tombs 151
 Mingji figurines 1313
Archaeology of ancient China 150
Archer, J. 352, 738
*Archetype and allegory in the 'Dream
 of the Red Chamber'* 1216
Architecture 99, 1302
 ancient cities 489
 Great Wall 53
 Ming tombs 140
Archives
 Hoover Institute 1357
 Library of Congress 1355
 Taiwan Bureau of Investigation 1353
Aristocracy 500
*Aristocratic families of early imperial
 China: a case study of the Po-ling
 Tsui family* 500
Arms limitation 793
*Arms of Kiangnan: modernization in
 the Chinese ordnance
 industry* 986
Armstrong, J. D. 771
Army 42, 673, 716, 718, 804
 Han 617
 officer education 561
 post Mao 674
*Army and masses in China: a Marxist
 interpretation of the Cultural
 Revolution and its aftermath* 297
Army Engineers 243
Army, Yunnan 634
Art 31, 39, 90, 96, 120, 175
 Avery Brundage Collection 1356
 bibliographies 1448
 Boston Museum of Fine Arts
 Collection 1354
 calligraphy 1278—1279, 1285, 1287,
 1289—1290
 ceramic tomb figurines 1313
 ceramics 1310—1311, 1315
 Cleveland Museum Collection 1359
 contemporary 1298
 criticism 1268
 engraved seals 1308
 folk 1297
 Freer Gallery Collection 1360
 Han motifs 447

Art *contd.*
  history 13, 409, 1271−1275, 1278,
    1284, 1299−1300
  Honolulu Academy of Arts
    Collection 1358
  jade treasures 1300, 1309
  lacquerwork 1303
  landscape gardening 1307
  landscape painting 1291, 1294−1296
  landscape scrolls 1283
  Metropolitan Museum
    Collection 1361
  Ming dynasty 1281
  painted porcelains 1292
  painting 1271, 1276, 1278−1282,
    1284, 1293, 1297−1299
  papercuts 1306
  photography 1317
  porcelain 1316
  Shanghai school 1286, 1288
  Stanford Museum Collection 1362
  Sui 204
  Tang 204
  theory 1279
  treasures 1, 75, 133, 141, 1270, 1301
  US trade 964
  watercolour painting 1286
  William Hayes Fogg Art
    Museum 1363
  William Rockhill Nelson
    Collection 1364
  woodcuts 1314
  Yuan dynasty 1280
Art and Archaeology in China 133
Art of painting on porcelain 1292
Art of war 724
*Artists and traditions: uses of the past
  in Chinese culture* 1271
Arts of China 1274
Arts of war 733
Ashley, R. K. 772
Asia
  bibliographies 1409
  Communist fifth-columnists 866
  relations with China 785, 826, 854
*Asia and the road ahead: issues for
  the major powers* 850
Asia, Central
  relations with China 56
Asia, Southeast
  Chinese immigrants 525, 531−533
  relations with China 801, 836

Asian Art Museum, Avery Brundage
  Collection 1356
Asian Home Gallery of the Asian
  Society and American Federation
  of Arts 1317
*Asian security in the 1980s: problems
  and policies for a time of
  transition* 854
Asian Survey 1373
Asian women in transition 508
*Aspects of Chinese sociolinguistics,
  essays by Yue Ren Chao* 1104
*Aspects of Sino-American relations
  since 1784* 745
*Astronomy in China: a trip report of
  the American Astronomy
  Delegation* 1042
Astronomy research and
  development 1042
Astrophysics 1050
Astrophysics research and
  development 1042
Athletics 1352
Atlas of China 65
Atlases and maps 38, 48, 64−69
  cities 487
  historical 63
  street maps 61
Attanasio, S. 526
Audio-visual materials
  bibliographies 1443
Auster, P. 226, 278, 310
Austin, P. B. 35
Australia
  Chinese immigrants 529
*Authority, participation and cultural
  change in China* 694
Autobiographies 695
  Kangxi 203
*Autocracy at work: a study of the
  Yung-cheng period,
  1723-1735* 173
Autopsy on the people's war 727
*Autumn in Spring and other
  stories* 1187
Aviation, Civil 912
Axilrod, E. 885
Ayers, J. 1305
Ayers, W. 549
Azalea mountain 1322
Aziz, S. 994

B

Ba Jin 1187—1188, 1214
Bachrack, S. D. 773
Backward toward revolution: the Chinese revolutionary party 236
Bai Hua 1126
Bailey, R. B. 1409
Baker, H. D. R. 498
Baldeschwieler, J. D. 1037
Ballad of the hidden dragon: Lu-Chih-Yuan Chu-Kung Tiao 1318
Ballets
 revolutionary 114
Balzer, R. J. 88
Ban, S. 346
Bandits 621
Bandyopadhyaya, J. 309
Bandyopadhyaya, K. 995
Bangladesh
 relations with China 818, 844
Bank of China 951
Bankers and diplomats in China, 1917-1925: the Anglo-American relationship 946
Banking 477, 921, 944—946, 948, 951
 Anglo-Indian 908
 Qian Zhuan 950
Bao plays 1323
Bao Ruo-Wang 70
Baopuzi 457
Barbarians and mandarins: thirteen centuries of western travellers in China 73
Barefoot doctors 301, 524
 acupuncture handbook 594
 manual 598
Barefoot doctor's manual: the American translation of the official Chinese paramedical manual 598
Barendsen, R. D. 550—551, 1410
Barke, W. 980
Barker, R. 886
Barnard, N. 1312
Barnds, W. J. 774
Barnes, A. C. 1232—1233
Barnett, A. Doak 270, 775—778, 793, 887, 956—957
Bartke, W. 389, 642, 779
Basic writings of Mo Tzu, Hsun Tzu, and Han Fei Tzu 464
Bastid, M. 155
Baterman, N. 1440

Battle hymn of China 513
Bauer, W. 4
Baum, R. 271, 643, 888
Bays, D. H. 152
Beal, J. Robinson 216
Bear at the gate: Chinese policy-making under Soviet pressure 812
Beattie, H. J. 467
Beeching, J. 1238
Beemer, H. L. Jr. 128, 130
Beers, B. F. 469
Beggerstaff, K. 1414
Beginning Chinese reader 1067
Behind the Great Wall: a photographic essay on China 76
Beijing 61, 75, 77, 97, 117, 161, 191, 353, 624
 Cultural Revolution 298
 history 51
 photographs 51
 politics 621
Beijing Foreign Language Institute 1091
Beijing opera 1324, 1326—1327, 1457
 character portraits 1282
Beijing street voices: the poetry and politics of China's democracy movement 663
Beijing Union Medical College 580
Belenstein, H. 617
Bell and the drum: a study of Shih Ching as formulaic poetry 1178
Bell, M. 217
Bemis, Polly 539
Bennet, G. A. 353
Bennet, L. B. 271
Bennett, E. M. 391
Bennett, G. A. 644, 944, 996
Bensky, D. 591
Benton, G. 297
Berg, A. 652
Bergere, Marie-C. 155, 226
Berling, J. A. 398
Bernal, M. 1239
Bernardo, R. M. 1026
Berninghasen, J. 1112
Bernstein, T. 486, 997
Bethelheim, C. 272
Bettelhelm, C. 981
Between tradition and modernity: Wang T'ao and reform in late Ch'ing 356

Beyond the crimson morning:
reflections from a journey
through contemporary China 106
Bianco, L. 217
Bible, Chinese translation 356
Bibliographical guide to Japanese
research on the Chinese economy
1958-1970 1427
Bibliographies 390, 1460
  archaeology 1413, 1448
  art 1448
  Asian Studies 1392, 1409
  audio-visual materials 1443
  Chinese studies 1447
  cities 1436
  Communist Party policy 1433
  Confucianism 440
  contemporary China 24
  Cultural Revolution 1449
  development strategy 1411
  Doctoral dissertations on China 1445
  drama 1457
  economic 1418, 1427
  education 554, 571, 578, 1410,
    1420−1421
  English-language Chinese
    studies 1435
  fiction 1454−1455
  folk tales 1415−1416
  foreign relations 284
  health care 579
  historical sources 1438
  history 1431
  industry 1423
  international law 604
  Japanese studies 1429
  linguistics 1453
  linguistics on computer 1450
  literature 1425
  maps 66
  music 1432
  newspapers and periodicals 1459
  novels 1456
  philosophy 1422
  poetry 1457
  political science 696
  politics 631, 1418−1419, 1440−1441
  prose 1442
  Qing government publications 1417
  reference works 1414
  research aids 1439
  Revolution of 1911 1452
  science 1039
  short stories 1456
  Sino-Soviet Conflict 1444

society 1446
sociology 495
Song dynasty 1428
technology 1039
US-China relations 1437
US scholarly sources on China 1434
writings of Mao 339, 348
Bibliography 1440
Bibliography of Asian Studies 1457
Bibliography of Chinese government
  serials, 1880-1949 1417
Bibliography of Chinese newspapers
  and periodicals in European
  Libraries 1459
Bibliography of secondary English
  language literature on
  contemporary Chinese
  politics 1441
Bibliography of studies and
  translations of modern Chinese
  literature, 1918-1942 1425
Bibliography on cities and city
  planning in China 1436
Bilancia, P. R. 599
Biographical dictionaries 390,
  393−394, 396, 1414
  authors 1458
  Ming dynasty 392
  Who's who 389, 397
Biographical dictionary of Chinese
  communism 1921-1965 393
Biographical dictionary of republican
  China, volume i-v 390
Biographies 1245
  Communist élite 395
  diplomats 391
  Lu Xun 1155, 1159
Biographies of eminent Chinese in the
  Republic of China 394
Birch, C. 1113−1114, 1222, 1247,
  1255
Birds 48
Birth control 301
Birth of landscape painting in
  China 1294
Bisson, T. A. 218
Blair, P. 1411
Blecher, M. 621, 645
Blofeld, J. 399−400, 425
Bloodworth, Dennis 618, 646
Bloodworth, Jingbing 618, 646
Bloomfield, L. P. 778
Blueshirts 636
Bo Zhuyi 1183
Boardman, R. 780

Boarman, P. M. 957
Bobrow, D. B. 781
Bodde, D. 5, 468, 600
Bodhisattva Guanyin 433
Bodhisattva of compassion: the mystical tradition of Kuan Yin 399
Bohdan, O. 958
Bollassen, J. 278
Bonavia, D. 6
Boodberg, Peter A. 1103
Book of Changes 432, 458, 466
 puzzles 444
Book of Songs 1114, 1457
Boorman, H. L. 390
Boorman, S. A. 721
Boorstin, R. O. 1412
Border conflicts 649, 881
 Manchuria 749
 Sino-Indian frontier 748, 756, 804, 813, 837, 868
 South China frontier 626
 Soviet frontier 770, 802, 806—807, 813
 Tibetan frontier 756
Borei, D. 468
Borg, D. 782
Borisov, O. B. 783
Born of the same roots: stories of modern women 1227
Borodin, Mikhail Markovich 372
Borodin: Stalin's man in China 372
Boston Museum of Fine Arts, Chinese Collection 1354
Botany 129, 131
Botjer, G. F. A. 219
Bouc, A. 310
Boundaries
 international law 611
Bourgeoisie 226, 278
Boxer Uprising 154, 162, 167, 191
Boyle, J. Hunter 739
Brachman, A. 354
Braun, Otto 248
Brecher, M. 784
Bredsdorf, J. 71
Breeze, G. 764
Brent, P. 153
Breslin, T. A. 401
Brewer, J. C. 253
Brief history of Chinese fiction 1152
Britain and East Asia, 1933-1937 767

Britain and the People's Republic of China 1949-74 780
Britain and the Sino-Japanese war 1937-39 754
British Broadcasting Corporation, China reports 1405
Broadbent, K. 889
Broken bits of old China: glimpses of China, 1912-1923 115
Broken image: essays on Chinese culture and politics 677
Broken wave: the Chinese communist peasant movement 1922-1928 1007
Bronze Age 135—138, 144, 147—148
Bronze working 1301
 Freer Collection 1304, 1312
Brown, C. 7
Brown, H. 785
Broyelle, C. 8, 507
Broyelle, J. 8
Bruer, H. 526
Brugger, B. 273—277
Brugger, W. 9, 982
Brundage, Avery
 Chinese Collection 1356
Buchanan, K. 10, 46
Buck, D. D. 619
Buck, P. 1038
Buck, Pearl 1220
Buddhism 28, 210, 399, 403, 409, 412—413, 418, 421, 424, 435, 453
 poetry 1181
Buddhism, Huayan 404
Buddhism under Mao 418
Buddhism, Zen 437
Buddhist leader in Ming China: the life and thought of Han-shan Te-ch'ing 421
Bueler, W. M. 786
Bullock, M. Brown 580
Bunge, F. M. 1240
Bunker, G. E. 220
Burchett, W. 72
Burdick, C. B. 221
Bureaucracy 485, 669, 688, 919
 Communist 8, 71, 83
 examination system 639
 Han 617
 local government 960
 origins 496
 political 651
 Tang 369

Bureaucracy of Han times 617
Burkatsky, F. 311
Burma
  relations with China 808
Burns, J. J. 581
Burns, R. D. 391
Burton, N. G. 272
Bush, R. C. 36
Bush, R. C. Jr. 402
Bush, S. 1279
Business contracts
  to trading partners 973
Business directories 962
Business interests, American 738
Business management 479
Buss, C. A. 787
Butler, D. 1252
Butler, S. 998
Butterfield, Fox 11
Buxbuam, D. C. 499
Byrd, W. 945

C

Cadres 629
Cadres, commanders and commissars:
    the training of the Chinese
    Communist leadership,
    1920-45 629
Cahill, H. A. 959
Cahill, J. 1280—1281, 1312
Call to arms 1154, 1158
Calligraphy 1110, 1264, 1278—1279,
    1285, 1287, 1289—1290, 1301
  and poetry 1147
  Daoist 442, 465
Cambodia
  Chinese aid 799
  relations with China 808
Cambridge history of China: late
    Ch'ing 1800-1911, part
    I 164—165
Cambridge history of China: Sui and
    T'ang China, 589-906 204
Camel Xiangzi 1206
Cameron, N. 73—74
Camileri, J. 788
Cancer 585
Cancer in China: the report of the
    American Cancer Delegation's
    visit to the People's Republic of
    China 585
Canton (see Guangzhou)

Cao Xueqin 1189—1190, 1215—1216
Cao Zhao 1301
Capital
  accumulation 939, 947
  consumption 939
  formation 894
  investment 895, 955
  oil investment by Japan 985
  oil investment by the US 985
Capital formation in mainland China,
    1952-1965 947
Capitalism 28
Capitalists
  Shanghai 227
Capon, E. 133, 1300
Captivity: 44 months in Red China 87
Careers 479
  incentives 697, 711
Careers in Shanghai: the social
    guidance of personal energies in a
    developing city, 1949-1966 711
Carrington Goodrich, L. 74, 140, 392
Carson, J. R. 963
Carter, Jimmy 747, 843
Carter, P. 312—313
Cartobibliographies 66
Castro, Fidel 820
Cat country: a satirical novel of China
    in the 1930s 1205
Catalogues
  Chinese-language collections in
    US 1460
Catchpole, B. 63
Catholic Church 416
  Jesuit missions 405, 414, 417
  missions 401
Cattle 1022
CCP (see Communist Party)
Cell, C. P. 647
Cement industry 943
Censorship 1366
Central Asia 102
  relations with China 56, 294
Central Intelligence Agency - CIA 61,
    67—68
Centrality and commonality: an
    exploratory essay on
    Chung-Yung 434
Century of Chinese revolution
    1851-1949 167
Ceramics 1292, 1301, 1305, 1311,
    1315—1316
  potter marks 1310
  tomb figures 1313

Chagatai 153
Chairman Hua: the new leader of the Chinese Communists 361
Chairman Mao and the Chinese Communist Party 333
Chairman Mao: education of the proletariat 314
Chairman's new clothes: Mao and the Cultural Revolution 324
Chan, G. F. 222—223
Chan, L. W. 983
Chan, M. 1161
Chan, Ming 224, 1027
Chan, S. 781
Chan, Wellington K. K. 960
Chan, Wing-tsit 1422
Chang (see Zhang)
Chang Chih-tung and educational reform in China 549
Chang Ch'un-ch'iao and Shanghai's January revolution 707
Chang Tso-lin in northeast China, 1911-1928: China, Japan, and the Manchurian idea 379
Char, Tin-yuke 527
Character indexes of modern Chinese 1106
Chaves, J. 1162—1163
Chean, Chu Don 314
Chelminski, R. 70
Chemical Engineering 1037
Chemical fertilizer industry 943
Chemical industry 989, 1056
  imported technology 1045
Chemistry 1047
  research and development 1037
Chemistry and chemical engineering in the People's Republic of China 1037
Chemotherapy 590
Chen (see also Zhen)
Chen, C. M. 1413
Chen Duxiu 238, 245, 723
Chen, J. Chester 722
Chen, Jack. 47, 307, 470, 528, 999
Chen, K. C. 789
Chen, Kenneth K. S. 403
Chen, Lili 1191
Chen, P. 1241
Chen, P. M. 601
Chen, Paul Xia 1148
Chen Pizhao 516—517
Chen Poda 345
Chen Qiyun 355
Chen Ruoxi 648

Chen Shixiang 1247
Ch'en Tu-hsiu and the Chinese communist movement 238
Chen Yi 96, 717
Chen Yi and the Jiangxi-Guangdong base area 717
Chen Yongfa 621
Chen Yuanzong 471, 1192
Chen Yun 911
Ch'en Yun's strategy for China's development: a non-Maoist alternative 911
Chennault, Claire L. 1253
Chenxia Huang 637
Chern, K. S. 225
Chesneaux, J. 154—155, 226, 278, 472
Chi-hua (see Jihua)
Ch'i: a Neo-Taoist approach to life 459
Ch'i Pai Shih 1288
Chiang Ching (see Jiang Qing)
Chiang Kai-shek (see Jiang Jieshi)
Chibelt, D. 822
Childhood in China 483
Children 483, 658
  education 565
China 2, 10
China, 1949-1976 7
China after the Cultural Revolution: politics between two congresses 652
China Aktuell 1397
China: alive in the bitter sea 11
China: all provinces and autonomous regions 60
China, American Catholicism, and the Missionary 401
China among the nations of the Pacific 785
China and Africa, 1949-1970: the foreign policy of the People's Republic of China 825
China and America: a bibliography of interactions: foreign and domestic 1437
China and America: the search for a new relationship 774
China and the foreign powers: the impact of and reaction to unequal treaties 743
China and the Great Powers: relations with the United States, the Soviet Union, and Japan 870
China and Inner Asia: from 1368 to the present day 56

China and Japan at war, 1937-1945:
    the politics of collaboration 739
China and Japan: emerging global
    powers 842
China and Japan: a new balance of
    power 811
China and Japan: past and
    present 764
China and Japan: a search for balance
    since World War I 741
China and the major powers in East
    Asia 775
China and the overseas Chinese: a
    study of Peking's changing policy,
    1949- 1970 532
China and Pakistan: diplomacy of an
    entente cordial 863
China and People's war in Thailand,
    1964-1969 833
China and Russia: the great game 795
China and the search for happiness:
    recurring themes in four thousand
    years of Chinese cultural
    history 4
China and South-east Asia since
    1945 801
China and Southeast Asia: Peking's
    relations with revolutionary
    movements 864
China and Southeast Asia: the politics
    of survival 808
China and the Taiwan issue 815
China and the three worlds 789
China and the West: comparative
    literature studies 1136
China and the West: Society and
    Culture, 1815-1937 497
China and the world food system 956
China and the world since 1949: the
    impact of independence,
    modernity and revolution 872
China: an annotated
    bibliography 1447
China: an anthropological
    perspective 143
China at the crossroads: nationalists
    and communists, 1927-1949 223
China beginner's/traveller's
    dictionary 1094
China briefing, 1980 36
China business manual, 1981 962
China Business Review 1374
China called me: my life inside the
    Chinese revolution 1241

China charts the world: Hsu Chi-yu
    and his geography of 1848 49
China city brief 61
China companion 124
China Council Report 1375
China: a country study 1240
China: day by day 88
China: development and challenge:
    proceedings of the fifth
    Leverhulme conference 915
China diary 107
China difference 45
China directory 396
China: the dream of man? 123
China enters the twentieth century:
    Chang Chih-tung and the issues
    of a new age, 1895-1905 152
China Exchange Newsletter 1376
China factor: Sino-American relations
    and the global scene 855
China: facts and figures annual.
    Volume iv 42
China Film Archives 1325
China for the West: Chinese porcelain
    & other decorative arts for
    export 1305
China from the 1911 revolution to
    liberation 226
China from Opium War to the 1911
    revolution 155
China: a general survey 39
China geographer. No. 11,
    agriculture 55
China: a geographical survey 58
China Guidebook 125
China: A Handbook 1262
China Handbuch 19
China hands: America's foreign service
    officers and what befell them 242
China historiography on the revolution
    of 1911: a critical survey and a
    selective bibliography 1452
China: a history in art 1272
China image 1264
China: the impact of the Cultural
    Revolution 274
China: the impacts of revolution 296
China in the 1920s: nationalism and
    revolution 222
China in antiquity 139
China in disintegration: the republican
    era in Chinese history,
    1912-1949 257
China in ferment: perspectives on the
    Cultural Revolution 271

China in the global community 876
China in maps, 1890-1960: a selective and annotated cartobibliography 66
China in old photographs, 1860-1910 469
China in world affairs: the foreign policy of the PRC since 1970 791
China: an index to European visual and aural materials 1443
China, India and the ruins of Washington 427
China: an interpretive history: from the beginnings to the fall of Han 182
China: an introduction 38
China, Iran, and the Persian Gulf 769
China: its history and culture 34, 111
China: the land and its people 15
China: land of charm and beauty 3
China: liberation and transformation 1942-1962 277
China lobby in American politics 753
China man 503
China: management of a revolutionary society 678
China as a model of development 907
China National Aviation Corporation 912
China notebook, 1975-1978 101
China as a nuclear power in world politics 832
China, oil, and Asia: conflict ahead 810
China: old and new 18
China on stage: an American actress in the People's Republic 114
China, Pakistan and Bangladesh 818
China passage 83
China: the People's Republic, 1949-1976 278
China: the People's Republic of China and Richard Nixon 787
China perceived: images and policies in Chinese-American relations 283
China Philately 1379
China Pictorial 1378
China policy: new priorities and alternatives 838
China policy: old problems and new challenges 776
China: a political history, 1917-1980 635
China: politics and government 692

China: the politics of revolutionary reintegration 696
China: the quality of life 72
China Quarterly 1380
China: radicalism to revisionism 1962-1979 276
China: rationalizing the domestic: theoretical approaches to the Chinese Communist world view 805
China reader, volume i, ii, iii and iv 43
China Reconstructions 658
China Reconstructs 1381
China: a resource and curriculum guide 1368
China returns 98
China revisited: after forty-two years 90
China: revolution continued 35
China scapegoat: the diplomatic ordeal of John Carter Vincent 1250
China Science Abstracts 1382
China: a second look 8
China since the Gang of Four 9, 275
China since Mao 272, 879
China, the Soviet Union and the West: strategic and political dimensions for the 1980s 857
China space report 1050
China 'spy' 121
China station, war and diplomacy, 1830-1860 169
China, the struggle for power, 1917-1972 865
China: this century 230
China to 1850 175
China today and her ancient treasures 75
China trade and US tariffs 959
China trade: export paintings, furniture, silver and other objects 964
China trade prospects and US policy 963
China: tradition and revolution 33
China under the four modernizations, part i 941
China under threat: the politics of strategy and diplomacy 807
China, the United Nations, and world order 823
China: US policy since 1945 884
China, a visual adventure 100

China-watch: toward Sino-American reconciliation 861

China: a world so changed 78

China yesterday and today 1242

Chinabound: a fifty-year memoir 285

China's African policy: a study of Tanzania 880

China's African revolution 817

China's allocation of fixed capital investment 1952-1957 955

China's changing map: national and regional development, 1949-71 57

China's changing role in the world economy 900

China's civilization and society: a source book 16

China's civilization: a survey of its history, arts, and technology 13

China's decision for rapprochement with the United States 802

China's development experience in comparative perspective 891

China's developmental experience 919

China's economic aid 779

China's economic development: growth and structural change 940

China's economic development: the interplay of scarcity and ideology 892

China's economic revolution 893

China's economy and the Maoist strategy 901

China's economy: a basic guide 904

China's economy in global perspective 887

China's energy: achievements, problems, prospects 926

China's examination hell: the civil service examinations of imperial China 639

China's fertilizer economy 1009

China's finance and trade: a policy reader 944

China's financial system: the changing role of banks 945

China's foreign aid: an instrument of Peking's foreign policy 799

China's foreign relations: new perspectives 883

China's foreign relations since 1949 826

China's Foreign Trade 1377

China's foreign trade statistics, 1864-1949 970

China's forty millions 518

China's four modernizations: the new technological revolution 888

China's future: foreign policy and economic development in the post-Mao era 935

China's global role 798

China's higher leadership in the socialist transition 715

China's hundred weeds: a study of the anti-rightist campaign in China 650

China's imperial past: an introduction to Chinese history and culture 174

China's industrial revolution: politics, planning and management, 1949 to the present 979

China's intellectual dilemma: politics and university enrollment, 1949-1978 573

China's intellectuals 665

China's intellectuals: a devise and dissent 556

China's international banking and financial system 951

China's modern economy in historical perspective 920

China's nation-building effort, 1927-1937: the financial and economic record 954

China's nationalization of foreign firms: the politics of hostage capitalism, 1949-57 929

China's new development strategy 666

China's nuclear and political strategy 804

China's oil future: a case of modest expectations 985

China's petroleum industry: output growth and export potential 992

China's policy on Africa, 1958-71 845

China's population: problems and prospects 519

China's population struggle: demographic decisions of the People's Republic 1949-1969 522

China's practice of international law: some case studies 603

China's quest for independence: policy evolution in the 1970s 659

China's Red Army marches 513

China's republican revolution: the case of Kwangtung 1895-1913 196

330

China's response to the West: a
documentary survey,
1839-1923 765
China's role in world affairs 877
China's school in flux: report by the
State Education Leaders
Delegation, US; US National
Committee on US-China
relations 565
China's Screen 1383
China's silk trade: traditional industry
in the modern world,
1842-1937 968
China's socialist revolution 279
China's sports 1352
China's trade with the West: a
political and economic
analysis 974
China's transition to industrialism:
producer goods and economic
development in the twentieth
century 989
China's turbulent quest 813
China's uninterrupted revolution: from
1840 to the present 1254
China's world: the foreign policy of a
developing state 853
Chinatowns 538, 540
Chine Antique 139
Chinese 6
Chinese agricultural economy 886
Chinese-American interactions: a
historical summary 235
Chinese Americans 536
Chinese and Americans 738
Chinese and exotic rugs 965
Chinese and the Japanese: essays in
political and cultural
interactions 750
Chinese approaches to family
planning 520
Chinese approaches to literature from
Confucius to Liang
Ch'i-chao 1135
Chinese bronze vessels in the Honolulu
Academy of Arts 1358
Chinese calculus: India and
Indochina 868
Chinese calligraphy 1289
Chinese calligraphy: an introduction to
its aesthetic and technique 1287
Chinese ceramics 1311
Chinese city between two worlds 477
Chinese civilization from the Ming
revival to Chairman Mao 156

Chinese classical prose: the eight
masters of the T'ang-Sung
period 1249
Chinese commissionship: the Ko Ku
Yao Lun: the essential criteria of
antiquities 1301
Chinese communism 1931-1934:
experience in civil
government 246
Chinese Communist materials at the
Bureau of Investigation archives,
Taiwan 1353
Chinese Communist Party in power,
1949-1976 667
Chinese Communist power and policy
in Xinjiang 1945-1977 681
Chinese communist treatment of
counter revolutionaries,
1924-1949 237
Chinese Communists: sketches and
autobiographies of the old
guards 395
Chinese cookery 1346
Chinese cooking the easy way, with
food processors 1345
Chinese cooking for the American
kitchen 1336
Chinese cooking on next to
nothing 1338
Chinese cooperative catalog 1460
Chinese Cultural Revolution 282, 305,
716
Chinese destinies 513
Chinese difference 91
Chinese domestic politics and foreign
policy in the 1970s 713
Chinese economic planning:
characteristics, objectives and
methods - an introduction 906
Chinese economic planning: translation
from Chi-hua Ching-chi 909
Chinese Economic Studies 1384
Chinese economy 890
Chinese economy: problems and
policies 921
Chinese Education 1384
Chinese education and society: a
bibliographic guide, the Cultural
Revolution and its aftermath 554,
1421
Chinese education since 1949:
academic and revolutionary
models 577
Chinese educational policy: changes
and contradictions 1949-79 563

Chinese elites: world view and
 perceptions of the US 1365
Chinese encounters 99
Chinese-English dictionary 1092
Chinese/English dictionary of China's
 rural economy 889
Chinese-English dictionary of
 Communist Chinese
 terminology 1083
Chinese-English dictionary of
 contemporary usage 1090
Chinese exclusion versus the Open
 Door policy, 1900-1906 247
Chinese experience 14
Chinese family and kinship 498
Chinese family law and social change
 in historical and comparative
 perspective 499
Chinese folk art: in American
 collections, from early 15th
 century to early 20th
 century 1297
Chinese folk narratives: a
 bibliographical guide 1416
Chinese folk tales 1195
Chinese for beginners 1068
Chinese foreign policy after the
 Cultural Revolution,
 1966-1977 860
Chinese foreign policy: the Maoist era
 and its aftermath 788
Chinese garden: history, art &
 architecture 1307
Chinese geomancy 446
Chinese gold murders, the Chinese
 lake murders 1223
Chinese herbs and therapy 584
Chinese herbs: their botany, chemistry
 and pharmacodynamics with
 special sections on mineral drugs,
 drugs of animal origin, 300
 Chinese prescriptions, toxic
 herbs 129
Chinese heritage: a new and
 provocative view of the origins of
 Chinese society 496
Chinese high command: a history of
 Communist military politics,
 1927-71 637
Chinese history and literature:
 collections of studies 1256
Chinese ideas of life and death: faith,
 myth and reason in the Han
 period 448

Chinese in America, 1820-1973, a
 chronology and fact book 530
Chinese in Indonesia: five essays 537
Chinese industrial society after
 Mao 476
Chinese jades 1309
Chinese Kung-Fu 1351
Chinese lacquer 1303
Chinese landscape painting 1291
Chinese landscape painting in the Sui
 and T'ang dynasties 1294
Chinese landscape painting, volume 2,
 the Sui and T'ang dynasties 1295
Chinese language 465
 calligraphy 1110
 character indices 1106
 Chinese-Chinese
  dictionaries 1099—1102
 Chinese-English
  dictionaries 1083—1084, 1086,
  1088—1093
 Chinese-English military
  dictionaries 1087
 Chinese-English political
  dictionaries 1085
 cursive script 1079
 English-Chinese
  dictionaries 1094—1096, 1098
 English-Chinese military
  dictionaries 1087
 English-Chinese technical
  dictionaries 1097
 flash cards for beginners 1062
 grammar 1065
 linguistic reform 1109
 linguistic studies 1103—1108, 1111
 Mandarin acoustic phonetics 1075
 Mandarin conversation textbook 1076
 particles 1082
 practice sheets for beginners 1067
 reader 1071, 1073—1074,
  1077—1078, 1081
 romanization systems 1080
 script 1103
 textbooks 1061, 1063—1064, 1066,
  1068—1070, 1072
Chinese Law and Government 1384
Chinese linguistics: a selected and
 classified bibliography 1453
Chinese literary scene: a writer's visit
 to the People's Republic of
 China 1143
Chinese literati on painting: Su Shih
 to Tung Chi-ch'ang 1279

Chinese Literature 1385
Chinese literature 19, 31, 39, 46, 368, 1138, 1194
  anthologies 1112–1113, 1119, 1130, 1142
  autobiography 695
  bibliographies 1425, 1442
  classical prose 1249
  classification 1134
  comic books 1263
  Confucian writings 355–356
  contemporary 447, 1116, 1124, 1144
  criticism 1136, 1143, 1203, 1215–1216
  Cultural Revolution 1126
  Daoist writings 400
  drama 1114, 1137, 1145, 1196, 1224, 1232, 1247, 1266, 1321–1323, 1328–1329
  fables 1150, 1152
  festivals 5
  fiction 695, 1122–1123, 1131, 1139, 1141, 1143, 1145, 1187, 1189, 1191, 1201, 1212, 1217, 1454–1455
  folk tales 1195, 1236–1237
  genres 1114, 1129
  ghost stories 1113
  historical epics 1211
  history 174–175
  Hundred Flowers Period 1133
  legends 1150, 1152
  Lu Xun 1148–1159
  May 4th Movement 1117
  narrative tradition 1255
  novels 197, 471, 1114–1115, 1121, 1137, 1140, 1188–1190, 1192–1193, 1197–1198, 1202, 1204–1207, 1209–1210, 1213–1214, 1219–1220, 1222, 1225–1226, 1228, 1230–1231, 1233–1235
  periodicals 1385
  poetry 210, 663, 695, 1113–1114, 1125, 1132, 1143, 1146–1147, 1160–1186
  political commentary 695
  religious themes 433
  short stories 1114, 1120, 1137, 1149, 1154, 1158, 1199–1200, 1208, 1218, 1227, 1229
  Six Dynasties Period 1127
  Tang 512
  theories 1128, 1135
  women 512
  World War II 1118
Chinese literature: an anthology from the earliest times to the present day 1130
Chinese literature for the 1980s: the fourth congress of writers and artists 1116
Chinese literature ii: nature poetry 1146
Chinese Literature Monthly
  index 1424
Chinese literature: popular fiction and drama 1145
Chinese local newspapers at SOAS 1426
Chinese look at literature: the literary value of Chou Tso-jen in relation to the tradition 1134
Chinese Machiavelli: 3,000 years of China statecraft 618
Chinese Maritime Customs report 970
Chinese medical modernization: policy continuity across revolutionary periods 588
Chinese menu cookbook 1333
Chinese migration and settlement in Australia 529
Chinese military system: an organizational study of the Chinese People's Liberation Army 684
Chinese mind 451
Chinese minority in Indonesia: seven papers 542
Chinese music: an annotated bibliography 1432
Chinese narrative: critical and theoretical essays 1255
Chinese novel at the turn of the century 1115
Chinese of America: from the beginning to the present 528
Chinese Opium Wars 1238
Chinese peasant economy: agricultural development in Hopei and Shantung, 1890-1949 1011
Chinese perception of the world 790
Chinese Pharmacology Delegation 581
Chinese poems 1177
Chinese poetic writing 1147
Chinese poetry: major modes and genres 1184
Chinese policy toward Indonesia 1949-1967 841

Chinese political thought in the
    twentieth century 723
Chinese politics and the Cultural
    Revolution 641
Chinese politics and the succession
    problems 661
Chinese porcelain 1305
Chinese porcelain of the 19th and 20th
    centuries 1316
Chinese: portrait of a people 37, 81
Chinese potter: a practical history of
    Chinese ceramics 1310
Chinese reader 1069
Chinese Red Army: campaigns and
    politics since 1949 649
Chinese revolutionary memoirs:
    1919-1949 1261
Chinese Revolutionary Party 236
Chinese rhyme-prose: poems in the fu
    form from the Han and Six
    Dynasties period 1182
Chinese road to socialism: economics
    of the Cultural Revolution 933
Chinese romanization self-study
    guide 1080
Chinese rural institutions and the
    question of transferability 1018
Chinese Science and Technology 1384
Chinese seals 1308
Chinese shadow 27
Chinese short story: studies in dating,
    authorship, and composition 1120
Chinese socialism to 1907 1239
Chinese Sociology and
    Anthropology 1384
Chinese Studies in History 1384
Chinese Studies in Philosophy 1384
Chinese technique: an illustrated guide
    to the fundamental techniques of
    Chinese cooking 1332
Chinese theatre in modern times: from
    1840-the present day 1326
Chinese theories of literature 1128
Chinese transformation of
    Buddhism 403
Chinese treaties: the post-revolutionary
    restoration of international law
    and order 614
Chinese vegetarian cooking 1339
Chinese vernacular fiction: the
    formative period, volume iii 1122
Chinese view of China 662
Chinese watercolors 1286

Chinese Watergate: political and
    economic conflict in China,
    1969-1977 664
Chinese way: life in the People's
    Republic of China 29
Chinese ways in warfare 180, 484
Chinese welfare system 475
Chinese worker 1029
Chinese writing: an introduction 1110
Ch'ing (see Qing)
I Ching games 444
Chinnery, J. 337
Chipp, S. A. 508
Choi, C. Y. 529
Chou (see Zhou)
Chou En-lai 352
Chou En-lai (see Zhou Enlai)
Chou: an informal biography of
    China's legendary Chou
    En-lai 381
Choudhury, G. W. 790−791
Christianity 402, 412, 455
Chronology of the People's Republic
    of China, 1949-1969 308
Chu (see Zhu)
Chu Dagao 426
Chu-hung (see Zhu Hong)
Chu Tongzu 473
Chu Yuan 1196
Chu Yuan 633
Chuang Tzu (see also Zhuan Zi)
Chuang Tzu: the inner chapters 437
Chuang Tzu: textual notes to a partial
    translation 438
Chung Ching O. 792
Chung-Kuo (see Zhongguo)
Church and China: toward
    reconciliation? 416
Churches, Christian 412
Ci 1114
Ci Hai 1099
Ci poetry 1162−1163, 1168, 1170,
    1186
CIA - Central Intelligence Agency 61,
    67−68
Cinema 1277, 1325
    periodicals 1383
Cities 487, 658, 913, 917
    ancient 489
    bibliographies 1436
    government 477
    guidebooks 124−125
    neighbourhood life 113
    Shang 147−148
    Zhou 148

City in Communist China 913
City in late imperial China 487
Civil aviation 912
Civil Service Examinations 639
Civil War 237, 249—251, 253, 255,
   313, 319, 717, 721, 738, 865,
   1244, 1261
 US involvement 761, 848
Civil war in China, the political
   struggle, 1945-1949 251
Civilization
 indigenous development 136, 150
 origins 144
Civilization of China: from the
   formative period to the coming of
   the West 183
Clan system 709
Clark, A. B. 393
Clark, C. M. 962
Clark, M. Gardner. 984
Clark, M. J. 1285
Class conflict in Chinese
   socialism 485
Class structure 83, 205, 278, 485, 710
Classic Chinese novel: a critical
   introduction 1140
Classical Chinese fiction: a guide to
   its study and appreciation, essays
   and bibliographies 1454, 1455
Clergy, Buddhist 418
Cleveland Museum of Art, Chinese
   Collection 1359
Cleveland Museum of Art -
   handbook 1359
Cleveland, Stephen 160
CLIBOC: Chinese linguistics
   bibliography on computer 1450
Climate 15, 48, 52, 61
Closing of the door: Sino-American
   relations 1936-46 768
Clough, R. N. 793—794, 1365
Clubb, O. E. 12, 795
Coal 1056
Coalitions 720
Coates, A. 427
Coble, P. M. 227
Coca-Cola Company 188
Cody-Rutter, E. 851
Cohen, A. P. 1103
Cohen, J. A. 75, 602—605, 796—797,
   963
Cohen, J. L. 75
Cohen, P. A. 356

Cohen, W. I. 228, 740
Cold mountain: 100 poems by the
   T'ang poet Han Shan 1181
Cold night: a novel by Pa Chin 1214
Coldest war: Russia's game in
   China 859
Coleman, E. J. 1268
Coleman, J. S. 706
Collaboration
 with Japan 739, 755
Collected writings of Mao Zedong 331
Collectivization 37, 511, 885, 999,
   1013
 agriculture 1021
Colleges
 entrance examinations 550
Colleges of Traditional Chinese
   Medicine of Beijing, Shanghai,
   and Nanjing 582
Collier, E. 279
Collier, J. 279
Colliti, M. 297
Columbus was Chinese: discoveries
   and inventions of the Far
   East 526
Combined Tai-chi Chuan 1350
Comic books 1263
Coming alive: China after Mao 286
Coming decline of the Chinese
   empire 294
Coming of grace 656
Comintern agents 248, 263, 372
Commentary on the Lao Tze 462
Commerce 165, 477, 658, 936, 977
 international law 611
 Qing 960
Commission on Critical Choices for
   Americans 811
Committee of One Million 773
Committee of one million 'China
   Lobby' politics, 1953-71 773
Commune: life in rural China 1012
Communes 72, 84, 91, 98, 110, 301,
   658, 996, 1012—1013
 economic enterprises 939
Communication and imperial control
   in China: evolution of the palace
   memorial system 1369
Communications 19, 42, 722, 1365,
   1367, 1370, 1372
 Qing dynasty 1369

Communications and national integration in Communist China 1367
Communism 525
  overseas Chinese 531—532
Communist China, 1949-1969: a twenty-year appraisal 303
Communist China and Latin America 1959-1967 820
Communist China's policy toward Laos: a case study, 1954-67 827
Communist conquest of Shanghai: a warning to the West 255
Communist Party 42, 217, 223, 234, 239, 249—251, 255, 258, 305, 330, 333, 345, 479, 676, 686, 716
  agricultural policy 654, 1021
  authoritarianism 297
  bibliographies 1433
  bureaucracy 8, 71, 91, 485, 651, 669, 688
  cadres 629
  Central Committee, 8th 683
  Central Committee, 11th 642
  class policy 710
  cliques 636
  discipline 702
  documents 628
  economic policy 932
  educational policy 575
  factionalism 278, 281, 289, 299, 353, 374, 628, 641, 643, 653—654, 664, 675, 687—688, 720
  history 265, 268, 290, 667, 691—692
  ideology 27, 736
  incentives policy 711
  labour policy 1028, 1030
  leadership 629, 643—644, 646, 671, 673, 693, 703, 715, 719
  official periodicals 1389
  organization 337
  origins 257, 319, 325, 723
  overseas Chinese policy 532
  planning 655
  policy towards women 511
  Politburo 363
  political strategy 268
  post Mao 674
  purges 702
  recruitment 680
  religious policy 402, 412, 416, 418, 423
  rural development policy 1010, 1014
  Second United Front 244
  Soviet advisors 248

  soviets 246, 264
  Yanan period 218, 237, 254, 256, 263, 268, 313, 319, 698
Communist Party, Soviet
  leadership 671
Communist régime 12, 22—24, 30, 37—38, 42, 45, 70, 81, 92, 172, 270, 272—276, 287, 303, 306, 308, 312, 317, 319, 719
  educational policy 555, 558—559, 563, 566, 568, 570, 573—574, 577
  foreign relations policy 781, 783, 881
  health policy 586, 589
  incentives policy 697
  local government 681, 699, 703
  minorities policy 518
  monetary policy 948
  official ideology 722
  opposition to 682
  policy documents 672
  policy evolution 659, 665
  population policy 516—517, 519—520, 522—523
  science policy 1053
Communist Revolution 7, 33, 44, 82, 104, 156, 167, 198, 217, 237—238, 242, 266, 285, 293, 300, 365, 481, 638, 647, 668, 701, 1000, 1254
  novels 378
  political theory 731
  social change 478
  women 513—514
Comparative politics: a developmental approach 706
Compass 526
Competitive comrades: career incentives and student strategies in China 697
Compilation of Chinese dictionaries 1089
Complete book of acupuncture 596
Complete stories of Lu Xun 1158
Complete works of Chuang Tzu 463
Comprador in nineteenth century China: bridge between East and West 215
Compradors 215
Comprehensive glossary of Chinese Communist terminology 1085
Comrade Chiang Ch'ing 384
Concept of man in contemporary China 452
Concise economic history of modern China, 1840-1961 908

Concise English-Chinese
    dictionary 1095
Concubines 506
Conference on Communications and
    Cultural Change 1370
*Conflict and control in late imperial
    China* 206
Confucian vision 449
Confucianism 28, 158, 199, 252, 333,
    351, 357, 388, 402, 434, 436, 449,
    453−455, 549, 601, 735, 1194,
    1249
  attitudes to 440
  origins 496
  writings 355−356, 441, 443
*Confucianism and Christianity: a
    comparative study* 455
Confucius 460
Confucius 456, 460
  attitudes to 440
  teachings 460
Confucius Campaigns 366
*Confucius: Confucian analects, the
    great learning and the doctrine of
    the mean* 443
Connally, Tom 225
*Connection: Roger S. Greene, Thomas
    W. Lamont, George E. Sokolsky
    and American-East Asian
    relations* 228
*Conquerors and Confucians: aspects of
    political change in late Yuan
    China* 158
Conroy, H. 741
Conservation 1054
Conservatism 436
*Consolidation of the South China
    frontier* 626
Constitutions 19, 627, 631
Construction industry
  imported technology 1045
Consumerism 6
Contemporary China 273, 277
Contemporary China Institute 1459
*Contemporary Chinese law: research
    problems and perspectives* 602
*Contemporary Chinese novels and
    short stories, 1949-1974: an
    annotated bibliography* 1456
Contemporary Chinese theater 1324
Contemporary law 602
*Continuing the revolution: the political
    thought of Mao* 338
Contraception 301, 516−517
Cook, D. J. 411

Cook, F. H. 404
Cookbook of famous dishes 1343
Cookery
  encyclopaedia 1340
  mandarin recipes 1335
  recipes 1332−1334, 1336−1338,
    1341−1343, 1345−1346
  recipes from the Tang period 1344
  restaurants 1335
  techniques 1332, 1334, 1337, 1339,
    1345
  vegetarian recipes 1339
Cooper, M. 405
Cooperativism 1014
Coox, A. D. 741
Copper, J. F. 798−799, 824
Cordell, A. 229
Corr, G. H. 649
Cosmology 5
Cotterell, A. 13
Cottevell, Young Yap 156
Cotton
  pest control 1023
Cotton textiles 899
Counter-revolution
  nationalist 237
Courtesan's jewel box 1229
Coye, M. J. 1242
*Cradle of the East: an inquiry into the
    indigenous origins of techniques
    and ideas of Neolithic and early
    historic China, 5,000-1,000
    BC* 136
Crafts 936
Crafts guilds 1034
Craig, A. M. 17
Credit
  pawnshops 953
Creel, Herlee G. 142, 157, 357, 428
Crespigny, R. R. C. De 15, 230
Crime 107, 490
*Crime and punishment in medieval
    Chinese drama: three judge Pao
    plays* 1323
*Crisis and conflict in Han China 104
    BC to AD 9* 186
*Crisis and prosperity in Sung
    China* 902
*Crisis of Chinese consciousness:
    radical anti-traditionalism in the
    May Fourth era* 245
Critique of Soviet economics 327
*Critiques of Confucius in
    contemporary China* 440
Croll, E. 474, 509−510

Crook, D. 1000
Crook, I. 1000
Cross, M. 76
Cross, T. 76
Crossman, C. L. 964
Crozier, B. 359
Crozier, R. C. 358
Cuba
  relations with China 820, 837
*Cult and canon: the origins and
  development of state Maoism* 328
*Cultural ecology of Chinese
  civilization: peasants and elites in
  the last of the agrarian
  states* 1017
Cultural Revolution 25, 35, 40, 43, 71,
  89, 94−95, 97−99, 121, 271,
  274, 278−282, 288−292,
  295−299, 301, 304−307, 320,
  324, 326, 328, 336−337,
  347−348, 353, 361−362, 366,
  470, 620, 641, 643, 645, 648, 650,
  653, 662, 665, 675−676, 679,
  690, 694, 707, 710−711, 716,
  725, 730, 778, 893
  bibliographies 1449
  economic planning 906, 933
  education 559, 566, 576
  literature 1126
  reading texts for language
    students 1078
  science 1041
  technology 1041
*Cultural Revolution and industrial
  organization in China: changes in
  management and the division of
  labour* 981
Cultural Revolution in China 299
*Cultural Revolution in China: an
  annotated bibliography* 1449
Culture 13, 17−18, 34, 36, 39, 65,
  103, 111−112, 143, 163, 174,
  226, 302, 421, 468, 480, 493,
  496−497
  contemporary 10, 22, 24, 27, 45, 303,
    337, 677
  Shang 138
  traditional 4, 10
*Cultures in collision: the Boxer
  rebellion* 162
Current Background 1386
*Current economic problems in
  China* 939
Cursive script
  textbook 1079

Curwen, C. A. 154
Customs
  exchange rates 970
Customs, Imperial Maritime 201

D

Da Liu 429
Da Zi Ran 1387
Daqing Oilfield 983
Dai Xiaoai 353
Daiji 1284
Daily life in People's China 84
Daily life in revolutionary China 95
Dalian 117
Daling Li 478
Dan, C. C. 723
Dance
  political communication 29
Dang Zou 621
Dao
  meaning 465
Dao De Jing 426
Dao of science 459
Daoism 28, 357, 399−400, 402, 412,
  419, 425, 428−429, 435, 442,
  453, 459, 461, 1194
  writings 426, 437−438, 463
Daoyuan 72
Dardress, J. W. 158
d'Argence, Rene-Y. L. 1356
Das, Naranarayan 650
Dastenay, A. 155
Daubler, J. 280
Daughters and sons 1231
David, Percival 1301
Davies, John Paton 242, 742
Davin, D. 511
Davis, L. 226, 278, 310
Dawn blossoms plucked at dusk 1151
Dawn wakes in the East 118
Dawson, R. 14
Day-care centres 107
Dayer, R. A. 946
Dazhai 72
Dazhai commune 110
De
  meaning 465
De Bary, B. 540
De Bary, William Theodore 430−431
De Beaufort, Simon 651
De Crespigny, R. R. C. 15, 230

De Francis, J. 1061—1062,
1073—1074
De Grazia, Sebastian 724
de Keijzer, A. J. 1368
De Pauw, J. W. 961
De-recognizing Taiwan 830
Dea Forges, R. V. 360
Dean, G. C. 1039
Death 140
 philosophy of 447—448
Death of woman Wang 1221
Debray, Regis 820
December Ninth Movement 620
Deeney, J. J. 1243
Defense 96
 government policy 1041
 naval policy 862
 policy in Asia 854
 post Mao 803
 weapons industry 986
Delahaye, H. 53
Deleyore, J. 890
Demarest, M. 100
Demieville, P. 139
*Democracy and organization in the
 Chinese industrial enterprise,
 1948-1953* 982
Democracy Movement 663
Democracy Wall 81, 286
Democratic People's Republic of
 Korea 108
Demography 6, 22, 38, 42, 46, 108,
 209, 516—523, 921
 overseas Chinese 529
Deng, S. Y. 159
Deng Siyu 1414
Deng Xiaoping 286, 326, 661, 666,
 689, 704
 fall 7
Dernberger, R. F. 891, 894, 935, 963
Destenay, A. 667
Determinism 461
Developing Nations
 Chinese aid 891, 907
 Communist fifth-columnists 866
 relations with China 789, 791,
 825—826, 849, 876, 881
*Development in the People's Republic
 of China: a selected
 bibliography* 1411
*Development of China's steel industry
 and soviet technical aid* 984
*Development of Chinese agriculture,
 1950-59* 1013

*Development of the Chinese collection
 in the Library of Congress* 1355
*Development of cotton textile
 production in China* 899
*Development of underdevelopment in
 China: a symposium* 905
*Deviance and social control in Chinese
 society* 490
Devillers, P. 315
Dewenter, K. L. 962
Dewey Experiment 552, 562
*Dewey experiment in China:
 educational reform and political
 power in the early republic* 562
Dewey, John 552
 lectures 552, 562
Dialectical materialism 323
Dian 953
Diananmen Square 286
*Dianying: electric shadow, an account
 of films and the film audience in
 China* 1325
Diary of a trip to Shu 1179
Dictionaries
 biographical 389—390, 392—394,
 396—397
 Chinese-Chinese 1099—1102
 Chinese-English 1083—1084, 1086,
 1088—1093
 Chinese-English military terms 1087
 Chinese-English political terms 1085
 Chinese particles 1082
 English-Chinese 1094—1098
 English-Chinese military terms 1087
 legal 599, 606
 political phrases 729
Dictionaries, Chinese-English
 rural economy 889
*Dictionary of Chinese law and
 government* 599
*Dictionary of the Chinese
 particles* 1082
*Dictionary of military terms,
 Chinese-English and
 English-Chinese* 1087
*Dictionary of Ming biography:
 1368-1644, two volumes* 392
Dil, Anwar S. 1104
*Dilemma in China: America's policy
 debate, 1945* 225
*Dimensions of China's foreign
 relations* 882
Dimond, G. E. 583
Ding Ling 44
Ding, Lixia Xu 1366, 1416

339

Ding, Naidong 1415—1416
Ding Wang 361, 1142
Diplomacy 116, 235, 1257
*Diplomacy and enterprises: British
    China policy: 1933-37* 744
Diplomacy, US 745
Diplomatic dispatches 234, 242, 253,
    762
Diplomats 391
Diplomats, British 946
*Diplomats in crisis: United
    States-Chinese-Japanese relations,
    1919-1941* 391
Diplomats, US 946, 1250
Directories
  business 962
  Chinese sources in Washington,
    DC 1430
  newspapers 1426
  professional societies 1412
  science institutes 1059
  trade 396
*Directory and guides to the galleries
    of the Asian Art Museum* 1356
*Directory of selected scientific
    institutions in mainland
    China* 1059
Dirlik, A. 231
*Discourse on the natural theology of
    the Chinese* 411
Discovery and Exploration
  America 526
Diseases 580
  acupuncture 596
  cancer 585
Dissent 682
*Dissent in early modern China: Ju-lin
    Wai-Shih and Ch'ing social
    criticism* 197
Dissent, Intellectual 556
*District magistrate in late imperial
    China* 208
Dittmer, L. 362
Divination 432, 444, 458, 466
  oracle bones 137
*Divine women: dragon ladies and rain
    maidens in T'ang literature* 512
Dixon, J. 475
Dobby, W. 1269
Dobson, W. A. C. H. 1082
*Doctoral dissertations on China,
    1971-75: a bibliography of studies
    in western languages* 1445
*Documents of the Chinese Communist
    Party, 1927-1930* 628

*Documents of dissent: Chinese
    political thought since Mao* 722
Dodge, E. S. 964
*Doing business with China: American
    trade opportunities in the
    1970s* 975
*Doing business with the People's
    Republic of China* 958, 977
Dolby, W. 1321
Dolezelova-Velingerova, M. 1115, 1318
Domes, J. 361, 652—654, 1001
Dong Chengsheng 1282
Dong Jichang 1279
Dong, Julia 1417
Dong, Master 1191
Dong, R. L. 476
Dong, T. K. 232
Dong, W. L. 530, 743
Donovan, P. 1353
Doolin, D. 568, 1083
Dorris, C. E. 1353
Dorwart, J. 160
Dou O Yuan 1266
Douglas, A. 432
*Dragon and eagle: United States-China
    relations, past and future* 846
Dragon Bones 137
*Dragon by the tail: American, British,
    Japanese, and Russian encounters
    with China and one another* 742
*Dragon empress: the life and times of
    Tsu-hsi Empress Dowager of
    China 1835-1908* 207
*Dragon wakes: China and the West,
    1793-1911* 171
Dragon's village 471, 1192
*Dragon's wings: the China National
    Aviation Corporation and the
    development of commercial
    aviation in China* 912
Drake, F. W. 49, 482
Drama 1114, 1137, 1145, 1196, 1224,
    1232, 1266, 1329, 1331
  20th century 1119
  anthologies 1119
  Bao plays 1323
  bibliographies 1457
  Communist 1322, 1328
  contemporary 37
  historical 1247
  history 1269, 1321, 1324
Drama, Western 292
*Drawing of an old cat and other
    stories* 1199
Dream and the destiny 229

Dream of the red chamber 1189,
    1215−1216
*Dream of the red chamber: a critical
    study* 1203
Dream of Red Mansions 1152, 1190
Drege, Jean-P. 53
Dreyer, E. L. 161
Dreyer, J. T. 518
Drugs 107
 military use 809
 mineral 129
Du Fu 1147, 1171, 1183
Du Mu 1183
Du Weiming 28, 434−435
Dual Nationality
 international law 611
Dubbridge, G. 1193
Dubois, A. M. 278
*Duel for the middle kingdom: the
    struggle between Chiang Kai-shek
    and Mao Tse-tung for control of
    China* 249
*Duel of the giants: China and Russia
    in Asia* 839
Duke, M. 1194
Dull, J. L. 473
Dulles, F. R. 800
Dunnigan, J. F. 553
Duobridge, G. 433
Durdin, T. 103
Dyer, N. A. 339
Dyiker, W. J. 162
*Dynamics of China's foreign
    relations* 797
Dynamics of Chinese politics 687
*Dynamics of factions and consensus in
    Chinese politics: a model and
    some propositions* 688
*Dynamics of revolution: a cybernetic
    theory of the dynamics of modern
    social revolution with a study of
    ideological change and
    organizational dynamics in the
    Chinese revolution* 481
Dynasties 163
 drama 1331
 Han 5, 149, 186, 355, 428, 448, 473,
    617, 1182
 history 38, 172
 Ming 56, 140, 149, 156, 161, 176,
    205−206, 208, 358, 398, 417,
    421, 424, 431, 467, 949, 1113,
    1270, 1281
 Qin 428, 448

 Qing 43, 149, 156, 159, 165, 173,
    178−179, 181, 192, 197, 203,
    205−207, 354, 356, 360, 385,
    467, 567, 749, 908, 949, 952, 960,
    966, 1113, 1115, 1152, 1270,
    1369, 1417
 Shang 137−138, 144, 147−148,
    709, 1270
 Song 149, 177, 189, 433, 902,
    1162−1163, 1167−1168, 1170,
    1180, 1249, 1290, 1299, 1428
 Sui 204, 211, 1294−1295
 Tang 135, 149, 204, 210, 369, 512,
    607, 1147, 1161, 1163, 1174,
    1176, 1181, 1183, 1185−1186,
    1249, 1270, 1294−1295
 Xia 709
 Yuan 149, 158, 161, 194, 1252, 1280,
    1299
 Zhou 144, 148, 157, 428, 709
Dynasties and treasures of China 1270

E

*Early Chiang Kai-shek: a study of his
    personality and politics:
    1887-1924* 377
*Early Chinese civilization:
    anthropological perspectives* 148
Early Chinese literature 1138
*Early Chinese revolutionaries, radical
    intellectuals in Shanghai and
    Chekiang, 1902-1911* 252
*Early Ming China: a political history,
    1355-1435* 161
*Early revolutionary activities of
    comrade Mao Tse-tung* 325
*Earthquake engineering and hazards
    reduction in China* 1044
Earthquakes 1044
*East Asia: tradition and
    transformation* 17
East is red: a simulation game 553
Eastern China dynasty 457
Eastman, L. E. 233
Eberhard, W. 163
Ebob, M. 1322
Ebon, M. 363
Ebrey, P. B. 16, 500
Ecke, G. 1358
Eckstein, A. 892−894, 963
Ecology 658
Economic Geography of China 58
*Economic growth and distribution in
    China* 910

Economic growth and employment in China 1033
Economic growth in China and India, 1952-1970: a comparative appraisal 927
Economic management in China 922
Economic organization in Chinese society 936
Economic policy 886, 939, 941, 951
Economic problems of socialism in the USSR 327
Economic reform in the PRC 931
Economic trends of China, 1912-1949 898
Economics 46
 periodicals 1388
Economy 7, 19, 23−24, 36, 39, 42, 57, 83, 112, 215, 270, 300, 303, 318, 332, 658, 672, 708, 886−887, 890−892, 904, 914, 921−923, 931, 936, 938−939, 942, 947
 balance of payments 971
 BBC reports 1405
 bibliographies 1411, 1418, 1427
 collective 885
 comparison with India 917−918, 927
 comparison with the Third World 917
 cotton textile production 899
 development theories 907, 917
 energy sector 926, 937
 growth 941, 1031, 1033
 growth rates 893, 927
 history 13−14, 21, 31, 174−175, 183, 196, 213, 226, 902, 908
 imperialist 897, 918, 920, 928
 inflation 365
 international 900
 macro-economic indicators 894
 Maoist planning 901, 910, 919, 933
 Mao's theories 932
 money supply 946, 948, 950
 overseas Chinese 527
 pawnshops 953
 periodicals 1374, 1391
 planning 906, 909, 944
 political 915, 930, 932−933
 post-Mao planning 661, 910−911, 925, 935, 945
 rebellions 898
 rural 889
 Shanghai 903
 Shen-Gan-Ning 924
 socialist planning 895, 901, 917, 934
 statistics 916
 structural change 940
 Sui 204
 Tang 204
 technology 896
 underdevelopment theories 905
Economy: a textbook 327
Edgar Snow's China 259
Education 6, 19, 22, 24, 39, 42, 90, 103, 120, 303, 555, 558−559, 562−563, 565, 568, 574, 577, 658, 691, 694, 708, 904, 921
 bibliographies 554, 571, 1410, 1420−1421
 college entrance examinations 550
 Communist cadres 629
 engineering 1049
 English language proficiency examinations 551
 history 560
 Maoist 314, 337
 mass resources 1368
 mathematics 572
 military 561
 political 643
 Qing 567
 reform 477, 549, 552, 557, 566, 570, 573, 576
 scientific 1049
 simulation games 553
 teacher recruitment 575
 theory of 452
 US-China exchanges 551, 578
 women 511
Education and popular literacy in Ch'ing China 567
Education and social change in the People's Republic of China 559
Education, Higher 578
Education in modern China 566
Education in the People's Republic of China: a selective annotated bibliography of materials published in the English language 1410
Education, Missionary 235
Education, Soviet 563
Education under Mao: class and competition in Canton schools, 1960-1980 574
Educators' source book on China: a selected list of information resources 571
Edwards, L. 1042
Edwards, R. 605, 1283

Eggleston, P. 300
Eight Chinese plays - from the 13'
century to the present 1321
Eight hundred million: the real
China 116
Eighth voyage of the dragon: a history
of China's quest for seapower 862
Eiland, M. L. 965
Elegant, R. S 281
Elementary Chinese 1070
Elementary Chinese 1069
Elementary Chinese comparison 1064
Elementary Chinese readers 1071
Eleventh Central Committee of the
Communist Party of China 642
Élites 177 – 178
  Communist 711
  discipline 702
  political 636, 676, 683, 687, 693,
    715, 1017
  rural 621
Élites in the People's Republic of
China 693
Ellman, M. 655, 895
Elvin, M. 477, 896, 905
Emergence of Maoism: Mao Tse-tung,
Ch'en Po-ta and the search for
Chinese theory 1935-1945 345
Emergence Salvation Campaign 265
Emerson, J. P. 1418
Emigration
  to Australia 529
  to Great Britain 547
  to Hawaii 527
  to Hong Kong 547
  to Indonesia 537
  to Southeast Asia 525, 531, 533
  to the US 528, 534 – 536, 538
  to Vietnam 531
  to Yunnan 531
Emigration and the Chinese lineage:
the man in Hong Kong and
London 547
Eminent Indonesian Chinese:
biographical sketches 543
Emperor of China: self-portrait of
K'ang-hsi 203
Employment 890, 904, 939, 1025,
  1031, 1033
  rural 1036
  structures 1029
Employment and economic growth in
urban China 1949-1957 1031
Encyclopedia of China today 24
Encyclopedia of Chinese cooking 1340

End of Isolationism - China's foreign
policy after Mao 878
Endicott, James G. 406
Endicott, S. 406, 744
Energy 926, 937, 1055
  minerals 1056
  periodicals 1401
Engineering 989
  education 1049
English-Chinese
  dictionaries 1094 – 1096, 1098
  military terms 1087
  technological 1097
English-Chinese dictionary of
idioms 1096
English-Chinese dictionary of
technology 1097
English-Chinese law dictionary 606
English-language teaching 71
Environment
  control structures 130
  protection 1054
Environmental protection in the
People's Republic of China 1054
Eoyang, E. Chen 1164
Episodes from the dream of the red
chamber 1074
Equality and development in the
People's Republic of China 934
Escape from predicament:
Neo-Confucianism and China's
evolving political culture 450
Esherick, J. 198, 234
Esmein, J. 282
Essays on China's legal tradition 605
Essays on Chinese civilization 468
Essays on the sources for Chinese
history 1431
Essential grammar for modern
Chinese 1065
Essentials of Chinese acupuncture 582
Ethics 451, 461
Ethnology 46
Etzold, T. H. 222, 745
Eunson, R. 364
Europe
  relations with China 860
Europe, Eastern
  relations with China 883
Europe, Western
  relations with China 883

Ever-Victorious Army 201
Every fifth child: the population of China 521
Evolution of Chinese Tz'u poetry: from late T'ang to Northern Sung 1186
Examinations
  college entrance 550
  English language proficiency 551
Excavations
  Great Wall 53
Excel in Chinese cooking 1342
Excerpts from the classical Chinese novels 1228
Exclusion Laws 528
Execution of Mayor Yin and other stories from the Great Proletarian Cultural Revolution 648
Exhibition of Archaeological Finds from China 133
Exorcisms 425
Extraterritorial system in China: final phase 262

F

Fables 1150, 1152
Face of China as seen by photographers and travellers, 1860-1912 74
Faces of China: tomorrow, today, yesterday 79
Facets of Taoism: essays in Chinese religion 419
Factional and coalition politics in China: Cultural Revolution and its aftermath 720
Factionalism 624, 627—628, 630, 632, 653—654, 664, 675—676, 687—688, 720
Factory-universities 98
Fading of the Maoist vision: city and country in China's development 917
Faience
  painting 1292
Fairbank, J. K. 17—18, 94, 164—165, 180, 235, 283—285, 407, 484, 765, 1209, 1429
Fairbank, W. 1244
Fall of imperial China 205
Fall of Shanghai 250
Families of Fengsheng: urban life in China 113

Family 1188
Family 120, 364, 473, 494, 498, 501, 503, 505—506, 658, 1214
  aristocracy 500
  father-son relations 690
  histories 502
  law 499
  women 507, 509, 511, 546
Family and kinship in Chinese society 501
Family planning 516—517, 520
Famine 198
Fan Dainian 1058
Fan, K. T. 316, 658
Fan, W. H. 658
Fanshen: a documentary of revolution in a Chinese village 1005
Far Eastern Economic Review 1388
Far Eastern politics: China, Japan, Korea, 1950-1975 1419
Far Eastern Review Yearbook 1388
Farming 469
Fashion 96
Father-son relations 690
Fauna 48
Fay, P. Ward 166
Feeney, W. R. 875
Fei Hsiao-tung: the dilemma of a Chinese intellectual 380, 564
Fei Xiaotong 134, 380, 564, 1002
Feminism 510, 514
Feminism and socialism in China 510
Fenn, C. H. 1084
Ferguson, A. 1419
Fertilizer industry 943, 1009
Fertilizers 1004, 1056
Festivals 5, 115, 1335
Festivals in classical China: New Year and other annual observances during the Han dynasty 206 BC-AD 220 5
Feudalism 144, 709, 726
Feuerwerker, A. 897—898, 905
Fiction 695, 1122, 1131, 1139, 1145, 1187, 1189, 1191, 1201, 1212, 1217
  20th century 1123, 1139, 1141, 1143
  bibliographies 1454—1455
  historical epics 1211
Field of life and death - tales of Hulan river 1226
Field of stones: a study of the art of Shen Chou 1427-1509 1283
Field, R. M. 1418

Fifty-five T'ang poems 1176
Film 1325
  criticism 1277
Finance 658, 914, 936, 944—945, 951
  government 949—950
  local 35, 621
  Ming 949
  Nationalist Government 954
  planning 906
  Qing 949
  revenue-sharing 922
  rural 1002
  US 972
Fingar, T. 659, 1420
Firearms 526
*First emperor of China: the politics of
  historiography* 184
*First revolution in China: a
  theory* 1265
Fisher, L. 77
Fitzgerald, A. 1040
Fitzgerald, C. P. 10, 78, 317, 531, 801
Fitzgerald, S. 532
Five Chinese Communist Plays 1322
*Five thousand dictionary:
  Chinese-English* 1084
*Flash cards for beginning Chinese
  reader* 1062
Fletcher, Merton D. 1028
Flood control systems 98
Flora 129, 131
*Florence Lin's Chinese regional
  cookbook* 1337
Flowers in the mirror 1228
*Flowers on an iron tree: five cities of
  China* 117
*Flowing plum and the palace lady:
  interpretations of Chinese
  poetry* 1165
Flying Tigers 1253
Fogg Art Museum, Greenville L.
  Winthrop Collection 1309
Fogg, William Hayes
  Chinese Collection 1363
Fok, P. 79
Fokkema, D. M. 80
Folk art 1297
*Folk Buddhist religion: dissenting
  sects in late traditional
  China* 413
Folk culture 5, 143, 1017
Folk medicine 129
Folk religion 402, 413

Folk songs 1371
Folk tales 633, 1195, 1218,
  1236—1237
  bibliographies 1415—1416
Fontein, J. 1354
Food 148—149
  prices 301
  world system 956
*Food for one billion: China's
  agriculture since 1949* 1021
*Food in Chinese culture:
  anthropological and historical
  perspectives* 149
Foreign aid 42, 804, 954
  from the US 963
  from the USSR 984
  to Africa 799, 817
  to Cambodia 799
  to medical groups 779
  to North Korea 799
  to North Vietnam 799
  to Pakistan 779, 799
  to Tanzania 779
  to textile mills 779
  to the Third World 891, 907
*Foreign establishment in China in the
  early twentieth century* 897
*Foreign intervention and China's
  economic development,
  1870-1911* 928
Foreign policy (see Foreign relations,
  specific countries)
Foreign relations 7, 19, 22—23, 36,
  96, 103, 163, 165, 226, 299, 303,
  337, 341, 659, 673, 813, 872
  anti-super power hegemony 789
  Chinese world view 790, 805, 877
  continuity 746
  defense policy 1041
  energy policy 937
  evolutionary diplomacy 789
  formulation of Communist
    policy 781, 788, 853, 881
  global role 797—798, 876
  international economic policy 900
  international law 608—609, 611—615
  militarism 640
  naval power 862
  nuclear weapons 793, 832
  periodicals 1403
  post Mao 661, 670, 878—879
  post Mao defense policy 803
  Qing 178, 181
  Sui 204

Foreign relations *contd.*
Tang 204
United Front doctrine 771
with Africa 817, 825, 845, 866
with Asia 56, 785, 826, 854, 866
with Bangladesh 818, 844
with Burma 808
with Cambodia 808
with Central Asia 294
with China 831, 834
with Cuba 820, 837
with Eastern Europe 883
with Europe 860
with France 883
with Great Britain 166, 169, 171,
    742, 744, 748, 756, 767, 780
with India 756, 832, 837, 844, 850,
    1259
with Indonesia 841, 850, 873
with Iran 769
with Israel 784
with Japan 379, 391, 739, 741−742,
    750, 752, 754−755, 757, 764,
    775, 811, 822, 828, 832, 842, 850,
    870−871, 882−883
with Korea 807, 821, 858, 868, 883
with Laos 827
with Latin America 820, 866, 882
with Malaysia 873
with the Middle East 852, 860, 882
with Nepal 882
with North Korea 792
with Pakistan 818, 863
with the Philippines 810
with Singapore 873
with South Korea 810
with Southeast Asia 785, 801, 836,
    864, 1257
with Taiwan 704, 713, 794, 796, 807,
    810, 816, 819, 821, 824, 830, 861,
    871
with Tanzania 880
with Thailand 808, 833, 873
with the Third World 789, 791,
    825−826, 849, 876, 881

with the US 6, 91, 102−103, 216,
    225, 234−235, 240, 247,
    283−285, 308, 311, 313, 359,
    375, 391, 670, 672, 704, 708, 713,
    738, 740, 742, 745, 747, 749, 751,
    753, 760−762, 768, 772−773,
    775−778, 782, 786−789, 791,
    793−794, 796, 800, 802, 815,
    821, 824, 830, 832, 835, 838, 840,
    843, 846, 848, 850−851,
    854−856, 858, 860−861, 870,
    874−875, 881−884, 887, 1365
with the USSR 6, 102, 108, 243,
    294, 311, 320, 372, 670, 687, 704,
    742−743, 758−759, 770, 772,
    775, 783, 791−792, 795, 802,
    806−807, 812−814, 816, 820,
    826, 829, 832, 837, 839, 844, 850,
    856−857, 860, 865, 868−870,
    881−883
with Vietnam 807, 1259
with Western Europe 883
with the Western powers 43, 159,
    201−202, 222, 743, 765, 847, 908
World War II 254
Foreign Relations Committee, US
    Senate 225
*Foreign relations of the People's
    Republic of China* 881
*Foreign trade of China: policy, law,
    and practice* 976
Foreign trade of mainland China 971
Forestry 55
*Forgotten ambassador: the reports of
    John Leighton Stuart,
    1946-1949* 253
Forman, B. 1286
Forman, S. 809
Fortress besieged 1202
Foster, J. R. 21
Four Modernizations 559, 687, 888,
    941
Four seasons of T'ang poetry 1183
France
    relations with China 883
Franco-Chinese War 171
Franke, W. 19, 167
Frankel, H. H. 1165
Fraser, J. 81
Fraser, S. E. 554
Fraser, Steward S. 1421
Free will 461
Freedman, M. 408, 488, 501
Freedom is a world 85
Freer Chinese bronzes, volume I 1312

Freer Chinese bronzes, volume II, technical studies 1304
Freer Gallery, Chinese bronzes 1304, 1312
Freer Gallery of Art, I China 1360
Freer Gallery of Art, Chinese Collection 1360
French literature
 on China 378
Friedman, E. 236
Frolic, B. M. 20, 32
From Canton to California: the epic of Chinese immigration 534
From muskets to missiles: politics and professionalism in the Chinese army, 1945-1981 561
From the other side of the river: a portrait of China today 658
Frontier defense and the open door: Manchuria in Chinese-American relations, 1895-1911 749
Fryer, J. 50
Fu, Charles Weixun 1422
Fu, Marilyn 1284 — 1285
Fu poetry 1182
Fu, Shen 1284 — 1285
Fu verse 1319
Fujian Province 679
Fulbright, J. W. 785
Fumei Zhang Chen 605
Fundamentals of the Chinese Communist Party 686
Fundamentals of political economy 930
Funerals 115
Fung, E. 660
Fung, K. K. 909, 939
Furth, C. 436
Fusang: the Chinese who built America 541
Future of China: after Mao 704
Future of the China market: prospect for Sino-American trade 972
Future of Taiwan: a difference of opinion 831

G

Gaan, M. 82, 365
Galbraith, J. K. 83
Galston, A. W. 84
Gamberg, R. 555
Games
 Yi Jing puzzles 444

Gandhi, Mohandas Karamchand 309
Gang and 900 million: a China diary 1259
Gang of Four 99, 101, 275, 326, 328, 685, 708, 713
 arrest 9
 trial 661, 692
Gang Zhao 899, 947, 1003
Ganiere, N. 1423
Gansu Normal University 1100
Gao E 1190
Gao Gang 265, 277
Gao, Michael Y. M. 366
Gao Ming 1329
Gao Shi 1161
Gao Zhi 1113
Gardens 1307
Gardner, J. 661
Garner, Harry 1303, 1311
Garside, E. 124
Garside, R. 286
Garth, B. G. 900
Garver, J. W. 802
Gas 810, 1056
Gascoigne, Bamber 1270
Gate of heavenly peace: the Chinese and their revolution, 1895-1980 44
Gau, M. Y. M. 789
Ge Hong 457
Ge Ku Yao Lun 1301
Geelan, P. J. M. 64
Gelber, H. G. 1041
Gelber, H. O. 803
Gemet, J. 21
Gen Ling 478
Genealogy 364, 498
General Gordon (see Gordon)
General Stilwell in China, 1942-1944: the full story 375
Genetics
 rice 132
 vegetables 130
 wheat 128
Genghis Khan 153
Genghis Khan 153, 373
Genius of China 146
Gentry 189, 269, 457
Gentzler, J. M. 31
Geography 19, 22, 24, 39, 46 — 49, 52, 54 — 57, 59 — 60, 209
 Great Wall 50, 53
Geography, Historical 65

Geography of China 58
Geology 15, 46
  earthquakes 1044
  soils 15
  vegetation 48
Geomancy 140, 446
Geomorphology 52
Gettens, J. 1304
Gettens, R. J. 1312
Ghosh, S. K. 804
Gibbs, D. A. 1424−1425
Ginneken, J. Van 367
Ginsburg, J. H. 805
Ginsburgs, G. 806
Gittings, J. 662, 746
*Glossary of Chinese political
    phrases* 729
Goats 1022
God, Chinese concept of 411
Godwin, P. 568
Gold Rush
  Chinese immigrants 534, 539
Goldberg, L. 1042
Goldblatt, H. 368, 1116, 1142, 1199,
    1226
*Golden age of Chinese drama: Yuan
    Tsa-chu* 1331
Golden Horde 153
*Golden peaches of Samarkand: a
    study of T'ang exotics* 1344
Golden road 1198
Goldman, M. 556, 665, 1117
Gongen, Henry Henne O. B. 1108
Gongfu 1351
Gongzhuan Xiao 168
Goodman, D. 652, 663
Goodman, D. S. G. 1426
Goodstadt, L. 318, 664
Gordon, Charles 159, 201
Gordon, E. 85
Gordon, L. H. D. 1445
Gou, Leslie T. C. 1004
Government 356, 452
  Communist 103
  soviets 246
*Government and politics in
    Kuomintang China
    1927-1937* 636
*Government and politics of China,
    1912-1949* 631
*Government and politics of the
    People's Republic of China* 708
*Government control of the press in
    modern China, 1900-1949* 1366

Graham, A. C. 437−438
Graham, G. S. 169
Grain
  pest control 1023
Grammar
  Chinese language 1065
*Grand titration: science and society in
    East and West* 1046
Granet, M. 408
Grant, C. 206
Grant, John B. 580
Gray, D. W. S. 1443
Gray, J. 666
Grayson, B. L. 747
Great Britain
  Chinese immigrants 547
  nationalization of Shanghai firms 929
  relations with China 166, 169, 171,
    742, 744, 748, 756, 767, 780
Great Leap Forward 320, 641, 893,
    906
*Great road, the life and times of Chu
    Teh* 698
Great Wall 53
Great Wall 526
  history 50, 53
Great Wall of China 50
Green, J. J. 508
Green, M. 957
Greenblatt, S. L. 479–480, 490–492,
    502, 734
Greene, F. 51
Greene, R. Altman 86
Greene, Roger S. 228
Greer, C. 52
Gresham, Walter 160
Grey, J. 1043
Grieder, J. B. 170, 439, 557, 1245
Griffin, F. K. 905
Griffin, P. E. 237
Griffith, S. B. 733
Gross National Product 894, 920
Grousset, R. 409
Guan Hanqing 1266
Guan Yin 399
Guandong 505
Guangli People's Commune 1012
Guangliang Xu 554
Guangtong 196
Guangxi clique 624
Guangzhou 61, 75, 222, 241, 353, 569,
    624
Guangzhou Fair 405

Guerrilla economy: the development of the Shensi-Kansu-Ninghsia border region, 1937-1945 924
Guevara, Ernesto 820
Guichi, Tanaka 757
Guide to Chinese philosophy 1422
Guide to Chinese poetry and drama 1409
Guide to Chinese prose 1442
Guide to the Hoover Institution archives 1357
Guide to the Metropolitan Museum of Art 1361
Guidebooks 1, 124—127
  to Chinese trade 978
Guilin 61
  photographs 62
Guillermaz, J. 667
Guisso, W. L. 369
Gunder, A. 905
Gungwu, W. 1431
Gunming 61
Gunn, E. 1118—1119
Guo, I. 1334
Guo, L. 1195
Guo Moruo 1196
Guo Muruo 382
Guo, T. C. 238
Guo, W. 1085
Guo, Y. 1195
Guomindang 82, 167, 219—220, 222—223, 227, 232—233, 237, 249—251, 257, 260, 262, 365, 372, 376—377, 423, 622, 624, 628, 636, 717, 721, 1244
  Northern Expedition 241
Gupta, K. 748
Gurley, J. G. 901
Gurtov, M. 807—808

H

Habits neufs du President Mao 324
Haeger, J. W. 902
Hai Jui dismissal from office 1224
Half the world: the history and culture of China and Japan 302
Hall, W. P. J. 1427
Halperin, M. H. 793
Hamburger, G. 809
Hammond, E. 656—657
Han dynasty 355
  army 617
  bureaucracy 617
  festivals 5
  food 149
  local government 617
  philosophy 428, 448
  poetry 1182
  politics 186
  society 473
Han Fei Zi 464
Han Ji 355
Han Ran 91
Han rhapsody: a study of the fu of Yang Hsiung 153 BC-AD 18 1319
Han Shan 1181
Han social structure 473
Han Suyin 280, 319—320, 668, 1197
Han Yu 1173, 1183
Hanan, P. 1120
Handbook of Chinese ceramic 1315
Handbook on Chinese language structure 1108
Hangzhou 61, 80, 117
Hannay, A. 453
Hansen, Lars J. 1108
Hanshan Deqing 421
Hansheng Zhuan 966
Hanyu Chengyu Cidian 1100
Hao Ran 1198
Happiness, persuit of 4
Harbert, M. A. 87
Harding, H. 299, 669
Hardy, R. W. 985
Harford, J. J. 1050
Harris, N. 287
Harris, P. 670
Harrison, J. P. 239
Harrison, S. E. 294
Harrison, S. S. 810
Harry Truman's China policy: McCarthyism and the diplomacy of hysteria, 1947-51 848
Hart, T. G. 481
Hasegawa, Tsuyoshi 458
Hawaii
  Chinese immigrants 503, 527
Hawkes, D. 1189
Hawkins, J. 558—559
Hay, J. 135
Hayden, G. A. 1323
Hayes, M. V. 838
He Bingdi 136
He Qifang 1172

He Zhiyou 1074
Health care 24, 39, 42, 72, 84, 113,
    516—517, 521, 524, 580, 583,
    589—590, 592—593, 891, 921,
    1018, 1055
  acupuncture 582—583, 590—591,
    594, 596—598
  barefoot doctors 301, 598
  bibliography 579
  cancer treatment 585
  modernization 586, 588
  rural 595
  women 511
*Health care in the People's Republic
    of China: bibliography with
    abstract* 579
Health of China 592
*Health policies and services in China,
    1974* 589
*Heathen Chinese: a study of American
    attitudes toward China,
    1890-1905* 187
*Heaven, earth and man in the book of
    changes: seven Eranos
    lectures* 466
*Heaven my blanket, earth my pillow:
    poems from the Sung
    dynasty* 1162
Heihues, M. F. Somers 533
Heiliger, W. S. 671
Heinnichs, W. 782
*Heirs apparent: what happens when
    Mao dies?* 646
Hellmann, D. C. 811
Hemenway, R. V. 482
Henderson, J. 565
Henderson, W. 303
Hengyan Xu 584
Henxiang Yuan 1136
Heoxter, C. K. 534
Herbal medicine 583—584, 598
Herbs 129
Hermitages
  Daoist 400, 425
*Heroes and villains in Communist
    China: the contemporary Chinese
    novel as a reflection of life* 1121
Hervouet, Y. 1428
Hibbert, C. 171
*Hidden history of the Sino-Indian
    frontier* 748
*Higher education and research in the
    People's Republic of China:
    institutional profiles* 1420

*Hills beyond a river: Chinese painting
    of the Yuan dynasty,
    1327-1368* 1280
Hiniker, P. J. 725
Hinton, H. C. 22, 672—673, 812—814
Hinton, W. 288—289, 1005—1006
Historical atlas 64
  20th century 63
Historical Geography 65
Historical monuments 1
*Historical relics unearthed in new
    China* 151
Historiography 26, 209, 224, 370
  Marxist 231
  Revolution of 1911 1452
*Historiography of the Chinese labor
    movement* 224, 1027
History 34, 39, 46—47, 72, 75, 78,
    111, 145, 182, 209, 302, 1242,
    1258
  6th century 204
  7th century 204, 409
  8th century 204
  17th century 202
  18th century 202
  19th century 152, 154—155,
    163—165, 175, 188, 202, 214
  20th century 152, 164—165, 188,
    202
  art 1271—1275, 1278, 1284, 1300
  Beijing 51
  bibliographies 1431, 1438
  Communist Party 268
  drama 1269, 1321, 1324
  economic 13—14, 21, 31, 174—175,
    183, 196, 213, 226, 902, 908
  educational 560
  epics 1211
  family histories 502
  Great Wall 50, 53
  intellectual 4, 21, 41, 44, 165, 170,
    174, 199, 204, 213, 351,
    355—356, 370, 380, 382, 388,
    424, 440, 552, 556—557, 564
  literature 1129, 1135
  maps 63
  military 180, 201, 484, 632, 637
  political 10, 13—14, 29, 31, 33, 38,
    43, 161, 172, 174—175, 183, 185,
    196, 205, 213, 226, 273, 364,
    618—619, 621, 625, 630—632,
    635, 638—639, 691—692, 696
politics 184, 662, 673
primary sources 16
religious 21

research guides 1451
science 190
simulation games 553
social 13—14, 16—19, 21—22, 26,
    33, 44, 174—175, 196, 205, 226,
    364, 477
technological 13, 21
theatre 1326—1327
History and will: philosophical
    perspectives of Mao Tse-tung's
    thought 304
History of China 163
History of Chinese civilization 21
History of the Chinese Cultural
    Revolution 280
History of Chinese drama 1269
History of Chinese political thought,
    volume i: from the beginning to
    the sixth century AD 735
History of imperial China, a research
    guide 1451
History of modern Chinese
    fiction 1139
Hixson, S. 1089
Ho (see He)
Ho Wan-Yee 729
Hofbreing, R. Jr. 1007
Hoffman, C. 1029—1030
Hojzlar, J. 1286
Hok-lam Chan 370
Holzman, D. 1166
Hom, Kem 1332
Home base of American China
    missions, 1880-1920 415
Homo erectus 135, 144
Hong Kong
  Chinese immigrants 547
  overseas Chinese 546
  women 546
Hong, William S. H. 606
Hong Xian porcelains 1316
Hongda Qiu 815
Hongqi 1389
Honolulu Academy of Arts, Chinese
    Collection 1358
Hookham, H. 172
Hoover Institution archives 1357
Hopei
  rural development 1011
Horses 1022
Horticulture 84
Hotchkis, A. M. 1293
Hou, F. W. 290
Hou-Han-Shu 5

How to approach the China
    market 978
How to consult the I Ching: the oracle
    of change 432
Howard, D. 1305
Howard, R. 321, 1324
Howe, C. 903—904, 1031—1032
Howe, F. 513
Howie, J. Marshal 1075
Hsi-liang (see also Xiliang)
Hsi-liang and the Chinese nationalist
    revolution 360
Hsi yu Chi 1193
Hsia Hung (see Xiao Hong)
Hsiang-Ya journal 86
Hsiao Hung 368
Hsin-lun and other writings by Huan
    T'an 1217
Hsu (see Xu)
Hsun Tzu (see Zun Zi)
Hsun Yueh: the life and reflections of
    an early medieval Confucian 355
Hu Jieqing 1206
Hu Shi 245, 439, 723, 1245
Hu Shih and the Chinese renaissance:
    liberalism in the Chinese
    revolution, 1917-1937 439, 1245
Hu Shiming 560
Hu Shuzhao 1355
Hua Guofeng 286, 666, 704
  career 361
Hua-yen Buddhism: the jewel net of
    India 404
Huaben 1131
Huadong commune 996
Huadong: the story of a Chinese
    people's commune 996
Huaibei 193
Huan Tan 1217
Huang Bei 173
Huang, Broong-Moo 807
Huang, C. C. 1224
Huang Hua 620
Huang, J. C. 1121
Huang Jieshan 494
Huang, P. C. C. 371, 905
Huang, Parker Bofei 1063
Huang, R. 949
Huang Xiao, Katherine 948
Huang Yongyu 1264
Huang Zhunming 1199
Huayan Buddhism 404
Huber, L. G. F. 1309

Hucker, C. O. 174—176
Hulcrants, G. 906
Human nature
  philosophy of 447, 461
Human resources 904
Human rights 45, 286
Human Rights Movement 723
Humanism, Confucian 436
Humphrey, T. 816
Hunan
  labour movement 1034
  rural development 1010
Hunan labour Movement 325
*Hundred day war: the Cultural
    Revolution at Tsinghua
    University* 288
Hundred Flowers Period 380
  literature 1133
Hunt, M. E. 749
Hurley, Patrick 225
Hurricane 1235
Hush, J. 1333
Hutchinson, A. 817
Huter, T. 1112
Hutton, B. 1358
Hyatt, I. T. Jr. 410
Hynes, M. 89

I

I-Ching (see Yi Qing)
Ichiko, Chuzo 1429
*Idea of China: myth and theory in
    geographic thought* 54
Idema, W. L. 1122
Ideology 725, 804
  anti-traditionalism 245
  Buddhist 404
  Confucianism 436
  economic 327
  educational 314
  Maoist 81, 287, 290, 303—304,
    310—311, 314, 322—323, 332,
    336—338, 340, 342, 345—347
  Marxist 280
  nationalist 236
  political 27, 54, 81, 158, 200, 309,
    672—673, 722, 725, 728, 732,
    736, 1348
  radical 306
*Ideology and culture: an introduction
    to the dialectic of contemporary
    Chinese politics* 732
*Ideology and politics in contemporary
    China* 728

*Ideology and practice: the evolution of
    Chinese Communism* 736
Ilkan 153
*Illustrated history of the Chinese in
    America* 538
Images of Asia 751
Imfeld, A. 907
Immigrants, Chinese
  to the US 247
Immigrants, Japanese
  to the US 247
*Imperial China: photography
    1850-1912* 1317
Imperial guard 194
Imperial law 600, 605
  Tang code 607
Imperial Maritime Customs 201
Imperial Ming tombs 140
Imperialism 152, 726
Imperialism and Chinese politics 726
Imperialism, Foreign 920, 928
Imperialism, US 410
Imperialism, Western 897, 918, 920,
    928
In the eye of the typhoon 94, 1209
In the footsteps of the Buddha 409
In the People's Republic 109
*In the People's Republic: an
    American's firsthand view of
    living and working in China* 110
Incentives system 1026, 1029—1030,
    1032
Incomes 891, 895, 904, 910, 920, 923,
    939, 1013
  socialist planning 655
*Index to Chinese archaeological works
    published in the People's
    Republic of China,
    1949-1965* 1413
*Index volume, beginning, intermediate,
    and advanced texts in spoken and
    written Chinese* 1061
India 309, 332, 404, 409, 427
  agricultural system 995
  banking in China 908
  border conflicts 748, 756, 804, 837
  development theories 917—918
  economy 927
  Red Army campaigns 649
  relations with China 756, 832, 844,
    850, 868, 1259

India, Russia, China and Bangladesh 844
India's China war 837
Individual and state in ancient China 456
Indochina War
  China's participation 868
Indonesia
  Chinese immigrants 537, 542–545
  relations with China 841, 850, 873
Industry 15, 22, 24, 84, 90, 96, 110, 120, 215, 290, 476, 658, 691, 890, 894, 910, 921, 927–928, 936, 941, 958
  bibliographies 1423
  chemical 989
  engineering 989
  fertilizer 1009
  growth 989
  iron 1056
  machine building 993
  management 694, 979, 981–982
  minerals 991, 1056
  Nationalist Government programme 988
  oil 980, 983, 985, 987, 992
  rural 943, 990
  state control 904, 982
  steel 91, 984, 1056
  steelmills 37
  technology 891
  weapons 986
Inflation 82, 365, 941
Information systems 906
Injustice to Tou O: a study and translation 1266
Inscriptions
  oracle bones 137
Insect control in the People's Republic of China 1023
Inside China 96, 122
Inside the Cultural Revolution 307
Inside Mao Tse-tung thought 346
Institutions 19, 31, 42, 120
  ancient 496
  economic 906, 940
  educational 479, 578
  Guomindang 636
  Han 186
  Jiangxi Soviet 264
  kinship 177
  local 189, 208
  medical 588
  military 194
  Ming 176

  political 625
  Qing 173, 212
  reform 700
  rural 1018
  scientific 1059
  social 886
  Song 189
  Sui 204
  Tang 204, 210
  urban 487
  Zhou 157
Instruments and future 1390
Intellectual history 4, 21, 41, 44, 165, 174, 199, 204, 213, 351, 355–356, 370, 380, 382, 388, 424, 440, 552, 556–557, 564
Intellectuals 116, 170, 178, 186, 189, 236, 245, 252, 305, 325, 658, 716
  political role 665
Intellectuals and the state in modern China 557
Intellectuals and the state in modern China, a narrative history 170
Interlingual critic: interpreting Chinese poetry 1169
Intermediate reader for modern Chinese 1077
Internal politics of China, 1949-1972 653
International energy relations of China 937
International law 603, 608
  bibliographies 604
  boundaries 611
  commerce 611
  dual nationality 611
  space 608
  trade 609
  treaties 611–615
International Military Tribunals for East Asia 754
International Rice Research Institute report 132, 1024
International Science Abstracts 1419
Introduction of socialism into China 445
Introduction to Chinese civilization 31
Introduction to Chinese cursive script 1079
Introduction to Chinese history: from ancient times to 1912 209
Introduction to Chinese literature 1129
Introduction to Chinese politics 673

Introduction to education in the People's Republic of China and US-China educational exchange 578
Inventions 526
Investment 895, 914, 929, 944—945, 947, 951, 955
  agriculture 1021
  local 35
  oil industry 985
  socialist planning 655
Invitation to Chinese philosophy: eight studies 453
Iran
  relations with China 769
Iriye, Akira 750
Iron Age 135—136
Iron industry 1056
Iron oxen: a documentary of revolution in Chinese farming 1006
Irrigation 1019
Isaacs, H. R. 751
Island China 794
Israel
  relations with China 784
Israel, J. 240, 620
Israel, the Korean War and China: images, decisions and consequences 784
Issues in Japan's China policy 871

J

Jackson, J. H. 1219
Jacobs, D. N. 372
Jade burial suits 151
Jade treasures 1300—1301, 1309
Jain, J. P. 674
Jain, R. K. 818
James G. Endicott: rebel out of China 406
James, J. M. 1204
Jamieson, J. C. 1064
Jansen, M. B. 752
Japan
  culture 17, 302
  history 302
  kinship 501
  occupation of China 220—221, 263, 354, 739, 755
  occupation of Manchuria 766
  relations with China 379, 391, 741—742, 750, 752, 754, 757, 764, 775, 811, 822, 828, 832, 842, 850, 870—871, 882—883
  use of drugs as weapons 809
Japan and China: from war to peace 1894-1972 752
Japan-China phenomenon 822
Japan-China relations
  oil investment 985
Japan-China Trade Handbook 978
Japan External Trade Organization 978
Japan faces China 828
Japanese army in north China, 1937-1941: problems of political and economic control 755
Japanese siege of Tsingtau 221
Japanese studies of modern China since 1953 1429
Java
  Chinese immigrants 544
Jencks, H. W. 561
Jenner, W. F. 1201
Jenner, W. J. F. 1246
Jennings, P. C. 1044
Jesuits 405, 414, 417
JETRO China Newsletter 1391
Jews 414
Jian Zhongshu 1202
Jiang, Cecilia Sunyun 1335
Jiang Feng 1306
Jiang, Gregory Guige 1109
Jiang Jieshi 92, 219, 227, 232, 249—250, 263, 352, 359, 375, 386, 721, 723
  foreign relations policy 782
  personality 377
  Sian Incident 267
  US assassination plans 761
  US support 753
Jiang Kui 1168
Jiang Qing 114, 274, 363, 685, 713, 720
  early life 384
Jiang Ye 90
Jiang Yi 1287
Jiang Zilong 1126
Jiangxi Soviet 237, 264, 623
Jie Xiong, James 322, 325
Jihua Jingji 909
Jin, Steven S. K. 323
Jing, F. 103
Jo Yung-Hwan 819
Johnson, C. 727—728, 820

Johnson, D. G. 177
Johnson, E. 1008
Johnson, G. 1008
Johnson, K. A. 508
Johnson, V. A. 128
Johnson, W. 607
Jones, M. 291
Jones, Susan Mann 621
Jordan, D. A. 241
Journal of Asian Studies 1392
Journey between two Chinas 119
Journey to the sun: folk tales from China 1236
Journey to the West 1230
Juan Ch'i (see Ruan Ji)
Junior English-Chinese dictionary 1098

K

Kahn, E. J. 242
Kaifeng
  Jewish community 414
Kala-azar 580
Kalicki, J. H. 821
Kallgren, J. K. 23
Kalyagin, A. Ia. 243
Kamachi, Noriko 1429
K'ang-hsi (see also Kangxi)
K'ang-hsi and the consolidation of Ch'ing rule, 1661-1684 178
Kang Youwei 44, 168
Kangxi, Qing Emperor 178, 192, 203, 212
Kao (see Gao)
Kao Shih 1161
Kaplan, F. 24, 125
Kaplan, H. S. 585
Karnow, S. 25
Karol, K. S. 291
Karst in China 62
Kataoka, Tetsuya 244
Kato, Shuichi 822
Kauz, H. 1347
Keenan, B. 562
Keightly, D. N. 137
Keijzer, A. de 125
Kelly, J. 1202
Kennedy, T. L. 986
Kessen, W. 483
Kessle, G. 35
Kessler, L. D. 178
Keswick, M. 1307
Key to Chinese cooking 1334

Keys, J. D. 129
Khan, H. L. 179
Khan, J. H. 793
Khubilai Khan 153, 1267
Kiangsi (see Jiangxi)
Kiangsi Soviet Republic: Mao and the National Congress of 1931 and 1934 264
Kierman, F. A. 139, 180, 484
Kim, Hong N. 1430
Kim Il-Soong
  interviews 108
Kim, Ilpyong J. 623
Kim, S. S. 823, 876
Kinderman, K. S. 94, 1209
King, C. 373
King, F. H. H. 908
Kingston, Maxine H. 503
Kinship 177, 473, 488, 493, 498, 501, 1002
Kintner, W. R. 824
Klein, D. W. 393
Knechtges, D. R. 1319
Knoerle, J. 1203
Ko Hung (see Ge Hong)
Koen, R. I. 753
Kolatch, J. 1348
Koloskov, B. T. 783
Kong Shan drama 1247
Kong Shangren 1247
Korea
  culture 17
  Red Army campaigns 649
  relations with China 821, 858, 868, 883
Korea, Democratic People's Republic 108
Korea, North
  Chinese aid 799
  relations with China 792
Korea, South
  relations with China 810
Korean War 738, 784, 807
Kouwie, Kan 440
Koxinga (see also Zheng Chenggong)
Koxinga and Chinese nationalism: history, myth and the hero 358
Kraar, L. 43
Kraft, J. 91
Kratochril, P. 1149
Kraus, R. A. 966
Kraus, R. C. 485
Krigen, J. A. 781

Ku Chieh-kang and China's new
    history: nationalism and the quest
    for alternative tradition 199
Kuala Lumpur riots 525
Kuan (see Guan)
Kuangqing Liu 165
Kubek, A. 255
Kubilai Khan 1267
Kuei-lin (see Guilin)
Kuhn, P. A. 621
Kungfu (see Gongfu)
Kuo Mo-jo: the early years 382
Kuomintang (see Guomindang)

L

Labour 84, 305, 325, 895, 1013, 1019,
    1025, 1035—1036
  allocation 1029
  Communist Party policy 1028
  in the US 187
  incentives 1026, 1029—1030, 1032
  industrial 1029
  political organizations 1034
  socialist planning 655
  urban 1031
  women 514
Labour movement 224, 1027, 1034
Labour relations 113
Labourers
  agricultural 1006
Lacquerwork 1303, 1356, 1358, 1364
Lacy, C. 92
Lai, T. C. 1288—1289
Lamont, Thomas W. 228
Lampton, D. M. 586
Land 467, 1035
  reform 15, 223, 471, 511, 654, 662,
    914, 995, 1001, 1013, 1020, 1036
  taxation 952
  use 128
Land and labor in China 1035
Land and lineage in China: a study of
    T'ung-Ch'eng county, Anhwei, in
    the Ming and Ch'ing
    dynasties 467
Land reform and economic
    development in China: a study of
    institutional change and
    development finance 914
Land reform in the People's Republic
    of China: institutional
    transformation in
    agriculture 1020

Land taxation in imperial China,
    1750-1911 952
Landscape 99
  gardens 1307
  painting 1283, 1291, 1294—1296
  photographs 3, 62
Lang, O. 1188
Language and linguistics in the
    People's Republic of China 1105
Language, Chinese 6, 19, 29, 31, 38,
    41, 183, 465
  calligraphy 1110
  character indices 1106
  Chinese-Chinese
    dictionaries 1099—1102
  Chinese-English
    dictionaries 1083—1084, 1086,
    1088—1093
  Chinese-English military
    dictionaries 1087
  Chinese-English political
    dictionaries 1085
  cursive script 1079
  English-Chinese
    dictionaries 1094—1096, 1098
  English-Chinese military
    dictionaries 1087
  English-Chinese technical
    dictionaries 1097
  flash cards for beginners 1062
  grammar 1065
  linguistic reform 1109
  linguistic studies 1103—1108, 1111
  Mandarin acoustic phonetics 1075
  Mandarin conversation textbook 1076
  particles 1082
  practice sheets for beginners 1067
  reader 1071, 1073—1074,
    1077—1078, 1081
  romanization systems 1080
  script 1103
  textbooks 1061, 1063—1064, 1066,
    1068—1070, 1072
Language, English
  proficiency examinations 551
  teaching 71
Language reform in China: documents
    and commentary 1109
Lanzhou 121
Lao, Joseph 1123, 1131, 1141, 1212
Lao She 1204—1207
Lao She and the Chinese
    revolution 1137
Lao Taitai 506

Lao Ze 1150
Lao Zi 462
Laos
 relations with China 827
Lardy, N. R. 909−911
Lardy, W. M. Jr. 912
Larkin, B. D. 825
Lary, D. 624
Last Confucian: Liang Shu-ming and the Chinese dilemma of modernity 351
Last emperor 354
Last moments of a world 82, 365
Latham, Ronald 1267
Latin America
 Communist fifth-columnists 866
 relations with China 820, 882
Lau, D. C. 441
Lau Yee-Fui 729
Law 6, 19, 28, 45, 490, 601, 610, 708
 business contracts 973
 dictionaries 599, 606
 family 499
 marriage 504, 510
Law and justice: the legal system in China, 2400 BC to 1960 AD 601
Law and policy in China's foreign policy 615
Law and politics in China's foreign trade 609
Law and politics in Chinese foreign trade 969
Law codes
 Tang 607
Law, Contemporary 602
Law courts 479
Law, Imperial 600, 605
 Tang code 607
Law in Chinese foreign policy: Communist China and selected problems of international law 608
Law in imperial China 600
Law, International 603, 608
 bibliographies 604
 trade 609
 treaties 611−615
Law of Treaties 612−613
Law without lawyers: a comparative view of law in the US and China 610
Lawrence, A. 826
Le Barbier, F. 226, 278
League of Women Voters, China conference 796
Leblanc, C. 468

Lectures in China, 1919-1920 552
'Lectures on basic knowledge of national economic plan' 909
'Lectures on national economic planning' 909
Ledderose, L. 1290
Lee, B. A. 754
Lee, Chae Jin 827−828
Lee, Hong Yung 675
Lee Ngok 915
Lee, R. H. G. 181
Lee, S. L. 1291
Left current in China 367
Legalists 357, 464
Legend of Miao-Shan 433
Legends 1150, 1152
 women 512
Legeza, L. 442
Legge, J. 443
Lehmann, W. P. 1105
Leibnitz, G. W. 411
Lein, D. W. 620
Leinman, A. 587
Leng, Shaozhuan 608, 967
Leon, N. H. 1106
Leong, S. C. 1076
Leong, Sow-Theng 829
Leriche, R. 890
Leslie, D. D. 1431
Letter on Chinese philosophy 411
Letters from China 89
Leung Chi-Keung 915
Levenson, J. R. 26, 182, 292
Leverhulme Conference, Fifth 915
Levine, S. 243
Levy, R. 327
Lewis, J. W. 676, 913
Leyda, J. 1325
Leys, S. 27, 324, 677
Li Bo 1147, 1171, 1183
Li Chih in contemporary Chinese historiography 370
Li, Dun J. 183
Li, H. Y. 444
Li He 1147
Li, K. 1336
Li Keran 1286
Li, L. 755
Li, L. H. 1074
Li, L. M. 968
Li, Leo Oufan 1124
Li Lisan
 labour policy 1034
Li Mankin 93
Li, P. 1454

Li Qi 138
Li Qingzhao 1167, 1175
Li Qingzhao: complete poems 1167
Li Rui 325
Li Shangyin 1147, 1183
Li Tianmin 374
Li, V. H. 609—611, 830—831, 969
Li Xin 394
Li Youming 184—185
Li Yu 1208
Li Yuanghong 627
Li Yuming 445
Li, Yunzhen 1425
Li Zhi 370
Li Zongren 232
Liang Ch'i-ch'ao and intellectual
   transition in China,
   1890-1907 388
Liang Ch'i-ch'ao and modern Chinese
   liberalism 371
Liang-Guang 385
Liang Jindong 375
Liang Qichao 371, 388
Liang Shuming 351
Liaozhai 1218
Liberalism 439, 450
Libraries, US
   Chinese collections catalogues 1460
Library of Congress, Chinese
   Collection 1355
Lieberman, F. 1432
Lieberthal, K. 293, 911, 1433
Liew Ki Siong 376
Life
   philosophy of 447—448
Life and customs 15, 18, 115, 183,
   496, 1241, 1264
   contemporary 2, 6, 10—11, 20, 32,
      76—77, 79, 84, 86, 100, 103, 112,
      117, 120, 1240
   marriage 474
Limestones
   photographs 62
Limits of change: essays on
   conservative alternatives in
   republican China 436
Limits of foreign policy: the West, the
   League and the Far Eastern crisis
   of 1931-33 766
Lin Biao 274, 328, 384
   career 720
   fall 366—367
   speeches 366
   writings 316, 363

Lin Chaoen 398
Lin, F. 1337
Lin Feng-mian 1286
Lin, H. C. 987
Lin, H. T. 1065
Lin, J. C. 1125
Lin Piao affair: power politics and
   military coup 366
Lin Piao: the life and writings of
   China's new ruler 363
Lin Qunxian 542
Lin Shuen-fu 1168
Lin, Xiaoliang 970
Lin Yusheng 245
Lin Yutang, 1086, 1337
Lin Yutang's Chinese-English
   dictionary of modern usage 1086
Lin Zongyuan 1146
Lindbeck, J. M. H. 678, 1434
Lindhoff, H. 906
Lindsay, M. 1248
Lineage 148, 467, 472, 498, 501
Ling, K. 679
Ling Zhun 1167
Linguistics 1105—1109, 1111
   bibliographies 1453
   bibliographies on computer 1450
   Peter Boodberg 1103
   Yue Ren Chao 1104
Link, P. 1126
Lip, E. 446
Lippit, V. 914, 925
Literacy 29
Literacy, Popular 567
Literary criticism 210
Literature
   Maoist theory 1251
   non-fiction 1238—1267
   Old Chinese 1256
Literature, Chinese 19, 31, 39, 46,
   368, 1138, 1194
   anthologies 1112—1113, 1119, 1130,
      1142
   autobiography 695
   bibliographies 1425, 1442
   classical prose 1249
   classification 1134
   comic books 1263
   Confucian writings 355—356
   contemporary 447, 1116, 1124, 1144
   criticism 1136, 1143, 1203,
      1215—1216
   Cultural Revolution 1126
   Daoist writings 400

358

drama 1114, 1137, 1145, 1196, 1224,
  1232, 1247, 1266, 1321—1323,
  1328—1329
fables 1150, 1152
festivals 5
fiction 695, 1122—1123, 1131, 1139,
  1141, 1143, 1145, 1187, 1189,
  1191, 1201, 1212, 1217,
  1454—1455
folk tales 1195, 1236—1237
genres 1114, 1129
ghost stories 1113
historical epics 1211
history 174—175
Hundred Flowers Period 1133
legends 1150, 1152
Lu Xun 1148—1159
May 4th Movement 1117
narrative tradition 1255
novels 197, 471, 1114—1115, 1121,
  1137, 1140, 1188—1190,
  1192—1193, 1197—1198, 1202,
  1204—1207, 1209—1210,
  1213—1214, 1219—1220, 1222,
  1225—1226, 1228, 1230—1231,
  1233—1235
periodicals 1385
poetry 210, 663, 695, 1113—1114,
  1125, 1132, 1143, 1146—1147,
  1160—1186
political commentary 695
religious themes 433
short stories 1114, 1120, 1137, 1149,
  1154, 1158, 1199—1200, 1208,
  1218, 1227, 1229
Six Dynasties Period 1127
Tang 512
theories 1128, 1135
women 512
World War II 1118
Literature, French
on China 378
Literature of the hundred
  flowers 1133
Literature of the People's Republic of
  China 1142
Literature, US
transmission to China 1243
Little Red Book (see Quotations from
  Chairman Mao)
Liu, A. P. L. 730, 1367
Liu Cunyang 1214
Liu, J. J. Y. 1128, 1169—1170
Liu, J. T. C. 28, 625
Liu Ling 35, 101

Liu Rongzhao 1009
Liu Shao-ch'i and the Chinese
  Cultural Revolution: the politics
  of mass criticism 362
Liu Shao-ch'i: Mao's first
  heir-apparent 374
Liu Shaoqi 278, 362, 374
labour policy 1034
political leadership 643
Liu Shishun 1249
Liu Wuji 1129, 1171, 1203
Liu Yijing 1127
Liu, Yueyun 832
Liu Zheng 519
Liu Zhun 1127
Liuchiyuan Zhukongdiao 1318
Living in China 120
Living standards 904, 941
workers 1029
Livingston, J. 1242
Lo, Irvin Yucheng 1171
Lo, R. E. 94, 1209
Local government 35, 189, 208, 264,
  681, 694, 699, 703
bureaucracy 960
finance 621
Han 617
Qing 385
tax 621
Loehr, M. 1309, 1363
Loescher, G. 29
Loewe, M. 186, 447—448
Loewen, J. W. 535
Lofstedt, Jan-I. 563
Logic of 'Maoism': critiques and
  explication 322
Loh, Pichon P. Y. 377
London, M. 478
Long Bow village
economy 1005
Long March 229, 239, 244, 248, 266,
  313, 319, 698, 1260
Long March 1935: the epic of Chinese
  communism's survival 266
Long March to power: a history of the
  Chinese Communist Party,
  1921-72 239
Long Revolution 301
Longtime California: a documentary
  study of an American
  Chinatown 540
Lord, B. 1210
Lost chance in China: the World War
  II dispatches of John S.
  Service 234

Lotta, R. 326
Lotveit, T. 246
Louis, V. 294
Love and struggle in Mao's thought 342
Lovelace, D. D. 833
Low, A. D. 834
Lowe, C. H. 1435
Lowe, J. D. 1087
Lu Guanghuan 1188
Lu Hsun's vision of reality 1155
Lu Xun 44, 245, 1150—1154, 1200
anthologies 1156—1157
biography 1155, 1159
short stories 1149, 1158
social criticism 1148, 1151, 1153—1155
Lu Xun: selected works 1157
Lu Xun: three stories 1149
Lu You 1194
Lu Yu 1179, 1194
Lucas, AnE. 588
Ludlow, N. H. 1045
Luo Guanzhong 1220
Luo Guanzhuan 1211
Luo, Kenneth 1338—1340
Luo Zewen 53
Luoyang 75
Lute: Kao Ming's Pi-Pachi 1329
Lyell, W. 1155, 1205
Lyman, S. M. 536

M

Ma, Fenghua 916, 971
Ma, L. J. C. 1436
Ma, Y. W. 1131, 1212
Macartney, Lord 171
McCarthyism 285, 800, 848
Macciochi, M. A. 95
McClellan, R. 187
McCormack, G. 379
McCough, J. P. 564
McCullough, C. 97
McCunn, Ruthanne L. 538—539
McCutcheon, J. M. 1437
McDonald, A. W. 1010
MacDonald, M. 96
MacDonald, W. L. 458
McDougall, B. S. 1172, 1251
McElderry, A. Lee 950
McFarlane, B. 933
MacFarquhar, R. 295, 835
McGough, J. P. 380
Machine-building industry 993

Machine-building industry in Communist China 993
Machtzki, R. 653
MacInnis, D. E. 412
McKee, D. 247
Mackerras, C. P. 188, 296, 1326—1327, 1431
Mackie, J. A. C. 537
Mackinnon, J. 513
Mackinnon, S. 513
McKnight, B. E. 189
McLaughlin, J. 87
McMahon Line 748, 756
McMahon line and after: a study of the triangular contest on India's north-eastern frontier between Britain, China and Tibet 1904-1947 756
McMillan, D. H. 681
McNaughton, W. 449, 1066, 1130
Macon, N. 594
Macquitty, W. 1300
Madam Mao (see Jiang Qing)
Madman of Ch'u: the Chinese myth of loyalty and dissent 633
Magazines 1399
Magic 5, 429, 442
Magistrates 208
Maitan, L. 297
Major lyricists of the Northern Sung, 960-1126 1170
Making green revolution: the policies of agriculture development in China 1015
Making of a model citizen in Communist China 568
Malaya
Chinese immigrants 548
Malaysia
relations with China 873
Malloy, Ruth Lor 126
Malraux, A. 378
Malthusianism 522
Man and the workers: the Hunan labor movement, 1920-1923 1034
Man, concept of 452
Man of many qualities 459
Man who lost China: the first full biography of Chiang Kai-shek 359
Management 1026
worker participation 1025

Manchukuo 220, 354, 739, 755
Manchuria
  border conflicts 749
  frontier 181
  Japanese occupation 766
  relations with China 56, 379
  Soviet influence 829
*Manchurian frontier in Ch'ing
    history* 181
Manchus 43, 159, 192, 354, 1265
  opposition to 252
  theatre 1327
Mandarin Chinese
  acoustic phonetics 1075
  conversation textbook 1076
Mandarin way 1335
*Mandarins, Jews and missionaries: the
    Jewish experience in the Chinese
    empire* 414
*Mandate of heaven: Marx and Mao in
    modern China* 287
Mangin, P. B. 571
*Manpower for science and engineering
    in China* 1049
Man's fate 378
Mao 312, 315
*Mao and China: from revolution to
    revolution* 25
Mao and the perpetual revolution 330
Mao: a biography 340
Mao Chronik 335
Mao Dun 1213
Mao, Isabella Bingyi 1077
Mao, Madam (see Jiang Qing)
Mao, N. K. 1202, 1208, 1214,
    1454—1455
Mao Tse-tung (see also Mao Zedong)
Mao Tse-tung and China 317
*Mao Tse-tung and the Chinese
    people* 321
*Mao Tse-tung and education: his
    thoughts and teachings* 558
*Mao Tse-tung and Gandhi:
    perspectives on social
    transformation* 309
Mao Tse-tung and his China 347
*Mao Tse-tung and Lin Piao:
    post-revolutionary writings* 316
Mao Tse-tung Chi 331
*Mao Tse-tung: a critical
    biography* 341
*Mao Tse-tung: a guide to his
    thought* 310
*Mao Tse-tung: an ideological and
    psychological portrait* 311

*Mao Tse-tung in the scales of
    history* 344
*Mao Tse-tung: the man in the
    leadership* 334
*Mao Tse-tung, the search for
    plenty* 318
*Mao Tse-tung selected works, volume
    v* 350
*Mao Tse-tung unrehearsed: talks and
    letters, 1956-1971* 337
Mao Zedong 30, 40, 43, 99, 156,
    249—250, 263, 265, 271, 278,
    281, 295, 298—299, 317,
    320—321, 324—327, 352, 362,
    481, 697, 700—702, 1260
  career 313, 319, 330, 333, 335, 340,
    345, 657, 865
  culture 98
  death 7, 9, 36, 272, 275, 666, 704
  economic thought 318, 327, 932
  educational policy 558, 566, 574
  family 340
  final years 12
  foreign relations policy 746,
    782—783, 876
  impact 341, 344
  interviews 218
  labour policy 1034
  leadership 25, 334
  literary theory 1251
  Long March 229, 244, 248
  personal life 312
  photographs 349, 657
  poetry 343
  policy 234
  political leadership 623, 643, 652
  political thought 304, 309—310, 314,
    322—323, 332, 336—338, 340,
    342, 345—347, 736
  psyche 311, 334
  role 691
  rural revolution strategy 1007
  sexual activities 343
  statements 315, 335, 337—338, 343
  strategy 721
  writings 315—316, 328—329, 331,
    333, 335—336, 338—339, 343,
    348, 350, 1073
*Mao Zedong and the political
    economy of the border region: a
    translation of Mao's economic
    and financial problems* 932
*Mao Zedong, a selection of
    photographs* 349

Mao Zedong 'Talks at the Yanan Conference on Literature and Art': a translation of the 1943 test with commentary 1251
Mao Zedong Text 1949-1976 329
Maoism 30, 412, 450, 718
  cultural values 27
  economic 930
  industrial planning 979, 981, 983
Maoist educational revolution 576
Mao's betrayal 265
Mao's China: a history of the People's Republic 30
Mao's great revolution 281
Mao's legacy: lessons for the future? 332
Mao's papers: anthology and bibliography 348
Mao's people 32
Mao's people: sixteen portraits of life in revolutionary China 20
Mao's revolution and the Chinese political culture 700
Mao's way 40
Map history of modern China 63
Maps and atlases 38, 48, 64—69
  cities 487
  historical 63
  street maps 61
March, A. J. 54
Marco Polo 1252
Marco Polo Bridge Commune 84
Marco Polo Bridge Incident 767
Marco Polo in China 93
Marine sciences 1060
Mark, Bow Sim 1350
Marketing 936
Markets 944
  for silk 968
  rice trade 966
Marriage 301, 473—474, 493—494, 501, 511, 658
  law 504, 510
  overseas Chinese 529
  women 546
Marriage and adoption in China, 1845-1945 494
Marriage law and policy in the Chinese People's Republic 504
Marshall in China 216
Marshall Mission 216, 768
Martial arts
  gongfu 1351
  Taiji 1347, 1350

Martin, E. 836
Martin, H. 328—329
Martin, R. 680
Marxism 30, 95, 280, 287, 290, 323, 347, 736
Masks of fiction in the dream of the red chamber 1215
Maspero, H. 139
Mass Media 1367, 1370—1372
  educational materials 1368
  government censorship 1366
  New China News Agency 1408
  presentation of the US 1365
Mass mobilization 223, 239, 293, 647
Mass movement in a Chinese village: ten mile inn 1000
Mass movements 644
Masses cookbook 1343
Master of Chinese political thought: from the beginning to the Han dynasty 724
Master Tung's western chamber romance, a Chinese chantefable 1191
Master who embraces simplicity: a study of the philosopher Ko Hung AD 282-343 457
Mathematics
  education 572
Mathematics education in China: its growth and development 572
Mather, R. B. 1127
Mathews' Chinese-English dictionary 1088
Mathews, R. H. 1088
Mathias, J. 1089
Matsu crisis 780
Matter of two Chinas: the China-Taiwan issue in US foreign policy 824
Mausolea
  Manch'eng 151
  Ming dynasty 140
Maxwell, N. 837
May 4th Movement 167, 219, 245, 257, 382, 629, 1239
  literature 1117
  women 510
May 7th Cadre Schools 91, 301
May, G. 1250
Mechanization
  agriculture 998, 1004, 1006, 1016
Media 1367, 1370—1372
  censorship 1366

Medical groups
  Chinese aid 779
Medicine 6, 39, 103, 120, 129, 516,
    521, 524, 580, 583, 587, 589,
    592–593, 595, 1055
  acupuncture 582–583, 590–591,
    594, 596–598
  barefoot doctors 598
  cancer treatment 585
  chemotherapy 590
  Daoism 429
  herbal 583–584, 598
  modernization 586, 588
  pathology 590
  pharmacology 581, 590
  women 511
Medieval Chinese oligarchy 177
Medley, M. 1310
Mehnert, K. 98
Mehra, P. 756
*Mei Yao-ch'en and the development of
    early Sung poetry* 1163
Meisner, M. 30, 621
*Memoir of China in revolution: from
    the Boxer Rebellion to the
    People's Republic* 1257
*Memoir of revolutionary China,
    1924-1941* 482
Memoirs of Li Tsung-jen 232
*Memories of Loyang: Yang
    Hsuan-chih and the lost
    capital* 1246
Mencius 441
Mencius 724
Meng Haoren 1146
Meng Qiao 1173
Mercenaries 201
*Mercenaries and mandarins: the ever
    victorious army in nineteenth
    century China* 201
*Merchants, mandarins and modern
    enterprises in late Ch'ing
    China* 960
Meserve, R. J. 1328
Meserve, W. J. 1328
Meskill, J. 31
Metallurgy
  imported technology 1045
Metals
  industrial 1056
Metaphysics 451
*Methodological issues in Chinese
    studies* 734
Metropolitan Museum of Art 1299

Metropolitan Museum of Art, Asian
    Collection 1361
Metropolitan Museum of Art, Chinese
    ceramics 1315
Metzger, T. A. 450, 492
Meyer, C. 1438
Meyers, W. 838
Mi Fu 1290
*Mi Fu and the classical tradition of
    Chinese calligraphy* 1290
Miao-shan legend 433
Michael, F. 330
*Micropolitics in contemporary China:
    a technical unit during and after
    Cultural Revolution* 645
*Mid-Ch'ing rice markets and trade: an
    essay on price history* 966
Middle East
  relations with China 852, 860, 882
*Middle East in China's foreign policy,
    1949-1977* 852
Middleton, D. 839
Midnight 1213
Miles, K. 1252
Militarism 622, 634, 640
  Guangxi clique 624
*Militarism in modern China: the
    career of Wu Peifu, 1916-39* 386
Militarism in Peking's policies 640
Military, The 479, 684, 703, 712, 718
  reform 660
Military Advisors, Soviet 243, 248
Military affairs 22, 194, 201, 303
*Military and political power in China
    in the 1970s* 712
Military campaigns 649
*Military dimension of the Chinese
    revolution* 660
*Military establishment of the Yuan
    dynasty* 194
*Military-gentry coalition: China under
    the warlords* 269
Military history 180, 269, 484, 632,
    637
  Great Wall 53
  Northern Expedition 241, 386
  simulation games 553
Military occupation
  by Japan 220–221, 354
Military technology 896
Military theory 727, 733
Military tribunals 754
Miller, A. 99
Miller, G. Bley 1341

Miller, L. 1215
Milton, D. 43, 298
Milton, N. 43, 298
*Mind of China: the culture, customs,
    and beliefs of traditional
    China* 41
Mineral industry 1056
Mineral resources 991, 1056
*Mineral resources and basic industries
    in the People's Republic of
    China* 991, 1056
Minford, J. 1189
Ming dynasty 56
  art 156
  biographical dictionaries 392
  decline 205, 358
  finance 949
  food 149
  institutions 176
  literature 156, 1113
  local government 208
  painting 1281
  philosophy 431
  politics 161
  porcelain 1270
  religion 398, 417, 421, 424
  society 206, 467
  tombs 140
*Ming dynasty: its origins and evolving
    institutions* 176
Mingji figurines 1313
Mining 928
  imported technology 1045
Ministry of Foreign Trade 976
Minorities 72, 120, 294, 518, 521, 626,
    708
Minoru, Takeuchi 331
Miserez-Schira, G. 1292
Missionaries 115
  education 235
Missionaries, American 401, 407, 410,
    415, 482, 738, 1239
Missionaries, British 1239
Missionaries, Canadian 406
Missionaries, European 416
Missionaries, Jesuit 405, 414, 417
Missionaries, Women 510
*Missionary enterprise in China and
    America* 407
*Mississippi Chinese: between black
    and white* 535
Mitayev, U. 640
Mitchell, P. H. 33
Mo Ze 1150
Mo Zi 456, 464

Mobilization campaigns 647
Mock, L. 1342
Modern China 1393
*Modern China, 1840-1972: an
    introduction to sources and
    resource aids* 1439
*Modern China and a new world: K'ang
    Yu-wei, reformer and utopian,
    1858-1927* 168
*Modern China: a chronology from
    1841 to the present* 188
*Modern China: from mandarin to
    commissar* 183
*Modern China: an interpretative
    anthology* 26
*Modern China: the story of a
    revolution* 198
*Modern Chinese fiction: a guide to its
    study and appreciation, essays
    and bibliographies* 1455
*Modern Chinese literature in the May
    Fourth era* 1117
*Modern Chinese poetry: an
    introduction* 1125
Modern Chinese readers 1072
*Modern Chinese society: analytical
    bibliography. Volume I,
    publications in western languages,
    1644-1972; volume II,
    publications in Chinese,
    1644-1969; volume III,
    publications in Japanese,
    1944-1971* 1446
Modern Chinese stories 1201
*Modern Chinese stories and novellas,
    1919-1949* 1123
Modern Chinese woodcuts 1314
*Modern drama from Communist
    China* 1328
Modern mandarin conversation 1076
Modernization 888, 893, 923, 941
  industry 982
  Nationalist programme 954
Modernization of China 923
Mohist school 464
*Monarchy in the emperor's eyes:
    image and reality in the
    Ch'ien-lung reign* 179
Monasteries
  Buddhist 412
  Daoist 412, 419, 425
Monde Chinois 21
Monetary system 946
  communist policy 948
  state control 950

Money and monetary policy in communist China 948
Mongolia
  relations with China 56
Mongolia, Outer
  Soviet occupation 829
Mongols 153, 176, 373, 1267
Monkey 1193
Monopolies 28
  salt 936
Montaperto, R. 353, 565
Monuments, Historical 1
Moody, P. R. Jr. 682—683
Moore, C. A. 451
Moore, J. 248
Moorsteen, R. 840
Moral behavior in Chinese society 492
Morals 492
Morath, I. 99
More than herbs and acupuncture 583
Morgan, D. 13
Morning deluge: Mao Tse-tung and the Chinese revolution, 1893-1954 319
Morning in Shanghai 1234
Morrill, S. S. 444
Morris, C. 600
Morris, M. 1346
Mortensen, R. 346
Morton, W. S. 34
Morwood, W. 249
Mose, E. 1271
Mosely, G. V. H. 626
Mote, F. W. 735
Mottahedeh Collection 1305
Moving a mountain: cultural change in China 737, 1370
Moxibustion 591, 594
Mozingo, D. 841
Mudan Ting 1222
Mueller, P. G. 842
Mules 1022
Mulligan, J. 1329
Mullikin, M. A. 1293
Munro, D. J. 452
Murk, C. F. 1271
Murphey, R. 332, 917—918
Museum of the American China Trade 469
Museums 37
Museums, Western
  Chinese art 1272

Music 1320
  ballad singing 1318
  bibliographies 1432
  fu 1319
Music and tradition: essays on Asian and other musics presented to Laurence Picken 1320
Musical instruments
  ancient zithers 1301
My house has two doors 668
Mydans, C. 100
Myers, R. H. 843, 1011
Myrdal, J. 35, 101—102
Mysticism
  Daoist 442
Myths
  women 512

N

Naess, A. 453
Nagel's encyclopedia-guide: China 127
Naik, J. A. 844
Nalty, B. C. 1253
Nanjing 220, 457
'Narcotic War' 809
Nath, Marie-L. 652
Nathan, A. J. 627, 1439
National Committee on US-China relations, China conference 796
National Congress of Writers and Artists, Fourth 1116
National development 57, 96, 270, 296, 341, 659, 872, 917
National Essence Movement 436
National Science Foundation 1059
National Soviet Congress 264
Nationalism 152, 358, 388, 423
Nationalist China during the Sino-Japanese war 1937-1945 988
Nationalist Government 156, 219, 227, 232—233, 260—262, 377, 387, 436, 622, 636
  fiscal policy 954
  industrial programme 988
Nationalist Party (see Guomindang, Civil War, Nationalist Government)
Nationalization
  foreign firms 929
Nations in darkness, China, Russia and America 856
Natural history
  periodicals 1387

Natural resources 88´
Naval battles 169
Navies 161, 862
Neare-Hill, W. B. R. 1311
Nee, V. 540, 1254
Needham, Joseph 190, 1046−1047
Neijer, M. J. 504
Neil, M. G. 1285
Neilan, E. 972
Nelsen, H. L. 561, 684
*Neo-Confucian thought in action:
    Wang Yang-ming's youth* 435
Neo-Confucianism 430−431, 435,
    450, 453
Neo-Daoism 459
Neolithic 135−136, 144
Nepal
  relations with China 882
Netsuke 1356
New China 1394
New China News Agency 1408
New Culture Movement 723
New earth 999
New Life Movement 223, 723
*New realism: writing from China
    1979-1980* 1144
New US policy toward China 777
*New York Times report from Red
    China* 103
Newhan, R. 1107
Newspapers 188, 1404−1408
  bibliographies 1459
  directories 1426
Newspapers, Chinese
  in the US 534
Ng Poon Chew 534
Nieh, Hualing 1133
Nien Rebellion 193
Nine sacred mountains of China 1293
*Nineteen seventy-eight college entrance
    examination in the People's
    Republic of China* 550
*Nineteen seventy-eight English
    language examination* 551
Nixon, Richard 91, 308, 320, 708,
    782, 787, 875
Noel, B. 250
Nolan, P. 934
Nomads 163
Northern Expedition 241, 386
*Northern expedition: the Chinese
    national revolution 1926-28* 241
Norton, W. Fitch 757

*Notable books on Chinese studies: a
    selected, annotated and
    subject-divided bibliography
    guide* 1435
Note, F. W. 370
Novelists 368
Novels 197, 1114, 1121, 1137, 1140,
    1187−1190, 1192−1193,
    1197−1198, 1202, 1204−1207,
    1209−1210, 1213−1214,
    1219−1223, 1225−1226, 1228,
    1230−1231, 1233−1235
  bibliographies 1456
  historical 1252
  literary criticism 1203, 1215−1216
  Qing 1115
Novels, Chinese
  set in China 471
Novels, French
  on China 378
Nuclear weapons 777, 793, 804, 813,
    832

O

Oboi Regency 192
Occult 442
Occupations
  incentives 697, 711
  overseas Chinese 529
Oceanography 1060
Oceanography in China 1060
O'Connor, J. 591
O'Connor, R. 191
Official guidebook of China 1
Ogunsanwo, Alaba 845
Oil 810, 941, 1056
  export to the US 967
*Oil in the People's Republic of China:
    industry structure production
    exports* 980
Oil industry 980, 985, 987, 992
  Daqing Oilfield 983
  imported technology 1045
Oksenberg, M. 846, 855, 919, 1418,
    1440−1441
*Old Madam Yin: a memoir of Peking
    life* 506
*Old man who does as he pleases:
    selections from the poetry and
    prose of Lu Yu* 1179
Old tales retold 1150
O'Leary, G. 847
Oliver, J. F. 278

On poetry 1160
'On the relationship of poetry and painting in China' 1162
Onate, A. D. 333
One of the great epics of our century - the rise to power of Mao Tse-tung and the land he led into the 20th century 313
Open Door Policy 240, 247, 749
Opera 1324, 1327, 1330, 1457
  character portraits 1282
  regional 1326
  revolutionary 114, 1371
Opium trade 634
Opium War, 1840-1842 166
Opium Wars 154—155, 166, 171, 198, 1238
Opposition and dissent in contemporary China 682
Oracle Bones 137
Oracle of Change 432
Oracles 425
Orchard boat, women poets of China 1175
Ordnance industry 986
Organization and support of scientific research and development in mainland China 1057
Organization behavior in Chinese society 479
Organizing China: the problem of bureaucracy, 1949-1976 669
Oriental Art 1354
Oriental Healing Arts Institute 584
Origins of the Chinese revolution, 1915-1949 217
Origins of the Cultural Revolution: contradictions among the people, 1956-59 295
Origins of statecraft in China: the western Chou empire 157
Origins of the war in the east: Britain, China and Japan, 1937-39 763
Orleans, L. A. 520—521, 589, 1048—1049
Ornithology 48
Otto Braun: Comintern agent in China, 1932-1939 248
Our ordered lives confess: three nineteenth-century American missionaries in East Shantung 410
Our world: the People's Republic of China 691
Outlaws of the marsh 1220

Outline of Chinese geography 48
Outsiders: the Western experience in India and China 918
Overmyer, D. L. 413
Overseas Chinese 881
  Australia 529
  demography 529
  economy 527
  fifth columnists 531—532
  Great Britain 547
  Hawaii 527
  Hong Kong 546—547
  Indonesia 537, 542—545
  Java 544
  Malaya 548
  marriage 529
  occupations 529
  politics 527
  religion 527
  Revolution of 1911 548
  Singapore 548
  society 488, 503, 527, 540
  Southeast Asia 525, 532—533
  US 528, 530, 534—536, 538—541, 738
  US attitudes to 187
  Vietnam 531
  Yunnan 531
Overseas Chinese and the 1911 revolution 548
Overseas trade 165, 804, 887, 890, 895, 904, 921, 944, 954, 957, 977
  assessment of the China market 958, 978
  business contracts 973
  compradors 215
  customs 201
  directories 396
  international law 609
  minerals 1056
  oriental rugs 965
  patterns 969, 971
  periodicals 1374, 1377
  regulation 976
  silk 968
  socialist planning 655
  statistics 970
  with Africa 817
  with Great Britain 780
  with Japan 871, 976
  with New England 235
  with the US 240, 778, 959, 961, 963—964, 967, 972, 975
  with the West 974

Owen, S. 1173—1174
Oxnam, R. B. 36, 192
Oxnam, R. O. 846

P

Pacific Affairs 1395
Painting 1268, 1278—1279, 1284,
    1293, 1301
  contemporary 1298
  essays on 1276
  faience 1292
  folk art 1297
  history 1271
  landscape 1291, 1294—1296, 1307
  landscape scrolls 1283
  Ming dynasty 1281
  of Beijing opera characters 1282
  porcelains 1292
  Shanghai school 1286, 1288
  Song dynasty 1299
  watercolours 1286
  Yuan dynasty 1280, 1299
*Painting in the People's Republic of
    China: the politics of style* 1298
*Paintings of Beijing opera
    characters* 1282
Pak, Hyobom 628
Pakistan
  Chinese aid 779, 799
  relations with China 818, 863
Pal, P. 1354
Palaces 1
Palm, C. G. 1357
Paludan, A. 140
Pannell, C. W. 55
Paper 526
Paper, J. D. 1442
Papercuts 1306
Parish, W. L. 505
Partai Kommunis Indonesia 841
*Parting at the shore: Chinese painting
    of the early and middle Ming
    dynasty, 1368-1568* 1281
*Party and professionals: the political
    role of teachers in contemporary
    China* 575
*Party leadership and revolutionary
    power in China* 676
Party recruitment in China 680
Pasqualini (see Bao Ruo-Wang)
*Passage to power: K'ang-hsi and his
    heir apparent, 1661-1722* 212
Pathology 590

*Paths in dreams: selected prose and
    poetry of Ho Ch'i-fang* 1172
*Patients and healers in the context of
    culture* 587
*Pattern of the Chinese past: a social
    and economic interpretation* 896
*Pattern of Sino-American crises:
    political-military interactions in
    the 1950s* 821
Pawnshop in China 953
Payne, R. 685
*Peace conspiracy: Wang Ching-wei and
    the China war, 1937-1941* 220
Peach blossom fan 1247
Peacher, W. S. 584
*Peacock maiden: folk tales from
    China* 1237
*Peasant China in transition: the
    dynamics of development toward
    socialism, 1949-1956* 1014
*Peasant life in China: a field study of
    country life in the Yangtze
    valley* 1002
*Peasant revolts in China,
    1840-1949* 154
Peasants 33, 46, 84, 198, 226, 305,
    365, 469, 716, 1002, 1017
  incentives 1014
  rebellion 28, 154, 325, 477, 1007,
    1035
Peck, J. 1254
Peeman, J.-P. 278
Peking 51
Peking (see also Beijing)
*Peking bomb: the psychochemical war
    against America* 809
*Peking diary: a personal account of
    modern China* 77
Peking man 135, 144
*Peking politics, 1918-1923:
    factionalism and the failure of
    constitutionalism* 627
Peking Review 658, 1396
*Peking's UN policy: continuity and
    change* 867
Peng Duhuai 277
*People of Taihang: an anthology of
    family histories* 502
Peoples
  names 47

People's China and international law: a documentary study 604

People's comic book: red women's detachment and other Chinese comics 1263

People's Daily 1404, 1406
  readings for language students 1081

People's emperor: Mao. A biography of Mao Tse-tung 343

People's Liberation Army 29, 301, 684, 698, 718
  officer education 561

People's Liberation army and China's nation-building 718

People's Republic of China, 1949-1979: a documentary survey 672

People's Republic of China: administrative atlas 67

People's Republic of China and the law of treaties 613

People's Republic of China: atlas 68

People's Republic of China cookbook 1343

People's Republic of China: a documentary history of revolutionary changes 300

People's Republic of China: a handbook 22

People's Republic of China Official Activities and Monthly Bibliography 1397

People's Republic of China: an overview 23

Pepper, S. 251

Peranakan Chinese politics in Java, 1917-42 544

Periodicals 1373—1403
  bibliographies 1459

Perkins, D. H. 920

Perrolle, P. M. 686, 1058

Perry, E. J. 193

Perspectives on the T'ang 210

Pest control 1023

Petroleum industry of the People's Republic of China 987

Petrov, V. 783

Peyrefitte, A. 37

Pfeffer, R. M. 778, 973

Pharmacology 590
  US-China symposium 581

Philanthropy 477

Philately 1379

Philippines
  Chinese immigrants 525
  relations with China 810

Philosophy 14, 41, 142, 168, 175, 183, 357, 447, 451, 456—458, 466, 658
  20th century 450
  bibliographies 1422
  Buddhist 404, 435, 453
  Christian 455
  concept of man 452
  Confucian 355, 357, 434, 440—441, 443, 449, 453—455, 601
  Daoist 357, 419, 425—426, 435, 437—438, 453, 461, 463, 465
  Han 428
  Indian 427
  Legalist 357, 464
  Maoist 304, 310, 314, 322—323, 332, 337—338, 340, 342, 345—347
  Ming 431
  Mohist 464
  Neo-Confucian 430—431, 435, 450, 453
  Neo-Daoist 459
  oriental 427
  periodicals 1400
  political 451, 721—728, 730—733, 735—736
  Qin 428
  religious 411, 420
  Tang 210
  Western 427
  Zhou 428

Philosophy of painting by Shih T'ao: a translation and exposition of his Hua-pu 1268

Photographs 2, 60, 74—76, 78—79, 88, 99, 105, 123, 259, 469, 701, 1317
  archaeological 151
  Beijing 51
  landscape 3, 62
  Mao Zedong 349, 657

Physics
  solid state 1040, 1050

Picken, L. 1320

Pictorial biography of Lu Xun, 1881-1936 1159

Pigs 1022

Pigtail War 160

Pigtail War: American involvement in the Sino-Japanese war of 1894-95 160

Pilgrimage to the West 1228

Pilgrims
  Buddhist 409

Ping-pong 1349
Pinkele, C. F. 806
*Pinyin Chinese-English
    dictionary* 1091
Pinyin romanization system
  Chinese-Chinese
    dictionaries 1099—1102
  Chinese-English dictionaries 1091
Pinyin-Wade-Giles romanization 1080
Pinyin-Yale romanization 1080
*Pivot of the four quarters: a
    preliminary inquiry into the
    origins and character of the
    ancient Chinese city* 489
Place-names 47, 59, 64
Plaks, A. H. 1216, 1255
Planned Birth Campaign 516—517,
    520
Plant breeding 1004
  rice 132
  vegetables 130
  wheat 128
*Plant studies in the People's Republic
    of China: a trip report of the
    American Plant Studies
    Delegation* 131
Plunknett, D. 130
*Pocket English-Chinese
    Dictionary* 1098
Poetry 695, 1113—1114, 1125, 1132,
    1160, 1164—1166, 1169,
    1171—1173, 1175, 1177, 1179
  20th century 1143
  and calligraphy 1147
  bibliographies 1457
  formulaic 1178
  Fu 1182
  genres 1184
  Han 1182
  Mao Zedong 343
  nature poetry 1146
  political 663
  reading 1176
  Six Dynasties Period 1182
  Song 1162—1163, 1167—1168, 1170,
    1180
  Tang 210, 1147, 1161, 1163, 1174,
    1176, 1181, 1183, 1185—1186
*Poetry and politics: the life and works
    of Juan Chi* 1166
Poetry of the early T'ang 1174
*Poetry of Meng Ch'iao and Han
    Yu* 1173
*Poetry of Wang Wei, new translation
    and commentary* 1185

Pokora, T. 1217
Poling Zu family 500
Politburo 363
*Political behavior of adolescents in
    China: the Cultural Revolution in
    Kwangchow* 690
*Political China observed: a western
    perspective* 670
Political commentary 695
*Political culture and group conflict in
    Communist China* 730
*Political economy of the Chinese
    revolution* 885
*Political economy of war and peace:
    the Sino-Soviet-American triangle
    and the national security
    problematique* 772
Political education 643
*Political imprisonment in the People's
    Republic of China: an Amnesty
    International report* 616
*Political institutions in traditional
    China: major issues* 625
*Political participation in Communist
    China* 705
Political phrases
  glossary 729
Political prisoners 70, 85, 87, 121, 616
Political refugees 616
Political science
  bibliographies 696
Political theory
  art of war 733
  civil war 721
  Communist Party 736
  contemporary 723, 728, 732
  Cultural Revolution 725, 730
  history 724, 735
  imperialism 726
  methodology 734
  people's war 727
  post Mao 722
  revolutions 731
*Political thinking of the Indonesian
    Chinese, 1900-1977: a source
    book* 545
*Political thought of Mao
    Tse-tung* 336
Politics 39, 46, 633, 1055
  ancient 496
  and sport 1348
  anti-imperialism 360, 423
  anti-traditionalism 245
  aristocratic families 500
  authoritarianism 690

bibliographies 631, 1418–1419, 1440–1441
border conflicts 626
bureaucracy 617, 639
coalitions 720
Communist régime 7–8, 12, 70, 270
conceptual models 734
Confucianism 158, 199
constitutionalism 627
contemporary 7–8, 22–24, 30, 37–38, 40, 42, 45, 80, 85, 112, 120, 230–231, 273, 276, 287, 290, 303, 306, 308, 312–313, 320–321, 330, 347, 366–367, 374, 384, 652–653, 658, 662, 664–665, 668, 672, 676–678, 683–684, 686, 688–689, 693–694, 700, 703, 705–706, 708, 712, 715, 722
criticism rituals 714
educational policy 573
factionalism 223, 236, 556, 569, 624, 627, 630, 632, 720
Guomindang 636
Han 617
history 10, 13–14, 29, 31, 33, 38, 43, 161, 172, 174–175, 183–185, 196, 205, 213, 226, 364, 618–619, 621, 630–632, 635, 638–639, 662, 673, 691–692, 696
ideology 27, 54, 81, 200, 280, 309
institutions 625
international law 609
Jiangxi Soviet 623
Manchus 192
militarism 622, 624, 634, 637, 640
minorities 626
opposition 682
overseas Chinese 527, 544–545
periodicals 1388, 1396–1397
post Mao 9, 12, 36, 81, 272, 274–275, 286, 326, 333, 361, 363, 640, 642, 646, 661, 663, 666, 670, 674, 680, 685, 687, 692, 704, 708, 713, 722, 737, 778, 909
purges 702
Qing 178, 192, 212, 360
Shang 147–148
Shanghai 903
simulation games 553
strategy 251, 268, 721
students 252
Sui 211
Tang 210, 369

youth 690
Zhou 148, 157
Politics and purges in China: rectification and the decline of party norms 1950-1965 702
Politics in China 706
Politics of agricultural mechanization in China 1016
Politics of Chinese Communism: Kiangsi under the Soviets 623
Politics of the Chinese Cultural Revolution: a case study 675
Politics of class and class origin: the case of the Cultural Revolution 710
Politics of the eighth central committee of the Communist Party of China 683
Politics of marriage in contemporary China 474
Politics of medicine in China: the policy process, 1949-77 586
Pollak, M. 414
Pollard, D. E. 1134
Pollution 107
  regulation 1054
Polo, Marco 93, 1252, 1267
Pope, J. A. 1312, 1360
Popular literacy 567
Popular management and pay in China 1026
Popular media in China: shaping new cultural patterns 1371
Popular movements and secret societies in China, 1840-1950 472
Population 6, 15, 22, 38, 108, 210, 518–519, 521–523, 890, 904, 921
  planned birth programme 516–517, 520
  rural resettlement programme 997
Population and health policy in the People's Republic of China 516
Population theory in China 523
Porcelain 1301, 1305, 1316
  painting 1292
Porkert, M. 590
Portraits of Chinese women in revolution 513
Ports, Treaty 477
Posner, A. 1368
Possession, spiritual 425
Post-liberation works of Mao Ze-dong: A bibliography and index 339

Post-Mao: China and US-China
    trade 967
Posters 1371
Poultry 1022
Poverty 33, 82, 365
Powell, G. B. 706
Power to politics in China 719
Practice sheets for beginning Chinese
    reader 1067
Pratt, K. L. 1443
Prayer mat of flesh 1208
Prehistory 144−145
Prehistory of China: an archaeological
    exploration 144
Prelude to revolution: Mao, the Party,
    and the peasant questions:
    1962-66 643
Present-day China: socio-economic
    problems 942
Presidency of Yuan Shih-k'ai:
    liberalism and dictatorship in
    early republican China 387
Press
  censorship 1366
Price, D. C. 758
Price, J. L. 629
Price, R. F. 566, 764
'Primitivist' essays 437
Princes of Jade 1300
Principle and practicability: essays in
    Neo-Confucianism and practical
    learning 431
Printing 526
Printz, P. 1012
Prisoner of Mao 70
Prisoners, Political 87, 616
Prisons 70, 87
Pritchard, W. 1050
Proceedings, US-China pharmacology
    symposium 581
Process of industrialization of China:
    primary elements of an analytical
    bibliography 1423
Productivity 1026
Professional societies in the People's
    Republic of China 1412
Progressivism and the open door,
    America and China,
    1905-1921 240
Propaganda
  Maoist 27
Property 28, 1002
Prose
  bibliographies 1442

Protestant Churches
  missions 406, 410, 415
Protracted game: a Wei-Chi
    interpretation of Maoist
    revolutionary strategy 721
Provinces of the People's Republic of
    China: a political and economic
    bibliography 1418
Provincial leadership in China: the
    Cultural Revolution and
    aftermath 703
Provincial militarism and the Chinese
    Republic: the Yunnan Army,
    1905-25 634
Pruitt, I. 506
Prusek, J. 1256
Prybya, J. S. 921
Psychiatry 587
Pu Songling 1218
Pu Yi, Qing Emperor 354
Purifoy, L. McCaroll 848
Puzzles, from Yi Jing 444
Pye, L. W. 38, 334, 630, 687−688,
    706
P'yongyang between Peking and
    Moscow: North Korea's
    involvement in the Sino-Soviet
    dispute, 1958-1975 792

Q

Qi Baishi 1286, 1288
Qi Wen 39
Qi Wenxun 1078, 1090
Qi Xin 689
Qi Xisheng 632
Qian Tuansheng 631
Qian Zhuan 950
Qianlong, Qing Emperor 179
Qijing Xiao 194
Qin dynasty
  philosophy 428, 448
Qinan 619
Qing Ci 1113
Qing dynasty 356, 360
  art 156, 1270
  bibliography of government
    publications 1417
  commerce 960
  communications 1369
  decline 159, 164−165, 205, 207
  economy 908
  education 567
  finance 949

food 149
foreign relations 749
institutions 173, 212
Kangxi 178, 192, 203, 212
land tax 952
literature 156, 1113, 1152
local government 385
novels 1115
politics 43, 181, 192, 212
Pu Yi 354
Qianlong 179
rice trade 966
society 197, 206, 467
Zuxi 207
Qing, J. 454—455
Qingdau 221
Qinghua University 288
Qinghua University Group 1097
Qiu Hongda 604, 608, 612—613
Quantitative measures of China's economic output 894
Quemoy crisis 780
Quotations from Chairman Mao Tse-tung 328
readings for language students 1073

R

Rabbits 1022
Rabe, V. M. 415
Racism 187, 247, 525, 528, 538
Raddock, D. M. 690
Radical change through communication in Mao's China 1372
Radicals 306
Radicals and radical ideology in China's Cultural Revolution 306
Radio-carbon dates 150
Rage for China 685
Railways
  Chinese labour 534
Railways, US
  Chinese labour 187
Rand McNally illustrated atlas of China 69
Rankin, M. Bakus 252
Rapp, R. 622
Rau, M. 691
Rawski, E. Sakakida 567
Rawski, T. G. 989, 1033
Rea, K. 253
Reading and writing Chinese 1066

Readings from the People's Daily 1081
Readings in the Chinese Communist Cultural Revolution 1078
Readings in Chinese geography 59
Readings in modern Chinese history 214
Reardon-Anderson, J. 254
Rebellions
  economic origins 898
  peasant 28
Rebels and bureaucrats: China's December 620
Rebels and revolutionaries in north China, 1845-1945 193
Red and expert: education in the People's Republic of China 555
Red Army 217, 305, 698
  authoritarianism 297
  in India 649
  in Korea 649
  in Tibet 649
  in USSR 649
Red detachment of women 114, 1074, 1322
Red Flag 1389, 1399
Red Guard 271, 281, 305, 353, 471, 675, 679
  education 568
  factionalism 569
  wall posters 662
Red Guard factionalism and the Cultural Revolution in Guangzhou 569
Red Guard: from schoolboy to 'Little General' in Mao's China 679
Red Guard: the political biography of Dai Hsiao-ai 353
Red lantern 114, 1322
Red Spear Society 193
Red star over China 229, 698
Reed, D. 1357
Reference works
  bibliographies 1414
Refugees
  interviews 20
Refugees, Political 616
Region and nation, the Kwangsi clique in Chinese politics 1925-1937 624
Regional development 57
Regional government and political integration in southwest China: a case study 699
Reischauer, E. O. 17, 778

Relief programmes 1019
Religion 31, 45, 120, 142, 175, 204,
    399, 402–416, 418–420,
    422–423, 433, 488–489, 493,
    496
  American Catholic missionaries 401
  history 21
  Ming 398, 417, 421, 424
  overseas Chinese 527
  Song 433
  Tang 210, 369
  traditional beliefs 5
*Religion and ritual in Chinese
    society* 420
Religion des Chinois 408
Religion in Chinese society 422
Religion in communist China 402
*Religion, nationalism and Chinese
    students: the anti-Christian
    movement of 1922-1927* 423
Religion of the Chinese people 408
*Religious policy and practice in
    communist China: a documentary
    history* 412
*Remaking China policy: US-China
    relations and
    government-decision-making* 840
Reminiscences 1330
Ren Yuwen 195
*Renewal of Buddhism in China:
    Chu-hung and the late Ming
    synthesis* 424
Renkou Lilun 523
Renmin Ribao 1404
Report from a Chinese Village 35
*Report from Peking: observations of a
    Western diplomat on Cultural
    Revolution* 80
Reports from China: 1953-1976 104
Republic of China 172, 205, 387, 436
Republic of China, Taiwan 36, 608,
    673, 704, 713, 774, 776, 786, 794,
    796, 807, 810, 815–816, 819,
    821, 824, 830–831, 861, 871
Research aids
  bibliographies 1439
  imperial history 1451
*Research and revolution: science policy
    and societal change in
    China* 1053
*Research guide to central party and
    government meetings in China,
    1949-1975* 1433
Researches on the I Ching 458

*Resistance and revolution in China,
    the communists and the second
    united front* 244
Resources 910, 920
Resources, Human 904
Resources, Mineral 991, 1056
Resources, Natural 886
Reston, J. 43, 103
*Revenge of heaven: journal of a young
    Chinese* 478
*Revolution and Chinese foreign policy:
    Peking's support for wars of
    national liberation* 866
*Revolution and cosmopolitanism: the
    Western stage and the Chinese
    stage* 292
*Revolution and history: origins of
    Marxist historiography in China:
    1919-1937* 231
*Revolution and tradition in Tientsin,
    1949-1952* 293
*Revolution at work: mobilization
    campaigns in China* 647
Revolution Culturelle Chinoise 282
*Revolution is not a dinner party: a
    feast of images of the Maoist
    transformation of China* 701
Revolution of 1911 167, 196, 226, 252,
    257, 261, 360, 371, 376, 387, 472,
    638, 660, 1265
  historiography 1452
  overseas Chinese 548
*Revolutionary diplomacy: Chinese
    foreign policy and the United
    Front doctrine* 771
*Revolutionary education in China:
    documents and commentary* 570
*Revolutionary ideology and Chinese
    reality: dissonance under
    Mao* 725
*Revolutionary leaders of modern
    China* 638
*Revolutionary literature in China: an
    anthology* 1112
Rexroth, K. 1167, 1175
Reynolds, P. D. 951
Rhoads, E. J. M. 196
Riboud, M. 105
Ricci, Matteo 414, 417
Rice 132, 1024
  pest control 1023
  trade 966

Rice, E. E. 40
Rice Improvement in China and other Asian countries 1024
Rice research and production in China: an IRRI team's view 132
Rickett, A. Austin 1135
Rickshaw: the novel Lo-T'o Hsiang Tzu 1204
Ridley, C. P. 1083
Ridley, M. 141
Riggs, D. A. 1147
Riley, C. P. 568
Rise and fall of Lin Piao 367
Rise of the Chinese Communist Party: autobiography of Chang Kuo-tao, Volume I, 1921-1927; Volume II, 1928-1938 268
Rise of modern China 213—214
Rise of the Peking opera 1770-1870: social aspects of the theatre in Manchu China 1327
Riskin, C. 905
Ritual, religious 420
Rivers
 Yangzi River 91
 Yellow River 52
Road to Communism: China since 1912 183
Road to confrontation: American policy toward China and Korea, 1947-1950 858
Roberts, M. 327, 1211
Robinson, J. 43, 104, 922
Robinson, T. W. 299
Rockefeller Foundation
 medical aid programme 580
Rockefeller, N. 1305
Rodrigues, Joao 405
Roman Catholic Church 416
 Jesuit missions 405, 414, 417
 missions 401
Romanization systems
 textbook 1080
Romantic generation of modern Chinese writers 1124
Ronan, C. A. 10
Ronning, C. 1257
Roosevelt administration
 expansionist policy 749
Roots, J. McCook 381
Ropp, P. S. 197
Rose, B. 886
Rosemount, H. Jr. 411
Rosen, S. 569
Ross, D. A. 842

Rossabi, M. 56
Rossi, P. 255
Rothenberg, M. 759
Roughton, A. 71
Roy, D. T. 142, 382
Rozman, G. 923
Ruan Ji 1166
Rubin, V. A. 456
Rubinstein, A. Z. 849
Rugs and rug-making 965
Rulin Waishi 197
Ruling from horseback: Manchu politics in the Oboi regency, 1661-1669 192
Rump, A. 462
Rural development 332, 1008, 1010, 1018
 to socialism 1014
Rural development: learning from China 994
Rural employment and manpower problems in China 1036
Rural health and birth planning in China 517
Rural health in the People's Republic of China 524, 595
Rural Health Systems Delegation, American 524
Rural industrialization in China 990
Rural industry 943, 990
Rural life 1002, 1005, 1012, 1017
Rural small-scale industry in the People's Republic of China 943
Rural Socialist Education Campaign 502
Rural transfer programme 486
Russia and the roots of the Chinese revolution 1896-1911 758
Rustication of urban youth in China 486
Ryga, G. 106

S

S. J. Rodrigues the interpreter: an early jesuit in Japan and China 405
Saich, T. 692, 1426
Sailey, J. 457
Sakamoto, Nobuko 1343
Salaff, J. W. 546
Salisbury, C. Y. 107
Salisbury, H. E. 108, 778, 1317

Salt monopoly 936
Salter, C. L. 55, 65
San Francisco
  Chinatowns 540
*Sandalwood mountains: readings and
  stories of the early Chinese in
  Hawaii* 527
Saran, V. 1444
Sariti, A. M. 325
Savage, J. 84
Scalapino, R. A. 693, 850, 963
Schafer, E. H. 512, 1344
Schaller, M. 760−761
Scharfstein, Ben-Ami 41
Scharping, T. 335
Schell, O. 43, 109−110, 198
Scherer, J. L. 42
Schirokauer, C. 639
Schloss Collection, Mingji
  figurines 1313
Schloss, E. 1313
Schneider, L. A. 199, 633
Scholars 1225
*Scholars' guide to Washington, DC,
  East Asian studies* 1430
School of Oriental and African Studies
  Chinese newspaper collection 1426
Schools 565, 697
  competition 574
  maths teaching 572
Schools, Secondary
  politics 569
Schram, S. R. 325, 336−337, 694
Schran, P. 924, 1013
Schurmann, F. 43, 182
Science 10, 22, 39, 103, 120, 890,
    1047
  and society 1046
  bibliographies 1039
  Daoism 459
  East-West relations 1046
  education 1037, 1049
  from the US 1038
  government policy 1041, 1051, 1053,
    1057−1058
  history 190
  marine 1060
  national science policy 1037
  periodicals 1376, 1382, 1387, 1390,
    1398
  research and development 1057
  US-China relations 1048, 1052

*Science and civilization in China,
  volume 5: chemistry and chemical
  technology, part 4: spagynical
  discovery and invention:
  apparatus, theories and
  gifts* 1047
*Science and socialist construction in
  China* 1058
*Science and technology in the
  development of modern China: an
  annotated bibliography* 1039
Science and Technology Review 1398
Science in contemporary China 1048
Science in traditional China 190
*Science, technology and China's drive
  for modernization* 1052
Scientific Institutions
  directories 1059
Scott, G. L. 614
Scott, M. W. 111
Scott, W. D. 1351
*Scratches on our minds: American
  views of China and India* 751
Seals 1308
Seaton, J. P. 1147
Seaver, R. 280
Second Chinese revolution 291
Second Hundred Flowers 1144
Second United Front 244
*Secret and sublime: Taoist mysteries
  and magic* 425
Secret societies 193, 472
Seidel, A. 419
Seifman, E. 560
Seismograph 526
Selden, M. 256, 300, 925
*Selected papers no. 3, proceedings of
  the NEH Modern China Project,
  1977-78: political leadership and
  social change at the local level in
  China from 1850 to the
  present* 621
Selected poems of Ai Qing 1164
Selected tales of Liaozhai 1218
*Selected works of Peter A.
  Boodberg* 1103
*Selections from China Mainland
  Magazine* 1399
Selections from PRC Magazines 1399
*Selections from records of the
  historian* 1258
Selling technology to China 1045
Sergeichuk, S. 851
'Serve the People' 72

Serve the people: observations on medicine in the People's Republic of China 593
Service, John S. 24, 234, 242, 762
'Seven sages of the bamboo grove' 1166
Sex 301
Seybolt, P. J. 486, 570, 695, 1109
Seymour, J. D. 696
Shabad, T. 57
Shachiapang 114
Shaffer, L. 1034
Shai, A. 763
Shandong 115, 221, 619
  rural development 1011
Shang civilization 147
Shang dynasty 709
  administration 138
  bronzes 1270
  chronology 147
  history 144
  oracle bones 137
  society 148
Shang Yang 185, 456
Shang Yang Pianfa 185
Shang Yang's reforms and state control in China 185
Shanghai 61, 75, 80, 117, 252
  capitalists 227
  Communist occupation 250, 255
  Cultural Revolution 707
  economy 903
Shanghai capitalists and the nationalist government, 1927-1937 227
Shanghai College of Traditional Medicine 591
Shanghai Electrical Machinery Factory 110
Shanghai old-style banks 1800-1935 950
Shanghai: revolution and development in an Asian metropolis 903
Shanghai school of painters 1286, 1288
Shansi 80
Shaping of Chinese foreign policy 847
Shapiro, S. 112, 1188, 1220, 1231
Shaw, M. 4
Shaw, Samuel 747
Shchutskii, Iulien 458
Sheeks, R. B. 1057
Sheep 1022
Shen-Gan-Ning
  economic development 924

Shen P'u-hai: a Chinese philosopher of the fourth century BC 357
Shen Puhai 357
Shen Zhou 1283
Sheng, H. 726
Shenjian 355
Sheridan, J. E. 257
Shewmaker, K. R. 258
Shi Jing 1178, 1184
Shi, Lilin 1064
Shi Naian 1219—1220
Shi, Paul K. T. 988
Shi Tau 1268
Shi, Vincent Y. C. 200
Shi Xiaoqing 1206
Shichor, Yitzhak 852
Shih-shuo Hsin-yu: a new account of tales of the world 1127
Shinn, Rinn-Sup 1240
Shipping 970
Shirk, S. L. 697
Shishuo Xinyu 1127
Shiyanzhi 1134
Short account of the maritime circuit 49
Short history of China 172
Short history of Chinese communism 290
Short history of nationalist China, 1919-1949 219
Short stories 1114, 1120, 1137, 1154, 1158, 1199—1200, 1208, 1218, 1227, 1229, 1371
  bibliographies 1456
Short story of Chinese art 1273
Shu Ch'ing 709
Shu Qing 709
Shue, V. 1014
Shulman, F. 1445
Sian 75
Sian incident 267
Sian incident: a pivotal point in modern Chinese history 267
Siberia
  relations with China 56, 294
Sichuan 622
Sidel, R. 113, 592—593
Sidel, V. W. 592—593
Sigurdson, J. 990, 1051
Sihanouk, Norodom
  interviews 108, 116
Silent China: selected writings of Lu Xun 1156
Silent invasion: the Chinese in Southeast Asia 525

Silk Road 102
Silk Road 93, 102, 526
Silk trade 968
Silverstein, M. E. 594
Sima Jian 1258
Simmons, J. D. 853
Simonsen, R. A. 553
Simulation games 553
Sinanthropus pekinensis 135, 144
Singapore
  Chinese immigrants 548
  relations with China 873
Singh, N. 1259
Sinha, R. 886
Sinkiang (see Xinjiang)
  relations with China 56
Sinkiang story 47
Sino-American detente and its policy
    implications 874
Sino-American normalization and its
    policy implication 875
Sino-American relations,
    1949-1971 835
Sino Chinese-English dictionary 1093
Sino-Indian Border War 160
Sino-Japanese War 160, 752, 754
Sino-Soviet confrontation: implication
    for the future 814
Sino-Soviet crisis politics 869
Sino-Soviet diplomatic relations,
    1917-1926 829
Sino-Soviet dispute 834
Sino-Soviet relations 6, 96, 102, 108,
    243, 294, 311, 320, 372, 687, 704,
    742—743, 758, 772, 775, 783,
    791—792, 795, 812, 814, 816,
    820, 826, 829, 832, 834, 837, 839,
    844, 850, 856, 860, 865,
    869—870, 881—883
  bibliographies 1444
  border conflicts 770, 802, 806—807,
    868
  post Mao 670, 859
  Soviet attitudes to China 759
  Western views 857
Sino-Soviet schism: a bibliography,
    1956-1964 1444
Sino-Soviet territorial dispute 770
Sino-Soviet territorial dispute,
    1949-64 806
Siu, R. G. H. 459
Six Dynasties Period
  literature 1127
  poetry 1182

Siyu Deng 765
Sizhuan University 89
Skinner, W. G. 477, 487–488, 1446
Skocpol, T. 731
Sladkovsky, M. I. 764
Slicher, C. P. 1040
Small groups and political rituals in
    China 714
Small incident 1155
Smedley, A. 513, 698
Smil, V. 926
Smith, B. 1272
Smith, C. R. 972
Smith, H. D. 460
Smith, R. J. 201
Smullyan, R. M. 461
Snow, Edgar 43, 229, 301, 698
  writings 259
Snow, Helen Foster 395
Snow, Lois Wheeler 114, 259
Sobin, J. N. 24
Social change 72, 90, 92, 95, 103, 109,
    116—118, 198, 206, 213, 215,
    290, 296, 301, 303, 305, 309, 332,
    369, 478, 480, 497, 499, 559, 621,
    690, 697, 701, 716, 737
  post Mao 661
Social criticism
  18th century 197
Social interaction in Chinese
    society 480
Social Science 380, 564
  periodicals 1393, 1400
Social Sciences in China 1400
Social thought of Lu Hsun,
    1881-1936 1148
Socialism 1239
Socialism in the Chinese
    countryside 654, 1001
Socialism, Western 445
Socialist planning 655, 895
Societies, Professional
  directories 1412
Society 17, 20, 468, 497, 658, 1055
  ancient 496
  and science 1046
  bibliographies 1411, 1446
  contemporary 2, 6—7, 11, 45, 92,
    106—107, 122, 287, 678, 1242
  history 13—14, 16—19, 21—22, 26,
    44, 174—175, 196, 205, 226, 477,
    1242
  industrial 476
  interaction 480

morals 492
Overseas Chinese 488, 503, 527, 540
protocols 506
rural 469–470, 482, 502
Shang 147–148
social control 490
stabilization 481
structure 163, 210, 467, 473, 479, 498, 501
Sui 204
Tang 204
traditional 28, 33, 41, 92, 143, 177, 183, 269, 356, 364, 421–422, 472, 474, 488, 493–494, 498, 501, 504, 506, 601, 1017
urban 487
values 120, 491, 506
village 35, 101, 470, 505
welfare system 475
women 507–511, 514
Zhou 148
Sociolinguistics
 Yue Ren Chao 1104
Sociology 495
Sociology and socialism in contemporary China 495
Soil conservation 1004
Soils 15
Sokolsky, George E. 228
Solar energy
 periodicals 1401
Solar Energy Journal 1401
Solid State Physics 1040
 microwave devices 1050
Solid state physics in the People's Republic of China 1040
Solinger, D. J. 699
Solomon, R. H. 700–701, 854–855
Song dynasty
 bibliographies 1428
 calligraphy 1290
 economy 902
 élites 177
 food 149
 institutions 189
 local government 189
 painting 1299
 poetry 1162–1163, 1167–1168, 1170, 1180
 prose 1249
 religion 433
Song Jian 519
Song Qiaoren 376
Song Shi poetry 1162
Songe, A. H. 571

Songs 126
Soong sisters 364
Source materials in Chinese history 1438
Sources of Shang history: the oracle-bone inscriptions of Bronze Age China 137
Southeast Asia
 relations with China 785, 801, 836, 864
Southeast Asia and China: the end of containment 836
Southeast Asia's Chinese minorities 533
Southern expansion of the Chinese people 531
Soviet and Chinese influence in the Third World 849
Soviet and Chinese personalities 671
Soviet-Chinese relations, 1945-1970 783
Soviet foreign aid
 steel industry 984
Soviets 623
Soviets, Chinese 246
Space
 international law 608
 research 1050
Spae, J. J. 416
Speaking of Chinese 1111
Spence, J. D. 44, 202–203, 1221, 1317
Spirit soldiers: a historical narrative of the Boxer rebellion 191
Spoken standard Chinese. Volume i, volume ii 1063
Sport 39
 and politics 1348
 athletics 1352
 gongfu 1351
 ping-pong 1349
 Taiji 1347, 1350
Sports, politics and ideology in China 1348
Spring moon 1210
Stahnke, A. A. 974
Staiger, B. 19
Stalin, Joseph 327, 372
Stamp, R. B. 1413
Stamps
 periodicals 1379
Stanford Museum, Chinese Collection 1362
Stanford Museum, volume II, volume III, volume IV 1362

Starr, J. B. 338—339, 732
State Education Leaders Delegation, US 565
State monopolies 28
State of American history and literature studies in the People's Republic of China 1243
States and social revolutions: a comparative analysis of France, Russia, and China 731
Stavis, B. 1015—1016
Steel industry 91, 984, 1056
  mills 37
Steiman, H. 1332
Steiner, S. 541
Steinle, P. 1012
Steurt, Marjorie Rankin 115
Stilwell and the American experience in China 1911-1945 261
Stilwell, Joseph 261, 375, 742
Stimson, H. M. 1063, 1176
Stoessinger, J. C. 856
Storm in a teacup 1155
Story of Genghis Khan 373
Story of the stone: the dream of the red chamber 1189
Stover, L. E. 143, 1017
Stover, T. K. 143
Strand, D. 621
Stranger in China 97
Strategic ridge, Peking's relations with Thailand, Malaysia, Singapore and Indonesia 873
Straw sandles: Chinese short stories, 1918-1933 1200
Strikes 1034
Strong, A. L. 43
Struggle for democracy: Sung Ch'iao-jen and the 1911 revolution 376
Stuart, D. T. 857
Stuart, John Leighton 253
Stubborn weeds: Chinese literature after the Cultural Revolution 1126
Students 252
  Cultural Revolution 89, 288, 353, 675
  factionalism 569
  in the US 551, 578
  incentives 697
  nationalist movement 222, 423
  rebellion 620

Studies in Chinese literary genres 1114
Studies in Chinese poetry and poetics, volume I 1132
Studies in Chinese society 493
Studies in connoisseurship: Chinese paintings from the Arthur M. Sacker collection in New York and Princeton 1284
Studies of Chinese society: essays by Maurice Freedman 488
Stueck, W. W. 858
Style in the arts of China 1275
Su Dongbo 1180
Su Shi 1279
Su Tung-po: selections from a Sung dynasty poet 1180
Subject and author index to Chinese literature monthly 1424
Sui dynasty
  history 204
  landscape painting 1294—1295
  politics 211
Sui dynasty: the unification of China, AD 581-617 211
Sullivan, L. R. 1353
Sullivan, M. 1273—1274, 1294—1296
Sulzberger, C. L. 859
Summary of world broadcasts, part 3, weekly economic report 1405
Summer Palace 1238
Sun, S. 1314
Sun Sibai 394
Sun Yat-sen (see Sun Yixian)
Sun Yat-sen: frustrated patriot 383
Sun Yat-sen 1074
Sun Yixian 196, 219, 222, 236, 372, 723
  career 383
Sun Zi 733
Sunflower splendor, three thousand years of Chinese poetry 1171
Sung and Yuan paintings 1299
Sung bibliography 1428
Sunrise 1232
Supplementary readers for intermediate Chinese reader, 5 volumes 1074
Survey of the China Mainland Press 1406
Survey of the PRC press 1406
Surveys & Research Corporation 1059
Suryadinata, L. 542—545
Sutter, R. G. 860—861
Suttmeier, R. P. 1052—1053

Sutton, D. S. 634
Suzhou 61
Swamy, S. 927
Swannack-Nunn, S. 1054
Swanson, B. 862
Swetz, F. 572
Syed, Anwar Hussain. 863
Sykes, C. 1292
Symbols of eternity: the art of landscape painting in China 1296
Syncretic Movement 398, 437
Syncretic religion of Lin Ch'ao-en 398
Szechwan and the Chinese Republic: provincial militarism and the central power, 1911-1938 622
Szuprowics, M. R. 958

T

T. L. Yuan bibliography of western writings on Chinese art and archaeology 1448
Tach'ing (see Daqing)
Tach'ing oilfield: a Maoist model for economic development 983
Taft administration
 expansionist policy 749
Tai Chi handbook 1347
Taibei 494
Taihang 502
Taiji 1347, 1350
T'aiping ideology: its sources, interpretations, and influences 200
Taiping Jing 419
Taiping Rebellion 154—155, 159, 167, 171, 195, 200—201, 472, 638
T'aiping rebellion and the western powers: a comprehensive survey 159
T'aiping revolutionary movement 195
Taiwan 36
 international law 608
 relations with China 704, 713, 774, 794, 807, 810, 815—816, 819, 821, 824, 830—831, 861, 871
 relations with the US 774, 794, 815, 821, 824, 830
Taiwan and American policy: the dilemma in US-China relations 796
Taiwan Bureau of Investigation Archives 1353
Taiwan Strait Crisis 807, 821

Taiwan's future? 819
Tajing 72
Taking mountain by strategy 114
Taking of bandits' stronghold 1322
Taking tiger mountain by strategy 1322
Tanaka Guichi and Japan's China policy 757
T'ang code: general principles 607
Tang dynasty 369, 1185
 cookery recipes 1344
 food 149
 history 135, 204
 institutions 210
 landscape painting 1294—1295
 law codes 607
 literature 512
 philosophy 210
 poetry 1147, 1161, 1163, 1174, 1176, 1181, 1183, 1186
 politics 210
 pottery 1270
 prose 1249
 religion 210
Tang Xianzu 1222
Tangshan earthquake 1044
Tanzania
 Chinese aid 779
 relations with China 880
Tao and Chinese culture 429
Tao is silent 461
Tao Magic: the Chinese art of the occult 442
Tao of architecture 1302
Tao Te Ching 426
Tao: the watercourse way 465
Taoism (see Daoism)
Taoism: the road to immortality 400
Tau Qian 1146
Tawney, R. H. 1035
Taxation 365, 949
 imperial 952
 Qing 952
Taxation and government finance in 16th century Ming China 949
Taxation, Local 621
Tay, W. 1136
Taylor, G. E. 778
Taylor, J. 864
Taylor, R. 573
Teachers
 recruitment 575

Teahouse 1207
Technical units 645
Technology 10, 22, 39, 106, 165, 886,
    888, 890, 934, 1046, 1055
  agriculture 1021
  ancient 526
  bibliographies 1039
  crops 130, 132
  economics 896
  English-Chinese dictionaries 1097
  government policy 1051, 1053, 1057
  history 13, 21
  imported to China 1045
  industrial 891
  military 896
  mineral industry 1056
  periodicals 1398
  research and development 1057
  US-China relations 1052
Technology and science in the People's
    Republic of China 1051
Technology, defense, and external
    relations in China, 1975-78 803,
    1041
Technology, politics, and society in
    China 1055
Teiwes, F. C. 702−703
Temples 1
  Buddhist 412
  Daoist 412
Ten great years: statistics of the
    economic and cultural
    achievements of the People's
    Republic of China 916
Ten Mile Inn 1000
Teng (see Deng)
Teng Hsiao-ping: a political
    biography 689
Terrill, R. 45, 79, 116−117, 340, 704
Textbooks, Elementary
  Chinese language 1061, 1063−1064,
    1066, 1068−1070, 1072
  Chinese language reader 1071
Textbooks, Intermediate
  Chinese language reader 1073−1074,
    1077−1078, 1081
  cursive script 1079
  Mandarin Chinese conversation 1076
Textile industry
  cotton 899
Textile mills
  Chinese aid 779
Textiles 1301
Thailand
  relations with China 808, 833, 873

Theatre 98, 114
  history 1324, 1326−1327
  opera 1326−1327, 1330
  Western plays 292
Theoretical foundations of Chinese
    medicine: system of
    correspondence 590
Third World
  Chinese aid 891, 907, 939
  Communist fifth-columnists 866
  development theories 917
  relations with China 789, 791,
    825−826, 845, 849, 876, 881
Thomas, S. C. 928
Thompson, T. N. 929
Thomson, J. C. Jr. 260
Thorne, C. 766
Thornton, R. C. 635, 865
Thought of Mao Tse-tung: form and
    content 323
Thousand pieces of gold 539
Thousand recipe Chinese
    cookbook 1341
Three Chinas, up close coming home -
    to China 92
Three Kingdoms 1228
Three kingdoms: China's epic
    drama 1211
Three People's Principles 219
Through Chinese eyes 695
Through Russian eyes:
    American-Chinese relations 851
Thunderstorm 1233
Tian, H. Yuan 522−523
Tian, Hongmao 636
Tianjin 61, 191, 293
Tibet
  border conflicts 756
  Red Army campaigns 649
Tien (see Dian)
Tigers over Asia 1253
Till morning comes 1197
Times atlas of China 64
To acquire wisdom: the way of Wang
    Yang-ming 454
To change China: western advisers in
    China, 1620-1960 202
To China and back 71
To embrace the moon 657
To Peking - and beyond: a report on
    the new Asia 108
Tomb figurines, Mingji 1313
Tombs
  Manch'eng 151
  Ming 140

Tongcheng 467
Tongming Hui 548
Topping, A. 103, 118
Topping, S. 103, 119
Tow, W. T. 857
Toward a New World outlook: a documentary history of education in the People's Republic of China, 1949-76 560
Toward a people's anthropology 134
Townsend, J. R. 705−706
Toynbee, A. 302
Traces the brush: studies in Chinese calligraphy 1285
Trade 42, 621
Trade, internal 960
  rice 966
Trade, Opium 166, 171, 634
Trade, overseas 165, 804, 887, 890, 895, 904, 921, 944, 954, 957, 977
  assessment of the China market 958, 978
  business contracts 973
  compradors 215
  customs 201
  directories 396
  international law 609
  minerals 1056
  oriental rugs 965
  patterns 969, 971
  periodicals 1374, 1377
  regulation 976
  silk 968
  socialist planning 655
  statistics 970
  with Africa 817
  with Great Britain 780
  with Japan 871, 976
  with New England 235
  with the US 240, 778, 959, 961, 963−964, 967, 972, 975
  with the West 974
Trade, Silk 526
Trade unions 1028−1029
Trade with China: assessment by leading businessmen and scholars 957
Traditional and contemporary painting in China 1278
Traditional China 28
Traditional Chinese stories: themes and variations 1131, 1212
Trager, F. N. 303
Trangrams 444

Transformation of the Chinese earth: aspects of the evaluation of the Chinese earth from earliest times to Mao Tse-tung 46
Transformation of the Chinese lyrical tradition: Chiang K'uei and Southern Sung tz'u poetry 1168
Transition to socialism in China 925
Translation of art: essays on Chinese painting and poetry 1276
Transport 24, 42, 126, 890, 921, 928, 954
Travel accounts 70−72, 74−92, 94−112, 114−123, 258
  18th century 74
  contemporary 13
  historical 73, 93
Travel guide to the People's Republic of China 126
Travel guides 125−127
Travels of Marco Polo 1267
Treadgold, D. W. 417
Treasures from China 141
Treaties, Law of 611−615
Treaties of the People's Republic of China, 1949-1978: an annotated compilation 611
Treatise on famous Chinese dishes 1343
'Treatises on rituals' 5
Treaty ports 477
Tregear, T. R. 58
Treistman, J. M. 144
Tribes
  names 47
Trotter, A. 767
True story of Ah Q 1155
Truman administration
  China policy 848
Tschirhart, E. 8
Tsien, Tsuen-Hsuin 1447
Tsinan (see Qinan)
Tsu-hsi (see Zuxi)
Tsuchitani, P. J. 581, 585
Tsuen-Hsuin Tsien 142
Tuchman, B. 261
Turning point in China: an essay on Cultural Revolution 289
Tuter, F. 1260
Twelve towers 1208
Twentieth century China 12
Twentieth-century Chinese drama: an anthology 1119
Twentieth-century Chinese stories 1141

Twentieth century Chinese writers and their pen names 1458
Twitchett, D. C. 64, 139, 164, 204, 210
Two Chinese states: US foreign policy and interests 843
Type of index of Chinese folktales 1415

U

Uhalley, S. Jr. 341
Ullerich, C. 1036
UN World Order Model Project 823
Uncertain passage: China's transition to the post-Mao era 270
Uncertain years: Chinese-American relations, 1947-50 782
Underdevelopment theories 905
Understanding business contracts in China, 1949-1963 973
Understanding China: an assessment of American scholarly resources 1434
Understanding foreign policy decisions: the Chinese case 781
Underwood, J. A. 409
Unemployment 941
Unequal Treaties 188, 262, 613, 743
Unfolding of Neo-Confucianism 430
Unger, J. 574, 1018
United Church of Canada
  missions 406
United Front Doctrine 771
United Front, First 628
United Nations 608, 708, 777, 791, 823, 867
  China lobby 773
United States and China 284
United States and China in the twentieth century 760
United States and China: the next decade 778
United States, China and arms control 793
Universities 98, 116
  enrollment 573
  entrance examination 550
Unknown war: North China 1937-1945 1248
Unwelcome muse, Chinese literature in Shanghai and Peking, 1937-1945 1118

Up to the mountains and down to the villages 997
Upper Felicity 470
Urban change in China: politics and development in Tsinan, Shantung, 1890-1949 619
Urban development 332
Urban origins of rural revolution, elites and the masses in Hunan province, 1911-27 1010
Urbanization 477
US
  China lobby 782
  Chinese immigrants 503, 528, 530, 534−536, 538−541, 738
  Chinese students 551, 578
  military involvement in Asia 777
  relations with Asia 751
US Air Force
  Flying Tigers 1253
US Animal Science Delegation 1022
US-China Pharmacology
  Symposium 581
US China policy and the problem of Taiwan 786
US-China relations 6, 91, 96, 102−103, 216, 228, 235, 240, 247, 253, 258, 260−261, 270, 283−285, 308, 311, 313, 359, 375, 391, 672, 704, 713, 738, 740, 742, 745, 751, 760−762, 768, 772, 775, 777−778, 782, 787−789, 791, 802, 821, 824, 830, 832, 835, 840, 843, 846, 848, 850, 855−856, 858, 860, 870, 874−875, 881−884
  aid projections 963
  American opinions on China 747
  anti-communism 800
  Asian security 854
  bibliographies 1437
  Chinese views 1365
  Democratic policy 838
  economic 887
  education 578
  finance 972
  nationalist lobby 753
  nuclear weapons 793
  oil investment 985
  open door policy 749
  periodicals 1375
  post Mao 670, 708
  scientific cooperation 1038, 1048, 1052
  Soviet view 851

Taiwan 774, 776, 786, 794, 796, 815, 861
technological cooperation 1052
trade 959, 963, 967, 972, 975
trade in art treasures 964
trade negotiations 961
UN influence 773
World War II 225, 234
US-Chinese trade negotiations 961
US crusade in China, 1938-1945 761
US Department of Health and Human Services 524
US Foreign Broadcast Information Service Reports 1407
US Foreign Service 1250
  China dispatches 234, 242
  diplomatic dispatches 762
US Insect Control Delegation 1023
US Medical Delegation to China 592
US National Academy of Sciences Committee for Scholarly Communication with the PRC 1048
US National Committee on US-China Relations 565
US Oceanography Delegation report 1060
US Pure and Applied Chemistry Delegation report 1037
US Rural Health System Delegation 595
US Senate, Foreign Relations Committee 225
US Solid State Physics Delegation report 1040
US State Department 225, 253
US Vegetable Farming System Delegation report 130
US Wheat Research Delegation report 128
USSR
  Communism 671
  educational policy 563
  Red Army campaigns 649
USSR-China relations 6, 96, 102, 108, 243, 311, 320, 372, 687, 704, 742−743, 758, 772, 775, 783, 791−792, 795, 812, 814, 816, 820, 826, 829, 832, 834, 837, 839, 844, 850, 856, 860, 865, 869−870, 881−883
  bibliographies 1444
  border conflicts 770, 802, 806−807, 813, 868
  post Mao 859

Soviet attitudes to China 759
steel industry 984
Western views 857

V

Valdelin, J. 906
Valenstein, S. G. 1315
Valley of decision 1277
Value change in Chinese society 491
Van Dort, H. A. 1316
Van Ginneken, Jaap 367
Van Gulik, R. 1223
Van Ness, P. 866
Vance, Cyrus 747
Vandenberg, Arthur 225
Vanderstappen, M. A. 1448
Varg, P. A. 768
Vegetable marketing systems in the People's Republic of China 130
Vegetables
  cropping systems 130
  pest control 1023
Vegetation 48
Vermeer, E. B. 1019
Vietnam
  Chinese immigrants 531
  culture 17
  relations with China 1259
  use of drugs as weapons 809
Vietnam, North
  Chinese aid 799
Vietnam War 738, 807
Vignell, M. 60
Village and bureaucracy in southern Sung China 189
Village and family in contemporary China 505
Villages 470, 505, 1000
  economy 1005
  social change 35, 101
Vincent, John Carter 242, 262, 1250
Visas 125−126
Vision of China: Photographs by Marc Riboud, 1957-1980 105
Vladimirov diaries: Yenan China, 1942-1945 263
Vladimirov, P. 263
Vocabularies
  Mandarin Chinese 1076
Vohra, R. 1137
Volti, R. 1055

W

Wade-Giles-pinyin romanization 1080
Wage patterns and the wage policy in modern China 1919-1972 1032
Wages 939, 1032
  incentives 1026
Waipiang 457
Wakeman, F. Jr. 205—206, 304
Walder, A. G. 707
Wales, N. 218
Waley, A. D. 1177
Walking on two legs: rural development in South China 1008
Wall Posters 81, 662
Waller, D. J. 264, 708
Waltham, C. 709
Wandering 1153
Wang Bi 462
Wang, C. H. 1178
Wang, Dee 1345
Wang Fangyou 1079
Wang Fanxi 1261
Wang, G. C. 930—931
Wang, James C. F. 1449
Wang Jingwei 220
Wang, K. P. 991, 1056
Wang Ming 265
Wang, N. 278
Wang Qingwei 739
Wang Tau 356
Wang, Wan-go 1272
Wang Wei 1146—1147, 1171, 1183, 1185
Wang, William S. Y. 1450
Wang Yang-ming 435, 454
Wang Zuoliang 1233
Ward, Frederick Townsend 201
Warfare 180, 198, 484, 496
  Daoism 429
  people's war 727
  political theory 733
  Red Army 649
  use of drugs 809
Warlord politics in China, 1916-1928 632
Warlords 222, 241, 257, 269, 379, 386—387, 477, 622, 632, 634
Warlords politics: conflict and coalition in the modernization of Republican China 630
Warlords, Yangzi 630
Warner, M. 207
Watch out for the foreign guests! China encounters the West 109
Water buffalo 1022

Water conservancy and irrigation in China: social, economic and agro-technical aspects 1019
Water conservation 1004, 1019
Water management 52, 98, 128, 130, 1019
Water management in the Yellow River basin of China 52
Water Margin 1152, 1219
Watson, A. 120, 932
Watson, B. 463—464, 1138, 1179—1182
Watson, J. L. 547
Watson, W. 145—146, 1275
Watt, G. 121
Watt, J. R. 208
Watt, James C. Y. 1276
Watts, A. 465
Ways to paradise: The Chinese quest for immortality 447
Weapons industry 986
Webb, G. 37
Wei Jingsheng 286
Weiner, R. R. 621
Weiqi 721
Welch, H. 418—419
Welfare 42, 475
Wen Fong 1299
Wen Tingyun 1183
Weng, Byron S. J. 867
West in Russia and China: religions and secular thought in modern times. Volume i, Russia, 1472-1917; volume ii, China 1582-1949 417
Weyi Zaidao 1134
What is Taoism? 428
Wheat
  cropping systems 128
Wheat in the People's Republic of China 128
Wheatley, P. 489
Wheelwright, E. L. 933
Whelan, J. S. 953
While China faced West: American reformers in Nationalist China, 1928-1937 260
White, G. 575, 645, 666, 710, 934
White-haired girl 1074, 1322
White Lotus Sect 413
White, Lynn 711
Whitehead, R. 342
Whither China: the view from the Kremlin 759
Whiting, A. 868

Whiting, A. S. 713, 935
Whitson, W. W. 637, 712, 975
Whittall, M. 209
Who's who in Communist China,
  volumes i and ii 397
Who's who in the People's Republic of
  China 389
Whyte, M. K. 505, 714
Wich, R. 869
Widdess, D. R. 1320
Wiethoff, B. 209
Wilbur, C. M. 383
Wilcox, F. O. 870
Wilcox, I. 1349
Wilhelm, H. 458
Wilkinson, E. 1263, 1451
Willhelm, H. 466
William Hayes Fogg Art
  Museum 1363
William Hayes Fogg Art Museum,
  Asian Collection 1363
William Rockhill Nelson Gallery,
  Chinese Collection 1364
William Rockhill Nelson Gallery of
  Art: Handbook of the Collections
  - volume 1 - Oriental 1364
Williams, J. F. 59, 66
Willmott, W. E. 936
Wilson, A. 479−480, 490−492, 734
Wilson, D. 53, 266, 343−344, 957
Wilson, R. 479−480, 490−492, 734
Wind in the tower: Mao Tse-tung and
  the Chinese revolution
  1949-75 320
Wind will not subside: years in
  revolutionary China, 1964-69 298
Wing-tsin Chan 462
Winthrop, G. L. 1309, 1363
Witke, R. 384, 514
Wo Soong kills a tiger 1074
Wolf, A. P. 420, 493−494
Wolf, M. 514, 871
Wolff, D. 1110
Wolpert, R. F. 1320
Womack, B. 322
Woman works: women and the Party
  in revolutionary China 511
Women 29, 113, 473, 496, 513−514
  liberation 35, 507, 509−510, 515,
    658
  periodicals 1402
  poetry 1175
  poets 1167
  political power 369
  status 508−509, 511, 546
Women in China 515
Women in Chinese societies 514

Women of China 1402
Women's Federation 511
Women's liberation in China 507
Women's Movement 509−511
Women's movement in China: a
  selection of readings,
  1949-1973 509
Wong, J. 1020
Wong, J. Y. 385
Wong, P. 715
Wong, Sui-lun 495
Woodard, K. 937
Woodcuts 1314
Work incentive practices and policies
  in the People's Republic of China,
  1953-1965 1030
Workers 716, 1027−1028
  incentives 1026, 1029−1030, 1032
  mobility 1029
  participation 1025
  political organizations 1034
  urban 1031
Workers and commissars: trade union
  policy in the People's Republic of
  China 1028
Workers and workplaces in
  revolutionary China 1025
Working daughters of Hong Kong:
  filial piety or power in the
  family? 546
World and China, 1922-1972 746
World food system 956
World Order Model Project-UN 823
World War I
  Japanese invasion 221
World War II 1244
  British policy in Asia 763
  Chinese literature 1118
  Communist Party 263
  Communist policy 254, 256
  diplomatic dispatches 234, 242
  Japanese occupation 220, 354, 739,
    755, 766, 1248
  US China policy 225
Worlds apart: China 1953-55, USSR
  1962-65 816
Worsley, P. 122
Worswick, C. 1317
Wou, Odoric Y. K. 386
Wright, A. 210−211
Wright, F. L. 1302
Writers 1129
  biographical dictionaries 1458
  contemporary 1116, 1124
  history 1135
  'stubborn weeds' 1126

Writing
  origins 496
Wu Dianwei 267
Wu Han 1224
Wu, J. C. H. 1183
Wu Jingrong 1091-1092
Wu, K. S. 496
Wu Peifu 386
Wu Qingzi 197, 1225
Wu, S. 212, 1369
*Wu Tse-tien and the politics of
  legitimization of T'ang China* 369
Wu, Wang Gung 872
Wu-wei
  meaning 465
Wu, Y. L. 1057
Wu, Yuanli 873, 1262
Wu Zetian 369
Wuhan 61, 117, 624
Wylie, R. F. 345

X

Xia, A. 305, 716
Xia, C. T. 1139-1141
Xia dynasty 709
Xian Democracy Wall 81
Xian Foreign Language Institute 120
Xiandai Hanyu Cidian 1101
Xiang Soviet 246
Xiangya Journal 86
Xiao, G. T. 874-875, 976
Xiao Gongzhuan 735
Xiao Hong 368, 1226
Xie Lingyun 1146
Xie Qiaomin 65
Xie, W. 1452
Xien Chen, T. 576-577
Xiju Ji 1230
Xiliang 360
Xin Fengxia 1330
Xingdeng 999
Xinhua News Agency Bulletin 1408
Xinhua Yuebao 1403
Xinhua Zidian 1102
Xinjiang 47, 681
Xinlun 1217
Xiong, J. C. 876
Xiong James Jie 615, 736
Xiynag county 621
Xu-Balzer, Eileen 88
Xu Beihong 1286
Xu, F. 88, 737

Xu, F. L. K. 1277, 1370
Xu, Guangliang 1421
Xu, Immanuel C. Y. 213-214
Xu Kaiyu 1142-1143
Xu Liangying 1058
Xu Qiyou 49
Xu, Robert C. 1021
Xu Shichang 627
Xu Songbang 421
Xu, Vivian Ling 1081, 1227
Xue Muqiao 938-939
Xue, Zhundu 638
Xun Yue 355
Xun Zu 464

Y

Yahuda, M. B. 877-878
Yale-pinyin romanization 1080
Yan Qinghuang 548
Yanan 218, 237, 254, 256, 263, 268,
  313, 319, 343, 698
Yanan Conference on Literature and
  Art 1251
Yan'an papercuts 1306
Yang 138
Yang 1162
Yang, C. K. 422
Yang, Gladys 1150-1154,
  1156-1158, 1190, 1201, 1225,
  1228-1229, 1258
Yang Guan 185
Yang, Marion 580
Yang, Paul Fumian 1453 ·
Yang Shangkui 717
Yang, Winston L. Y. 1454-1455
Yang Xianyi 1150-1154,
  1157-1158, 1190, 1225,
  1228-1229, 1258
Yang Xiong 1319
Yang Xuan Ji 1246
'Yangist Miscellany' 437
Yangze valley
  rural life 1002
Yangzi bridge 91
Yanping Hao 215
Ye Mingzhen 385
Ye Qing 346
*Year in Upper Felicity: life in a
  Chinese village during the
  Cultural Revolution* 470
Yee, D. 1080
Yee, Lee 1144

Yeh Ming-chen: Viceroy of Liang-Kuang, 1852-1858 385
Yellow earth, green jade: constants in Chinese political mores 651
Yellow River 52
Yenan (see Yanan, Communist Party)
Yenan and the Great Powers: the origins of Chinese Communist foreign policy, 1944-46 254
Yenan in June 1937: talks with the Communist leaders 218
Yenan way in revolutionary China 256
Yeqian Wang 952
Yeung, E. 1226
Yeung Sai-Cheng 729
Yi Jing 411, 432, 458, 466
  puzzles 444
Yim, Kwan Ha 879
Ying Huan Zhilue 49
Yingmao Gau 718
Yingxiong Zhou 1136
Yip, Ka-Che 423
Yip, Wai-lim 1184
Yiyazaki, Ichisada 639
Yoga
  Daoist 400
Yonfan, Manshih 1264
Yong Deng Jia-Yee 1074
Yong Deng Jiaye 59
Yong-Zheng Emperor 173
Young, A. H. 954
Young, E. P. 387
Young, M. 515
Younghusband, Francis
  Tibet expedition 756
Youth 72, 658, 716
  education 568
  political behaviour 690
  resettlement programme 997
  rural transfer programme 486
Yu, A. C. 1230
Yu, G. T. 880
Yu, P. 1185
Yu Zhunfang 424
Yuan dynasty 1252
  drama 1331
  food 149
  military affairs 194
  painting 1280, 1299
  politics 158, 161
Yuan, F. L. 1418
Yuan Mei 1113
Yuan Qing 1231

Yuan San Zhu 1113
Yuan Shikai 205, 376, 387
  death 632
Yue Ren Chao 1104
Yundong: mass campaigns in Chinese Communist leadership 644
Yunnan
  Chinese immigrants 531
Yunnan Army 634
Yuyitung case 525

Z

Zai, Meishi 1456
Zao Yu 1232−1233
Zen Buddhism 437
Zeng Yuhe Ecke 1297
Zetterholm, T. 123
Zhai, Winberg 881
Zhan, R. 188
Zhang, A. 1298
Zhang Chunqiao 707
Zhang, Diaon Amos Ih. 1302
Zhang Gangyi Sun 1186
Zhang Guodao 268
Zhang Guoxin 347
Zhang, H. C. 1145−1146
Zhang Hao 388
Zhang, J. L. 1289, 1308
Zhang Kuangzhi 147−150
Zhang, M. 1111
Zhang, P. H. 306, 719
Zhang, R. 1111
Zhang, S. T. 596
Zhang, Simon 1067
Zhang, Y. C. 720
Zhang, Yilok 594
Zhang Zhidong 152, 549
Zhang Zuolin 379, 386
Zhangsha 61
Zhangzhou 61
Zhao Yingfang 392
Zhejiang 252, 999
Zhen, Jerome 269, 348, 497
Zhen Yi 96
Zheng Chenggong 358
Zheng, F. 1147
Zheng, James K. M. 1447
Zheng, Peter 308
Zheng, R. 1346
Zheng, Ronald Yelin 1265
Zheng Shifeng 60
Zheng Zhuyuan 955, 992−993

Zhili clique 386
Zhong Ling 1175
Zhong Qi 48
Zhong Shang University 94
Zhong Yong 434
Zhongguo Zhenjuxue Gaiyao 582
Zhongqing 61, 1244
Zhongwen Shi 1331
Zhou dynasty 709
  history 144
  institutions 157
  philosophy 428
  society 148
Zhou Enlai 37, 96, 326, 352, 381, 646,
    656
  death 286, 704
  foreign relations policy 782
  interviews 103, 108, 116, 119, 816
  novels 378
  receptions 118

Zhou Erfu 1234
Zhou Libo 1235
Zhou Zouren 1134
Zhu, Baoliang 1458
Zhu De 698
Zhu, G. C. 737, 1370—1372
Zhu Hong 424
Zhu Shuzhen 1175
Zhuang Ze 1150
Zhukongdiao 1191, 1318
Zhundu Xue 882—883
Zhungwen Shi 1266
Zhuyuan Zheng 940
Zithers 1301
Zuan, T. H. 346
Zuan Zi 437—438, 456
  complete works 463
Zun Zi 724
Zuxi, Empress Dowager 207

Map of China

This map shows the more important towns and other features.

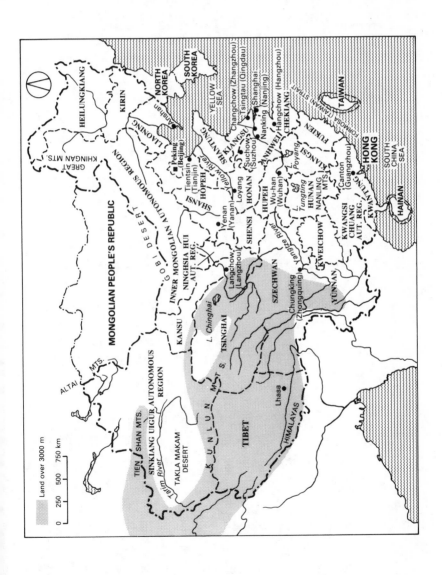